SENTENCE PRODUCTION:
Developments in Research and Theory

Contributors

J. Kathryn Bock, University of Oregon, Eugene, Oregon

Joseph H. Danks, Kent State University, Kent, Ohio

Suitbert Ertel, Universität Göttingen, Göttingen, West Germany

Georges Gosnave, I.N.S.E.R.M., Paris, France

Joseph Jaffe, College of Physicians & Surgeons of Columbia University, New York

Robert J. Jarvella, The Rockefeller University, New York

Gerard Kempen, University of Nijmegen, Nijmegen, The Netherlands

Daniel C. O'Connell, S.J., Saint Louis University, Saint Louis, Missouri

Charles E. Osgood, University of Illinois, Urbana, Illinois

Sherry R. Rochester, Clarke Institute of Psychiatry, Toronto, Canada

Sheldon Rosenberg, University of Illinois at Chicago Circle, Chicago, Illinois

Judith Rupp, Clarke Institute of Psychiatry, Toronto, Canada

I.M. Schlesinger, The Hebrew University of Jerusalem, Jerusalem, Israel

Ola A. Selnes, University of Rochester, Rochester, New York

Sharon Thurston, Clarke Institute of Psychiatry, Toronto, Canada

Harry A. Whitaker, University of Rochester, Rochester, New York

SENTENCE PRODUCTION:

Developments In Research And Theory

EDITED BY

Sheldon Rosenberg

UNIVERSITY OF ILLINOIS AT CHICAGO CIRCLE

 LAWRENCE ERLBAUM ASSOCIATES, PUBLISHERS
1977   Hillsdale, New Jersey

DISTRIBUTED BY THE HALSTED PRESS DIVISION OF

JOHN WILEY & SONS

New York   Toronto   London   Sydney

Lawrence Erlbaum Associates, Inc., Publishers
62 Maria Drive
Hillsdale, New Jersey 07642

Distributed solely by Halsted Press Division
John Wiley & Sons, Inc., New York

Library of Congress Cataloging in Publication Data

Main entry under title:

Sentence production.

Includes bibliographical references.
1. Grammar, Comparative and general—Sentences.
2. Languages—Physiological aspects.   3. Speech,
Disorders of.   I. Rosenberg, Sheldon.
P295.S43   415   77-1754

ISBN 0-470-99114-3

Printed in the United States of America

To Irma, my mate of twenty-five years,
and our sons, Eric and Jason,
with all my love

Contents

Preface

For some time now I have been concerned about the general neglect of the problem of sentence production (or more generally, speech production) in psycholinguistics. True, there is a body of research and theory on sentence production in the literature, but next to sentence comprehension, sentence perception, and sentence memory, the offerings are meager at best. The present volume is an attempt to begin the task of remedying this situation. In it will be found original, invited contributions that represent a number of the major trends of research and theory in this area. We hope these papers will stimulate other students of language and language behavior to become involved with the problem of understanding the organization and operation of man's productive linguistic capabilities. Thus, there was no attempt in preparing the present volume to create a handbook of ongoing research and theory in sentence production. The reader will note, for example, the absence of papers concerned exclusively with the current work on articulatory programming, the speech monitoring function, or speech errors.

The order in which the papers in this volume appear reflects my own perceptions of topic overlap. Thus, the papers by Selnes and Whitaker, Gosnave, and Jaffe have to do with the biological foundations of language production; the paper by Rochester, Thurston, and Rupp has to do with pausal phenomena in speech and their possible disruption; the papers by Osgood and Bock and by Ertel deal mainly with motivational determinants of sentence structure in speech; the papers by Schlesinger, Rosenberg, Danks, Kempen, and Jarvella are all concerned in one way or another with the problem of understanding how ideas are translated into utterances; and the paper by O'Connell is addressed to the problem of identifying the units of speech production.

The introduction and overview chapter was designed to serve two functions: first, to introduce the reader who is unfamiliar with this area to some of the major theoretical accounts of speaking in the literature; second, to present an overview of the contents of the individual contributions to the volume.

SHELDON ROSENBERG

1
Introduction and Overview

Sheldon Rosenberg
University of Illinois at Chicago Circle

There are available in the literature a number of reviews of various segments of the research and theory in the area of sentence or speech production (Fodor, Bever, & Garrett, 1974; Laver, 1970; Rochester, 1973; Valian, 1971) and, moreover, certain of the papers in the present volume contain reviews of portions of this material (see, particularly, the paper by Danks and the one by Rosenberg), so I have no intention of attempting to survey the field in this Introduction. What I will attempt to do, rather, is describe some of the major directions of thinking about sentence or speech production in the literature and then present a brief overview of the contributions to the present volume. It will be noted that I have not included in what follows a description of accounts that make use of associative-probabilistic principles in the treatment of sentence or speech production (e.g., Lounsbury, 1965; Osgood, 1963; Wickelgren, 1969).

THEORETICAL REVIEW

We owe a debt of gratitude to Blumenthal (1970) for making those of us, who were unfamiliar with it, aware of Wundt's thinking about sentence production. Blumenthal included in his historical work, *Language and Psychology*, a translation of some passages from the 1912 edition of Wundt's *Die Sprache* which show him to have been a major forerunner of not only Lashley (1951), but Chomsky (e.g., 1957, 1959) as well. Wundt begins his account of sentence production—the sentence and not the word or some smaller unit was primary for him—by rejecting the classical view of a sentence as consisting of a sequence of associated conceptual units or lexical items. Briefly, according to Blumenthal's translations, Wundt's view of the sentence production process can be characterized in the following fashion. At the first stage in the process a whole

1

mental configuration or idea (whose components exist simultaneously) is generated. This configuration is then organized into logically or grammatically related segments (i.e., subject and predicate) and the segments in question further expanded into hierarchically organized constituents. Transformations may then operate on the output of the initial stages of the process so as to produce orderings of constituents in overt production that are different from the orderings that would result from the initial structuring. Finally, a phonological configuration is produced which becomes part of a simultaneous hierarchically organized structure that controls the process of articulation.

It is clear from Blumenthal's translations that Wundt, like Chomsky, was influenced by Von Humboldt's distinction between the inner and the outer form of utterances, and felt that no theory which emphasized only the latter could hope to account for either sentence production or language structure. It is not surprising, therefore, that his account of sentence planning and execution is similar to the models that have been inspired by Chomskian transformational grammar (see, e.g., Katz & Postal, 1964, pp. 169–172).

Unfortunately, with the coming of the behaviorist revolution in psychology and linguistics, Wundt's ideas about sentence production were lost to students of language production. Some, however, began to think again in such terms when Lashley's (1951) influential article on serial organization in behavior appeared. Lashley, however, was evidently unaware of Wundt's psycholinguistic work for he makes no mention of it in the article in question.

Generalizing on the then available data on the neuromuscular organization of behavior, and the facts of language structure, bilingualism, and speech errors, Lashley was led to speculate on speech production and other kinds of serially organized activities. Briefly, according to Lashley, (a) the serial organization of speech is not the result of word-to-word associations but, rather, hierarchically organized neural action schemata (that are more general than the particular syntactic patterns the language permits) which determine serial order all the way from the level of discourse to the level of the vocal movements of articulation; (b) words are not selected one at a time as needed for execution but readied, or activated partially, in larger groups prior to articulation; and (c) the elements and relations of the idea that underlies an utterance exist simultaneously rather than sequentially.

What of the nature of the control of the movements of the vocal apparatus? Lashley speculated, first, that the control mechanism is central rather than peripheral; second, that it involves essentially the translation of spatial patterns derived from systems of spatial coordinates into temporally organized movements; and third, that it is intimately related to the control of speech rhythms.

From a substantive research standpoint, Lashley's greatest contribution has been the result of his suggestions concerning the control of the movements of the vocal apparatus. According to MacNeilage (1970) and Sussman (1972), it is a combination of a spatial representation of phonological input that specifies the targets of articulatory movements ahead of time, and closed-loop feedback during articulation, which is responsible for the motor control of serial order in speech. Lashley's influence, however, is also evident in recent work on the hierarchic control of syllable duration in speech production (e.g., Lackner & Levine, 1975; MacKay, 1974).

Both Wundt and Lashley proposed that the speech planning and execution unit is larger than the individual word. According to Wundt, it is a linguistic unit, the sentence, while for Lashley it is more general than any particular linguistic unit. What is important, however, is that for both theorists speech is planned in hierarchically organized terminal units that encompass more than an individual word. In recent years, Boomer and Laver (Boomer, 1965; Boomer & Laver, 1968; Laver, 1970) appear to have been the chief proponents of the view that the basic unit of speech planning and execution is a linguistic one. These investigators, moreover, adopted the phonemic clause (Trager & Smith, 1951) as the typical unit of spontaneous speech.

According to Laver (1970), the phonemic clause, or what he prefers to call the "tone group" (after Halliday, 1967), is marked by its length (in syllables), the presence of a highly stressed syllable generally at or in the neighborhood of its terminus, the presence of a terminal pitch contour, and boundary pauses. Also, the phonemic clause frequently corresponds to the syntactic clause, and is involved in intonation and rhythm. It is to be noted, finally, that on the above view, the phonemic clause is not only the typical unit of speech planning, but the typical unit of speech execution as well, since it is thought that this unit is spoken as a whole.

It is of interest to note here that the view that a certain type of linguistic structure is strategic for speech planning and execution is consistent with a number of different views of the relation between thought and speech. Thus (briefly), on one view the thought that underlies speech is organized in such a fashion that it is best expressed in linguistic units the size of, for example, syntactic clauses. Note that in this case thought precedes clausal planning in the speech production process, and it is the organization of thought which is responsible for certain of the decisions made in the course of speech planning and execution.

A second view is that thought precedes clausal planning and is organized and constrained in ways that have no necessary implications for speech planning and execution, but that constraints on information-processing load, communicative effectiveness, output monitoring, and the like peculiar to speech planning and execution are what make the syntactic clause strategic.

Third, there is the view that the development (for whatever reason) of speech planning and execution strategies that favor a particular type of linguistic "packaging" serves to constrain subsequently the organization of ongoing thought. In other words, on this view, thought comes to be organized with a view toward how it is best realized linguistically.

Last, there is the view that thought, as we know it, is made possible by the acquisition of our speech capability, and therefore the units of speech planning are the units of thought and the units of speech execution the means by which our thoughts are externalized.

This last view, and its variants (e.g., Vendler, 1970), is clearly the most radical of the lot and the one which students of, for example, nonhuman animal cognition, the development of cognition in prelinguistic humans, and the relationship between nonlinguistic environmental-perceptual input and speech production are most likely to object to. Osgood (1971), for example, has found reason to reject the view "that there can be no thinking without language [p. 499]," and appears to reject as well (if I read him correctly) the claim that a certain type of linguistic structure is strategic for speech planning and execution. For Osgood, who has studied the relationship between nonlinguistic environmental input and the form and content of the sentences used to describe that kind of input, nonlinguistic perceptual—motor activity and speech are controlled by the same nonlinguistic cognitive system. This system, moreover, which has its origin in the prelinguistic perceptual—motor behavior that relates to objects, actions, events, locations, etc., in the world, has both a semantic and an organizational component.

McNeill (1975) has recently attempted to develop a performance (as opposed to a competence) model of the origin and organization of speech which emphasizes prelinguistic perceptual—motor activity, but for some reason he makes no mention of Osgood's work or of his own earlier (e.g., McNeill, 1966, 1970a, b) claims concerning the psychological reality of the structures and operations of Chomskian transformational grammar. Briefly, according to McNeill (1975), speech production mechanisms develop out of the cognitive action schemas of Piaget's sensory-motor stage of intellectual growth and their subsequent "interiorization" (i.e., differentiation from overt action). In addition, he rejects the notion that the organizational unit of speech production is a linguistic unit such as the phonemic clause or the syntactic clause, on the grounds that such units are not semantically motivated, and proposes instead that for both children and adults, it is the syntagma of Kozhevnikov and Chistovich (1965). A syntagma is a unit of speech articulation (i.e., a speech segment which is pronounced as a whole) that corresponds to a single underlying unit of meaning. Thus, McNeill (1975) feels, as Lashley did, that the mechanism which controls the serial organization of speech production is ". . . more general than the notion of a grammatical rule . . . [p. 355]."

Children's syntagmas, in McNeill's view, undergo a process of enrichment as they are extended to express more abstract thoughts, a process which ". . . makes distortions possible in the process of thought itself, higher levels of mental functioning conforming too directly to the structure of the speech mechanisms [p. 352]."

Lashley, as I pointed out earlier, was influenced in his thinking about serial order by, among other things, facts about the organization of speech errors. In recent years, however, some students of linguistic performance, the most noteworthy being Fromkin (1971; but see also Garrett, 1975), have proposed that observations about the organization of speech errors have implications for the entire process of speech production. I would like to end this section of my Introduction, therefore, by outlining Fromkin's model of the process by which a single sentence (basically a clause of the type that interested Boomer & Laver, 1968) is produced. It is to be noted in the summary presented below, which is based upon her 1971 paper, that the processing is serial. In a more recent paper (Fromkin, 1973, pp. 11–45), she considers certain possibilities for parallel processing:

Stage 1. At the first stage in the sentence production process a semantic component generates an idea or a meaning to be expressed and stores it in a buffer store.

Stage 2. The task of mapping internal semantic relations, emphasis, and the like onto terminal linguistic entities begins at this stage. Here, a syntactic generator structures the elements of the meaning syntactically and a semantic generator assigns semantic features to elements of the syntactic structure. Thus, at the end of this stage the content of the buffer store is "... a syntactic structure with semantic and syntactic features specified for the word slots [p. 49]."

Stage 3. At this stage a sentence intonation contour (including the location of primary stress) is generated and added to the information in the buffer. Thus, according to Fromkin, syntactic structuring precedes and lexical selection follows the generation of an appropriate intonation contour.

Stage 4. The language user now enters his internal lexicon with the semantic and syntactic featural information in the buffer and engages in the process of lexical selection, the details of which I will omit here. Suffice it to say that the output of this stage is basically a syntactically bracketed and syllabically ordered string of feature-specified phonological segments.

Stage 5. Finally, at Stage 5, the stored output of Stage 4 is acted upon, if necessary, by certain "morphophonemic constraints of the language" and the automatic process of phonetic coding and articulatory programming takes place.

OVERVIEW

Ola A. Selnes and Harry A. Whitaker. These authors review what is known (from clinical and other observations) and what can reasonably be hypothesized concerning the neurological organization of language functions including speech production. Thus, it appears that the most important cortical areas for language functions are Broca's area (speech production, among other things), Wernicke's area (receptive language; i.e., auditory reception, recognition, and interpretation), and the angular region (serving, among other things, a cross-modal associative function). There is also some evidence which suggests that certain subcortical structures (especially the thalamus) are involved in the control of some of the features of expressive language (e.g., voice volume, speaking rate). Third, it seems (as one would anticipate) that the cortical tracts interconnecting the primary language areas as well as the cortical tracts that connect the primary language areas with their surrounding cortical areas play a role in speech and other language functions. Fourth, there is evidence of involvement of the basal ganglia and the cerebellum in the motor control of speech, with the cerebellum serving, for example, to regulate prosody and the fine movements of articulation.

These investigators also address themselves to the major question that interested Lashley, namely, that of the specific mechanisms by which the brain controls the movements of articulation, and stress in their treatment of this question the importance of the feedback the cerebellum and cortical control areas receive from the articulatory system. Thus, there are both central and peripheral aspects to the motor control of speaking. What I found most interesting, however, in Selnes and Whitaker's discussion of the control of articulation was the observation that "the rapid and precise motor control required for speech by far exceeds any other type of motor behavior in terms of its level of sophistication" (page 27).

Selnes and Whitaker end their paper by making some observations about the maturation of the language areas of the brain (e.g., that they are in general late-maturing areas) and reviewing what little is known at present about the dominance of language functions by the left cerebral hemisphere.

Georges Gosnave. Much of the information on the neurological organization of speech production comes from studies of aphasia such as Gosnave's. Under the stimulation of Hécaen's important work on the differentiation of subgroups within the classification of sensory (speech reception) aphasias, Gosnave studied the performance of aphasic patients with varying locations of temporal lobe damage, nonaphasic brain-damaged patients, and normals on a controlled sentence production procedure. This procedure involved presenting subjects with several sets of words and asking them to use each set in a single short sentence. The sets were constructed so as to permit the investigator to study how subjects handle semantic restrictions and syntactic constraints in producing sentences. The procedure itself is interesting because it bears some relationship to the research paradigm used by Danks, by Jarvella, and by Rosenberg in their studies reported on in the present volume to gain access to certain of the semantic and syntactic planning components of the sentence production process.

What was interesting in the responses of the aphasics as a whole was "the predominance of semantic over syntactic errors" (page 43) on the sentence production test which was associated with a low repetition rate for the lexical input. Also, there was evidence that the aphasics were less task oriented than the other groups in their performance on the sentence production test. In general, then, I believe these results suggest that an information-processing performance deficit may be involved in the sentence production behavior of sensory aphasics. However, it is to be noted that the sentence production performance of the aphasic subgroups (which had been defined in terms of localization of lesion) showed both similarities and differences.

Joseph Jaffe. The Markovian communication rhythms of verbal and nonverbal behavior and their biological significance is the topic of Jaffe's paper, a case in point being the rhythms of dialogue (the alternations of states of speaking and listening). One thing Jaffe has observed is an appreciable degree of intraindividual consistency in such rhythms across "experiential fluctuations," a fact which he suggests might possibly serve to "enhance interpersonal predictability in one sphere of social interaction and conceivably aid in the linguistic decoding process as well" (page 52). In the course of his exposition, Jaffe presents a mathematical–statistical treatment of "rhythm control" at the level of behavior and then speculates about its underlying physiological organization and biological significance.

S. R. Rochester, Sharon Thurston, and Judith Rupp. The purpose of the study reported on by these investigators was to determine whether speakers who have difficulties making their speech understandable at the levels of multiclause sentences and connected discourse (thought-disordered schizophrenics) also show characteristic patterns of hesitation pauses between and within clauses. The view that guided their research was that the location of hesitation pauses signals when the speaker is engaging in certain speech planning activities, and therefore, speakers having difficulty putting clauses together should differ from other speakers in the hesitation pauses of their speech at clause boundaries. Speech samples were collected in interviews and in the cartoon description-followed-by-interpretation task of Goldman-Eisler (1961). The subjects were thought-disordered schizophrenics, nonthought-disordered schizophrenics, and normals, and a variety of measures of hesitancy was used.

Goldman-Eisler, in her study of description and interpretation (i.e., cognitive difficulty) found that speakers spent relatively more time pausing during interpretation than they did during description. The present authors, however, found just the opposite to be the case for all of their subject samples. Difficulties in manipulating the demand characteristics of speech-eliciting tasks and differences between their study and Goldman-Eisler's (educational level of subjects, instructions) were cited as possible factors responsible for the observed reversal. (See, however, the paper by Rosenberg in the present volume for a discussion of what he feels are fundamental methodological problems with Goldman-Eisler's original procedure.)

To return to the main concern of the present investigators, it seems that there is evidence, at least from the interviews, that thought-disordered speakers produce longer silent pauses (absolutely and relatively) at clause boundaries than other speakers but not within clauses. Thus, speakers of the sort that had previously been shown to have difficulty producing coherent sequences of clauses tend to pause more at clause boundaries during spontaneous speech. Herein lies a paradox, however, according to the present authors, for "if pauses indicate cognitive processing time, then why does the greatest amount of pausing produce the least coherent discourse?" (page 81). The remainder of their paper is devoted to an attempt to answer this question and related ones.

Charles E. Osgood and J. Kathryn Bock. Osgood's (1971) view of sentencing and its relation to nonlinguistic perceptual-motor events which I summarized earlier is discussed further and elaborated upon in the present paper. In it a unified account of linguistic performance is presented which includes information-processing components that serve both sentence production and sentence comprehension, and makes use of a *performance* rather than a *competence* grammar. In the main, however, the present paper "is concerned with some production principles which, in different ways, modulate the relative salience of the meaning components of the ideas (intentions) to be expressed" (page 90). Three such principles are mentioned, *Naturalness* ("the *inherent* salience of the *meaning components as wholes*"), *Vividness* ("the *inherent* salience of the *semantic features* of the meaning components to be expressed [i.e., their affective intensity . . .]"), and *Motivation-of-speaker* ("interest, concern, ego-involvement, etc.–the notion of 'focus' generally"). The significance of Naturalness for sentence production "is that the natural order of constituents will correspond to that most frequently experienced in prelinguistic, perception-based comprehending" (page 90), while the expected effect of the two other variables is for the constituents that express them to show a tendency to shift toward the left and appear earlier in sentence productions.

The present paper includes a review of literature relevant to the foregoing principles (which includes the work Ertel reports on in the present volume), a report of a reanalysis of some of Osgood's earlier (1971) data from the standpoint primarily of the principle of Naturalness, and a report of a study by Bock which was concerned primarily with the principle of Vividness.

Suitbert Ertel. The studies reported on by Ertel are relevant to Osgood's proposal that many of the grammatical properties of the sentences we produce can be traced to the organization of the cognitive representations of our nonlinguistic perceptual–motor activities. Ertel's particular interest, however, is in the phenomenon *grammatical subject-of-sentence,* and he begins his paper with a critique of available linguistic accounts of this phenomenon, offering in their place a psychological interpretation based upon certain speculations about the sentence planning process. According to Ertel, sentences have their origin in the speaker's view of the world ("phenomenal field"), a view that includes the speaker's perception and conception of himself or herself (i.e., his or her "ego"). The utterances produced, however, are considered to be a selection from among the possibilities in the phenomenal field at any given time.

The first step in the planning of a particular sentence, according to Ertel, is "nominal seizing," that is, selection of the nominal unit present in the phenomenal field which is closest to the ego component. Subsequently, the product of nominal seizing becomes "the primary reference point" for the planning of the sentence and the element that will appear as the first noun phrase when the sentence is uttered and serve the role of grammatical subject.

The studies reported on by Ertel were designed to evaluate predictions derived from his view of sentence planning.

I. M. Schlesinger. Linguistic theory, the facts of (normal and disrupted, child and adult) language processing, and some plausible assumptions constitute the background for the speculative model of the components of speech performance that Schlesinger sketches out in his paper. Briefly, the semantic elements and their interrelations which are viewed as being the immediate input to utterance planning are termed the *input-marker* by Schlesinger. The origin of a particular utterance, however, is not to be found in the input marker but in the speaker's current (nonlinguistic) cognitive structure. Thus, input-markers reflect the structuring of certain selected aspects of ongoing perception and thought preparatory to speech. Schlesinger, then, unlike Osgood, argues for different organizations for thought and speech planning and execution, and offers many observations which he feels support his position.

Realization rules, including *lexicalization* (word selection), take an input-marker as input and convert it into a structure suitable for articulatory programming. A given input-marker, however, can have different surface realizations, with each one serving a different communicative function. Thus, Schlesinger's model includes a component (*communicative considerations*) that makes a selection from among them. Realization rules involve, in addition to lexical selection, grammatical category marking, serial ordering, inflectional and function word selection, and intonational and phonological structuring. Last, the output of the operation of the realization rules is the input to an articulatory component.

Sheldon Rosenberg. Rosenberg's paper begins with a rather critical review of a sample of the descriptive—correlational literature on the significance of pauses in spontaneous speech, the experimental literature in speech production, and the attempts to develop models of speech performance from observations on the organization of speech errors, citing problems of theory, methodology, data analysis, and data interpretation. However, he believes that questions about the determinants and organization of the speech production process can be resolved if "we turn our attention toward the development of manipulative research paradigms which (a) insure adequate control over input, (b) limit information processing demands, and (c) constrain the speaker's responding" (page 196). His review, however, did lead him to formulate a number of hypotheses about the organization and operation of the speech production process which envisage (a) flexibility in regard to when and where speech planning can take place, (b) flexibility in regard to the requirements of speech planning, (c) multiple determination of pauses in speech, (d) flexibility in regard to the units of speech planning and execution, (e) the availability of shortcutting strategies for speech planning and execution, and (f) differences in the ease of sentence planning associated with differential input demands and content relations. The remainder of Rosenberg's paper is a report of a series of experiments on item (f) and its relation to sentence processing time and complexity which ends with a proposal concerning the operation of differential, overlearned linguistic programming strategies for talking about semantically related and semantically unrelated input that is not unrelated to Kempen's (this volume) proposal concerning the importance of syntactic constructions in speech planning.

Joseph H. Danks.   Danks distinguishes two models of the speech production process, the discrete processing model (idea generation, syntactic structuring and lexical selection, phonological representation, monitoring for communicative effectiveness, articulatory programming, articulation), in which idea generation precedes and is independent of linguistic coding, and an alternative model which he appears to favor. Thus, according to Danks,

> In typical speech production situations, sentences and ideas are produced simultaneously in an abstract code corresponding to speech. That is to say, our response mode determines the symbolic code used in thinking and influences the direction and structure of thought. Thought is possible in several modes, but one of the most common is speech. (page 230)

It seems clear, then, that Danks shares some of Kempen's views with respect to the relations between thought and sentence construction.

Danks' paper consists largely of a report of investigations that were designed to evaluate features of these alternative views of sentence production that have to do with the relationship between thought and sentence construction, the results of which he takes as supporting the view that "idea generation and sentence production represent the same functional process" (page 231).

Gerard Kempen.   According to Kempen, there are three major components to the process of speech production, content selection (conceptualization), syntactic form selection (formulation)—including the conversion of content into morpheme strings and a selection from among alternative syntactic forms for a given content—and phonetic realization (speaking). However, Kempen argues that there are circumstances under which the decision about the syntactic form of an utterance, or some portion of it, is made *prior* to the decision concerning its content, that the former decision can serve to constrain the latter, and that the origin of such syntactic decisions is to be found in the situational context (theme) in which the speaker is operating. Thus, with Kempen's view thought comes to be influenced by the syntactic organization of the linguistic devices available for its expression. Support for this view, according to Kempen, comes from both informal and experimental observations, including the results of an experiment of his own on the production of previously learned sentences.

Robert J. Jarvella. Jarvella's paper is concerned mainly with the question of the nature of the syntactic decisions that convert speaker semantic judgments (via predications) into sentence productions, and he, like Rosenberg and like Danks, utilized a lexical-input strategy for initiating, and gaining access to the ideational and linguistic components of, the sentence production process. Thus, with the view "that verbs in English correspond roughly to (some of the) predicates underlying English sentences" (page 278) Jarvella undertook to carry out a series of experiments in which complement- and noncomplement-taking verbs were presented to speakers for use in sentences and their effects on sentence processing time and structure determined. His findings led, among other things, to some suggestions concerning the importance of the early portions of sentences (see also Osgood & Bock in this regard) in the expression of mood, person, and tense, and the form of the performance rules and strategies speakers use in syntactic planning during the process of sentence production.

Daniel C. O'Connell. O'Connell's concerns in the area of speech production have been with such problems as semantic influences on pausing (O'Connell, Kowal, & Hörmann, 1969) and the development of pausing in spontaneous speech (Kowal, O'Connell, & Sabin, 1975). However, O'Connell chose in the present instance to concern himself with a critical analysis of the definition of the sentence and its status as a unit in speech production, and in the course of his analysis he finds reason to reject traditional, linguistic, and psycholinguistic (behavioral) views of the sentence and its primacy as the unit of speech production. He is particularly critical of linguistic accounts that "ignore the reality of paragraphs" and other discourse structures, behavioral accounts that tend to use pauses to bracket (isolate) sentential units in spontaneous speech, and descriptions of language development that revolve around the sentence.

REFERENCES

Blumenthal, A. L. *Language and psychology.* New York: Wiley, 1970.

Boomer, D. S. Hesitation and grammatical encoding. *Language and Speech,* 1965, 8, 148–158.

Boomer, D. S., & Laver, J. D. M. Slips of the tongue. *British Journal of Disorders of Communication,* 1968, 3, 2–11.

Chomsky, N. *Syntactic structures.* The Hague: Mouton, 1957.

Chomsky, N. Review of Skinner's *Verbal behavior. Language,* 1959, **35**, 26–58.

Fodor, J. A., Bever, T. G., & Garrett, M. F. *The psychology of language.* New York: McGraw-Hill, 1974.

Fromkin, V. A. The non-anomalous nature of anomalous utterances. *Language,* 1971, **47**, 27–52.

Fromkin, V. A. (Ed.) *Speech errors as linguistic evidence.* The Hague: Mouton, 1973.

Garrett, M. F. The analysis of sentence production. In G. Bower (Ed.), *Advances in learning theory and motivation.* Vol. 9. New York: Academic Press, 1975.

Goldman-Eisler, F. Hesitation and information in speech. In C. Cherry (Ed.), *Information theory.* London: Butterworth, 1961. Pp. 162–174.

Halliday, M. A. K. *Intonation and grammar in British English.* Janua Linguarum, Series Practica, 48. The Hague: Mouton, 1967.

Katz, J. J., & Postal, P. M. *An integrated theory of linguistic descriptions.* Cambridge, Massachusetts: MIT Press, 1964.

Kowal, S., O'Connell, D. C., & Sabin, E. J. Development of temporal patterning and vocal hesitations in spontaneous narratives. *Journal of Psycholinguistic Research,* 1975, **4**, 195–207.

Kozhevnikov, V. A., & Chistovich, L. A. *Speech, articulation, and perception.* Washington, D. C.: U. S. Department of Commerce, Joint Publication Research Service, 1965.

Lackner, J. R., & Levine, K. B. Speech production: Evidence for syntactically and phonologically determined units. *Perception and Psychophysics,* 1975, **17**, 107–113.

Lashley, K. S. The problem of serial order in behavior. In L. A. Jeffress (Ed.), *Cerebral mechanisms in behavior.* New York: Wiley, 1951.

Laver, J. D. M. The production of speech. In J. Lyons (Ed.), *New horizons in linguistics.* England: Penguin, 1970. Pp. 53–75.

Lounsbury, F. G. Transitional probability, linguistic structure and systems of habit-family hierarchies. In C. E. Osgood & T. A. Sebeok (Eds.), *Psycholinguistics: A survey of theory and research problems.* Bloomington, Indiana: Indiana University Press, 1965.

MacKay, D. G. Aspects of the syntax of behavior: Syllable structure and speech rate. *Quarterly Journal of Experimental Psychology,* 1974, **26**, 642–657.

MacNeilage, P. F. Motor control of serial ordering of speech. *Psychological Review,* 1970, **77**, 182–196.

McNeill, D. Semiotic extension. In R. L. Solso (Ed.), *Information processing and cognition.* Hillsdale, New Jersey: Lawrence Erlbaum Associates, 1975.

McNeill, D. Developmental psycholinguistics. In F. Smith & G. A. Miller (Eds.), *The genesis of language: A psycholinguistic approach.* Cambridge, Massachusetts: MIT Press, 1966. Pp. 15–84.

McNeill, D. *The acquisition of language.* New York: Harper and Row, 1970.   (a)

McNeill, D. The development of language. In P. Mussen (Ed.), *Carmichael's manual of child psychology.* Vol. 1. New York: Wiley, 1970. Pp. 1061–1161.   (b)

O'Connell, D. C., Kowal, S., & Hörmann, H. Semantic determinants of pauses. *Psychologische Forschung,* 1969, **33**, 50–67.

Osgood, C. E. On understanding and creating sentences. *American Psychologist,* 1963, **18**, 735–751.

Osgood, C. E. Where do sentences come from? In D. D. Steinberg & L. A. Jakobovits (Eds.), *Semantics: An interdisciplinary reader in philosophy, linguistics, and psychology.* Cambridge, England: Cambridge University Press, 1971. Pp. 497–529.

Rochester, S. R. The significance of pauses in spontaneous speech. *Journal of Psycholinguistic Research,* 1973, **2**, 51–81.

Sussman, H. M. What the tongue tells the brain. *Psychological Bulletin,* 1972, **77**, 262–272.

Trager, G. L., & Smith, H. L. *Outline of English structure.* Norman, Oklahoma: Battenburg Press, 1951.

Valian, V. V. Talking, listening, and linguistic structure. Unpublished doctoral dissertation, Northeastern University, Boston, Massachusetts, 1971.

Vendler, Z. Say what you think. In J. L. Cowan (Ed.), *Studies in thought and language.* Tucson: University of Arizona Press, 1970. Pp. 79–98.

Wickelgren, W. A. Context sensitive coding, associative memory, and serial order in (speech) behavior. *Psychological Review,* 1969, **76,** 1–15.

2

Neurological Substrates
of Language and Speech Production

Ola A. Selnes
Harry A. Whitaker

University of Rochester

INTRODUCTION

In this chapter we will outline some of the major characteristics of those areas of the brain which have been shown to be involved with language, how these areas are interconnected, and some speculations as to how the integrated action of these areas exerts control over the peripheral structures involved in language or speech production. Although emphasis is on the central mechanisms and their structural correlates, some aspects of the peripheral anatomy of speech production are discussed. A few developmental principles are mentioned, as well as some current research relating to cerebral dominance and the equipotentiality of the two hemispheres.

It would be somewhat optimistic to assume that our present knowledge of the neuroanatomy of the cerebral cortex and subcortical structures enables us to provide an exhaustive description of the neurological correlates of language and speech. Some might argue that such a description, in order to be complete, should be nothing short of a description of the entire nervous system. It is true that language is a highly complex form of behavior and that the entire cerebral cortex is more or less "active" during language behavior (as well as during any other type of behavior). However, there is evidence from recent EEG studies that certain areas of the brain are more active than others during language behavior, and furthermore, there is abundant clinical evidence that the neurological integrity of certain areas of the brain is crucial for maintenance of normal language; lesions outside of these areas do not normally interfere with language.

BROCA'S AREA

Broca's area is located in the inferior frontal gyrus (F 3) of the language-dominant hemisphere. This is most frequently the left hemisphere, irrespective of handedness. Some of the clinical evidence suggesting that Broca's area is intimately involved in expressive aspects of language has been reviewed by Hécaen and Consoli (1973), and Whitaker and Selnes (1975a) reevaluated some of the negative evidence, that is, cases of destruction of Broca's area reportedly without any expressive aphasia, and concluded that this area is an important part of the language mechanism of the brain.

The clinical case material available to Broca did not allow him to precisely specify the boundaries of the frontal speech area, and he therefore qualified his conclusions regarding the anatomical localization of the center for expressive speech, stating that it is located in the posterior portion of the third frontal convolution (Broca, 1865). Subsequent observations, purportedly showing that expressive aphasia may occur with lesions outside the area of F 3, led some to postulate that the frontal speech area was much larger than what Broca had originally proposed. Leading authorities in the field of aphasia, like Von Monakow, Mingazzini, Dejerine, and others, argued that the speech area included parts of F 2, the triangular part of F 3, and parts of the insula.

Henschen, in his monumental *Pathologie des Gehirns* (1922), specifically addressed the question of the boundaries of Broca's area. He reviewed about 1350 cases of aphasia, but could find no support for the notion of an "extended" Broca's area, and concluded that the opercular part of the third frontal convolution constitutes the speech area proper of the frontal lobe. Some present-day textbooks of neurology still include the triangular part of F 3, located immediately anterior to the opercular part, as being part of Broca's area, but the bulk of clinical evidence suggests that the integrity of this region of the brain is less crucial for normal motor control of expressive language. This view was also favored by Dandy (1932), who wrote: "From several cases of pure motor aphasia it is my impression that the area concerned in motor speech is somewhat farther posterior than that shown in textbooks [p. 222]."

The inferior frontal gyrus in the dominant hemisphere is usually more highly convoluted than the contralateral one (Gray, 1973). The surface area of the part of the inferior frontal gyrus constituting Broca's area is somewhat larger than the corresponding area in the opposite hemisphere (Blinkov & Glezer, 1968), and the cortex of this region of the brain has also been found to be markedly thicker on the left side than on the right side (Lindon Mellus, 1911). A more recent study of cerebral asymmetries, however, found the surface area of Broca's area to be somewhat smaller than the corresponding contralateral region (Wada, Clarke, & Hamm, 1975). The authors note, however, that differences in the density of packing of the gyri on the two sides could have been a source of possible error: "We suspect that, in spite of our measurement, the total cortical surface area of the operculum could be larger on the left in most brains [p. 245]."

In terms of cytoarchitecture, Broca's area corresponds roughly to Brodmann's Area 44, and von Economo's Area FCBm. It is characterized by the presence of large pyramidal cells in layers IIIc and V, and a thin granular layer. The triangular part (Area 45) differs from Area 44 in that the cells of its Layer V are not as prominent as in the latter. According to Brodmann (1908), Area 44 is a "well-differentiated and sharply delineated field, that on the whole corresponds quite precisely with the opercular part of F 3 [p. 241]." In a later publication, he subdivided Area 44 into 44a and 44b (Brodmann, 1914). A similar distinction was also made by investigators belonging to the Vogt school, who designated Broca's area as Areas 56 and 57 (Knauer, 1909; Kreht, 1936 a & b; Riegele, 1931; Strasburger, 1938). However, more recent investigations of the cytoarchitecture of the frontal lobes suggest that while there may be detectable differences within the opercular part, these may not be worth emphasizing. Bonin (1949) gives the following description of Broca's area:

> The architecture of area 44 . . . differs in many respects from that of the rest of the precentral subsector. It shows a well discernable internal granular layer, and the third and fifth layers, too, show definite substrata, not recognizable in the areas described thus far. It is in keeping with this tendency towards a more "elaborate" lamination that the myeloarchitecture, too, shows a definite stratification with a separation of the two stripes of Baillarger (p.53). . . . The histological differences between the dysgranular area 44 and the agranular portion of the precentral motor cortex may be assumed to express functional differences between these two parts [p. 57].

One of the reasons why the exact boundaries of Broca's area have been difficult to establish is the fact that there may be rather striking individual variations in the amount of cortex devoted to a particular cytoarchitectural area. It has been known for quite some time that the pattern of gyri and sulci of the brain differ widely from one individual to another (Cunningham, 1892; Eberstaller, 1890; Retzius, 1896), and there is also evidence that the more prominent sulci in most cases represent fairly reliable demarcations of cytoarchitectural areas (Sanides, 1962). The inference can thus be made that the size of different cytoarchitectural areas varies from one brain to another. This is true for Broca's area (Knauer, 1909; Kreht, 1936a, b; Riegele, 1931) as well as for other areas of the brain (Whitaker & Selnes, 1975b). This variability in the size of cortical area 44 may be, as noted by Bolton (1911), one of the reasons why clinicopathological correlations of disease of the frontal lobes have been subject to such divergent interpretations.

The inferior frontal gyrus derives its blood supply from branches of the middle cerebral artery. Broca's area is most commonly supplied by the orbitofrontal branch, which is one of the first branchings of the middle cerebral artery, and thus a prime candidate for receiving traveling emboli. There are, however, considerable individual variations in the angioarchitecture of the cerebral cortex

(Waddington, 1974), and it is therefore not possible to generalize beyond the fact that the frontal speech area is normally supplied by one or more branches of the middle cerebral artery.

WERNICKE'S AREA

Not long after Broca's proposal concerning the role of the inferior frontal gyrus in expressive language, Wernicke correlated disorders of receptive language with a lesion in the posterior part of the dominant temporal lobe. For some reason, the status of this region of the brain, later to become known as Wernicke's area, as a true language "center" has been much less disputed than the frontal language area. In fact, some of the most ardent opponents of Broca's theory proclaimed that Wernicke's aphasia was the only true form of aphasia (Moutier, 1908).

Wernicke's area, a specialized type of auditory association cortex, is located in the posterior portion of the superior (first) temporal gyrus. Just like Broca, Wernicke himself did not specify the exact boundaries of the area in the temporal lobe which he believed to be essential for receptive language functions. Later investigators, while agreeing on the general location of the posterior language area, have held different opinions concerning its size. Some differences in terminology should also be noted; for example, in French, the term Wernicke's area is used collectively for the posterior part of the superior temporal lobe and the angular region of the parietal lobe. The variability in size of what different investigators consider as constituting Wernicke's area may in part be explained in terms of different views of what constitutes Wernicke's aphasia. If, for example, anomic or amnestic aphasia is included in this syndrome, as is done by Penfield and Roberts (1959), the middle temporal gyrus becomes part of Wernicke's area. Another factor which could be partly responsible for the somewhat divergent views on the exact location and size of Wernicke's area is that of individual variation. Although nobody appears to have addressed this question directly with regard to Wernicke's area per se, it has been known for a long time that both the primary auditory region (Heschl's gyrus), immediately adjacent to Wernicke's area, and the *planum temporale* (part of Wernicke's area) are subject to rather large individual variations (De Crinis, 1934; Minckler, 1972; Pfeifer, 1920), and it is therefore reasonable to assume that similar variations may exist for Wernicke's area as a whole.

It is well documented that the planum temporale is normally larger in the left than in the right hemisphere. This was first pointed out by Geschwind and Levitsky (1968), and their findings have later been corroborated by Teszner, Tzavaras, and Gruner (1972). The anatomical asymmetry of the planum temporale has also been shown to be present in newborn infants (Witelson & Pallie, 1973) and in fetuses (Teszner *et al.*, 1972; Wada *et al.*, 1975). There is as yet no direct evidence that this asymmetry of the temporal lobes is causally related to language. Von Economo and Horn (1930) noted that no asymmetries have been found in the gyral pattern of the superior part of the temporal lobes in the orangutan and chimpanzee, and Wada *et al.* (1975) could not find any asymmetries in the brains of the rhesus monkey and baboon. However, Le May and Geschwind (1975) have recently reported that the brain of the orangutan shows rather conspicuous asymmetries in the temporal region. This leaves the question of a possible relationship between morphological asymmetries of the two hemispheres of the brain and language open to further research.

Data from different investigators are not in entire agreement concerning the cytoarchitectural parcellation of the temporal lobe (Crosby, Humphrey, & Lauer, 1962), but a few areas are generally considered to be readily identifiable. These include Brodmann's Areas 41 and 42, the primary auditory area, and the surrounding Area 22, which occupies the remainder of the posterior part of the superior temporal convolution. Wernicke's area basically comprises the posterior part of Area 22, but some also prefer to include Area 42 as part of Wernicke's area. The cellular arrangement of the primary auditory cortex is characterized among other things by the width of the granular layers and by the relatively small size of the majority of its cells. One of the chief distinguishing features of the surrounding parakoniocortex (Wernicke's area) is the large size of the pyramidal cells of Layer III, presumably reflecting the associative nature of this type of cortex (Sanides, 1975). Functionally, Area 41 has been characterized as the auditory receiving area, Area 42 as the (auditory) recognition area, and area 22 as the (auditory) interpretive area (Krieg, 1966). Others prefer to talk about areas 41 and 42 as being receptive, and Area 22 as being associative in nature.

Wernicke's area is supplied by the temporal branches of the middle cerebral artery. The number and branching pattern of these temporal branches show considerable individual variations, in part explaining why vascular lesions involving the superior temporal lobe are so variable in terms of severity of and degree of recovery from language problems.

THE ANGULAR REGION

A third region of the brain which has been demonstrated to be of importance for symbolic functions is located in the parietal lobe, and comprises the angular and supramarginal gyri. The supramarginal gyrus surrounds the termination of the ascending part of the fissure of Sylvius, and the angular gyrus that of the (ascending) superior temporal sulcus (Fig. 1). Collectively, they are referred to as the inferior parietal lobule or the angular region. As can be seen from Fig. 1, the inferior parietal lobule is strategically located for purposes of cross-modal association, being contiguous with the association cortex of the somatosensory, auditory, and visual areas.

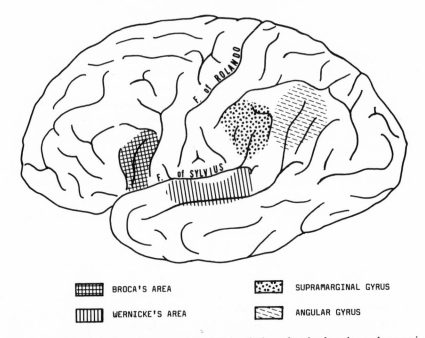

FIG. 1   Drawing of the lateral aspect of the left hemisphere showing location and approximate size of the four major language areas. (Fissural pattern after Eberstaller, 1890.)

The gyral pattern of the angular region tends to be highly variable, possibly related to the fact that this area of the brain is of recent phylogenetic origin. There are a few descriptions in the literature of brains showing interhemispheric asymmetry in the degree of development of the angular region (Guszman, 1901), but so far nobody appears to have established whether this difference consistently favors one or the other hemisphere. Von Economo has published maps showing how the various cortical areas differ in thickness, but he apparently did not look for interhemispheric differences. His data do indicate, however, that the upper part of the inferior parietal lobule is one of the most highly developed regions of the brain in terms of cortical thickness.

According to von Economo, the supramarginal gyrus, Area PF (Brodmann's Area 40) shows most clearly the characteristics of parietal (Type 3) cortex, being characterized by a well-defined six-layered structure. The granular layers are quite dense, and the cells of Layers III and V somewhat smaller but larger in number than those of the corresponding layers in the frontal lobes. Area PG (Brodmann's Area 39), the angular gyrus, shows a similar structure, with perhaps an even more conspicuous columnar arrangement of the cells. Cytoarchitecturally, there is a rather gradual transition from Area PG to the occipital and temporal lobes.

SUBCORTICAL STRUCTURES

Broca's area, Wernicke's area, and the angular region constitute the three cortical areas of most importance for language functions. Lesions of any of these regions will interfere with normal linguistic behavior. A discussion of aphasic syndromes following lesions to the left hemisphere can be found in Whitaker and Whitaker (in press). Although aphasic syndromes are rarely, if ever, pure, frontal lesions may be said to produce disorders primarily expressive in nature, and posterior lesions disorders of a receptive type. Lesions of the angular and supramarginal gyri may produce different types of syndromes, depending on how much subcortical white matter is affected. In general, injury to the angular gyrus produces anomic aphasia and a variety of alexic and/or agraphic symptoms. A lesion of the supramarginal gyrus may be highly disruptive, particularly if it interrupts the underlying long association tracts, in which case a conduction type aphasia is likely to ensue.

While it was formerly thought that only lesions involving cortical matter could interfere with the language system, there is now some evidence suggesting that pathology of the thalamus may also have a disruptive effect on language behavior. This evidence is derived from case studies of spontaneous lesions of the thalamus, surgical lesions for the treatment of movement disorders, and electrical stimulation preparatory to or during surgery of the thalamus.

It was not until Penfield and Roberts (1959) published data from their stimulation experiments that the possibility that subcortical structures may participate in language functions began to receive serious attention. Prior to that time, reports of cases of thalamic tumors had suggested that a left-sided tumor in a left-hemisphere dominant patient may sometimes be associated with language disorders; it is generally accepted, however, that intracranial tumors provide a rather unreliable basis for localization studies.

Various disorders of speech and language have been reported as sequels to stereotaxic surgery for the treatment of Parkinson's disease or intractable pain. The most common target in these operations has been the ventrolateral (VL) area, but there are also some data from surgical lesions of the pulvinar. In the case of VL-lesions, the most commonly observed postoperative deficits have been reduced voice volume and dysarthria. Language deficits are much less common, although some expressive difficulties have been noted (Botez & Barbeau, 1971). Receptive aphasia has not been observed as a sequel to thalamotomy.

There are also numerous reports of alterations in speech functions during electrical stimulation of thalamic nuclei. The most commonly reported effects of stimulation of the ventrolateral area include arrest or acceleration of speech, and sometimes a progressive decrease in voice volume (Guiot, Hertzog, Rondot, & Molina, 1961; Hassler, Riechert, Mundinger, Umbach, & Ganglberger, 1960; Schaltenbrand, 1965). Ojemann and Ward (1971) reported that stimulation of the left VL evoked alterations in object naming in 6 of 13 patients. They also found that anomic responses were more frequently elicited from left pulvinar stimulation than from VL stimulation. Effects on object naming were not seen with stimulation of right thalamic nuclei.

It thus appears that any interference with the normal activity of particularly the left VL nucleus will have some detrimental effect on speech, and possibly also language. On the basis of the known anatomical connections of this nucleus, with inputs from the cerebellum and basal ganglia, and projections to the precentral motor cortex, it is not surprising that stimulation or coagulation of the VL nucleus will affect speech. How the effects on language are brought about is not, however, entirely clear. Mohr, Watters, and Duncan (1975) reported on two living and four autopsied cases of thalamic hemorrhage and found that the patients' language performance varied considerably with degree of alertness. When fully alert, "the patients appeared virtually intact in language function, including intact repeating from dictation, but quickly lapsed into a state of unwonted logorrheic paraphasia resembling delirium [p. 3]." The language deficits seen in these cases thus appear to be secondary to a malfunction of thalamically related arousal mechanisms, and are not comparable to any of the classical aphasic syndromes.

Fedio and van Buren (1975), on the other hand, have argued for a more specific role of the thalamus in linguistically related functions. They suggest that although the disorders resulting from lateral thalamic lesions are not usually clinically prominent, they are nevertheless cognitive in nature: ". . . we argue that the lateral thalamus enters cognitive processing at a pre-perceptual stage. Coding and perception of verbal and non-verbal stimuli are reserved for neocortical association areas where insult creates obvious intellectual deficits. In contrast, lateral thalamic lesions generate different language and memory disorders which are clinically less evident [p. 98]."

Several other theories have been proposed to account for the data so far available on thalamically related speech and language disorders (see *Brain and Language,* 2(1), 1975). Further study of thalamic syndromes and application of neuro- and electrophysiological techniques to this important collection of nuclei will hopefully soon allow some more specific conclusions to be made about the relationship between the thalamus and language. At this point, the statement by Penfield and Roberts (1959) "that the functions of all three cortical speech areas in man are coordinated by projections of each to parts of the thalamus and that by means of these circuits the elaboration of speech is somehow carried out [p. 207]" remains to be challenged, and to be further specified.

THE INTERCONNECTIONS

The manner in which different cortical areas are interconnected follows certain general principles, one of which was formulated by Flechsig (1901), essentially stating that no primary cortical area receives or sends long cortical association fibers. This implies that the primary areas communicate chiefly through their surrounding association areas, from where the long association tracts (or fasciculi) originate. (For an exception to Flechsig's principle, see Selnes, 1974.) One of the most important of these association tracts for language is the arcuate fasciculus, whose inferior part interconnects among other things the posterior language area with the frontal language area (Fig. 2). Rather than being made up of single or continuous axons, the arcuate fasciculus consists of a number of shorter fibers synapsing with others to form a long bundle (Rosett, 1933). The superior part of this bundle, also known as the superior longitudinal fasciculus, connects the superior part of the frontal lobes with the parietal and occipital lobes. A separate bundle of fibers courses from Wernicke's area posteriorly to the region of the angular gyrus (Krieg, 1966). Another projection from the temporal lobe runs from the anterior part of Area 22 to the prefrontal and orbital regions. The significance of this connection, known as the uncinate fasciculus, for language is not clear. The angular region also communicates with areas in the frontal lobe, including Broca's area and Exner's center, via a prominent bundle of fibers, the occipitofrontal fasciculus.

Although the nature of the information transmitted by these association

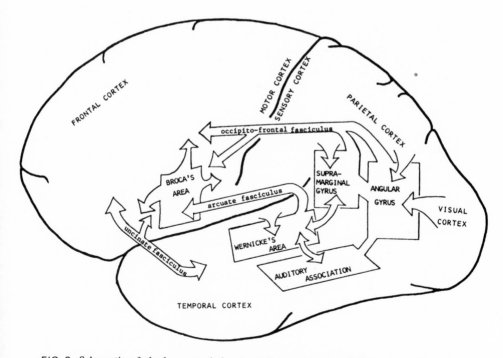

FIG. 2 Schematic of the long association tracts interconnecting the language areas of the left hemisphere. (Modified from Whitaker, 1971.)

tracts, or the type of coding the messages undergo, is by no means known, the clinical symptoms associated with lesions or total interruption of these pathways clearly indicate their importance for language functions. For a detailed discussion of such syndromes, the reader is referred to Geschwind (1965, 1969). In addition to the long association fibers connecting the language areas of the brain with each other, they are obviously also interconnected with the surrounding cortical areas, and depend on the integrity of these areas for proper functioning. A case which illustrates this rather dramatically was reported by Geschwind, Quadfasel, and Segarra (1968). They studied the language behavior of a young woman who survived for about 10 years following accidental carbon monoxide poisoning. Her language output was restricted to a few stereotyped phrases, and she showed no evidence of comprehension. She was, however, able to repeat words and sentences fluently and without any articulatory problems. At post mortem, the patient's brain showed intactness of the language areas and their interconnections, but the cortical areas surrounding the language areas were essentially destroyed.

Considerable exchange of information also takes place between the two halves of the brain, via so-called commissural fibers, the most important of which is the corpus callosum. Despite a large number of both anatomical and functional studies of this structure, no general agreement exists as to its exact function in man. The possibility that the corpus callosum may play some part in the mechanisms underlying the establishment of functional cerebral dominance for language will be discussed later. The two hemispheres are also connected via some smaller commissures, including the anterior, posterior, and hippocampal commissures. Even less is known about the function of these structures than about the corpus callosum.

Exchange of information between the cerebral cortex and subcortical structures is carried out via so-called projection fibers. These originate largely from the deeper layers of the cortex, and are commonly named according to their origin and destination, for example, corticothalamic, corticospinal, etc. They mediate among other things motor functions, modulation of reflex activity and sensory input, regulation of attention, and state of arousal. Most of these fibers come together in the internal capsule, a lesion of which may have devastating effects. If the lesion includes the pathways to lower motor neurons innervating the vocal tract musculature, a spastic type of dysarthria will result.

BASAL GANGLIA AND CEREBELLUM

In addition to the highly specialized neocortical areas, there are other parts of the brain which participate in speech functions. One such structure, a collection of nuclei in the depth of the brain, is the basal ganglia. These nuclei, the caudate, putamen, and globus pallidus, are part of the extrapyramidal system, which is phylogenetically older than the pyramidal system. Because of their numerous interconnections with other parts of the central nervous system it has proved difficult to obtain data on their specific functions. The so-called basal ganglia syndromes are all chiefly motor in nature, including disturbances of muscle tonus, derangement of movements, loss of automatic associated movements, etc.

The globus pallidus sends projections to the motor and premotor cortex via the thalamic fasciculus and the ventral anterior and ventral lateral nuclei of the thalamus, and some fibers also descend, via the subthalamic nucleus and the reticular formation, to the spinal cord. The caudate sends most of its fibers to the putamen, which in turn projects to the globus pallidus. Another source of input to the globus pallidus (and putamen) is from the substantia nigra. Projections back from the motor and premotor cortex to the caudate have been demonstrated in the monkey, and these fibers are probably also present in man.

The disorders of speech associated with basal ganglia lesions may be separated into two groups, those associated with lesions of the substantia nigra and globus pallidus (pallidal) and those associated with lesions of the putamen and caudate (striatal). The pallidal syndrome is characterized by resting tremor, problems in initiation of movements, and a reduction in the range of movements. The speech sometimes appears to be speeded up in rate in such cases. The striatal syndrome is chiefly characterized by extraneous, involuntary movements superimposed on the articulatory movements, such as a sideways jerk of the head, protrusion of the tongue, or facial grimaces (Whitaker, in press a).

The cerebellum is a relatively well explored region of the brain, both in terms of its anatomy and physiology (Larsell & Jansen, 1972; Eccles, Ito, & Szentagothai, 1967). It may be considered an integrating structure, where information from different levels of the central nervous system is received, processed, and then returned to its origin, presumably to be used in a regulatory manner. It receives input from the spinal cord, vestibular and brainstem nuclei, and from diencephalic and cortical structures. Clinical data indicate that the cerebellum plays some role in the regulation of the fine motor movements required for speech. Attempts have been made to localize the areas within the cerebellum that are concerned with speech, and there is some agreement that lesions of the posterior lobe, particularly if bilateral, are usually associated with disorders of speech. Even extensive pathology of other regions of the cerebellum has not been reported to produce any speech deficits (Minckler, 1972).

Cerebellar speech disorders, referred to as ataxic dysarthrias, are characterized by imprecise articulatory movements occurring at irregular intervals. The inaccuracy manifests itself as errors in timing of movements as well as in errors in the range and direction of movements. In addition to articulatory inaccuracies, the prosodic aspects of speech are usually also affected. This may take the form of reduction of, alteration of, or absence of word and sentence stress, and a tendency to equalize syllable durations.

The structures described so far are all part of the central nervous system. Some

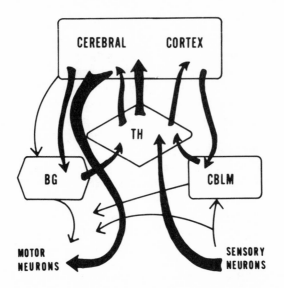

FIG. 3 Diagrammatic representation of some of the major tracts connecting the cerebral cortex, basal ganglia (BG), thalamus (TH), and cerebellum (CBLM) with each other. (Adapted from Whitaker, in press a.)

of their major interconnections are diagrammatically depicted in Fig. 3. Before turning our attention to a few aspects of the peripheral nervous system, passing mention should be made of the syndrome of akinetic mutism. This is a clinical condition characterized by total mutism and complete immobility, apart from the eyes. It may be caused by lesions of different central nervous system structures, with some part of the reticular activating system most frequently being involved. Mutism does not as a rule occur as a result of lesions restricted to the cortical language areas.

PERIPHERAL ASPECTS

The peripheral nervous system comprises the cranial and spinal cord nerves and parts of the autonomic nervous system. Since a detailed description of the innervation pattern of the cranial nerves may be found in most textbooks of neurology, only a schematic representation of those cranial nerves relevant for speech will be given here (Fig. 4). Lesions of the nuclei of the cranial nerves innervating the vocal tract musculature, their axons, or the neuromuscular junction result in a flaccid type of dysarthria. This disorder is characterized by reduced muscle tone and a considerable reduction of the force of muscle contraction. The specific features of the speech impairment depend on what part of the vocal tract is most seriously affected. Involvement of cranial nerves V,

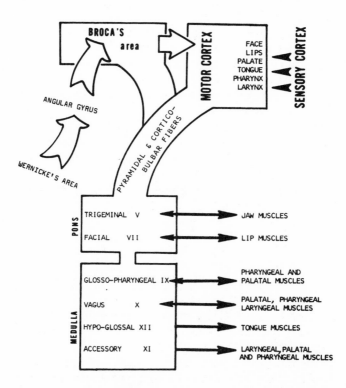

FIG. 4 Diagram representing neural circuits involved in expressive language, including the cranial nerves relevant to speech and their innervation. (Modified after Whitaker, 1971.)

VII, and XII, for example, will result in inaccuracies of consonant articulation due to weakness of either the tongue or the lip–facial muscles.

The ease with which we can articulate the sound sequences of our native language tends to obscure the fact that the rapid and precise motor control required for speech by far exceeds any other type of motor behavior in terms of its level of sophistication. Researchers in the field of speech production and related areas have, however, recently been able to map out some of the neurophysiological mechanisms which may explain how the brain is able to adequately program the vocal tract musculature with sufficient speed and accuracy to make articulate speech possible. Because the configuration of the vocal tract is constantly changing during speech, the central control mechanisms must be kept informed at all times about the length, location, and velocity of every muscle group used in articulation, in particular those of the tongue, the most important of the articulators. A major portion of this information, or feedback, is provided by small receptors within the muscles, known as muscle spindles. While the muscle spindles, or gamma system, of skeletal muscles relay their information to the cerebellum, those of the vocal tract musculature apparently project directly back to the cortex. If this is the case, the gamma system of speech may be able to operate somewhat more rapidly than the classical gamma system which is involved in mechanisms of postural control. An outline of how the gamma system may work in speech may be found in Bowman (1971) and Sussman (1972). Another source of feedback used in speech is provided by cutaneous or tactile receptors, which project both to the sensory-motor cortex and to the cerebellum. This type of feedback may be particularly important for articulation of consonants. Whatever the precise mechanism of tactile and proprioceptive feedback, it is clear that the cerebellum is intimately involved in the fine motor control of speech. Lesions of the cerebellum may produce ataxic dysarthria with little or no involvement of other motor systems (Kent & Netsell, 1975; Whitaker, in press b).

DEVELOPMENTAL ASPECTS

Knowledge about the development of the nervous system may provide important information as to the neuronal mechanisms underlying language, and a background against which behavioral data on language acquisition may be interpreted. Furthermore, it may provide clues as to which components of language may be innate and which may be acquired. Although far from being complete, the knowledge which is available so far on the maturation of the nervous system is sufficiently rich to allow for several interesting hypotheses.

Neuronal maturation from birth onward progresses in a cephalic direction, starting at the level of the brainstem, which is relatively mature and functional at birth, and terminating in the cerebral cortex, which attains complete functional maturity only some time around puberty, and further development probably goes on until about the age of 20 years. In terms of development of individual nerve cells, Jacobson (1970) has proposed a theory of neuronal specificity in which three classes of neurons are distinguished on the basis of their developmental characteristics. Class I neurons originate early in embryonic life and are generally large neurons with long axons that form the primary afferent and efferent pathways in the brain. Class II neurons are interneurons which originate later, and they are usually smaller and continue to differentiate well into postnatal life. Class III neurons are specified even more slowly during postnatal life, as the organism continues to develop. Both Class II and III neurons depend upon adequate sensory stimulation for their full and normal development and for the maintenance of their connections. The importance of early stimulation has been demonstrated most clearly in the case of the visual system; a large body of behavioral, neurophysiological, and anatomical evidence suggests that early visual deprivation exerts rather profound influences on the developing visual system (Bondy, 1973; Sherman, 1973; Wiesel & Hubel, 1963). In the case of the auditory system cases of congenital deafness have provided some information about the effects of inadequate stimulation. Siebenmann and Bing (1907) looked at the gross morphology and cell size of the superior temporal convolution in a deaf-mute, and found it to be both macro- and microscopically poorly developed. Similar findings were reported by Horn (1930). Stengel (1930) looked at the structure of Broca's area in the same brain as that reported on by Horn (1930). He found the left F 3, in particular the opercular region, to be poorly developed, but no prominent cytoarchitectural abnormalities were identified. This could be related to the fact that this particular patient had not been congenitally deaf, but became deaf at the age of four years.

Maturation within a cortical area starts with the innermost layers (VI and V) and progresses toward the outer layers (II and I). This implies that the first major connections to be established are those between the periphery and primary cortical areas (sensory—motor, visual, and auditory cortices). The next connections to develop are those between these primary areas and their respective association areas. The last pathways to become fully developed are the ones between the different association areas. These long association tracts, including the arcuate fasciculus and the corpus callosum, do not become fully myelinated until about the age of puberty. One implication of this particular sequence of maturation is that sensory inputs can be processed before they can become appropriate stimuli for perceptions and motor responses.

In terms of the sequence of maturation of different cortical areas, the sensory—motor cortex matures first, and remains the most mature area of the cerebral cortex up to about six years after birth (Conel, 1939–1967). Based on anatomical criteria, the visual cortex is next in order of maturity, and the last primary region to develop fully is the auditory cortex. Electrophysiological data suggest, however, that auditory evoked potentials show adult characteristics at an earlier age than visual evoked potentials (Ellingson, Danahy, Nelson, & Lathrop, 1974). Within the sensory-motor cortex, maturation starts in the region of the hand area and progresses upward toward the leg and downward toward the head area. It simultaneously proceeds anteriorly in the direction of Broca's area and posteriorly toward the parietal region. The language areas which are last to develop are Broca's area, the angular gyrus, and the supramarginal gyrus. Further details on the ontogenesis of the language areas of the brain, in particular cytoarchitectural data and myelogenesis, may be found in Aranovich (1939) and Whitaker (1973).

An intact auditory system is a prerequisite for development of normal language. The feedback provided through the auditory modality is quite important for speech production, particularly during language acquisition. The maturation of the auditory system is, however, quite slow, and although no specific age can be given for its full development, it is known that children do not attain adult scores on several tests of auditory function before the ages of 7–11 years (Fior, 1972). It is also known that the disruptive effect on speech of delayed auditory feedback is age dependent, with this effect becoming less prominent with increasing age. These functional studies are corroborated by anatomical studies which indicate that the auditory system has a rather prolonged period of maturation. Myelination of the acoustic radiations is probably not complete until about 4 years postnatally, compared with about 5 months for the visual system (Yakovlev & Lecours, 1967), and Conel's data (1939–1967) indicate that the association areas of the auditory cortex are still not fully mature at the age of four years.

These data impose certain constraints on the interpretation of recent studies of infant speech perception indicating that 4-week-old infants show evidence of dishabituation to linguistically contrasting elements. The maturational state of the auditory cortex at four weeks makes it unlikely, however, that the infants' capacity for linguistic discriminations has a cortical basis. There are also reports to the effect that some subhuman species are able to perform similar linguistic discriminations (Kuhl & Miller, 1974, 1975), and a study by Walker and Halas (1972), using electrophysiological techniques, would suggest that the neural mechanisms involved could be at the brain-stem level.

The mechanisms underlying development of unilateral cerebral dominance for language, and possibly other functions, are still poorly understood. It has been suggested that the difference in size between the language areas in the left hemisphere and the corresponding areas in the right hemisphere could be one factor, but it is probably not the case that a quantitative difference alone between the two brain-halves could be the basis for language laterality. Compare the fact that only about 65% of the brains in the Geschwind and Levitsky (1968) and Teszner *et al.* (1972) series had a larger left hemisphere with the well-known fact that something in excess of 90% of the population have left-hemisphere dominance for language.

The fact that language develops most frequently in the left hemisphere could conceivably be related to the observation that the left hemisphere appears to develop more rapidly than the right hemisphere. This suggestion was first made by Broca (1865), who quoted the work of two of his colleagues on the development of the fissural pattern of the two hemispheres: ". . . in the development of the brain, the convolutions of the left side appear earlier than those of the right. The first ones are already delineated at a point when the others are not yet apparent [p. 383]." Although no reference to a difference in the rate of maturation of the two hemispheres has been found in the more recent developmental literature, Broca's suggestion that the precocious development of the left hemisphere may relate to language lateralization remains an interesting one.

It has also been proposed that the corpus callosum, the largest of the interhemispheric commissures, may play some part in establishing cerebral dominance (Selnes, 1974). On the assumption that either hemisphere could theoretically participate in language functions, one might expect to find some mechanism which allows one hemisphere to gain exclusive control over linguistic functions. The corpus callosum has been shown to be at least partly inhibitory in function, and it is therefore possible that it may serve to suppress activity in the hemisphere contralateral to the one subserving language. The most compelling evidence for this view derives from the fact that all published cases of congenital absence of the corpus callosum in which language laterality has been investigated have reported bilateral distribution of language. This theory does not attempt to explain why language develops most frequently in the left hemisphere, it merely suggests that the corpus callosum could be the neural substrate of a mechanism involved in preventing duplication of a function which can be unilaterally subserved.

According to standard neurological teaching, the two hemispheres at birth are equally capable of subserving language. This view is based chiefly on cases of infantile hemiplegia which demonstrate that even with massive lesions of the left hemisphere, language will still develop, presumably in the right hemisphere. Dennis and Whitaker (1975) reviewed most of the published cases of infantile hemiplegia, and concluded, contrary to the above, that the two hemispheres are not equally at risk with regard to language disorders following early cerebral insults. Early left hemisphere damage is much more frequently associated with language disorders than lesions of the right hemisphere. Furthermore, tests of linguistic abilities in subjects who have had one hemisphere removed shortly after birth indicate that those subjects who have undergone left hemispherectomy have lower scores that those who have had the right hemisphere removed (Dennis & Kohn, 1975). These data thus suggest that while both hemispheres can subserve language, the left hemisphere appears to be inherently better equipped for this particular function. It is probable that this left superiority for language has some structural or physiological correlates, but apart from the gross morphological differences mentioned above, no differences between the two hemispheres which could be related to language have been identified. The language areas in the left hemisphere and the corresponding areas in the right hemisphere do not appear to differ in terms of their cytoarchitectural structure, and so far, no differences have been found on the neurochemical level. The left hemisphere is, however, more highly vascularized than the right, and there are also characteristic differences between the hemispheres in terms of blood flow, but whether or not these differences have anything to do with the left hemisphere's apparent specialization for language remains to be established.

REFERENCES

Aranaovich, J. Ontogenia de los centros del Lenguaje. *Revista Neurologica de Buenos Aires,* 1939, **4**, 3–54.

Blinkov, S. M., & Glezer, I. I. *The human brain in figures and tables.* New York: Plenum Press, 1968.

Bolton, J. S. A contribution to the localization of cerebral function based on the clinico-pathological study of mental disease. *Brain,* 1911, **33**, 26–148.

Bondy, S. C. The regulation of regional blood flow in the brain by visual input. *Journal of Neurological Science,* 1973, **19**, 425–432.

Botez, M. I., & Barbeau, A. Role of subcortical structures and particularly the thalamus in the mechanisms of speech and language. *International Journal of Neurology,* 1971, **8**, 276–299.

Bowman, J. P. *The muscle spindle and neural control of the tongue.* Springfield, Illinois: Thomas, 1971.

Broca, P. P. Sur Le Siège de la Faculté du langage Articulé. *Bulletin de la Societe d'Anthropologie,* 1865, **6**, 377–393.

Brodmann, K. Beiträge zur histologischen localisation der grosshirnrinde. VI. Mitteilung: Die Cortexgliederung des Menschen. *Journal für Psychologie und Neurologie,* 1908, **10**, 231–246.

Brodmann, K. Physiologie des gehirn. Die anatomische feldertopographie der grosshirnober-flache. In F. Krause (Ed.), *Die Allgemeine Chirurgie der Gehirnkrankheiten.* Stuttgart: Enke, 1914.

Conel, J. L. *The postnatal development of the human cerebral cortex.* Cambridge, Massachusetts: Harvard University Press, 1939–1967.

Critchley, M. *The parietal lobes.* London: Arnold, 1953.

Crosby, E. C., Humphrey, T., & Lauer, E. W. *Correlative anatomy of the nervous system.* New York: Macmillan, 1962.

Cunningham, D. J. *Contribution to the surface anatomy of the cerebral hemispheres.* Dublin: Royal Irish Academy, 1892.

Dandy, W. E. Effects of total removal of left temporal lobe in right-handed person: Localization of areas of brain concerned with speech. *Archives of Neurology and Psychiatry,* 1932, **27**, 221–224.

de Crinis, M. *Anatomie der hörrinde.* Berlin: Springer-Verlag, 1934.

Dennis, M., & Kohn, B. Comprehension of syntax in infantile hemiplegics after cerebral hemidecortication: Left hemisphere superiority. *Brain and Language,* 1975, **2**, 472–482.

Dennis, M., & Whitaker, H. A. Language acquisition in the right and left hemisphere. Paper presented at a Conference of Language Development and Neurological Theory, Brock University, St. Catharines, Ontario, May 9–10, 1975.

Eberstaller, O. *Das Stirnhirn.* Wien and Leipzig: Urban & Schwarzenberg, 1890.

Eccles, J. C., Ito, M., & Szentagothai, J. *The cerebellum as a neuronal machine.* New York: Springer-Verlag, 1967.

Ellingson, R. J., Danahy, T., Nelson, B., & Lathrop, G. H. Variability of auditory evoked potentials in human newborns. *Electroencephalography Clinical Neurophysiology,* 1974, **36**, 155–162.

Fedio, P., & van Buren, J. M. Memory and perceptual deficits during electrical stimulation in the left and right thalamus and parietal subcortex. *Brain and Language,* 1975, **2**, 78–100.

Fior, R. Physiological maturation of auditory function between 3 and 13 years of age. *Audiology,* 1972, **11**, 317–321.

Flechsig, P. Developmental (myelogenetic) localization of the cerebral cortex in the human subject. *Lancet,* 1901, **II**, 1027–1029.

Geschwind, N. Disconnexion syndromes in animal and man. *Brain,* 1965, **88**, 237–294, 585–644.

Geschwind, N. Problems in the anatomical understanding of the aphasias. In A. L. Benton (Ed.), *Contributions to clinical neuropsychology.* Chicago: Aldine, 1969.

Geschwind, N., & Levitsky, W. Human Brain: Left–right asymmetries in temporal speech region. *Science,* 1968, **161**, 186–187.

Geschwind, N., Quadfasel, F., & Segarra, J. Isolation of the speech area. *Neuropsychologia,* 1968, **6**, 327–340.

Gray, H. In C. M. Goss (Ed.), *Anatomy of the human body*. Philadelphia: Lea & Febiger, 1973.

Guiot, G., Hertzog, E., Rondot, R., & Molina, P. Arrest or acceleration of speech evoked by thalamic stimulation in the course of stereotaxic procedures for Parkinsonism. *Brain*, 1961, **84**, 363–369.

Guszman, J. Beitrag zur morphologie der genirnoberflache. *Anatomischer Anzeiger*, 1901, **19**, 239–249.

Hassler, R., Riechert, T., Mundinger, F., Umbach, W., & Ganglberger, J. A. Physiological observations in stereotaxic operations in extrapyramidal motor disturbances. *Brain*, 1960, **83**, 331–349.

Hécaen, H., & Consoli, S. Analyse des troubles du langage au cours des lesions de l'aire de Broca. *Neuropsychologia*, 1973, **11**, 377–388.

Henschen, S. E. Über motorische Aphasie und Agraphie. In *Klinische und Anatomische Beiträge zur Pathologie des Gehirns*. Vol. VII. Uppsala: Almquist & Wiksell, 1922.

Horn, L. Die Supratemporalflachen eines Taubstummengehirns. *Zeitschrift für Neurologie und Psychiatrie*, 1930, **130**, 758–774.

Jacobson, M. *Developmental neurobiology*. New York: Holt, Rinehart, & Winston, 1970.

Kent, R., & Netsell, R. A case study of an ataxic dysarthric: Cineradiographic and spectrographic observations. *Journal of Speech and Hearing Disorders*, 1975, **40**, 115–134.

Knauer, A. Die myeloarchitektonik der Brocashen region. *Neurologisches Zentralblatt*, 1909, **28**, 1240–1243.

Kreht, H. Zur volumengrösse der Architektonischen Felder 55–66 einiger Menschlicher Gehirne im vergleich zu der Schimpansen und Orang-utan. *Zeitschrift für Mikroskopisch-Anatomische Forschung*, 1936, **39**, 409–414. (a)

Kreht, H. Cytoarchitektonik der motorisches Sprachzentrums. *Zeitschrift für Mikroskopisch-Anatomische Forschung*, 1936, **39**, 331–354. (b)

Krieg, N. J. S. *Functional neuroanatomy*. Evanston, Illinois: Brain Books, 1966.

Kuhl, P. K., & Miller, J. D. Discrimination of speech sounds by the chinchilla: /t/ vs /d/ in CV syllables. *Journal of the Acoustical Society of America*, 1974, (Suppl.) **56**: S 52, Abstr. Z 5.

Kuhl, P. K., & Miller, J. D. Speech perception by the chinchilla: Phonetic boundaries for syntactic VOT stimuli. *Journal of the Acoustical Society of America*, (Suppl.) 1975, **57**, S49. (Abstr. X 13)

Larsell, O., & Jansen, J. *The comparative anatomy and histology of the cerebellum*. Vol. 3. Minneapolis: University of Minnesota, 1972.

LeMay, M., & Geschwind, N. Hemispheric differences in the brains of great apes. *Brain, Behavior & Evolution*, 1975, **11**, 48–52.

Lindon Mellus, E. A contribution to the study of the cerebral cortex. *Anatomical Record*, 1911, **5**, 473–482.

Minckler, J. Communication disorders. In J. Minckler (Ed.), *Pathology of the nervous system*. Vol. 3. New York: McGraw-Hill, 1972. Ch. 206.

Mohr, J. P., Watters, W. C., & Duncan, G. W. Thalamic hemorrhage and aphasia. *Brain and Language*, 1975, **2**, 3–17.

Moutier, F. *L'Aphasie de Broca*. Paris: Steinheil, 1908.

Ojeman, G. A., & Ward, A. Speech representation in ventrolateral thalamus. *Brain*, 1971, **94**, 669–680.

Penfield, W., & Roberts, L. *Speech and brain mechanisms*. Princeton, New Jersey: Princeton University Press, 1959.

Pfeifer, R. A. *Myelogenetisch-anatomische Untersuchungen über das Kortikale ende der Hörleitung*. Leipzig: Teubner, 1920.

Retzius, G. *Das Menschenhirn.* Stockholm: Norstedt, 1896.

Riegele, L. Die cytoarchitektonik der Felder der Brocaschen region. *Journal für Psychologie und Neurologie,* 1931, **42,** 496–514.

Rosett, J. *Intercortical systems of the human cerebrum.* New York: Columbia University Press, 1933.

Sanides, F. Die Architektonik des Menschlichen Stirnhirns. *Monographien aus dem Gesamtgebiete der Psychiatrie.* No. 93. Berlin: Springer-Verlag, 1962.

Sanides, F. Comparative neurology of the temporal lobe in primates including man with reference to speech. *Brain and Language,* 1975, **2,** 396–419.

Schaltenbrand, G. The effects of stereotaxic stimulation in the depth of the brain. 1965, **88,** 835–840.

Selnes, O. A. The corpus callosum: Some anatomical and functional considerations with special reference to language. *Brain and Language,* 1974, **1,** 111–139.

Sherman, S. M. Visual field defects in monocularly and binocularly deprived cats. *Brain Research,* 1973, **49,** 25–45.

Siebenmann, F., & Bing, R. Ueber den Labyrinth- und Hirnbefunde bei einem an retinitis pigmentosa erblindeten angebornen aubstummen. *Zeitschrift für Ohrenheilkunde,* (Wiesb.) 1907, **54,** 265–280.

Stengel, E. Morphologische und Cytoarchitektonsiche studien ueber den Bau der unteren Frontalwindung bei Normalen und Taubgestummen. *Zeitschrift für Neurologie und Psychiatrie,* 1930, **130,** 631–677.

Strasburger, E. H. Vergleichender myeloarchitektonsiche studien an der erweiteren Brocaschen Region der Menschen. *Journal für Psychologie und Neurologie,* 1938, **48,** 477–511.

Sussman, H. M. What the tongue tells the brain. *Psychological Bulletin,* 1972, **77,** 262–272.

Teszner, D., Tzavaras, A., & Gruner, J. L'asymetrie droite-gauche du planum temporale; a propos de l'etude anatomique de 100 cerveaux. *Revue Neurologique,* 1972, **126,** 444–449.

Von Bonin, G. Architecture of the precentral motor cortex and some adjacent areas. In P. C. Bucy (Ed.), *The precentral motor cortex.* Urbana, Illinois: University of Illinois Press, 1949.

Von Economo, C., & Horn, L. Über Windungsrelief, Masse und Rindenarchitektonik der Supratemporalflache, ihre Individuellen und Seitenuterschiede. *Zeitschrift für Neurologie und Psychiatrie,* 1930, **130,** 678–757.

Wada, J. A., Clarke, R., & Hamm, A. Cerebral hemispheric asymmetry in humans. *Archives of Neurology,* 1975, **32,** 239–246.

Waddington, M. M. *Atlas of cerebral angiography with anatomic correlation.* Boston, Massachusetts: Little, Brown, 1974.

Walker, J. L., & Halas, E. S. Neural coding at subcortical auditory nuclei. *Physiology and Behavior,* 1972, **8,** 1099–1106.

Whitaker, H. A. *On the representation of language in the human brain.* Edmonton: Linguistic Research, Inc., 1971.

Whitaker, H. A. Comments on the innateness of language. In R. W. Shuy (Ed.), *Some new directions in linguistics.* Washington, D.C.: Georgetown University Press, 1973. Pp. 95–120.

Whitaker, H. A. Disorders of speech production mechanisms. In E. C. Carterette & M. Friedman (Eds.), *Handbook of perception.* Vol. 7. New York: Academic Press, in press. Chapter 17. (a)

Whitaker, H. A. Levels of impairment in disorders of speech. To appear in: *Proceedings of the 8th International Congress of Phonetic Sciences.* (b)

Whitaker, H. A., & Selnes, O. A. Broca's area: A problem in language brain relationships. *Linguistics,* 1975, 154/155, 91–103.

Whitaker, H. A., & Selnes, O. A. Anatomic variations in the cortex: Individual differences and the problem of the localization of language functions. Paper presented at the New York Academy of Sciences' Conference on Origins and Evolution of Language and Speech, New York City, September 22–25, 1975. (b)

Whitaker, H. A., & Whitaker, H. A. Language disorders. In H. D. Brown & R. Wardhaugh (Eds.), *A survey of applied linguistics.* Ann Arbor: University of Michigan Press, in press.

Wiesel, T. N., & Hubel, D. H. Effects of visual deprivation on morphology and physiology of cells in the cat's lateral geniculate body. *Journal of Neurophysiology,* 1963, 26, 978–993.

Witelson, S. F., & Pallie, W. Left hemisphere specialization for language in the newborn: Neuroanatomical evidence of asymmetry. *Brain,* 1973, 96, 641–646.

Yakovlev, P. I., & Lecous, A. R. The myelogenetic cycles of regional maturation of the brain. In A. Minkowski (Ed.), *Regional development of the brain in early life.* Philadelphia: Davis, 1967.

3

Sentence Production Test in Sensory Aphasic Patients[1]

Georges Gosnave

I.N.S.E.R.M.
Laboratoire de Pathologie du Langage

From the time of the classic writings on aphasia to the present, Wernicke's left temporal lobe area has held a predominant place in the localization of language function in the cortex. Brain damage in this region is likely to disturb all speech modalities. Around the central Wernicke's area, two main poles of language localization have been admitted: an anterior part, in the frontal lobe (Broca's area), the impairment of which may induce motor aphasia; and on the other side, a parietotemporal posterior zone which seems to be preferentially involved in reading. The present study—an investigation of the effects of left temporal lesions on sentence production—deals basically with Wernicke's aphasia.

Although sensory aphasia had been classically characterized by disturbance of speech reception and comprehension, the frequency of defects in other linguistic performances is striking. The verbal expression of the patients is almost always impaired, but difficulties in comprehension may not be restricted to speech. In many cases they have been known to appear in reading. Moreover, since comparisons among patients show that the various language functions are not always disturbed to the same degree, "sensory aphasia" shows a marked variability.

To account for this variability in the syndrome, Hécaen (1969) has studied the performances of a group of sensory aphasics in response to a neurolinguistic test battery. Statistical comparison of the data has permitted the isolation of three relatively homogeneous groups of patients, demonstrating three forms of aphasia

[1] Work of l'Unité de Recherches Neuropsychologiques et Neurolinguistiques (U-111) de l'I.N.S.E.R.M., Laboratoire de Pathologie du Langage de l'E.H.E.S.S.; E.R.A. N° 274 au C.N.R.S.—2ter, rue d'Alésia, 75014 PARIS.

corresponding to the classic distinction between verbal deafness, sensory aphasia, and transcortical sensory aphasia (see Wernicke, 1903):

1. Sensory Aphasia with Predominant Word-Deafness. In this first form, performances are primarily affected by severe defects in verbal reception. Phonemic discrimination, verbal item repetition, comprehension of spoken orders, and writing following dictation are nearly impossible. Comprehension of written orders and transcribed writing are more easily performed. Conversational speech, which is remarkably fluent, shows relatively few paraphasias, especially phonemic ones. Despite the grammatical anomaly of sentences, speech topic remains sufficiently coherent.

2. Sensory Aphasia with a Predominant Comprehensive Disturbance. This second form contrasts with the preceding in being essentially characterized by comprehension disorders of both spoken and written orders. Although impaired, repetition is possible, the response remaining relatively close to the presented item. Phonemic discrimination is only slightly affected. Conversational speech reveals quite an important number of paraphasias, in particular semantic substitutions. Produced sentences are ungrammatical, often stereotyped, and incomplete. The conversational thread is frequently lost in a discourse marked by an important logorrhea.

3. Attentional Disorganization. This last form can be distinguished by the absence of notable sensory defects. Verbal reception and comprehension are almost unimpaired. However, conversational speech displays striking disturbances. Discourse flow is overfluent, the topic being hardly comprehensible. Speech, which shows numerous perseverative phenomena and paraphasic substitutions, is marked by considerable asemantism. Writing is impaired only under spontaneous expressive conditions in a similar way to that of conversational speech. Damage of the left temporal tip was found to be involved in this form of aphasia (Hécaen, Marcie, & Dubois, 1967).

Contrast among these three forms is clearly shown by the varying intensity of verbal receptive and comprehensive defects as well as by the different types of paraphasias in utterances. With regard to expression, logorrhea and the predominantly semantic anomalies in sentences produced in conversational speech tend to appear as the two main tendencies common to all three profiles. In fact, given the idiosyncratic differences of expression between the patients, comparative analysis of data from a relatively free context of communication may prove ambiguous, causing variations due to the specific effects of different forms of aphasia to be hardly interpretable.

In order to reduce the complexity of factors associated with speech elaboration in a free communicative context and to simplify the grammatical analysis of the responses, Dubois and Irigaray (1966) have designed a sentence production test in which the responses are based on verbally presented sequences of words.

Using this test, Assal (1968) showed, in a population of left and right unilaterally brain-damaged subjects, that patients with temporal lesions produced sentences of significantly greater length than those of other nontemporal groups, notwithstanding the hemispheric localization of injuries. Left temporal patients displayed a higher ratio of agrammaticality and failures in the sentence production test than all other groups.

This study investigates the combined effects of aphasia and the intratemporal localization of lesions in a group of patients with left temporal injury. Given the implications of the anterior zone of the temporal lobe for an "attentional" form of aphasia, this localization will be used as a clue to the study of sensory aphasics' performance.

PROCEDURE

Subjects

Forty-four brain-damaged patients and 10 normal subjects, all right-handed, 39 males and 15 females aged from 18 to 67, were tested. All patients underwent neurosurgical operations at the Centre Neuro-chirurgical, Hôpital Sainte-Anne, in Paris. Surgical reports provided information about the localization of lesions.

The following groups were constituted:

Group 1: temporal, N = 25, mean age 41.08 years.

Group 2: nontemporal, N = 19, mean age 39.8 (frontal and rolandic: N = 10; parietal and occipital: N = 9).

Group 3: normal, N = 10, mean age 38.2.

In order to exclude the possibility of an anterior extension of temporal lesions, subjects with temporal damage but showing clinical signs of a motor defect were not selected in Group 1. All patients performed a standard neuropsychological test battery less than one month after operation. None of them displayed intellectual deterioration or confusion. On the basis of their test performance, none of the patients in Group 2 received diagnosis of aphasia. The education level of each patient was established on a three point scale.

Intratemporal selection

Group 1A (N = 4): subjects with temporal damage limited to the temporal lobe tip.

Group 1B (N = 10): subjects with temporal damage including the lobe tip.

Group 1C (N = 11): subjects with temporal damage excluding the lobe anterior part.

Material

The subject is requested to utter a single sentence which must be as simple and short as possible, based on each of nine verbally presented word sequences. This instruction leads the subject to reduce the number of clauses in the produced sentence (simple) as well as the number of word additions (short). Such a restriction permits one to use sentence length to measure the propensity of some subjects to elaborate fluent utterances. In case of failure following the first presentation, the subject is allowed two more trials. Each input sequence includes two, three, or four high-frequency words. The presented sequences are the following:

1. Fauteuil (armchair), docteur (doctor), asseoir (to sit down).
2. Bureau (desk, office), ouvrir (to open), tiroir (drawer).
3. Crayon (pencil), écrire (to write), bleu (blue), feuille (sheet).
4. Arbre (tree), voir (to see), feuille (leaf), vert (green).
5. Maison (house), mère (mother).
6. Maison (house), chat (cat).
7. Feuille (sheet, leaf), voler (to fly), détacher (to detach).
8. Enfant (child), père (father), absent (absent).
9. Cheval (horse), voir (to see), rouge (red).

These word sequences have been chosen so as to constitute approximate sentences which are either asyntactic given the particular order of constituents (for instance Sequence 1), or semantically anomalous with respect to the lexical compatibility between items (for instance Sequence 9). Such variability permits us to establish the subject's ability to separate the semantic restriction of the words themselves from the syntactic implications of the order of the words in the presented sequence.

SCORING PROCEDURE

Sentences

All indices concerning sentences were calculated in proportion to the number of presented sequences.

Correct Sentences

Grammatically correct sentences use at least one of the words from the presented sequence.

Types of Errors

Response Failure. This occurs when there is no response, simple repetition of the presented words, or incomplete fragment of a phrase.

Digressive Production. Here there is a demonstration of a tendency to neglect the test situation in favor of free communication, some of the presented words or the meaning of the sequence being used as a conversational basis.

Grammatical Errors. Provided the patient showed no immediate autocorrection, grammatically anomalous sentences were classified in three types: (1) semantic errors (erroneous sentences with respect to lexical compatibility or semantic agreement among clauses, and incomplete sentences with comparable characteristics); (2) syntactic errors (sentences with deficient concordance, lack or incorrect use of syntactic constituents and similarly incorrect incomplete sentences); and (3) mixed.

Others. These consisted of incorrect sentences showing defects nonassociated to a grammatical error (that is, paraphasias, marked hesitation, etc.).

Words

All indices concerning words were rated in proportion to the number of presented words.

Integrated Correct

Here the number of presented words were integrated in correct sentences.

Types of Errors

Missing Words. Some of the presented words were missing in the produced sentences which were correct.

Lexical Approximations. Nonparaphasic substitutions of presented words took place.

Integrated Incorrect. A number of presented words were integrated in incorrect sentences.

Nonintegrated. A number of the presented words were not used because of response failures.

Paraphasias.

Perseverations.

Sentence Length

The mean number of clauses was a function of the number of presented verbs.

The following data from five neurolinguistic tests were selected for correlation with sentence production performances:

1. Conversational Speech. The number of paraphasias over a 500-word corpus.

Percentage of correct responses in:

2. Repetition Test. 200 words and nonsense syllables.

3. Phonemic Discrimination Test. Elicited by the associative identification of a verbal input with an image in a multiple-choice picture.

4. Comprehension Test. Judged from the execution of verbal and written orders.

5. Object Naming Test.

RESULTS AND DISCUSSION

In both brain-damaged groups, a significant age effect[2] was found, the older subjects' performance being more affected.

Performance of Brain-Damaged Patients without Aphasia

Owing to a greater difficulty in elaborating sentence structures, particularly on the first presentation of the word sequence, brain-damaged patients without aphasia displayed poorer performance than normal subjects: 74% of these patients versus 40% of normal subjects failed at the first trial. Higher means of "response failures" and "nonintegrated words" reflect this fact.

The mean numbers of correct responses and types of errors in sentence production are shown in Tables 1 and 2.

On the other hand, the less accurate integration of presented words was due to a greater proportion of items missing: 58% of nonaphasic patients versus 80% of normal subjects integrated all input words in their sentences (Table 2). In t-test analysis, no statistical difference was found between Groups 2 and 3 concerning grammatically incorrect sentences (Table 1) and lexical approximation errors (Table 2).

[2] Group 1 (aphasic): $r = .48$, $p < .05$. Group 2 (nonaphasic): $r = .42$, $p < .05$. Group 3 (normal): $r = .50$, nonsignificant.

TABLE 1

Mean Percentage of Correct Sentences and Types of Errors
for Aphasic (Group 1), Nonaphasic (Group 2), and Normal (Group 3)
Subjects

Sentences		Group 1 (aphasic)	Group 2 (nonaphasic)	Group 3 (normal)
Correct		25.30	76.06	89.18
Response failure		28.14	13.45	6.54
Digressive		7.25	–	–
Agrammatical	Syntactic	7.94	5.90	2.80
	Semantic	23.26	4.15	1.45
	Mixed	1.00	–	–
	Total	32.20	10.05	4.25
Others		7.20	.42	–

TABLE 2

Mean Percentage of Correct Words and Types of Errors
for the Groups Already Mentioned in Table 1

Words	Group 1 (aphasic)	Group 2 (nonaphasic)	Group 3 (normal)
Integrated correct	31.56	75.17	88.60
Missing	22.47	5.87	3.80
Lexical approximations	3.83	1.79	1.10
Integrated incorrect	10.18	3.80	2.30
Nonintegrated	29.09	13.34	3.00
Paraphasias	2.71	–	–
Perseverations	1.00	–	–

Performance of Sensory Aphasic Patients

The aphasic patients were strongly characterized by the grammatical anomaly of their sentences. One interesting point was the predominance of semantic over syntactic errors: 64% of the subjects in Group 1 (versus 26 and 20% in Groups 2 and 3, respectively) produced predominantly nonsemantic sentences. This was confirmed by the fact that aphasics differed from nonaphasics only when asemantic sentences obtained in both groups were compared ($t = 4.05, p <$ .001), while no difference between these groups was found when comparing syntactic errors. Since aphasic patients tended to correct their syntactic errors, very few mixed types of ungrammatical sentences were found.

TABLE 3
Mean Number of Clauses as a Function of the Number
of Presented Verbs for the Same Groups as in Table 1

	Group 1 (temporal)	Group 2 (nontemporal)	Group 3 (normal)
Mean number of clauses	1.89	1.05	1.16

Added to a high proportion of nonintegrated items resulting from a serious difficulty in sentence structure elaboration, the report of presented words was distinctly affected by paraphasic and perseverative defects in production. However, even in the absence of these last disturbances, the integration of presented words in sentences was impaired by numerous omissions and lexical approximation errors (see Table 3).

The examination of sentence length illustrated another characteristic aspect of the performance of aphasic patients. These subjects were found to differ from nonaphasic and normal subjects in generally producing complex sentences, in spite of the restrictive test instruction to utter simple (that is, kernel) sentences. Together with digressive productions (see Table 1), this variable demonstrates a high fluency in utterances.

Effects of the Intratemporal Localization of the Lesions

In order to determine to what extent the aphasics' responses could be affected by the intratemporal localization of the lesions, data have been collected from three groups (1A, anterior/temporal tip; 1B, antero-posterior/including the tip; 1C, posterior/excluding the tip). Figure 1 shows the mean percentage of correct responses and types of errors.

Examination of the data indicates that the performance within each subgroup generally conforms to the overall profile of the temporal group. However, the performance found in Group 1A tends to gather around a pole characterized by a low proportion of response failures (mean: 13.85, SD 14.15; nonaphasics: mean 13.45, SD 17.13) and few paraphasic sentences. In this group, the "lexical approximation" errors are numerous and the produced sentences complex (see Fig. 1b: sentence length), and digressive productions frequent. On the other side, the performances of Group 1C concentrate around an opposite pole characterized by a high proportion of response failures and paraphasias, while the produced sentences appear to be generally less complex.

Performances of Group 1B settle between the two preceding poles: the high frequency of "lexical approximation" errors and the production of complex sentences relates it to Group 1A, while the proportion of response failures and paraphasic sentences draws it closer to Group 1C.

TABLE 4
Performances of Three Temporal Subgroups in Responses to
Five Neurolinguistic Tests[a]

	Intratemporal Localization Subgroups		
	1A	1B	1C
Object naming[b]	92.50	42.00	52.09
Comprehension[b]	88.75	64.05	59.40
Repetition[b]	83.25	72.35	75.63
Phonemic discrimination[b]	94.66	87.12	91.63
Conversational speech: mean number of paraphasias over 500 words	5.20	5.00	5.36

[a]Group 1A (temporal tip); Group 1B (including the tip); Group 1C (excluding the tip).
[b]% correct.

The differences among the three subgroups with respect to the distribution of responses appeared to be due to a combined influence of both aphasia severity and lesion localization. Table 4 shows the performances of the intratemporal groups on a set of five neurolinguistic tests. The subjects with damage circumscribed to the anterior part manifested only slight defects in naming, comprehension, and verbal reception. Such a fact clinically confirms the distance of the lesions from Wernicke's area and their limited dimension. These patients displayed a quite exclusive impairment in speech expression underlined by the number of paraphasias in conversation. On the other hand, subgroups 1B and 1C displayed performances comparably impaired in all tested modalities of aphasia. "Response failures," a variable clearly characterizing performances of subjects within Groups 1B and 1C were found to be strongly related to comprehension, repetition, and phonemic discrimination tests.[3] The absence of notable receptive defects in Group 1A is accordingly accompanied by a lack of response failures.

On the other hand, despite their distinctly opposing results concerning both lesion size and aphasia severity, the fact that Groups 1A and 1B performed very similarly with respect to sentence length and digressive errors indicates a specific effect due to the anterior localization of damage. The reduction of this type of production in subjects with posterior injury gives support to a localization factor. Finally, no correlations were found between either digressions or complex sentences in performances and the other tests.

[3]Correlation analysis between sentence production variables and the set of five neurolinguistic tests for the subjects of the whole temporal group. All r values significant at a $p < .01$ level.

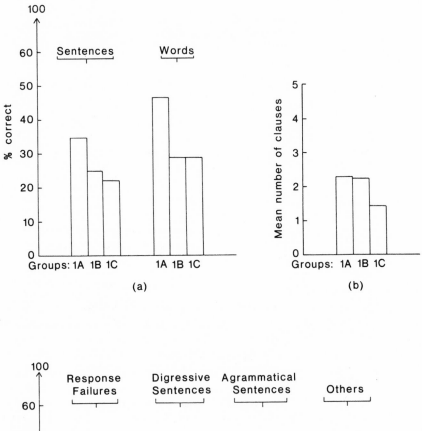

(a)

(b)

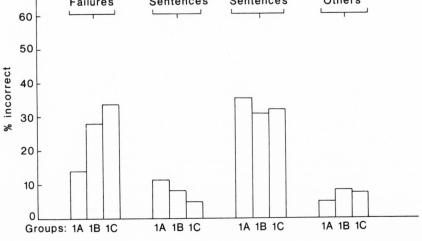

(c)

FIG. 1a, b, c.

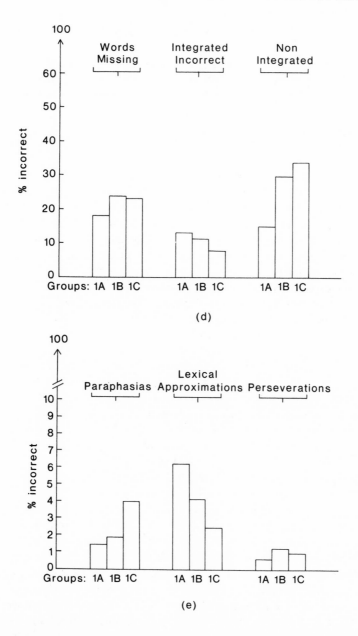

FIG. 1 Mean correct responses and types of errors for three temporal subgroups. Subgroups are: 1A (temporal tip), 1B (including the tip), 1C (excluding the tip). Variables are: (a) mean percentage of correct sentences and correct words; (b) mean number of clauses as a function of the number of presented verbs; (c) mean percentage of incorrect sentences; (d) mean percentage of incorrect words; (e) mean percentage of incorrect words.

The three subgroups were approximately equivalent with regard to grammatical errors.

No differences in types of agrammatical sentences were found among these groups (75% of the subjects in all groups produced predominantly asemantic sentences).

CONCLUSION

The results of the present study showed a marked effect of brain damage on sentence production. Patients with lesions not followed by aphasia displayed significantly poorer performances than those of normal subjects. As could have been foreseen, sentence production was more distinctly affected by temporal lobe lesions. The impoverishment of responses already manifested in nonaphasic subjects was found to be aggravated in temporal group patients. Though performance was impaired on the first presentation of the sequence in nonaphasics, the possibility of elaborating a sentence structure was distinctly ameliorated after successive trials. On the other hand, similar "response failure" types of errors remained quite stationary over all trials in aphasic patients. Four subjects in this group failed to produce any sentence from the input words.

The temporal and nonaphasic groups were equally well distinguished by the former's low accuracy in reporting the presented words in their sentences, due to a high rate of words missing and "lexical approximation" errors, interfering with more specifically expressive disturbances (paraphasias, perseverations).

Digression, a type of error strongly characterizing sensory aphasia, underlined a propensity to neglect the test situation in favor of conversational communication. Related to this behavioral tendency, sentence length measures revealed a marked fluency in production. The high number of added clauses indicated a relatively constant elaboration of complex sentences.

Finally, the responses of aphasic patients were characterized by their "semantic" anomaly, these subjects having displayed a smaller proportion of errors and more frequent corrections at the level of the syntactic constituents in their sentences. A similar predominantly lexical impairment has been shown in previous studies on conversational speech (Dubois, Hécaen, Cunin, Daumas, Lerville-Anger, & Marcie, 1970). However, asemantism may have been exaggerated by the test procedure—an auditory presentation involving the amnesic ability to recall and process the sequence constituents (a significant correlation was found in Group 1 exclusively between the variables "words missing" and "semantic errors"; $r = .63, p < .01$).

Performances obtained from three groups of aphasic subjects selected with respect to varying localizations of lesions appeared to conform to the overall profile of the temporal group's sentence productions. The means of grammatical errors among these subgroups were roughly equivalent. However, the influence of the intratemporal localization may have been responsible for some contrasts among the groups shown by some types of errors in sentence production. Patients with limited temporal tip damage displayed few "response failures," numerous "lexical approximations," and complex sentences. Conversely, patients with posterior temporal injury showed a high ratio of failed and paraphasic responses but few complex sentences with regard to the number of produced clauses. One may argue that such a difference is possibly due to the mere opposition in aphasic severity among these two groups. And indeed patients with an anterior lesion demonstrated an almost exclusive disorder in conversational speech, while those with posterior injury were found to be distinctly impaired in all aphasia modalities. However, a third group with anterior temporal damage followed by a global sensory aphasia shares characteristics with both preceding groups: a high proportion of substitutions and complex sentences draws it close to the group with similar anterior injury, while on the other hand responses were frequently affected by failed and paraphasic productions, a tendency manifested by the group of patients comparably affected by sensory speech defects.

This fact can be interpreted as a combined effect of intratemporal localization and aphasia. Regarding the types of errors in sentence production, the indications provided by the subjects with temporal tip lesions are consistent with an "attentional" form of speech disorganization. Some aspects found to characterize this form of aphasia—perseverations, substitutions, paraphasias, and considerable fluency in conversational flow—appeared to be reflected in the sentence production test.

ACKNOWLEDGMENTS

The author is grateful to Drs. Henri Hécaen and Jean Dubois for their helpful criticism, and to Mr. Hervé Le Bras for the statistical analysis of the collected data.
The research was carried out with the aid of a grant from the Grant Foundation.

REFERENCES

Assal, G. Étude neurolinguistique des productions de phrases chez des malades neuropsychiatriques. Paris: Mémore pour le titre d'assistant étranger, 1968.
Dubois, J., & Irigaray, L. Approche expérimentale des problèmes intéressant la production de la phrase noyau et ses constituants immédiats. *Langages,* 1966, 3, 90–125.
Dubois, J., Hécaen, H., Cunin, S., Daumas, M., Lerville-Anger, B., & Marcie, P. Analyse d'énoncés d'aphasiques sensorielles. *Journal de Psychologie Normale et Pathologique,* 1970, 2, 185–206.

Hécaen, H. Essai de dissociation du syndrome de l'aphasie sensorielle. *Revue Neurologique, Paris*, 1969, **120**, No. 4, 229–237.

Hécaen, H., Marcie, P., & Dubois, J. Aspects linguistiques des troubles de la vigilance au cours des lésions temporales antéro-internes droites et gauches. *Neuropsychologia*, 1967, **5**, 311–328.

Wernicke, C. Der aphasische symptomencomplex. *Die Deutsche Klinik*, 1903, **6**, 487–556.

4

The Biological Significance of Markovian Communication Rhythms

Joseph Jaffe

College of Physicians and Surgeons of Columbia University
and
The New York State Psychiatric Institute

For more than a decade, our laboratory has been investigating Markovian communication rhythms (Jaffe, Cassotta, & Feldstein, 1964; Jaffe & Norman, 1964). We have gradually realized that they are not unique to speech, but characterize certain nonverbal communication rhythms as well (Buchsbaum, 1972; Jaffe, Stern, & Perry, 1973; Natale, 1976). The resultant sense of a more general phenomenon prompts this inquiry into their biological significance.

Rhythms of dialogue have been of interest to behavioral scientists for almost forty years—the history has been reviewed elsewhere (Jaffe & Feldstein, 1970). Fundamentally, conversation is an alternation of speaking and listening states, but the speaking–listening cycle is rhythmic only in a weak sense, for example, the "rhythm" of peace and war or that of economic boom and bust. In ritual or highly structured conversations such as responsive prayers or verbal questionnaires, rhythmicity may increase markedly. However, in casual, social dialogue the variance among response durations is huge.

Speech rates of individual conversationalists are nevertheless remarkably constant whether they are healthy or diseased. The straight lines of Figure 1 mean that the average rate of syllable production over the course of a minute is subject to some regulatory mechanism. We know that the brain is an excellent metronome for speech rhythm when reciting verse or during singing. It is even suspected that Galileo employed his own singing voice as a chronometer to discover the law of falling bodies (Drake, 1975). It should not be surprising that conversational speech rate could be a very stable individual characteristic, being partly under the control of prosody. But the underlying regulatory mechanism remains a mystery.

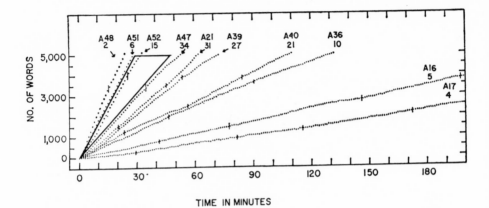

FIG. 1   Rate of emission of words for several aphasic patients. The ordinate specifies the cumulative number of words spoken after successive minutes of interview. A *straight line* represents a constant rate of speech. *Vertical markers* indicate the termination of one interview and the onset of another at a later date. The *triangular area* at the left indicates the range of rates in 12 normal subjects. (From Howes & Geschwind, 1964.)

We know that the impulse to communicate fluctuates from minute to minute and certainly from day to day as a function of motivation, fatigue, attention, and especially mood. The latter is seen most dramatically in manic-depressive psychosis. Yet rate and rhythmicity of communication seem less perturbed by these experiential fluctuations than might be expected. Behavioral constancy in the face of vicissitudes of subjective experience would enhance interpersonal predictability in one sphere of social interaction and conceivably aid in the linguistic decoding process as well.

Nevertheless, rhythmicity of speech in casual discourse is not a strong perceptual phenomenon despite the maintenance of an average rate over minutes. Short-term memory being what it is, we tend to focus on the variation of successive intervals rather than upon longer term averages. This can be illustrated by a simple artificial example. First, some definitions:

Characterizing Simple Rhythms

A rhythm is a sequence of two or more states (a temporal pattern) that recurs with detectable regularity, that is, more or less *periodically*. For simplicity, we restrict our sequence to two component states.

Suppose I type at a rate of one digit per second for three runs of 16 sec each, yielding the following[1]:

(a)   1 0 0 0 1 0 0 0 1 0 0 0 1 0 0 0

---

[1] The first digit of each run is understood to begin a period and the last to end one.

(b)　1 0 0 0 0 1 0 0 0 1 0 0 1 0 0 0

(c)　1 0 1 0 1 0 0 0 0 0 0 0 0 1 0 0

In each run the digit "one" recurs at the *same mean rate* (tempo) of once every four seconds. The reciprocal, the *mean period,* is four seconds in each run. Yet rhythmicity clearly decreases from (a) to (c) as the period durations become progressively irregular. Conversely, consider the following patterns produced in the same manner:

(d)　1 0 0 0 1 0 0 0 1 0 0 0 1 0 0 0

(e)　1 0 1 0 1 0 1 0 1 0 1 0 1 0 1 0

Here we have two *different* mean rates (the reciprocals of mean periods of 4 and 2, respectively), both with the *same* degree of rhythmicity.

This demonstrates that sequences having identical rates can differ in rhythmicity and vice versa. The distribution of rhythmic periods may be characterized by two independent descriptors, the mean and the variance around that mean. Each of the component states is likewise characterized by a mean duration and a variance about its mean, respectively. I introduce some notation:

Let M_P　=　mean duration of a period;

$\quad M_1$　=　mean duration of sequences of ones;

$\quad M_0$　=　mean duration of sequences of zeros;

$\quad \sigma_P^2$　=　variance of duration of periods;

$\quad \sigma_1^2$　=　variation of duration of sequences of ones;

$\quad \sigma_0^2$　=　variation of duration of sequences of zeros.

Generally, the mean and variance of distributions are independent parameters. Utilizing these ingredients, we desire a single index of *rhythmic control.* It is the coefficient of variation of the period:

$$CV_P = \sigma_P/M_P \qquad (1)$$

This statistic combines both descriptors, simply by taking the ratio of the standard deviation to the mean. One of its interesting properties is that it permits comparison of rhythmic control among systems with widely different mean periods. Long intervals might be expected to vary more than short intervals (for example, the absolute height of giants may vary more than that of pygmies) but the coefficient of variation corrects for this. Thus, the smaller the ratio the tighter the control.

To understand Eq. (1), note the necessary relationship:

$$M_P = M_1 + M_0 \qquad (2)$$

However, it is not necessary that $\sigma_P^2 = \sigma_1^2 + \sigma_0^2$ when these three quantities are nonzero.

In Example (a) above $M_P = 4$, $M_1 = 1$, $M_0 = 3$, and $\sigma_P^2 = \sigma_1^2 = \sigma_0^2 = 0$. (If the components of a period do not vary the period cannot vary.)

In Example (b), M_P, M_1, and M_0 are the same as in example (a) whereas $\sigma_P^2 > 0$, $\sigma_1^2 = 0$, and $\sigma_0^2 > 0$. (If only one component of a period varies while the other remains constant, the period variance is attributable to the former.)

Now modify Example (a) so that sequences of ones begin at the same time as previously but are no longer of constant duration:

(f)   1 0 0 0 1 1 0 0 1 1 1 0 1 1 0 0

In example (f), $M_P = 4$ as before but now $M_1 = M_0 = 2$, whereas $\sigma_P^2 = 0$ as before but now $\sigma_1^2 = \sigma_0^2 > 0$. (In order to keep the period duration constant, the durations of ones must be inversely correlated with durations of zeros within periods, so-called "temporal compensation.")

Finally, we modify Example (b) above so that sequences of ones also begin at the same time as previously but are no longer of constant duration:

(g)   1 1 0 0 0 1 1 1 0 1 0 0 1 1 1 0

In Example (g), $M_P = 4$ as before but now $M_1 = 2.25$ and $M_0 = 1.75$, whereas σ_P^2, σ_1^2 and σ_0^2 are all > 0.

The relationship among the three variances is governed by a correlation coefficient, r, between durations of one and zero sequences within periods (Anderson, 1975):

$$r = \frac{\sigma_P^2 - \sigma_1^2 - \sigma_0^2}{2\sigma_1\sigma_0} \tag{3}$$

such that

$$
\begin{aligned}
\sigma_P^2 &> \sigma_1^2 + \sigma_0^2 \quad &\text{when } r > 0, \\
\sigma_P^2 &= \sigma_1^2 + \sigma_0^2 \quad &\text{when } r = 0, \\
\sigma_P^2 &< \sigma_A^2 + \sigma_B^2 \quad &\text{when } r < 0.
\end{aligned}
$$

The final Example (g) above is typical of the sloppy type of rhythm encountered in natural communicative behavior.

Stochastic Rhythms

My ultimate aim is to reveal the molecular character of the underlying rhythmic mechanisms of conversation. That goal is distant although a start has been made (Allen, 1973; Anderson, 1975). In the search for clues to underlying mechanisms one descriptive strategy is to give a probabilistic (stochastic) account of the sequence of ones and zeros. Stochastic modeling addresses itself to the macroscopic properties of these mechanisms without our knowing the microscopic organization in detail. At the very least, such models establish the gross statistical behavior which must follow from any hypothesized molecular mechanism and thus serve as criteria for the assessment of such hypotheses.

Specifically, it is assumed that the rhythm is produced by a discrete-time, two-state stochastic process. This is a process which makes decisions at evenly spaced time intervals, such as in our typing demonstration. Each decision, of unspecified nature but involving a random element, is either to remain in its previous state or change to the other.

For the general class of these stochastic rhythms the coefficient of variation of the rhythmic period (CV_P) can be derived from the equations above. Recall that this statistic is our composite index of rhythmic control. Substituting Eqs. (2) and (3) in Equation (1) we get

$$CV_P = \frac{\sigma_P}{M_P} = \frac{\sqrt{\sigma_1^2 + 2r\,\sigma_1\,\sigma_0 + \sigma_0^2}}{M_1 + M_0} \tag{4}$$

The sole purpose of including this cumbersome expression is to indicate that the desired statistic has five independent parameters: $M_1, M_0, \sigma_1, \sigma_0,$ and r. I make use of this fact presently.

Markovian Rhythms

These are a special case of stochastic rhythms in which the probability of the next decision depends only on the present state, hence a one-step memory. In our simple two-state example, the necessary and sufficient conditions for the rhythm to be Markovian are:

1. *Constant probability of prolonging the duration of each state.* This is mathematically equivalent to the statement that the process has a short (one-step) memory (longer memory would be redundant), and also dictates that the distribution of ones and zeros each be negative exponentials.

2. *Successive state durations are independent.* This means that component state durations within periods are uncorrelated. If $r = 0$,

$$\sigma_P^2 = \sigma_1^2 + \sigma_2^2$$

The immediate significance of these special Markovian constraints is the reduction of parameters of Eq. (4). In an exponential distribution the mean and variance can be derived from each other. Coupled with the fact that $r = 0$, CV_P for the Markovian rhythm has two parameters instead of five.

Some Examples of Markovian Communication Rhythms

The ones and zeros of the preceding theoretical discussion are now given a concrete interpretation. If "one" means vocalization above the threshold of a speech detector and "zero" means a pause $\geqslant 200$ msec, then a fluent monologue exhibits Markovian rhythm as defined above (Jaffe & Breskin, 1970a; Jaffe, Breskin, & Gerstman, 1970, 1972; Jaffe et al., 1964; Schwartz & Jaffe, 1968). Typical distributions are shown in Figs. 2 and 3. The "goodness of fit" of the

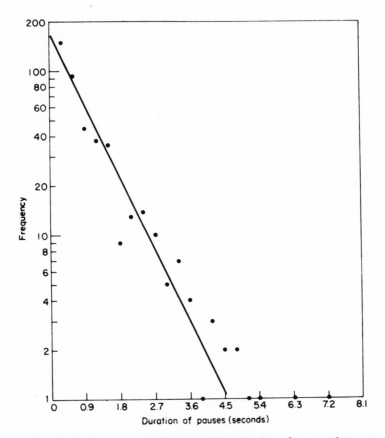

FIG. 2 A typical log-frequency distribution of the duration of pauses that occur in a monologue. The straight line represents the predicted distribution based upon a first-order Markov chain. The distribution is derived from a monologue lasting 20 min. (From Jaffe & Feldstein, 1970.)

model in this and the subsequent examples is not at issue here since a more general point is being made. It has been previously argued that discussion of the fit of a single model to data is unfruitful (Jaffe & Feldstein, 1970, p. 83).

Now, disregarding pauses as just defined and decomposing the vocalizations into their microstructure, let "one" represent the presence of any stressed (accented) vowel and "zero" the lower energy, unstressed segment which separates the stressed segments (Anderson, 1975). This more strictly linguistic rhythm also demonstrates Markovian characteristics. Typical distributions are shown in Fig. 4.

The next example shows that the phenomenon is not confined to speech rhythm. Let "one" represent an infant's gaze at mother's face and "zero" a gaze away from the face. This system also displays Markovian features (Jaffe et al.,

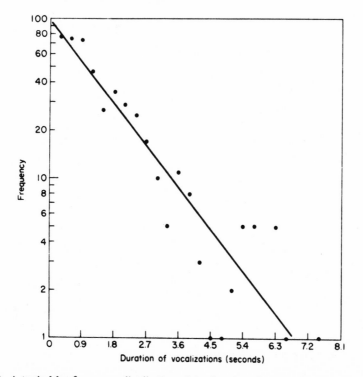

Duration of vocalizations (seconds)

FIG. 3 A typical log-frequency distribution of the duration of vocalizations that occur in a monologue. The straight line represents the predicted distribution based upon a first-order Markov chain. The distribution is derived from a monologue lasting 20 min. (After Jaffe & Feldstein, 1970.)

1973). The distributions are shown in Figure 5. This finding has recently been replicated in adult verbal conversations (Natale, 1976). The distributions are shown in Fig. 6.

A Possible Physiological Mechanism.   This was suggested by Gustafson (1969) and is here condensed with the related notions of Lenneberg (1967) and Schaltenbrand (1975). Speech onset involves activation of a six-per-second generator in the left thalamus which operates at two different impulse strengths: Let q_0 be the probability of a stressed level of response to any specified impulse given an *unstressed* level at the prior impulse; let q_1 be the probability of stressed response given a *stressed* level at the prior impulse. In other words, q_0 is the probability of initiating and q_1 the probability of continuing a stressed response level. This mechanism generates a Markovian rhythm, the two parameters yielding all the desired statistics for the three-per-second stress pattern.

Recomposing the syllabic stress rhythm into undifferentiated phonation (that is, lumping states of the microstructure), the more macroscopic two-state system

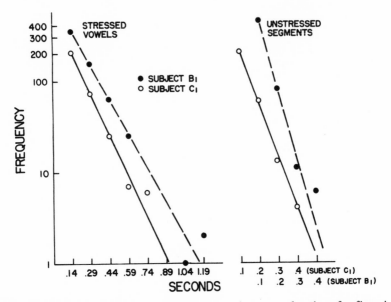

FIG. 4 Distribution of stressed vowel and unstressed segment durations for five-minute monologues of two randomly selected normal subjects. Summed over 150-msec intervals, the midpoints of which are shown on the abscissa. The last point of each plot represents less than 1% of the data (linear fit by eye).

is recovered. Now q_0 is interpreted as the probability of initiating a vocalization (terminating a pause) and q_1 as the probability of continuing it. The microstructure is nested in the macrostructure.

The temporal pattern produced can be thought of as a varying set of rhythmic opportunities which can be used by a linguistic process that did not create them (Butterworth, 1975). Equally speculative is the possibility of varying settings of the underlying pacemaker, say for "allegro" or "lento" styles, suggested by the known thalamic mechanisms for step-down transformation of six-per-second stimulation to three-per-second response (Purpura, 1970, personal communication). Parameters q_0 and q_1 can similarly be interpreted as probabilities of initiating and terminating a gaze, respectively.

Families of Markovian Rhythms: An Explanatory Finding?

In attempting to fathom the import of Markovian rhythms, the proposal of intelligible physiological mechanisms that might generate them and the fact that they eliminate three of the five parameters of Equation (4) is doubly mysterious. What biological function is being fulfilled?

A Markovian rhythm posits no necessary relationship between its parameters, but these parameters do change under varying circumstances. Correlational

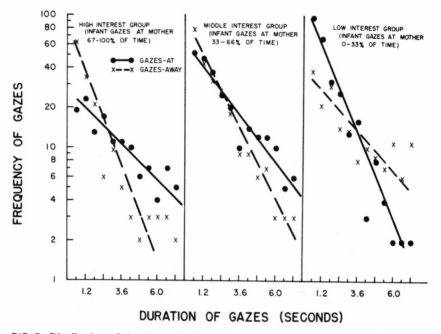

FIG. 5 Distribution of durations of infant's gaze "at" and "away" from mother's face at three different motivational levels, summed over infants and occasions. This demonstrates both the general form of the distributions and the reciprocal changes in slope (linear fit by eye). (From Stern, 1974.)

studies were therefore undertaken in the various families of stochastic processes described previously, in search of empirical relationships.

In the gross vocalization-pause rhythm (Jaffe & Breskin, 1970b), in the infant face-gaze rhythm (Stern, 1974), and in the syllabic stress rhythm (Anderson, 1975) a similar pattern emerged, namely, a *positive* correlation between q_0 and q_1. This says that the probability of initiating a run in a given state varies concomitantly with the probability of continuing it. Equivalently, the correlation is negative between the probabilities of remaining in each of the two states, q_1 and $1 - q_0$, respectively. If their mean durations vary inversely the mean period is held constant.

One can now sense the biological significance of a Markovian rhythm, but only in the light of this empirical finding. We see:

1. The correlation of the two remaining parameters in Eq. (4) under changing circumstances stabilizes the rhythm even more than would be the case if q_0 and q_1 were statistically independent. If the correlation were +1.0 the rhythm would be highly stable. In fact r varies in the +.3 to +.5 range which is statistically significant but permits flexibility.

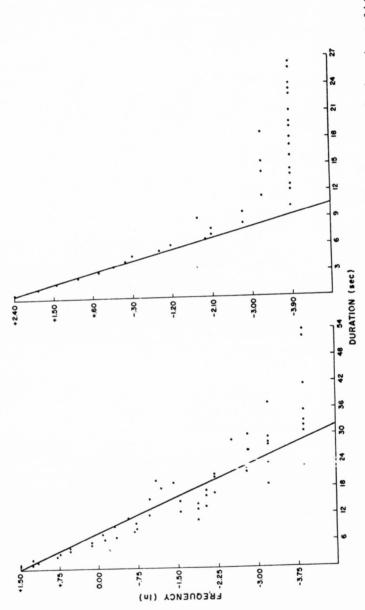

FIG. 6 Distributions of durations of "face gaze" (left) and "away gaze" summed over the 48 subjects in a conversational experiment of 4.5 min duration. (From Natale, 1976.)

2. The effect of the correlation is to counteract change in the mean period M_P, in the face of changing impulse toward or away from a given state, by means of a complementary change in the other state.

3. Concomitantly, a change in the variance of duration in a given state tends to be accompanied by an opposite change in the variance of the other state since variances grow and shrink with the mean, for example,

$$M_1 = \frac{1}{1 - q_1} \quad \text{and} \quad \sigma_1^2 = \frac{q_1}{(1 - q_1)^2}$$

The net effect is to counteract changes in period variance since $\sigma_P^2 = \sigma_1^2 + \sigma_0^2$.

4. It follows that the index of rhythmic control CV_P is a final common path for the highly coordinated effects of all these mechanisms, and a likely locus for future research. Thus, the concept continues to be of heuristic value (Hayes, Meltzer & Wolf, 1970; Brähler & Zenz, 1975; Butterworth, 1975; Henderson, 1974).

Discussion. A previous linguistic application of the coefficient of variation was reported by Kozhevnikov and Chistovich (1965) who required speakers to utter a two-clause sentence repeatedly, the clauses being separated by a juncture pause. The *CV* for the pause was over ten times greater than that for the first clause and over 20 times greater than that for the second. Thus, successive executions of articulatory programs are apparently under tighter timing control than are intervening pauses, during which the program is temporarily turned off. This is a likely explanation for the finding that average length of vocalizations by one speaker in a conversation is not influenced by that of the other speaker. In contrast, the intervening pauses are exquisitely sensitive to interpersonal influence, pairs of speakers showing a strong tendency to match the average pause durations displayed as they alternately "hold the floor" (Jaffe & Feldstein, 1970). Yet, however productive of phonetic insights, repetition experiments yield an automatic performance with the rhythmicity of doggerel, divorced from the cognitive roots of the language generating process. They are, in general, unsatisfactory models of the naturalistic communication treated herein.

In our studies of uncontrived events a powerful mechanism has been described which is common to both verbal and nonverbal communication rhythms. It has an intelligible though speculative physiological basis. By reducing what is potentially a system with five independent parameters to one with two highly coupled variables, both tempo and degree of rhythmicity are simultaneously regulated. The homeostatic effect of this highly unified mode of control is to efficiently stabilize the communication rhythms of the organism despite fluctuations in the impulse to communicate. Such fluctuations are seen in mood changes, most dramatically in manic-depressive psychosis. But to a lesser degree, the varying energy levels of everyday life invoke this mechanism which would serve to maintain interpersonal predictability in one sphere of social behavior.

Behavioral stability is obviously an important part of what we call personality style. In the sense that a solid baseline of expectancy permits others to recognize us and to accurately assess our moods as departures from expectancy, the mechanism may be important in the communication of emotion. By analogy to other species-specific communication patterns, it may play a role in human assortative mating.

Most relevant to the present volume is the possible role of this mechanism in linguistic decoding. We know that participants in conversation match tempo to a marked degree but the communicative payoff attained thereby has not yet been specified. It is an old idea that rhythm is a very early stage of the sentence generating process (Anderson, 1975). Its role in the decoding process is equally probable and it is not hard to imagine the utility of conversationalists being literally on the same wavelength.

ACKNOWLEDGMENTS

This work was supported in part by the Department of Mental Hygiene of New York State and a general research support grant from the Research Foundation for Mental Hygiene, Inc. I am indebted to Drs. Samuel Anderson, Daniel Stern, Joseph Fleiss and Michael Natale for invaluable assistance.

REFERENCES

Allen, G. D. Segmental timing control in speech production. *Journal of Phonetics,* 1973, 1, 219–237.

Anderson, S. W. Ballistic control of rhythmic articulatory movements in natural speech. In D. R. Aaronson & R. W. Reiber (Eds.), Developmental psycholinguistics and communication disorders. *Annals of the New York Academy of Sciences,* 1975, 263, 236–243.

Brähler, E., & Zenz, H. Artifacts in the registration and interpretation of speech-process variables. *Language and Speech,* 1975, 18, Pt. 2, 166–179.

Buchsbaum, M. Individual differences in eye movement patterns. *Perceptual Motor Skills,* 1972, 35, 895–901.

Butterworth, B. Hesitation and semantic planning in speech. *Journal of Psycholinguistic Research,* 1975, 4, 75–87.

Drake, S. The role of music in Galileo's experiments. *Scientific American,* 1975, 232, No. 6, 98–104.

Gustafson, H. W. Model for the analysis of talkspurt and silence durations in conversational interaction. *Proceedings of the 77th Annual Convention of the American Psychological Association,* 1969, 43–44.

Hayes, D. P., Meltzer, L., & Wolf, G. Substantive conclusions are dependent upon techniques of measurement. *Behavioral Science,* 1970, 15, 265–269.

Henderson, A. Time patterns in spontaneous speech: Cognitive stride or random walk? A reply to Jaffe *et al. Language and Speech,* 1974, 17, 119–125.

Howes, D., & Geschwind, N. Quantitative studies of aphasic language. In D. McK. Rioch & E. A. Weinstein (Eds.), *Disorders of communication.* Association for Research in Nervous and Mental Disorders. Vol. XLII. Baltimore, Maryland: Williams & Wilkins, 1964. Pp. 229–244.

Jaffe, J. & Anderson, S. W. One of the most neglected physiological signals in psychopathology. Annual meeting of the Society of Biological Psychiatry, New York City, 1975.

Jaffe, J., & Breskin, S. Further consequences of a Markov model of speech rhythms. *Computers and Biomedical Research,* 1970, **3,** No. 2, 174–177. (a)

Jaffe, J., & Breskin, S. Prediction of an individual speech pattern from dynamic interaction. *Perceptual and Motor Skills,* 1970, **30,** 363–368. (b)

Jaffe, J., Breskin, S., & Gerstman, L. J. Range of sequential constraint in monologue rhythms. *Psychonomic Science,* 1970, **19,** No. 4, 233.

Jaffe, J., Breskin, S., & Gerstman, L. J. Random generation of apparent speech rhythms. *Language and Speech,* 1972, **15,** 68–71.

Jaffe, J., Cassotta, L., & Feldstein, S. A Markovian model of time patterns of speech. *Science,* 1964, **144,** 884–886.

Jaffe, J. & Feldstein, S. *Rhythms of dialogue.* New York: Academic Press, 1970.

Jaffe, J., & Norman, D. A simulation of the time patterns of dialogue. Scientific Report CS-4. Center for Cognitive Studies, Harvard University, 1964.

Jaffe, J., Stern, D. N., & Peery, J. C. "Conversational coupling" of gaze behavior in prelinguistic human development. *Journal of Psycholinguistic Research,* 1973, **2,** 321–329.

Kozhevnikov, V. A., & Chistovich, L. A. *Speech, articulation, and perception.* Vol. 30. Washington, D.C.: Joint Publications Research Service, 1965. P. 543.

Lenneberg, E. H. *Biological foundations of language.* New York: Wiley, 1967.

Natale, M. A Markovian model of adult gaze behavior. *Journal of Psycholinguistic Research,* 1976, **5,** 53–63.

Schaltenbrand, G. The effects on speech and language of stereotactical stimulation in thalamus and corpus callosum. *Brain and Language,* 1975, **2,** 70–77.

Schwartz, J., & Jaffe, J. Markovian prediction of sequential temporal patterns in spontaneous speech. *Language and Speech,* 1968, **11,** 27–30.

Stern, D. N. Mother and infant at play: the dyadic interaction involving facial, vocal and gaze behaviors. In M. Lewis & L. Rosenblum (Eds.), *The effect of the infant on its caregiver.* New York: Wiley, 1974. Pp. 187–213.

5

Hesitations as Clues
to Failures in Coherence:
A Study of the
Thought-Disordered Speaker

S. R. Rochester
Sharon Thurston
Judith Rupp

Clarke Institute of Psychiatry

What must a speaker do to produce utterances which are coherent, that is, readily understood by a listener? In an attempt to answer this question, we have investigated speakers who fail to be coherent, namely, thought-disordered schizophrenics. These speakers are interesting because their discourse breaks down in a specific area: while their lexicon and syntax are adequate, the ties between their propositions are weak. Or, to say this another way, they seem able to string words together to form clauses, but unable to string clauses together to form comprehendable sentences or paragraphs.

In previous studies, we have established that this breakdown does occur (Martin & Rochester, 1975; Rochester & Martin, in press) and that it is discernable to lay observers as well as to psychiatrists (Rochester, Martin, & Thurston, 1976). In the present investigation, we determine whether this breakdown seen in the segmental systems is observable in hesitation patterns as well. Hesitations are often taken as indicators of cognitive processing because they tend to increase with an increase in the difficulty of cognitive tasks (e.g., Goldman-Eisler, 1961; Reynolds & Paivio, 1968). The location of hesitations seems to reveal which production decisions are being made: within major constituents, pauses precede uncommon words and point to lexical decision-making (Blankenship & Kay, 1964; Goldman-Eisler, 1958a, b; Tannenbaum, Williams, & Hillier, 1965); between constituents, hesitations seem to reflect decisions on a larger scale, relating to the overall direction of the discourse (Goldman-Eisler, 1961; Hawkins, 1973) or to syntactic structure (Rochester & Gill, 1973). If thought-disordered speakers are somehow aberrant in their decision processes *between* clauses, then they should differ from other speakers in the hesitations produced at clause boundaries. And, since their failures in coherence are rarely found *within* clauses, thought disordered speakers should resemble other subjects in their pattern of within-clause hesitations.

In this study, thought-disordered (TD) speakers are compared to two other subject groups: non-thought-disordered schizophrenic (NTD) speakers and normal subjects (N). The important comparison is between TD and NTD speakers. These groups are identical on several potentially important variables such as drug dosage, length of hospitalization, and verbal IQ. However, they are clearly different in the coherence of their discourse in interviews: on the basis of lay judges' ratings of coherence, we correctly identified 75% of TD interview transcripts and falsely identified only 5% of NTD transcripts. Normal subjects are included as a secondary control group, to provide a baseline of performance in the several contexts examined.

Hesitation patterns were studied in three situational contexts. All were dyadic. One context was an unstructured interview in which the subject was asked to select the topics discussed. The two contexts of a second task were both structured. In these, the subject was shown a set of ten cartoons. He or she was asked to describe the cartoon and then interpret why it was supposed to be funny. These contexts were designed to replicate Goldman-Eisler's (1961) well-known experiment in which subjects describe and formulate the meaning of sets of New Yorker cartoons. Goldman-Eisler found that the proportion of silent pauses to total speech time was higher in the interpretative task and concluded that hesitations increase with increases in the difficulty of the cognitive task. This conclusion, though widely credited (e.g., Bernstein, 1962, 1973; Paivio, 1971; Silverman, 1973), has never been replicated.[1] Since it is important to the claim that pauses may be behavioral concommitants of brain processes concerned with verbal planning (Goldman-Eisler, 1964, p. 99), we sought to establish its replicability with normal speakers and its generality to NTD and TD subjects.

To summarize, we have attempted to study the production of coherent discourse by examining the speech of subjects who fail to be coherent across clausal boundaries but maintain coherence within clauses. Using recordings previously analyzed on the verbal level, we focus here only on hesitation characteristics. That is, we study the location and distribution of silent pauses, voiced hesitations such as filled pauses and word repetitions, and (in cartoon

[1] Although the original paradigm was repeated in a subsequent study (Goldman-Eisler, Skarbek, & Henderson, 1965), no data are reported that would demonstrate a replication of the 1961 investigation.

contexts only) latencies. We assume that the pattern of hesitations in unrehearsed discourse is indicative of the location of the decisions required to produce that discourse.

We are concerned with the general question of whether TD speakers differ from other subjects, both NTD and N, in the pattern of their hesitations. If such a difference exists,

1. Does it depend on location, that is, on whether the hesitation falls at clausal boundaries or within a clause?

2. Does it depend on the type of hesitations, that is, on whether we measure silent pause duration, silent pause frequency, or voiced hesitation frequency?

3. Does it depend on situational context, that is, on whether hesitations occur in an unstructured interview or in structured cartoon contexts?

4. Does latency to respond in cartoon contexts differ across subject groups?

I. METHOD

A. Subjects

Subjects were 40 inpatients in a short-term psychiatric hospital, who received a discharge diagnosis in any of the schizophrenias, and 20 volunteers from the community with no reported history of psychiatric disturbance. All were either native English speakers, or had adopted English by the age of 12. They were between the ages of 15 and 52 years, had completed at least seven school grades, and were paid to participate in the study.

Thought disorder was said to be present when two senior psychiatrists, separately viewing an unstructured video-taped interview with a patient, concluded that the patient showed clear signs of thought process disorder. Thought disorder was said to be absent when the judges were unanimous in that opinion. The judges used Cancro's (1969) Index of Formal Signs of Thought Disorder to guide their evaluations. A total of 71 videotaped interviews was seen: of these, judges were agreed on 40, yielding 20 subjects each in the TD and NTD groups.

Table 1 summarizes several salient characteristics of the sample. The groups do not differ in composition according to sex (χ^2 = 2.9, df = 2, p = 0.23) or age (one-way analysis of variance yields F = 2.1, df = 2,57, p > 0.10). However, as might be expected, the patients' educational level and IQ scores are lower than those of the normals. Normals have about three more school grades than the patients (one-way analysis of variance yields F = 13.4, df = 5,57, p < 0.001) and score about ten points higher than patients on the Shipley-Hartford (transformed to WAIS equivalents) (analysis of variance yields F = 15.7, df = 2,57, p < 0.001). Nevertheless, Scheffé tests indicate that TD and NTD subjects are homogeneous with regard to both education and IQ level.

TABLE 1
Subject Characteristics

Group	Age $\bar{X}$	Age SD	Education $\bar{X}$	Education SD	Shipley–Hartford $\bar{X}$	Shipley–Hartford SD
TD	24.3	6.4	11.2	2.6	101.5	8.4
NTD	26.8	7.9	11.9	2.6	104.1	10.4
N	29.9	10.9	15.0	2.1	117.8	6.8

Patients were invited to participate in this study when they received an admission diagnosis of schizophrenia uncomplicated by alcoholism or organic syndrome. Those who had received electroconvulsive therapy within the previous four months were not approached. Informed consent was obtained after the procedure had been fully explained. For both TD and NTD subjects, about 70% had no more than two previous admissions. The average length of stay for both groups was 2.0 months (SD = 1.1). All but two patients were taking phenothiazines. For both groups, subjects were receiving a mean chlorpromazine equivalent (Hollister, 1970) of 550 mg daily (one-way analysis of variance between groups yields $F < 1$). About half the patients had been receiving medication for no more than two weeks, and about 80% of all patients for no more than three weeks (the groups did not differ, as indicated by $\chi^2 = 10.1$, $df = 7$, $p = 0.18$).

B. Speech Contexts

Interview. All subjects participated in an unstructured interview (with SR or ST) of about a half-hour in duration. The interview was videotaped for patients, but not for normal subjects (costs prohibited taping all subjects). Subject and interviewer sat facing each other, and the subject was told to speak about anything he or she found interesting. If the subject requested help, topics were suggested (e.g., what you've been doing in the past two years; a trip you'd like to take; things which make you happy or sad).

Discourse was recorded through Uher M822 low-impedance lavelier microphones input to a Uher Royal Deluxe Stereophonic tape recorded at 7.5 ips. The stereo recordings permitted judges to listen separately to experimenter and subject. For each subject, 3-min speech samples were sought. These were actually about 2.6 min and about 468 words in duration (SD = 113). Where possible, samples of uninterrupted speech were taken; otherwise, shorter samples were selected and combined. Ideally, samples from TD and other subjects would have been selected at random from the discourse. However, this procedure would ignore the fact that only small portions of the TD subjects' discourse show signs of thought disorder. Thus, for TD subjects, the most thought-disordered sections (as indicated by the judges' comments) were selected. For other subjects "informal" sections involving slang, laughter, and/or increased tempo (Labov, 1973) were chosen.

Cartoon tasks. All subjects were shown a set of 10 cartoons. The cartoons were chosen in three steps. First, 35 cartoons were selected, each of which contained no more than one word, required only general knowledge for its interpretation, and contained no more than five panels. Then three judges (two female, one male) indicated why the cartoon was suppoed to be funny. Unanimous agreement occurred in 26 cartoons. Finally, each judge selected 15 of the remaining cartoons which were most clearly humorous. Ten of these were chosen by all judges and these became the experimental materials. They were redrawn to 7 in X 7 in. size and mounted on beaverboard.

In the experimental task, subjects were instructed that they would be shown a series of cartoons. For each one, they were to describe the picture (s) as fully as possible (cartoon descriptions) and then explain why the cartoon was supposed to be funny (cartoon interpretations). Two samples were shown. Then the ten test cartoons were presented in a systematically counterbalanced order so that no more than two subjects per group received the same sequence of cartoons. With the subject seated opposite the experimenter, the experimenter dropped each cartoon picture into a wooden box. This activated a microswitch which discharged a click onto the tape recorder.

C. Dependent Measures

Latencies. Latency to describe a cartoon was the time elapsed between microswitch discharge and the subject's first word. Latency to interpret a cartoon was the time elapsed between the subject's last word of description and first word of interpretation. If the subject did not offer an interpretation, the experimenter asked "And why is that funny?" In this event, latency was the time between the experimenter's final word and the subject's first word. Full recordings were taken of the cartoon descriptions (about 2.8 min and 395 words) and interpretations (about 1.5 min and 244 words) for each subject.

Clausal units. The basic unit of analysis was the independent clause (any combination that can be generated from a noun phrase and verb phrase). Relative clauses, sentence complements, and other subordinate structures were treated as parts of this basic unit. For example, the following is one unit:

(1)   Sharon saw Ruth while she was in Ottawa//

Sentence modifiers were treated as separate units, as were independent clauses linked by *and, or,* and *but.* For example,

(2)   Snoopy is a human dog// which makes him a laughable character//

(3)   A dog arrives on the scene with usual barrel of wine around his neck//
       but this time with 25 cents written on it//

Pauses. The full cartoon tapes and interview samples were rerecorded twice; once onto cassettes via a Sony Secutive Transcriber BM-25 for transcription by a typist, and once onto a monaural reel via a Sony TC 330 recorder. The cassette tapes were typed in conventional orthography without any punctuation. The reel tapes were analyzed through a Honeywell 1508 Oscillograph coupled with a fundamental frequency extractor[2] (cf. Léon & Martin, 1969). Output was recorded on Kodak Linograph paper at a rate of .1 mm per 40 msec.

Silent pauses longer than 250 msec were determined by measuring millimeter lengths along the Linograph paper.[3] Silent pauses were recorded as either *initial* silent pauses preceding or following the first word of a clausal unit or *within-*clause silent pauses occuring at any other location within the clausal unit.

Hesitations. Hesitations other than silent pauses were also measured. These were filled pauses [ð], [r], [m], exact word and phrase repetitions, stutters, word corrections, and tongue slips (Mahl, 1956). So-called false starts in which the speaker changes the sentence form and appears to begin again are not considered hesitations but are included as part of the clause. In general, where several hesitations occur or where one hesitation was repeated at a given location, each occurrence was recorded; for example,

3 Hesitations: it *uh uh uh* signifies that the couple are keeping their fingers
                crossed
2 Hesitations: and *ah the* the insect goes into a pile of leaves

However, where a stutter effect occurred, only one hesitation was recorded, for example,

the *bbb*bottle just looks the same

Reliability between coders was high: there was about 92% agreement on location of hesitations between coders, and about 95% agreement on number of hesitations. There were no differences in these proportions across groups or contexts.

---

[2] We are most grateful to Professor Pierre Léon, Dr. Philippe Martin, and Mr. Michael Dobrovolsky of the Laboratoire de Phonétique, University of Toronto for the generous loan of their pitchmeter.

[3] Silences less than 250 msec are considered part of articulation itself. As Goldman-Eisler (1968, p. 12) has argued, failure to measure silences less than 250 msec might mean loss of some data but this "ensures the clear separation of hesitation pauses from phonetic stoppages." (See also Rochester, in press.)

TABLE 2
Comparison of Cartoon Data
with Those of Goldman-Eisler (1961)[a]

Variable (mean per subject per cartoon)	Goldman-Eisler (N = 9)	Present data[b] (N = 60)	
		$\bar{x}$	SE
1. Mean words			
Description	56.5	39.9	0.97
Interpretation	13.1	22.5	0.82
2. Latency to begin task (sec)	19.2	19.7	0.70
3. Total pause time/total time			
Description	.51	.35	
Interpretation	.66	.27	
4. Total pause time/"speech time"			
Description	1.24	.54	
Interpretation	2.03	.37	
5. Within pause time/"speech time"			
Description	.87	.29	
Interpretation	1.25	.23	
6. Initial pause time/"speech time"			
Description	.36	.28	
Interpretation	.76	.17	

[a]Our calculations are from Goldman-Eisler (1961, Tables I and II).
[b]In Entries 3–6, Description and Interpretation differ according to t tests with $t > 2.53$, p at least $< .05$.

II. CARTOON CONTEXTS AS A REPLICATION

The present cartoon contexts were designed as a replication of Goldman-Eisler's (1961) study. Table 2 presents comparison data for that study and the present findings.

The first two entries show the general performance of subjects in the two studies. In the present study, speakers used almost twice as many words in describing as in interpreting cartoons. In Goldman-Eisler's data, descriptions were about four times longer than interpretations. In both studies, latencies to respond to the experimenter's signal to begin were about 19 sec.

Entries 3–6 in Table 2 demonstrate our failure to replicate Goldman-Eisler's central findings. Where she found significantly greater proportions of speech time devoted to pausing in cartoon interpretations, we found significantly more time devoted to pausing in cartoon descriptions. These results hold for all pauses over total time (from onset of the first word of a response to termination: Entry 3), for all pauses over "speech time"[4] (total time minus pause time: Entry 4), and for both initial pauses and within-clause or within-sentence pauses (Entries 5 and 6).

These results are the same whether we use data for all 60 subjects in the present study, or only for the 20 normals. For example, Entry 3 is the relative hesitancy measure reported below in Tables 5 and 6. Over all subjects, pausing is greater with this measure in descriptions than in interpretations (analyses of variance of context effects for cartoons yield $F = 24$ with $p < .001$). With normal subjects only, pausing is again greater in descriptions (t tests between descriptions and interpretations for both initial and within-clause pauses yield $t = 2.53$ with $p < .01$).

Our failure to replicate this classic study is remarkable because it emphasizes a problem already at issue in the pause literature (cf. Rochester, 1973). That is, what does it mean when an experimenter manipulates task "difficulty" or "cognitive demands on the speaker?" What processes are intended by these terms? What procedures are available to confirm that more or different or more rapid cognitive processing is involved in two presumably different verbal contexts? There are no such procedures apart from postexperimental self-reports.

There were, of course, some differences between the present experiment and Goldman-Eisler's original study. The cartoons themselves differed, our subjects were almost certainly less educated than Goldman-Eisler's, and our instructions differed in a small but possibly significant way. Where Goldman-Eisler asked her subjects to formulate "the general point, meaning or moral of the story in as concise a form as you can," we directed our subjects to "explain why it (the cartoon) is supposed to be funny." With this instruction, we hoped to involve our subjects in the process of abstract thinking which seems required in stating the general point of cartoon stories, while at the same time making the instructions easy to understand by our unsophisticated subjects. In retrospect, this might have been satisfactory if we had demanded that the interpretation be "as concise as possible." Aaron Siegman (1975, personal communication) in an unpublished experiment, found that this aspect of the instructions was critical to the finding of longer silent pauses in cartoon interpretations. Goldman-Eisler (1975, personal communication) suggests that it may be necessary to repeat all the instructions exactly as given.

Our uncertainty about what is critical in instructions to the speaker echoes the broader uncertainty of how to manipulate cognitive demands on the speaker. With instructions as with other variables, we do not yet know how to ensure that different levels of cognitive processing are being used.

---

[4] Goldman-Eisler's figures for "speech time" are always smaller than the result of total time minus pause time, but she does not describe how these figures are computed.

III. RESULTS

A. Silent Pause Duration

1. Initial Pause Duration

For each subject, the durations of all initial silent pauses were summed and divided by their frequency of occurrence. In the interview, there were approximately 25 initial silent pauses per subject; in cartoon descriptions there were about 24 pauses and in cartoon interpretations there were about 10. These numbers did not differ across subject groups.

Mean initial pause durations and standard deviations over groups and contexts are shown in Table 3 along with the results of a 3 groups X 3 contexts analysis of repeated measurements.

There are two clear-cut observations to be made. First, regardless of context, TD speakers pause longer (1.28 sec) than other speakers (NTD = 1.03 sec; N = 0.55 sec). In cartoon contexts, NTD subjects fall between TD and N speakers; in the interview, however, TD subjects are clearly different from both NTD and N speakers (Scheffé tests yield $p < .05$). Unless otherwise noted, a difference between two contexts or between two subject groups is reported only if the probability of its having occurred by chance (using a Scheffé t test) is $\leqslant .05$. Second, there is a significant context effect: speakers pause longer in cartoon contexts (cartoon descriptions = 1.03 sec; interpretations = 1.06 sec) than in

TABLE 3
Mean Initial Pause Durations (units in seconds)

	Duration of initial pauses/frequency of initial pauses					
	Cartoon description		Cartoon interpretation		Interview	
Groups	$\bar{X}$	SD	$\bar{X}$	SD	$\bar{X}$	SD
TD	1.41	(.54)	1.31	(.69)	1.11	(.63)
NTD	1.23	(.45)	1.08	(.64)	0.79	(.37)
N	0.46	(.35)	0.79	(.39)	0.40	(.12)

Analysis of variance

Effect	df	F	p	ω^2
Groups/subjects within groups	2,57	33.45	.001	.29
Contexts/error	2,114	20.98	.001	.18
Groups X contexts/error	4,114	<1		

interviews (.77 sec). Speaker effects and context effects are fairly strong here, accounting for 29 and 18%, respectively, of the total variance of initial pause durations ($\hat{\omega}^2$ computed according to Winer, 1971).

2. Within-Clause Pause Duration

Mean within-clause duration was computed as above. There were about 28 pauses per speaker in the interview sample, 33 in cartoon descriptions, and 16 in cartoon interpretations. Again, frequencies did not differ across speaker groups.

Table 4 presents mean within-clause pause durations, standard deviations, and a summary of the 3 groups X 3 contexts analysis of repeated measurements.

Both speaker effects and context effects are significant. However, in the present case speaker effects account for a negligible 3% of the total variance. Nonthought-disordered speakers do not differ significantly from the TD or N subjects. Thus, while there is a small effect, there is no evidence that TD speakers differ from other schizophrenic subjects in the duration of their within-clause pauses.

Context accounts for 62% of the total variance in these data. As with initial pauses, durations are long in cartoon descriptions and interpretations (.93 and .83 sec, respectively) and short in the interview context (.24 sec; Scheffé tests between cartoon contexts and interview yield $p < .001$).

To summarize, mean pause durations vary with context and speakers. This is true regardless of pause location. However, pause location determines the strength of the effects: Context effects increase and speaker effects drop when pause location changes from the clause boundary to within the clause. In

TABLE 4
Mean Within-Clause Pause Durations (units in seconds)

Duration of within-clause pauses/frequency of within-clause pauses

Groups	Cartoon description		Cartoon interpretation		Interview	
	$\bar{X}$	SD	$\bar{X}$	SD	$\bar{X}$	SD
TD	1.11	(.54)	0.93	(.53)	0.26	(.13)
NTD	0.89	(.28)	0.78	(.36)	0.23	(.15)
N	0.80	(.24)	0.77	(.36)	0.22	(.08)

Analysis of variance

Effect	df	F	p	$\hat{\omega}^2$
Groups/subjects within groups	2,57	6.38	.005	.03
Contexts/error	2,114	106.94	.001	.62
Groups X Contexts/Error	4,114	1.27	ns	—

TABLE 5
Initial Relative Hesitancy

	Duration of initial silent pauses/total speech duration per subject					
	Cartoon description		Cartoon interpretation		Interview	
Groups	$\overline{X}$	SD	$\overline{X}$	SD	$\overline{X}$	SD
TD	.21	(.08)	.16	(.10)	.30	(.15)
NTD	.18	(.09)	.12	(.05)	.26	(.12)
N	.12	(.05)	.06	(.04)	.14	(.15)

Analysis of variance

Effect	df	F	p	$\hat{\omega}^2$
Groups/subjects within groups	2,57	18.27	.001	.10
Contexts/error	2,114	81.94	.001	.48
Groups X contexts/error	4,114	5.99	.001	.06

general, context effects are noteworthy at both locations but speaker effects are strong only with initial pauses.

3. Relative Hesitancy. Initial Pauses

It is not clear how best to measure pause duration. While mean pause duration has the merits of common use, it does not allow us to take speech rate into account. So speakers producing a few long pauses with only a few sentences are indistinguishable from those producing a few long pauses with many sentences. This is especially relevant in the present data where TD speakers pause longer than other subjects. Perhaps the long pauses of TD subjects are accompanied by little text. If this is true, then in quantitative terms the pauses of TD speakers may be as "valuable" as those of other subjects. To assess this, one may divide pause duration by total words produced, by clauses produced, or by total speech time. We examined each variable using discriminant function analyses. Total speech time was the divisor which yielded the best discriminations between groups, so analyses with this divisor are reported here.

Table 5 shows the relative hesitancy of initial pauses divided by total duration[5] of the speech sample. Means, standard deviations, and an analysis of variance summary are given.

---

[5] Total duration is the time in sec from onset to offset of the speech sample. It includes both speech and silent pauses.

Group effects account for a moderate 10% of the total variance and must be interpreted in the light of a significant interaction between groups and contexts. Thought-disordered speakers use more of their total speech time in initial pausing (22%) than normal speakers (11%). However, this difference is significant only in the interview context where TD subjects use 30% of their speech time for initial pauses while other speakers use significantly less time (NTD subjects use 26% and N subjects use 14%). Thus, TD speakers' initial pauses are not only longer than the pauses of normal subjects (Section III, A.1) but TD pauses occur only half as frequently (relative to total speech time) as the pauses of normal subjects. It might be the case that pauses for the TD speaker are less "valuable" contributors to the production of subsequent sentences than the pauses of normal subjects. This assumes that pauses are responsible for the production of subsequent speech, an assumption which is at least tenable on the basis of Butterworth's (1975) recent work.

Context effects are strong, accounting for an impressive 48% of the variance of initial relative hesitancy. Speakers use about 11% of their speech time in initial pausing in cartoon contexts and 23% in interview contexts. Scheffé tests between each cartoon context and the interview yield $p < .01$. This is a reversal of the findings for mean pause time noted above (Sections III, A.1 and 2). Mean pause time is *longer* in cartoons than in interviews but the total proportion of time spent in initial pausing is *less* in cartoons than in interviews. This is due to two things: initial pauses are relatively infrequent in cartoon contexts, and these contexts are longer than interview samples. This disparity between mean pause duration and relative hesitancy is noteworthy because it indicates that mean pause durations must be interpreted in conjunction with information about the total speech production.

4. Relative Hesitancy. Within-Clause Pauses

Table 6 presents mean proportions for within-clause pauses divided by total duration of the speech sample, and a summary of a 3 groups × 3 contexts analysis of variance for these data.

Context effects account for a moderate 13% of the total variance. Speakers use the smallest portion of their speech time on within-clause pauses in interviews (11%), the next largest in cartoon interpretations (13%), and the largest in cartoon description (17%). These results contrast with findings for initial relative hesitancy but correspond to results with mean pause durations. Both initial and within-clause pause durations are longer in cartoons than in interviews (Sections III, A.1 and 2); and, within-clause pauses occupy more speech time in cartoons. Thus, initial pauses are exceptional in occupying less time in cartoon contexts than in interviews.

There are no group effects or interaction effects here. All speakers use about equal speech time for the same within-clause pause duration. Thus, when total speech production is taken into account, the modest group differences seen in

TABLE 6
Within-Clause Relative Hesitancy

| Groups | Duration of within-clause silent pause/total speech duration per subject | | | | | |
| | Cartoon description | | Cartoon interpretation | | Interview | |
	$\bar{X}$	SD	$\bar{X}$	SD	$\bar{X}$	SD
TD	.17	(.08)	.10	(.06)	.13	(.07)
NTD	.16	(.07)	.14	(.09)	.10	(.05)
N	.18	(.06)	.14	(.07)	.10	(.04)

Analysis of variance

Effect	df	F	p	$\hat{\omega}^2$
Groups/subjects within groups	2,57	<1		
Contexts/error	2,114	10.31	.001	.13
Groups X contexts/error	4,114	1.17	ns	–

mean pause durations (Section III, A.2) disappear. In terms of the quantity of speech produced, all speakers appear to get about the same "value" from within-clause pause.

To summarize, relative hesitancy measures present a broader view of the function of pauses than can be seen with only mean pause times. In particular, group differences are significant only for initial pauses, and context effects depend on pause location. Initial pauses occupy more speech time in interview contexts than in cartoon contexts; for within-clause pauses, the findings are reversed.

B. Voiced Hesitations

Frequencies of initial and within-clause voiced hesitations are presented in Tables 7 and 8, respectively. Means, standard deviations, and analysis of variance summaries are given for frequencies per 100 words of discourse.

1. Initial Voiced Hesitations

About 15% of the variability in Table 7 is due to context effects: speakers use almost twice as many initial hesitations in cartoon contexts (2.1 and 1.7 hesitations per 100 words for descriptions and interpretations, respectively) as in interviews (1.0 hesitations). In addition, there is a very small speaker effect, accounting for only 4% of the total variance and moderated by an interaction

TABLE 7
Initial Voiced Hesitations

Groups	Initial voiced hesitations per 100 words					
	Cartoon description		Cartoon interpretation		Interview	
	$\bar{X}$	SD	$\bar{X}$	SD	$\bar{X}$	SD
TD	2.5	(2.1)	2.0	(2.0)	0.6	(0.6)
NTD	1.4	(1.3)	1.4	(1.6)	1.1	(1.0)
N	2.4	(1.3)	1.6	(1.0)	1.5	(0.9)

Analysis of Variance

Effect	df	F	p	$\hat{\omega}^2$
Groups/subjects within groups	2,57	3.95	.05	.04
Contexts/error	2,114	12.61	.001	.15
Groups × contexts/error	4,114	3.45	.001	.06

TABLE 8
Within-Clause Voiced Hesitations

Groups	Within-clause voiced hesitations per 100 words					
	Cartoon description		Cartoon interpretation		Interview	
	$\bar{X}$	SD	$\bar{X}$	SD	$\bar{X}$	SD
TD	2.9	(2.6)	2.0	(2.0)	1.2	(1.1)
NTD	2.2	(1.2)	2.6	(2.4)	1.0	(0.9)
N	3.7	(2.4)	3.5	(2.5)	1.4	(0.9)

Analysis of variance

Effect	df	F	p	$\hat{\omega}^2$
Groups/subjects within groups	2,57	7.57	.005	.07
Contexts/error	2,114	24.82	.001	.27
Groups × contexts/error	4,114	1.97	ns	—

between speaker and context. In interview contexts only, thought-disordered speakers produce fewer voiced hesitations at clause boundaries than other speakers.

2. Within-Clause Voiced Hesitations

Context effects account for 27% of the variance in Table 8 data. Again, speakers use more voiced hesitations in cartoon descriptions and interpretations (2.9 and 2.7 hesitations per 100 words, respectively) than in interviews (1.2 hesitations). Speaker effects account for only 7% of the data variability, but differences between speakers are not dependent on context effects: normal speakers use slightly more voiced hesitations than other subjects in all contexts.

Thus, moderate context effects and small speaker differences are seen with voiced hesitations regardless of the location of the hesitations. More voiced hesitations are used in cartoon contexts than in interviews and there is a trend for normal subjects to use more and TD subjects to use fewer voiced hesitations.

C. Latencies

Latency of response in seconds was recorded in the two cartoon contexts for each of ten cartoons. Table 9 gives the means, standard deviations, and analysis of variance summary for total response times divided by ten cartoon frames.

There is a massive context effect accounting for about 58% of the variance in latencies. This probably reflects the constraints of the task, in which cartoon

TABLE 9
Latencies in Cartoon Contexts

	Latencies per cartoon (sec)			
	Cartoon description		Cartoon interpretation	
Groups	$\bar{X}$	SD	$\bar{X}$	SD
TD	2.48	(0.96)	1.53	(1.01)
NTD	2.67	(0.96)	1.41	(0.71)
N	1.96	(0.54)	1.07	(0.41)

Analysis of variance

Effect	df	F	p	$\hat{\omega}^2$
Groups/subjects within groups	2,57	10.74	.001	.06
Contexts/error	2,114	99.8	.001	.58
Groups × contexts/error	4,114	1.27	ns	—

descriptions were always given first and cartoon interpretations always second. The differences between speakers are small ($\hat{\omega}^2$ = .06) but more interesting. Schizophrenic speakers, both TD and NTD, take longer than normal subjects. That is, thought disorder per se is not associated with longer response time.

D. Discriminant Function Analyses

The variables examined above can be formed into a single weighted composite score to distinguish between groups in each context. Since mean pause duration and relative hesitancy measures use the same numerator (total pause duration) the two sets of variables were not included in the same discriminant function analysis.[6] Rather, one analysis per context was performed with mean pause durations included, and then separate analyses were done with relative hesitancies included and mean pause durations omitted.

Initial silent pauses are clearly the most efficient discriminators between the three groups overall, and between TD and other subjects. For both mean pause durations and relative hesitancies, initial pauses (a) account for the largest proportion of variance, regardless of context; and (b) identify TD speakers with a hit rate (correct identification) of about 50–65% and a false alarm rate (false identification as TD) for NTD subjects of 20–35% and for normals of 0–15%.

After initial silent pauses, the discriminative power of variables depends on the speech context. In general, within-clause silent pauses do not discriminate between speakers. The exception is the contribution made by mean within-clause pause durations in cartoon descriptions, where the false alarm rate for TD is slightly reduced (by 15% for NTD and by 5% for N subjects although the hit rate does not change.

Voiced hesitations are clearly less successful than silent pauses in discriminating between speakers. These variables yield insignificant univariate F values in every case except the interview. In that context, initial voiced hesitations enter the analysis but do not contribute to a distinction between TD and other speakers.

Finally, latencies are not helpful in distinguishing among speakers. The univariate F is insignificant in cartoon interpretations, as we saw in Section III.C above, and the multivariate f is insufficient for computation of hit and false alarm rates in cartoon descriptions.

[6] Relative hesitancy measures correlate highly with mean silent pause measures: Pearson product moment correlations of initial relative hesitancy with initial mean silent pause durations are about +.80 across, and the corresponding correlations for within-pause measures are about +.60. In general, the measurement variables used in the separate discriminant function analyses are not highly correlated. The consistent exceptions are voiced hesitations: initial and within-clause voiced hesitations yield correlations of about +.70 in all contexts. In addition, in cartoon contexts, initial silent pause measures correlate significantly with latency, yielding values of about +.45 (n = 60, p < .001).

Across contexts, the discriminative power of these pause variables is similar. The best discrimination of TD speakers is found in interviews using mean pause durations rather than relative hesitancies. Under this circumstance, TD speakers are selected with a 60% hit rate and an impressively low false alarm rate of 20% for NTD subjects and 0% for normals. It is remarkable that this level of discrimination can be achieved using only silent pause durations. And, what may be even more noteworthy, this level of discrimination is not confined to one context and one measurement variable, but is almost matched by the discrimination possible in other contexts with either mean pause duration or relative hesitancy as measurement variables.

IV. DISCUSSION

To answer the question posed initially, we find that TD speakers do have hesitation patterns different from other speakers. The difference is seen in initial silent pause durations (with measures of mean duration and relative hesitancy) but not with other hesitations. The difference is most clear in the interview context and appears as only a trend in cartoon contexts.

Only *initial* silent pauses differentiate TD speakers from other subjects. This fact rules out the hypothesis that TD subjects pause longer because they are generally slow information processors, that is, that they are slower to process incoming information (e.g., Hawks & Marshall, 1971; Yates, 1966), slower to retrieve recent information (e.g., McGhie, Chapman & Lawson, 1964; Zubin, 1975), or slower to respond to signals (e.g., Broen, 1966). Thought-disordered speakers are comparable to other schizophrenic subjects in response latency, so their input processing and response timing are not unusually slow: they pause about as long as other speakers at within-clause locations so their general language processing and information retrieval seem unimpaired.

What is problematic, then, must be production processes which occur at *clause boundaries.* Recall that our earlier work showed that TD subjects fail to be coherent across clauses, but maintain coherence within clauses. Silent pause measures reflect these results: they distinguish TD subjects at clause boundaries but not within clauses. This correspondence between hesitation measures and coherence ratings is impressive because it occurs over three situational contexts with measures of mean pause duration and relative hesitancy.

Within this consistency, however, lies a paradox: if pauses indicate cognitive processing time, then why does the greatest amount of pausing produce the least coherent discourse? Surely, if pause time is even a monotonic function of decision time, longer pauses should signal higher quality productions. Thought-disordered subjects, according to this view, should produce the briefest pauses and use the smallest proportion of speech time in pausing.

The assumption behind this paradox is that all speakers in all situations are equally efficient in producing coherent discourse. Certainly this is too simple, and its simplicity is not restricted to TD or to schizophrenic speakers. Recently, Hawkins (1973) reported that among the children he studied, the most fluent subjects produce the highest quality narratives. In a detailed analysis, he discovered that these fluent subjects paused less than other subjects at clause boundaries. That is, those with the shortest initial pause durations produced the "best" stories.

Hawkins' data mirror our own and again indicate that coherence or quality of discourse is not a direct function of initial pause duration. Hawkins accounts for his results by suggesting that long initial pauses (5 sec and longer) are not so productive in planning discourse as shorter pauses: "they are not giving 'value' for the amount of time they consume [p. 244]." Our data may merit a stronger claim. With long initial pauses, there appears to be an inverse relation between coherence and pause duration. The present results show that a clause is two to three times[7] more likely to be judged low[8] in coherence when it is preceded by a long ($\geq$ 5 sec) rather than a short ($<$ 5 sec) pause. It is possible, therefore, that initial pause duration is a U-shaped function of coherence: for brief durations, coherence increases as duration increases, but for long durations, coherence drops as duration increases.

Regardless of whether Hawkins is correct in assuming that long initial pauses are only partially productive, or we are correct in assuming that long initial pauses are counterproductive, the question remains: What is the speaker doing during this extra pause time? Why do *initial* pauses discriminate TD speakers?

Initial pauses are probably critical because they occur at the boundaries of major organizational units in speech processing. There is fairly extensive support for the view that clauses serve some significant role in the comprehension of speech: there seem to be "lulls in processing" at clausal boundaries when sentences are presented to listeners (Holmes & Forster, 1970, 1972), and segmentation into clausal units when sentences are recalled (e.g., Aaronson, Lorinstein, & Shapiro, 1971; Jarvella, 1972; Lackner, 1974). In sentence production, Spoonerisms, voiced hesitations, and latencies have been offered as evidence that clauses serve as one kind of organizational base in processing (Lindsley, 1975; MacKay, 1970).

If clauses serve as a planning base in discourse production, then hesitations at the boundaries of this base probably indicate what is happening in the planning

----

[7] This is true for both NTD and TD subjects (N subjects had no clauses of low coherence). For NTD subjects, 3% of all short initial silent pauses ($n = 538$) were rated as low coherent, but 10% of all long silent pauses ($n = 19$) were rated that way. For TD subjects, 15% of short initial pauses ($n = 501$) and 26% of all long pauses ($n = 31$) were rated as low in coherence.

[8] Low coherent ratings are defined as those in which seven out of ten judges found a clause disruptive.

process. This need not mean that hesitations reflect efficient processing, however. During long initial pauses, the speaker may be efficiently planning ahead, or distracted from production of the subsequent clause, or still occupied with the clause just uttered. These possibilities are discussed below.

A. Planning during Long Initial Pauses

There is evidence that normal speakers use longer pauses and more voiced hesitations when the bonds between clauses are weak. In these circumstances, the frequency and duration of hesitations seem to reflect extended utterance planning, performed efficiently. For example, Mott (1972) had judges rank the semantic relationship between adjacent clauses along a five-point scale (where 1 indicated a topic change and 5 indicated a close semantic connection). He found a strong inverse correlation (−.84) between the judges' semantic ratings and the number of voiced hesitations occurring between clauses. Goldman-Eisler (1972) and Rochester and Gill (1973) report that clauses with weak structural ties to a main clause are preceded by longer pauses and more voiced hesitations than clauses with strong ties. Goldman-Eisler suggests that the additional hesitations in these cases reveal that the speaker is attempting to form a new "sentence-whole" or thought unit. She argues that fluent transitions occur only "where no new thought has entered the utterance [p. 111]."

Conceivably, the thought-disordered speaker also plans as efficiently as possible during long initial pauses. However, the planning may require more time than normal productions because thought-disordered speakers have difficulty integrating new concepts into their discourse. Bleuler's (1950) classic view of thought disorder exemplifies this argument. In normal discourse, Bleuler observed, the speaker organizes and interrelates many single thoughts in order to put forward a guiding idea. The speaker is able to tie topics to other topics and sentences to other sentences by using "associative threads." In thought disorder, there is a breaking of some, or all, of the associative threads. This results in ideas becoming split off or isolated from each other. If all the associative threads for the ideas being discussed are broken, there is "blocking": the train of ideas stops suddenly and the speaker is unable to continue discussing a topic. When a new train of thought is chosen, it is likely to have no obvious relationship to the earlier discourse.

This account provides an excellent description of many of our TD speakers. Moreover, the account is valuable because it clearly places responsibility for incoherence in the underlying propositional structure of the discourse—in thought, not in response bias or perception or memory.

As yet, no adequate experiments have tested this notion, although many studies have been performed examining word associations (compare Cohen & Camhi, 1967; Lisman & Cohen, 1972). It is a difficult hypothesis to test because, phrased in the psychology of J. S. Mill, it is not clear what predictions should be made. In a general way, this hypothesis can account for some of our earlier findings. With a failure in proposition structure, speakers might fail to tie a new clause to an old one with a conjunction, and instead resort to the simple word repetition which characterizes the cohesive devices of TD speakers (Rochester *et al.*, 1976). However, there are alternate explanations for this finding, as discussed below.

B. Distraction during Long Initial Pauses

Thought-disordered speakers may lose their attentional focus at clause boundaries and fail to plan the subsequent clause. Maher (1972), for example, hypothesizes that thought-disordered speakers are unable to inhibit associations from intruding into their utterances, and that this failure is especially evident at "terminal points in an utternace such as commas, full stop or period points [p. 13]." Terminal points are vulnerable, he speculates, because they mark the boundaries of coherent attentional units for the speaker.

This proposal places responsibility for the TD speaker's incoherence in the early stages of information processing. The speaker, it is argued, cannot filter out inappropriate responses. This view is consistent with a variety of studies in the literature: with Holmes and Forster's (1970, 1972) account of a lull in processing at the boundaries of clauses; with the work of Shakow and his colleagues (e.g., Shakow, 1963) showing that schizophrenic subjects become increasingly distractable after preparatory periods of 4 sec or longer; and with a host of other studies (e.g., Lisman & Cohen, 1972) indicating that schizophrenic subjects fail to edit out responses inappropriate to the situation.

In fact, this hypothesis explains too much. An important aspect of our findings using segmental analyses is that TD subjects are not incoherent, but rather resemble normal speakers in many respects. For example, TD speakers usually provide adequate referents for noun phrases, and provide as many cohesive ties in their discourse as other schizophrenic speakers (Rochester *et al.*, 1976). Thus, their failures are not pervasive throughout a clause but are limited to making connections between clauses. Sometimes TD speakers provide ambiguous or obscure referents for noun phrases (in about 9% of their total noun phrases); and the *type* but not the quantity of cohesive ties differs for TD speakers. Thus, while Maher's postulate accounts nicely for the present hesitation data, it fails to predict the restricted impairments in coherence seen in our earlier work.

C. The Problem of Lingering

There is a construct related to the distraction hypothesis which provides a more plausible explanation of the present data. This is the notion that the schizophrenic speaker has difficulty "clearing the slate" to process subsequent inputs. This has been demonstrated in a number of studies (cf. Chapman & Chapman,

1973). For example, in a reaction-time task with various preparatory intervals, schizophrenic subjects perform as if they were prepared to respond to the preparatory interval of the immediately prior trial (Zahn, Rosenthal, & Shakow, 1963). Similarly, schizophrenic subjects have trouble divesting themselves of the influence of earlier stimuli. This possibility has been formulated in Salzinger's (1973) immediacy hypothesis and in Cromwell & Dokecki's (1968) formulation of a failure of the schizophrenic subject to disattend.

According to this view, longer pauses at the beginning of new clauses might reflect an aftereffect of the previous clause, an inability to withdraw attention from that clause. Richard Steffy (1975, personal communication) terms this the "problem of lingering." This account does not overpredict failures of the schizophrenic speaker, if we assume that clauses are primary planning bases in discourse production. With this assumption, failures to disattend should occur only at clause boundaries and should be reflected in long, unproductive pauses.

It is not difficult to find explanations of why initial pauses, but not latencies or within-clause pauses, are distinctive for TD speakers. The source of difficulty can be placed in early information processes, or in higher order cognitive organization. The interesting problem is to find an account which does not overpredict impairment. Such an account would also be a description of the cognitive planning process underlying the production of coherent discourse. At this point, such an account would seem to require recognition of the central role of integral planning units for the speaker, planning units which approximately coincide with the boundaries of independent clauses in the surface structure of the grammar.

ACKNOWLEDGMENTS

The authors gratefully acknowledge the support of the Benevolent Foundation of Scottish Rite Freemasonry, Northern Jurisdiction, United States, and the Clarke Institute Associates' Research Fund.

The authors express their profound appreciation to Dr. Alexander Bonkalo and Dr. Mary Seeman, both of the Department of Psychiatry of the University of Toronto, for their painstaking efforts in serving as clinical judges for thought disorder. We are also grateful to Dr. Ron Langevin, Dr. Richard Steffy, and Dr. Stan Feldstein for their valuable comments on an earlier draft of this chapter.

REFERENCES

Aaronson, D., Lorinstein, I. B., & Shapiro, H. Cognitive and linguistic aspects of sentence coding. Paper presented at the 42nd meeting of the Eastern Psychological Association, New York City, April, 1971.

Bernstein, B. Linguistic codes, hesitation phenomena and intelligence. Language and Speech, 1962, 5, 31–46.

Bernstein, B. (Ed.) *Class, codes and control.* Vol. 2: *Applied studies towards a sociology of language.* London: Routledge & Kegan Paul, 1973.

Blankenship, J., & Kay, C. Hesitation phenomena in English speech: A study in distribution. *Word,* 1964, **20,** 360–372.

Bleuler, E. *Dementia praecox; or, the group of schizophrenias.* New York: International Universities Press, 1950. (Originally published: 1911.)

Broen, W. E., Jr. Response disorganization and breadth of observation in schizophrenia. *Psychological Review,* 1966, **73,** 579–585.

Butterworth, B. Hesitation and semantic planning in speech. *Journal of Psycholinguistic Research,* 1975, **4,** 75–88.

Cancro, R. Psychological differentiation and process-reactive schizophrenia. *Journal of Abnormal Psychology,* 1969, **74,** 415–419.

Chapman, L., & Chapman, J. *Disordered thought in schizophrenia.* Englewood Cliffs, New Jersey: Prentice-Hall, 1973. Pp. 271–276.

Cohen, B. D., & Camhi, J. Schizophrenic performance in a word-communication task. *Journal of Abnormal Psychology,* 1967, **72,** 240–246.

Cromwell, R. L., & Dokecki, P. R. Schizophrenic language: A disattention interpretation. In S. Rosenberg & J. H. Koplin (Eds.), *Developments in applied psycholinguistic research.* New York: Macmillan, 1968.

Goldman-Eisler, F. Speech production and the predictability of words in context. *Quarterly Journal of Experimental Psychology,* 1958, **10,** 96–106.   (a)

Goldman-Eisler, F. The predictability of words in context and the length of pauses in speech. *Language and Speech,* 1958, **1,** 226–231.   (b)

Goldman-Eisler, F. Hesitation and information in speech. In C. Cherry (Ed.), *Information theory.* London: Butterworth, 1961. Pp. 162–174.

Goldman-Eisler, F. Discussion and further comments. In H. Lennenberg (Ed.), *New directions in the study of language.* Cambridge, Massachusetts: MIT Press, 1964. Pp. 109–130.

Goldman-Eisler, F. *Psycholinguistics: Experiments in spontaneous speech.* New York: Academic Press, 1968.

Goldman-Eisler, F. Pauses, clauses, sentences. *Language and speech,* 1972, **15,** 103–113.

Goldman-Eisler, F., Skarbek, A., & Henderson, A. The effect of chlorpromazine on speech behavior. *Psychopharmacologia,* 1965, **7,** 220–229.

Hawkins, P. R. The influence of sex, social class and pause-location in the hesitation phenomena of seven-year-old children. In B. Bernstein (Ed.), *Primary socialization, language and education; class, codes and control.* Volume 2. Boston, Massachusetts: Routledge & Kegan Paul, 1973.

Hawks, D. V., & Marshall, W. L. A parsimonious theory of overinclusive thinking and retardation in schizophrenia. *British Journal of Medical Psychology,* 1971, **34,** 75–83.

Hollister, L. E. Choice of antipsychotic drugs. *American Journal of Psychiatry,* 1970, **127,** 186–190.

Holmes, V. M., & Forster, K. I. Detection of extraneous signals during sentence recognition. *Perception and Psychophysics,* 1970, **7**(5), 297–301.

Holmes, V. M., & Forster, K. I. Perceptual complexity and underlying sentence structure. *Journal of Verbal Learning and Verbal Behavior,* 1972, **11,** 148–156.

Jarvella, R. J., & Herman, S. J. Clause structure of sentences and speech processing. *Perception and Psychophysics,* 1972, **11**(5), 381–384.

Labov, W. *Sociolinguistic patterns.* Philadelphia: University of Pennsylvania Press, 1973.

Lackner, J. R. Observations on the speech processing capabilities of an amnesic patient: Several aspects of H. M.'s language function. *Neuropsychologia,* 1974, **12,** 199–207.

Léon, P. R., & Martin, P. *Prolégomènes a l'étude des structures intonatives.* Montreal: Didier, 1969.

Lindsley, J. R. Producing simple utterances: How far ahead do we plan? *Cognitive Psychology*, 1975, 7(1), 1–19.

Lisman, S. A., & Cohen, B. D. Self-editing deficits in schizophrenia: A word-association analogue. *Journal of Abnormal Psychology*, 1972, 79(2), 181–188.

MacKay, D. G. Spoonerisms: The structure of errors in the serial order of speech. *Neuropsychologia*, 1970, 8, 323–350.

Maher, B. The language of schizophrenia: A review and interpretation. *British Journal of Psychiatry*, 1972, **120**, 3–17.

Mahl, G. F. Disturbances and silences in the patient's speech in psychotherapy. *Journal of Abnormal and Social Psychology*, 1956, **53**, 1–15.

Martin, J. R., & Rochester, S. R. Cohesion and reference in schizophrenic speech. In A. & V. Makkai (Eds.), *The first LACUS forum*. Columbia, South Carolina: Hornbeam Press, 1975. Pp. 302–311.

McGhie, A., Chapman, J., & Lawson, J. S. Disturbances in selective attention in schizophrenia. *Proceedings of the Royal Society of Medicine*, 1964, 57, 419–422.

Mott, O. Unpublished manuscript. University of Toronto, 1972.

Paivio, A. *Imagery and verbal processes*. New York: Holt, Rinehart & Winston, 1971.

Reynolds, A., & Paivio, A. Cognitive and emotional determinants of speech. *Canadian Journal of Psychology*, 1968, **22**, 164–175.

Rochester, S. R. Defining the silent pause in speech. *Journal of the Ontario Speech and Hearing Association*, in press.

Rochester, S. R. The significance of pauses in spontaneous speech. *Journal of Psycholinguistic Research*, 1973, **2**, 51–81.

Rochester, S. R., & Gill, J. Production of complex sentences in monologues and dialogues. *Journal of Verbal Learning and Verbal Behavior*, 1973, **12**, 203–210.

Rochester, S. R., & Martin, J. R. The act of referring: The speaker's use of noun phrases to instruct the listener. In R. Freedle (Ed.), *Dialogues and discourse analysis*. Hillsdale, New Jersey: Lawrence Erlbaum Associates, in press.

Rochester, S. R., Martin, J., & Thurston, S. *Thought process disorder in schizophrenia: The listener's task*. Manuscript. University of Toronto, 1976.

Salzinger, K. *Schizophrenia: Behavioral aspects*. New York: Wiley, 1973.

Shakow, D. Psychological deficit in schizophrenia. *Behavioral Science*, 1963, 8, 275–305.

Silverman, G. Redundancy, repetition and pausing in schizophrenic speech. *British Journal of Psychiatry*, 1973, **122**, 407–413.

Tannenbaum, P. H., Williams, F., & Hillier, C. S. Word predictability in the environment of hesitations. *Journal of Verbal Learning and Verbal Behavior*, 1965, **4**, 134–140.

Winer, B. J. *Statistical principles in experimental design*. New York: McGraw-Hill, 1971.

Yates, A. J. Data processing levels and thought disorder in schizophrenia. *Australian Journal of Psychology*, 1966, 18, 103–117.

Zahn, T. P., Rosenthal, D., & Shakow, D. Effects of irregular preparatory intervals on reaction time in schizophrenia. *Journal of Abnormal and Social Psychology*, 1963, 67, 44–52.

Zubin, J. Problem of attention in schizophrenia. In M. Kietman, S. Sutton, & J. Zubin (Eds.), *Experimental approaches to psychopathology*. New York: Academic Press, 1975. Pp. 139–166.

6

Salience and Sentencing: Some Production Principles

Charles E. Osgood
University of Illinois at Urbana-Champaign

J. Kathryn Bock
University of Oregon

The major goals of psycholinguistics are to specify the antecedents of utterances in language production and the consequents of utterances in language comprehension. However, apart from studies of language acquisition, there seems to have been little concern with "where do sentences *come from*?", as one of the authors put it (Osgood, 1971)–the production problem. Rather, the focus of research interest has been on "where do sentences *go to*?"–the comprehension problem. In his *Annual Review of Psychology* chapter on experimental psycholinguistics, Johnson-Laird (1974) opens with the assertion that "the fundamental problem in psycholinguistics is simple to formulate: what happens when we understand sentences? [p. 35]." This emphasis in a review chapter on comprehension, to the exclusion of production, can be justified only on the ground that most of the research available in the literature *is* on language comprehension. As Fodor, Bever, and Garrett (1974) observe, "practically anything that one can say about speech production must be considered speculative even by the standards current in psycholinguistics [p. 434]."

The difficulty has been primarily methodological–to devise controlled experimental procedures that maximize linguistic production variables and minimize linguistic comprehension variables, that is, to "force" subjects into Speaker rather than Listener roles. But if the subject is to be in a natural Speaker role, how is the investigator to exercise any control over what he is to speak *about*? To sit subjects down individually in a completely bare room and tell them "O.K.–just talk about something" is not a very appealing procedure and it is not one likely to provide comparability across speakers. However, there are *naturalistic* methods by which the ideas to be expressed can be constrained across speakers without using linguistic inputs. One of these has been dubbed "Simply Describing" (Osgood, 1971)—an ordinary communicative skill, brought to an artistic peak by sports broadcasters, in which what is comprehended (and hence constrains what is to be expressed) is entered via nonlinguistic, perceptual channels. If one is to exercise *experimental* control within a strictly *linguistic* mode, and still maximize production (Speaker) variables, then the comprehension and production phases must somehow be separated—the "how" of which, of course, has been the stumbling block for research on speech production.

As its title indicates, this chapter is concerned with some production principles which, in different ways, modulate the relative "salience" of the meaning components of the ideas (intentions) to be expressed. One of these principles is what we call *Naturalness:* this refers to the *inherent* salience of the *meaning components as wholes,* and the principle is that the natural order of constituents will correspond to that most frequently experienced in prelinguistic, perception-based comprehending. Another principle is what we call *Vividness:* this refers to the *inherent* salience of the *semantic features* of the meaning components to be expressed (i.e., their affective intensity, as in *the vampire* versus *the man*), and the principle is that constituents having relatively high Vividness will tend to shift "leftward" in sentencing—thus earlier in expression. A third principle is *Motivation-of-Speaker:* this refers to the salience *attributed* by the speaker to the *meaning components as wholes,* and the principle is that constituents having relatively high speaker motivation (interest, concern, ego involvement, etc.—the notion of "focus" generally) will tend to shift "leftward" in sentencing and thus be earlier in expression.

Following a brief presentation of the relevant aspects of a general theory of cognizing and sentencing (see Osgood, 1976, for details) and a brief review of the most relevant literature, two studies will be reported: (1) a reanalysis of data obtained in a naturalistic investigation of "Simply Describing" (Osgood, 1971), which mainly illuminates the Naturalness principle; (2) an experimental investigation of constituent ordering in sentence reconstruction, conducted by the second author (Bock, 1975), which primarily tests the Vividness principle. Although the Motivation-of-Speaker principle is only obliquely approached in these two studies, we shall report some research by others which does focus on this principle.

THEORETICAL ORIENTATION

The general theory of cognizing and sentencing that the first author has been developing over the past couple of decades postulates three levels of information processing on both sensory (comprehending) and motor (producing) sides. The *Projection Level* (linking peripheral inputs and outputs to sensory and motor projection areas of the cortex) and the more central *Integration Level* (in which sensory and motor integrations are formed on the basis of frequency of co-occurence of sensory signals and (via feedback) of motor signals from the Projection Level, thus reflecting redundancies or patternings in perceiving and behaving) have been discussed in detail elsewhere (see, e.g., Hebb, 1949; Lashley, 1951; Osgood, 1957a, b, 1963; Osgood & Hoosain, 1974). The main relevance here is that the sensory integrations (perceptual forms to be comprehended) and motor integrations (motor programs for behaviors to be produced) are, respectively, the inputs to and outputs from the *Representation Level,* which *is* our main concern. This is the level at which sensory integrations are coded into meanings and these meanings organized into the cognitive structures involved in thinking and sentencing. At least the following "mechanisms" (by which are meant *functional* types of information processing by some as yet unspecifiable means in the CNS) must be postulated at this level of cognizing—and all of them are "memories" in one sense or another.

What is called the LEXICON is a semantic encoding and decoding mechanism; it is a "process" rather than a "storage" memory, roughly analogous to the long dial-bank of an old-fashioned desk calculator which spins to that particular set of readings (here, strip of codings on N semantic features) which corresponds to the momentary key-punched input (here, either from the sensory integration level in comprehension or from the OPERATOR in production). Such a process memory has the advantage that it can be used and reused at a very fast clip, becoming reusable as soon as a given feature code-strip has been outputed to another location (to the OPERATOR in comprehending or to the motor integration system in expressing).

The OPERATOR is the system which gives structure to related sets of outputs from the LEXICON and within which the dynamic semantic interactions among such sets occur (see below). It is also a short-term and reusable "memory." Inputs to the OPERATOR may be from either the LEXICON or from the MEMORY (and we speak of "cognizing" in the former case and "re-cognizing" in the latter); outputs from the OPERATOR may be to either the MEMORY (in comprehending) or to the LEXICON (in producing).

In order to handle transformations of diverse types (particularly optional ones)—in which the "natural" order of meaning components required in the OPERATOR does not correspond to the order of constituents in the received input or intended output—what is called a BUFFER must also be postulated. This is a *very* short-term "storage" memory, temporarily holding semantic strip-codes for meaning components that would "naturally" be prior but, for the transformational moment, are subsequent in either inputing or outputing. In effect, the ordering of semantic information in the OPERATOR in interaction with the BUFFER constitutes the transformational syntax of this model.

What is called the MEMORY is a "real" memory in the lay sense of long-term storage. For the present, at least, it is assumed that it is organized in terms of ordered sets of semantic features representing the "topics" of cognitions (M_1 s from the OPERATOR—see below), each associated with its "commentary" $(- - (M) - \rightarrow$'s and M_2s from the OPERATOR—see below).

In the total cognizing process—whether via nonlinguistic perceptuomotor channels (comprehending perceptual events and behaving appropriately) or via linguistic channels (comprehending and producing sentences)—sensory integrations (meaningless forms) are the *input* to the Representational (meaningful) Level and motor integrations (central programs for overt behaving) are the *output*. The use of the terms *encoding* (for the inputing of information to the Representational System via the LEXICON) and *decoding* (for the outputing of information to the motor expressive systems via the LEXICON) seems entirely apropos here: *nonmeaningful,* analogically represented perceptual forms are being *en*coded into *meaningful,* digitally (but not necessarily binary) represented semantic-feature sets on the input side and the identical semantic-feature sets are being *de*coded into *nonmeaningful* motor programs on the output side. It should also be emphasized that everything that transpires at the Representational Level is based upon transfers of and operations on the semantic code-strips outputed "upward" from the LEXICON—thus the "semantic component" has been fully substituted for the syntactic "deep structure" of the standard (Chomsky, 1965) transformational grammar of linguistics—as a step toward an abstract *performance* grammar.[1]

The most critical "mechanism" for present purposes is the OPERATOR, where the dynamic interactions both within and across cognitions occur. A simple cognition (we will often use COG for short) is defined as the representation in the OPERATOR of a perceptual event or linguistic sequence involving a single action or stative relation between two perceived entities (perceptual) or noun phrases (linguistic). It is thus assumed that *simple cognitions are tripartite in structure,* the three constituents being M_1 (the meaning of one perceived entity, later of a subject NP), $- - (M) - \rightarrow$ (the meaning of the perceived action or stative relation, later of a verb phrase), and M_2 (the meaning of another perceived entity, later of an object noun phrase).[2] It is also assumed that *all complex cognitions are analyzable into conjoined sets of simple cognitions,* represented as parallel COGs in the OPERATOR, the set of simplexes being a paraphrase of the complex (e.g., that *the ball the boy hit broke the window* has the same meaning as *the boy hit the ball* (and then) *the ball broke the window*). Indeed, we assume that complexes *must* be so analyzed in order to be comprehended (and for economy in expression, simplexes may be synthesized into

---

[1] The behavior-theoretic process whereby componential $r_M$$- - -$$s_M$, elicited by signs (i.e., semantic-feature sets in the general theory), are derived from the total behaviors elicited by the things signified in the history of the organism has been described many times elsewhere (for example, Osgood, 1954, 1957a, b, 1963, 1971) and need not be redescribed here.

[2] That this basic structure of simple COGs is not a happenstance of English being an SVO-type language and the authors being speakers of English is supported by some evidence (Radulović, 1975); see the Discussion section of this paper.

complexes in sentence production). With these structural notions in mind, we may now consider certain dynamics of cognitive interaction—particularly those which relate to the temporal ordering of information in comprehending and expressing, that is, to salience.

The idea that the focus of a speaker's interest or attention is likely to be expressed as early as possible in sentencing has a long history. In 1900 we find that Wundt, for example, formulated a "principle of placing emphasized concepts first":

> Where word positioning is free, not bound by a hard and fast traditional rule, etc., the words follow each other according to the degree of emphasis on the concepts. The strongest emphasis is naturally on the concept that forms the main content of the statement. It is also the first in the sentence [1970, p. 29].

Descriptivist Bloomfield in 1914 also noted that:

> The emotional relations of the elements . . . affect the sentence in various ways in different languages. A method in English, for instance, is to place the emotionally dominant element in some way out of its usual position, preferably first or last [pp. 113–14].[3]

And many other early expressions of the same notion could be cited. The three "salience" principles being considered here—Naturalness, Vividness, and Motivation-of-the-Speaker—are interrelated and reflect one of Clark Hull's principles of behavior (1943, p. 229), namely (and to paraphrase): *reaction potential* (his symbol would be sEr for mediational processes) *is a multiplicative function of prior learning* (his symbol sHr) *and motivation* (his symbol D for drive). When we add to this his postulated "indexing functions"—that the greater the reaction potential, the greater the probability, amplitude, *and speed of reaction*—it follows that, in both comprehension and production of language and at all levels of the cognitive system, *more highly motivated elements will tend to be processed earlier* (even if in terms of milliseconds) *than less motivated elements* (see Osgood, 1954, for more detail).

Naturalness. An underlying assumption of the first author's theory is that the cognitive structures underlying comprehension (where sentences "go to") and production (where sentences "come from") develop in prelinguistic, perception-based experience, these already available structures quite naturally being "taken over" by the linguistic system as it develops later. The basic structure of a simple COG is assumed to be $[M_1 - - (M) - \rightarrow M_2]$, as already indicated. But what determines the content of this structure? Putting oneself back in one's "booties" of early childhood, it seems intuitively obvious that, for Action relations, the natural order will be ACTOR–ACTION–RECIPIENT, and that, for Stative

---

[3] Bloomfield's ". . . first or last" here is an interesting anticipation of the important distinction now being made between Speaker-oriented (where the salient tends to be "first") and Listener-oriented (where the salient tends to be "last") communications.

relations, the natural order will be FIGURE–STATE–GROUND. Not only does one usually perceive Actors before the Recipients, with the Action more associated with the former than the latter (for example, THE RABBIT IS RUNNING INTO THE BUSHES), but the $^+$Animacy (and often $^+$Human) and $^+$Movement features frequently associated with Actors have more motivational salience than the $^-$Animacy and $^-$Movement features frequently associated with recipients (there is hardly any way to express THE BUSHES acts upon THE RABBIT). And for Stative relations there is much gestalt-type evidence that Figures somehow "stand out" from Grounds (THE CUP IS ON THE TABLE is somehow "natural" while THE TABLE IS UNDER THE CUP is clearly not); and, again, note that Figures are typically characterized by motivational $^+$Animacy $^+$Movement (potential).

Of all determinants of ordering, we consider such perception-based Naturalness to be the most important, being based not only on regularities in prelinguistic experience but also upon a whole succeeding lifetime of perceptual cognizing as a parallel to linguistic cognizing. In this connection, it is interesting that Greenberg (1963) reports that the dominant surface structures of languages are almost universally VSO, SVO (most frequent), or SOV–thus practically never of a type whose dominant structure has O prior to S. Of course, Naturalness of ordering is not restricted to the structure of simple COGs; in conjoined complexes, for example, it is natural for clauses which express temporally prior COGs to precede those which express temporarily subsequent COGs–for example, *after he got dressed he went to work is more natural* than *he went to work after he got dressed* (Opačić, 1973).

Vividness. This principle states that meaning components which include more polarized semantic codings, particularly on the dominant affective features (±Evaluation, ±Potency, and ±Activity), will tend to be processed more quickly, and hence the constituents in which they are expressed will tend to appear earlier in sentence production. The close affinity of the affective E, P, and A–found to be universals in human languages (Osgood, May, & Miron, 1975)–to emotional and motivational variables has often been noted. We assume that more intense affective meaning (here, inherent in the semantic codings of word forms) is therefore a direct indication of speaker motivation. This can also be picked up in sentential stress patterns: one is more likely to say *the vámpire took the key* than *the mán took the key* (when no special contrastive emphasis is involved). It should be noticed that this Vividness principle will often be in conflict with the Naturalness principle, and this comes out clearly in the study on constituent ordering in sentence reconstruction to be reported here.

Motivation of Speaker. Although speaker motivation has been emphasized as underlying all determinants of "salience," in this principle we point to *attributed* rather than to *inherent* motivation (either on the basis of perceptual experience–Naturalness–or the coding of forms on affective features–Vividness). Here we expect wide individual differences (one man's concern with the object of an active construction, *the visitor took the key,* may be much greater than another's, leading the former along the path toward passivization). The general principle, again, is that the more motivation associated with a meaning component for a speaker, the earlier the constituent expressing that component is likely to be in sentencing. This Motivation-of-Speaker principle is also often likely to be in conflict with the Naturalness principle.

CONTEXT OF THE PRESENT RESEARCH

While there is little direct evidence for the notion that the most salient conceptual contents will be expressed early in an utterance, numerous studies have hinted in various ways that the salient is somehow the foremost. In this section we review the most relevant evidence available in the literature. We will report evidence from studies of word order in child language, constituent and word order in adult language, and investigations of the conditions for shifting from active to passive modes—the latter, by all odds, being the most heavily tilled plot. In passing, we will relate this literature to the three salience principles— Naturalness, Vividness, and Motivation of Speaker—with which this chapter is primarily concerned.

Word Order in Child Language

Bates (1974) has argued for the operation of a salience principle to account for word order in child language. Like Carroll (1958) and Gruber (1969), Bates suggests that perceptual organization in terms of the gestalt distinction between figure and ground may have a linguistic correlate, and that in early stages of language acquisition, names of things assuming figural properties will be given ordering preference over names of things assuming ground properties. Thus, at the one-word stage, the single expressed form should tend to be figural in reference; at the two-word stage, the first word should be more figural than the second. This tendency is hypothesized to originate in the operation of the infant's orienting system—which selects novel stimuli for attention from a familiar background, resulting in the organization into figure and ground in perception. This is one aspect of the Naturalness principle.

Several studies of the development of language in very young children support this view. Greenfield and Smith (in press, cited by Bates, 1974) investigated children in the one-word stage of language acquisition and found that the single element of a situation which the child chose to express was regularly that undergoing greatest change or emphasis. Thus, if a child is putting a series of objects into a bucket, the child will name the changing objects rather than saying "bucket" or "put." When several different agents successively perform the same action, the child will most probably name the agent, but if a single agent carries out several different activities, the verb usually appears as the one-word utterance.

At the two-word stage, Bates (1974) and Baroni, Fava, and Tirandola (1973, cited by Bates, 1974) report that young Italian children frequently appear to express new, high-information elements before old, low-information elements. MacWhinney (1975) also reports evidence that some of the utterances of children acquiring Hungarian conform to a pattern of "expressive focusing," in which an interesting or important word precedes the other word in the utterance. MacWhinney notes further that other observers of children acquiring Hungarian have reported a short period of verb fronting early in acquisition, and a similar tendency has been found in children acquiring other languages, despite the fact that this often violates basic adult word order (although the imperative in adult English reflects the same principle). MacWhinney suggests that this period of verb fronting represents a "basic tendency to put the most interesting thing first [1975, p. 162]."

There is virtually no evidence that children acquiring English follow a similar rule (of placing the most interesting thing first) in the two-word stage. However, Bloom (1970) suggests that children rather rigidly observe a rule to place animate nouns in subject position and inanimate nouns in object position, which again reflects our Naturalness principle (here, the Actor—Recipient notion). Similar preferences for animate-first placement have been noted by Bowerman (1973) for children acquiring Finnish, and by Schlesinger (1968) for children acquiring Hebrew. In English, since there is significant overlap with the ordering of agent—action—object in adult language, the evidence is not clear. However, Radulović (1975) reports that young children learning Serbo-Croation—a highly inflected language with extreme word-order variation in adult performance—rigidly adhere to an Actor—Action—Recipient sequence. Bates (in press) has suggested a pragmatic ordering principle to account for word order in child language in variable word—order languages. The basis of Bates' pragmatic ordering principle is a strategy to place the more salient element first: "the novel, high information element is essentially 'blurted out' first, with other information added on with the child's remaining processing capacity [Bates, in press, p. 45]."

Placing salient information first in an utterance thus appears to be a very early development in language acquisition, and may persevere into adulthood. A logical consequence of such a tendency is that certain grammatical devices should be employed in order to allow placement of salient information early in the sentence. Along these lines, Osgood (1971) has proposed that "the job of syntax is not central but rather peripheral in ordinary language—merely accomodating lexical decisions made on the basis of the fleeting interests and motivation entertained by speakers [p. 520]."

Constituent and Word Order in Adult Language

Perhaps surprisingly, there seems to be little experimental research reported on ordering phenomena in adult language—that is, other than on the conditions for passive constructions (see below). However, the next chapter by Ertel ("Where Do the Subjects of Sentences Come From?") does much to fill this gap. He presents four highly relevant experiments, all designed to test his hypothesis that in sentencing the speaker focuses on that nominal constituent which is closest to his ego in the phenomenal field (a process which Ertel terms "nominal seizing") and makes it the subject of his sentence. This can be freely translated as a salience principle, specifically what we have referred to as *Motivation of Speaker*—although the fourth experiment reported (on the role of affective meaning polarization of nonsense forms in determining sentence subject choice) gets more at our *Vividness* principle.

In the first experiment, subjects were shown a drawing in which there were two girls, one on each side of a fence, four boys in a row, a speaker (indicated by a cartoon-style, but empty, balloon coming out of his mouth) and a listener—the two girls and the four boys all having names printed above them. This drawing was rotated 180° for half the subjects. When given sentences like *Hans is watching the girl standing in front of the fence* and asked to name the girl being referred to (Inge or Gisela) by the pictured speaker, the results indicate that the subjects tended to adopt the perspective of the "speaker." The lack of significant differences when the picture is rotated 180°—thereby reversing the subject's own relations to the characters—clearly controls for the possibility that the viewers' own location contributed to the findings.

In an experiment on kinship reasoning, male and female subjects were given statements like *my sister is your daughter* or *my nephew is your brother* and then asked: "who can say this to whom?" To reverse ego-closeness from sentence subject to sentence object, the synonymous sentences *your daughter is my sister* and *your brother is my nephew* were also given. Solution speeds were recorded: for each pair of synonymous sentences for each subject, a (+) was recorded if the congruent sentence ("My" X in sentence–subject position) was processed quicker than the incongruent sentence ("Your" X in sentence–subject position) and a (−) if the speed difference went the other way. Across all 40 sentence-pairs, 25 subjects had positive and only 5 negative indices, indicating that kinship reasoning is faster when the ego-related concept is in the sentence-subject role. There were four possible correct answers to each reasoning problem (thus, for the first example in this paragraph, the answers could be *a son to his father, a son to his mother, a daughter to her father,* and *a daughter to her mother*); most significantly, male subjects selected *male* speakers and hearers in their answers while female subjects selected *female* speakers and hearers.

Ertel's third "experiment" was actually a content analysis—of sports writers' reports of identical soccer games, the writers (and their newspapers) being close to team A in one case and close to team B in the other. Only sentences including references to players of both teams were analyzed, and the prediction, of course, was that the home-team player would be more likely to appear in sentence-subject position. This expectation was clearly borne out.

The fourth experiment, as noted above, was more related to our Vividness principle than our Speaker-Motivation principle (Closeness to Ego in Ertel's terms). In an earlier study, 20 concepts had been rated on semantic differential scales defined by nonsense strings of phonemes (e.g., OKAR–ELIN, FANGO–MNUHF), along with three E–P–A marker scales, and the results factor analyzed (yielding the usual three dominant factors). In the present experiment, subjects were asked to write simple sentences about pairs of hypothetical people whose "names" were the pairs of nonsense strings from scales having high loadings on a given factor (E, P, or A) and low loadings on the other two factors. Ertel's prediction was that the Positives of scales (E^+ P^+, and A^+) would be more likely to be used as sentence subjects than the Negatives. This prediction was borne out most clearly (for both gymnasium and university students) for P, only for gymnasium subjects for E, and only for university subjects for A–but the overall prediction for all subjects clearly holds up.[4]

Very recently, Cooper and Ross (1975), in a paper entitled "World Order" (and this is not a printer's error!), brought together a tremendous amount of linguistic data on "freezes" of word orders in conjoints (e.g., *no more ands or buts/*no more buts or ands; fore and aft/*aft and fore*) which are generally consistent with Ertel's notion of Ego-Closeness as well as our three salience principles. Only a few examples must suffice here.

What Cooper and Ross refer to as the "Me First" principle is very much like Ertel's Ego Closeness or our Speaker Motivation: spatial deixis (*they hunted here and there/*there and here; they talked about this and that/*that and this*); temporal deixis (*I think of him now and then/*then and now; sooner or later/*later or sooner they'll arrive*); generational closeness (*my son and grandson/*grandson and son take after me*); WASPness (!) (*they played cowboys and Indians/*Indians and cowboys*); humanness (*'taint a fit night out for man nor beast/*beast nor man*). *Naturalness* appears in a wide variety of ways, for examples: Actor to Recipient (*they played cat and mouse/*mouse and cat*); Figure to Ground (*Snow White and the Seven Dwarfs/*the Seven Dwarfs and Snow White*; and, of course, *figure and ground/*ground and figure* itself). Positive affective polarity, an aspect of *Vividness* (see Ertel's fourth experiment above), appears as a major determiner: Good to Bad (*are you for or against/*against or for me; the pros and cons/*cons and pros of it; I'm in it, win or lose/*lose or win*); Dynamic to Insipid (*a scotch and soda/*soda and scotch,*

---

[4] Our Vividness principle would predict that *affective intensity*, regardless of polarity and over all factors, would be the best predictor–but still with the Positive polarity bias (see below). Since this would require materials in which the nonsense items had been rated as *concepts* on the usual meaningful scales, this prediction cannot be tested with his data.

please; dollars and cents/*cents and dollars; the quick and the dead/*dead and the quick; horse and buggy/*buggy and horse).

That these are only universal tendencies *in a statistical sense* is evident from the many exceptions one can find (e.g., *we want him, dead or alive/*alive or dead; it swung to and fro,* but also *it swung back and forth/*forth and back).*[5] Cooper and Ross describe a number of phonological factors that interact with semantic (and salience) determinants and may countermand them. One of these is that, other things being equal, place 2 elements will typically have more syllables than place 1 elements (Panini's Law); thus *kit and caboodle/*caboodle and kit,* and this may work to make *dead or alive* more acceptable than *alive or dead.* Another is that, other things being equal, place 2 elements will have vowels containing a lower second formant frequency; thus *spic and span* and *hem and haw,* and this may be why we have *it swung back and forth* as well as *it swung to and fro.*

It is also interesting that many constructions with "frozen" order tend to be idiomatic and to function like single words, resisting insertions within their borders; Cooper and Ross provide a cute example: we can say *both mouse and cat were exhausted after the chase* but we cannot say *Tip never plays mouse and cat with Teddy;* note also that *Tip never plays cat and little mouse with Teddy* loses the force of the idiom (as do *spic and quite span* and *hem and then haw).* The same resistance to insertion appears for nominal compounds as contrasted with ordinary noun phrases; thus *it's an old wishing well/*it's a wishing old well* as compared with *it's an old dirty well/*it's a dirty old well.*

Conditions for Passive Constructions

The most frequently cited example of reordering of constituents for emphasis is the passive transformation (e.g., Jesperson, 1924; Osgood, 1954; Pillsbury, 1915; Rommetveit, 1968). Accordingly, considerable research has been devoted to investigating the determinants of passive constructions. Two major areas of concern have been, first, the semantic characteristics of the subjects of active and passive sentences (our Vividness) and, second, the contextual conditions under which passives are employed (our Motivation of Speaker). As we pointed out earlier, both Vividness and Speaker-Motivation principles often work against the Naturalness principle—and the passive transformation is a clear case in which they prevail.

Vividness. If earlier constituents of sentences represent more salient elements, then it might be expected that the surface subjects of *both* active and passive sentences would be more vivid than the surface objects. A number of studies suggest this to be the case. Segal and Martin (1966) reported that the surface

---

[5] And, of course, it will have to be demonstrated that the same principles have statistical validity cross-linguistically; Ross and Cooper plan to make such checks.

subjects of active and passive sentences were rated as the "most important" elements in the sentences. Johnson-Laird (1968) asked subjects to illustrate sentences such as "Red follows blue" and "Blue is followed by red" by coloring in areas of long thin rectangles. For both active and passive sentences, the area assigned to the surface subject tended to be larger than that given to the surface object. While these studies are difficult to interpret—for example, there are several ways in which a sentence constituent can be "most important," particularly if one considers satisfying the different needs of speaker and listener ("new" first versus "given" first)—they tend to confirm the intuition that there is something "different" about surface subjects.

Some suggestions as to what this difference might be have been offered by H. Clark (1965), Johnson (1967), Ertel (1971), and Flores d'Arcais (1974). Clark (1965) reports that surface subjects of both active and passive sentences tend to be more animate than surface objects. Similarly, Johnson (1967) found that semantic differential ratings of CVCs presented as subjects and objects in active and passive sentences showed differences in Activity ratings attributable to their surface grammatical functions: surface subjects tended to be rated more active than surface objects. These results converge with the developmental finding that animate nouns come first in children's utterances.

Ertel (1971) asked subjects to select which members of pairs of sentences they preferred, when the pairs consisted of active and passive versions of the same content. Sentences in which the nouns used as surface subjects were more Valued, Potent, and Active than the nouns used as surface objects were more likely to be chosen than their alternatives. Flores d'Arcais (1974) showed that the tendency to prefer passive sentences could be increased by manipulating the sizes of different components of pictures for which subjects had to choose either an active sentence or its corresponding passive as the "best" description.

Motivation of Speaker.   Perhaps the earliest study investigating the contextual conditions for active and passive sentences was performed by J. B. Carroll (1958). High school students were asked to describe two situations in response to different question forms, which varied across subjects. In the first situation a man (introduced as "the professor") manipulated blocks on a table; in the second, the same man motioned for a student confederate to erase a blackboard, and when the student refused, he was ordered by the man to report to the principal's office. The various question forms corresponded to "what did the professor do?", "what happened?", "what was done to (the blocks/the classmate)?" When asked to describe what the professor did, the subjects produced predominantly active constructions; in response to "what happened?" most of the constructions remained active, but the number of passives increased. More passives than actives were produced when the subjects were questioned about the blocks, but when questioned about the classmate, three types of constructions were used: slightly less than half of the responses were passive, and of the remainder, most used active sentences with the professor as subject. However, many subjects responded to this question with active constructions having the classmate as the subject. The sentence types used by the subjects were thus rather easily manipulated simply by changing the question—and hence, the *focus* of the speaker subjects. Turner and Rommetveit (1967) report similar effects of asking questions about the objects of actions.

Somewhat similar conclusions can be drawn from production studies carried out by Prentice (1967), Tannenbaum and Williams (1968), Turner and Rommetveit (1967), and Flores d'Arcais (1974). In each of these experiments, subjects were asked to produce sentences describing pictures. It was found that more passives were produced in conditions in which the object of the action was given as a type of cue, either by presenting a picture of the object before a picture of the situation (Prentice, 1967) or by seeing the object of an action before seeing the actor in a simply-describing situation (Turner & Rommetveit, 1967). Other studies have found that the latency of producing a passive sentence as a description of a picture decreases when an introductory paragraph emphasizes the object of the action (Tannenbaum & Williams, 1968) or when the name of the object is provided prior to exposing the picture of a situation (Flores d'Arcais, 1974).

Critique. Although these studies could be interpreted as providing evidence for the hypothesis that increasing the salience of the cognitive object (either via inherent vividness or attributed speaker focus) facilitates use of the passive, there are serious difficulties with this conclusion. One problem is that all of the methods used to elicit passive sentences may have the effect of making the object of the action *given* (or old) *information.* Chafe (1970) has suggested that passive sentences are primarily used when the object of the action is old information, and Bock (1975) found that old information tends to occur earlier in the sentence than new information in a question-answering task. A second problem is that providing a picture of the object or the name of the object should obviously tend to reduce the latency of producing the object label; showing the picture in advance gives the subject the opportunity to retrieve the name before the entire situation is presented—and actually presenting the name makes even *this* step unnecessary.

The salience-of-object interpretation also assumes that a sentence must be entirely formulated cognitively before production is initiated. Although this assumption, as applied to simple cognitions (clauses, sentoids), is also made by the authors, Lindsley (1975) has reported data which he interprets as implying that sentence production is initiated shortly after the surface subject is selected— actually after the subject is selected and the verb "partially" selected. However, Lindsley's experimental conditions were highly artificial and the *prescribed* utterances for the speaker-subjects were nonsentences in many cases (e.g., *the man, greeting, the man greeting*), even though the pictures to be described provided perceptually complete cognitions (e.g., MAN GREETS WOMAN).

Various recall studies are subject to similar objections (e.g., Prentice, 1966;

Turner & Rommetveit, 1968). However, one recall study by James, Thompson, and Baldwin (1973) found that when the imagery value of the nouns used to construct active and passive sentences was varied, shifts from active to passive were more likely when the surface-structure object was higher in imagery value than the surface subject. Because of the parallels that can be drawn between recall and sentence production, the James *et al.* study does suggest that increasing the salience of the cognitive object contributes to its earlier occurrence in the sentence, and thus a higher probability of a passive. The criticism that might be leveled against this study is that higher imagery values typically operate to increase recallability of words (cf. Paivio, 1969), so that the results could be accounted for by the fact that one part of each sentence was better remembered than the other. However, since salience must be defined broadly enough to include some such thing as the degree of clarity and codability of a cognitive representation, this criticism is not particularly serious. Without the mediation of memory, however, it is doubtful that imageability would correlate well with salience (where salience corresponds to our notion of Vividness): the word CAR, for example, is very imageable ($I = 6.87$, Paivio, Yuille, & Madigan, 1968) but it is not particularly vivid; on the other hand, ATROCITY is not particularly imageable ($I = 3.67$) but it is intuitively very vivid.

On the whole, in view of the amount of effort that has gone into the investigation of salience effects, there is surprisingly weak evidence for it. The least contestable support comes from a sentence recall study (James *et al.*, 1973) rather than from sentence production studies, and most of the research (including that of James *et al.*) is restricted to the passive transformation. There are many other constructions—in English as well as in languages with less restricted word orders—that allow movement of constituents within sentence frames without changing underlying logical or semantic relations.

SIMPLY DESCRIBING: A NATURALISTIC APPROACH

One of the few issues in psycholinguistics that has been addressed primarily with production procedures is how the form and content of utterances are influenced by nonlinguistic, situational variables. The first author's study of Simply Describing ("Where Do Sentences Come From?," Osgood, 1971) was a sentence production experiment under naturalistic conditions, and it provides many compelling illustrations of the ways in which sentencing is determined by perceptually-induced cognizing. Unlike most prior and subsequent studies of linguistic responses to nonlinguistic stimuli (e.g., Carroll, 1958; Flores d'Arcais, 1974; Olson, 1970; Prentice, 1967; Turner & Rommetveit, 1967) the subjects' sentencings were entirely unconstrained, except in so far as the perceptual inputs naturally constrained what there was to talk about—these being the source of independent variables, of course. Furthermore, the perceptual inputs ("demonstrations") varied widely in type and complexity, giving opportunity for diversity in the form and content of sentencing.

Method

The materials for this study were a variety of objects (balls of varying colors and sizes, plates, tubes, poker chips, etc.) that were manipulated by the experimenter standing at one end of a large table (seminar classroom size) in a series of 32 demonstrations. These demonstrations were designed and sequenced with "psycholinguistic malice aforethought," for example, to induce certain presuppositions, to provide for implicit contrasts (over time) as well as explicit contrasts (over space), and so forth. The 26 subjects were graduate students and the instructions were very simple: for each demonstration (announced by its number), to open their eyes on the cue "open," to close them on the cue "close," and then describe the perceptual event(s) that had transpired in a single sentence that a (hypothetical) six-year-old "just outside the door and not able to see what is happening" would be able to understand; if the experimenter was visibly involved in an event, they were to refer to him as *the man*.

Examples of the "malice aforethought": D(emonstration)3 was THE BALL IS ROLLING ON THE TABLE[6] and the following D4 was THE BALL IS ROLLING SLOWLY ON THE TABLE, designed to induce adverbial qualification of the verb phrase; D6 was THE MAN IS HOLDING TWO SMALL BLACK BALLS and the following D7 was ONE BALL ROLLS AND HITS THE OTHER, designed to induce both conjoining of verb phrases and use of semireflexives (here, *the other, another,* etc.); D15 was A BALL, A SPOON, AND A POKER CHIP ARE ON THE PLATE and the following D16 was THE PLATE IS EMPTY, designed to induce some form of negation (... *is empty, there is nothing ...,* etc.).

Among the findings reported in the 1971 paper were the following: *shifting determiner* from indefinite *a* to definite *the* was an abrupt function of immediate reappearance of an entity, with shifting back toward *a* being a continuous function of delays (over demonstrations) in reappearance; use of determiner was also a function of whether an entity was a member of a set of identicals (*a*) or unique from others (*the*); *richness of qualification* (modifying) in noun phrases was a continuous, decreasing function of the number and temporal closeness of reappearances of entities; *pronominalization of entities* required that they enter into more than one action or stative relation within the same demonstration (e.g., *the man bounced the ball and IT hit the plate; a ball is on a tube WHICH is*

---

[6]We use ALL CAPS for statements describing nonlinguistic, perceptual events; the wordings for each demonstration title are simultaneously a description of the event and a prediction of what will be the dominant linguistic sentencing of it; the D-numbers refer to the demonstration orders in the original study (Osgood, 1971).

standing on a plate); both *explicit contrast* within the same demonstration (e.g., for D10, *a small black ball hits the big blue ball*) and *implicit contrast* across demonstrations (e.g., after eight demonstrations involving only squash balls, for D9 saying *the man is holding a celestial big blue ball*) maintain or increase qualification, even though the entities in question (e.g., A SMALL BLACK BALL in D10) may be familiar "old" information.

Naturalness

It will be recalled that the essence of the first author's theory of cognizing and sentencing is that the deep cognitive structures which interpret sentences received and initiate sentences produced have their origins in prelinguistic perceptuomotor comprehending and behaving—which, by the way, is not to deny that there may be innate as well as experiential factors involved. "Naturalness" was defined as that ordering of constituents within clauses which corresponds to the *inherent salience* of the components of simple cognitions $[M_1 -- (M) - \rightarrow M_2]$ as determined in experience with perceived entities in their action and stative relations. The higher this correspondence, the greater the Naturalness in sentencing. In the Simply Describing situation, it is assumed that having perceptual events as the inputs to cognizing serves both to constrain cognitions across speakers and to amplify inherent salience; hence the role of Naturalness in determining the sentences produced.

Stative Relations. In perceived stative relations (for example, CAT/ BE ON/ PILLOW) it is assumed that the M_1s of cognitions will most naturally be the Figures (typically Mobile, often Animate, usually more Variable than Constant, etc.) and that the M_2s will be the Grounds, with the relation often expressed by some form of the verb *to be;* thus here, for familiar entities, the expected sentence would be *the cat is on the pillow.* In D2 (THE BALL IS ON THE TABLE) we find the Naturalness principle holding 25/1/0 for the 26 subjects,[7] with nine speakers using simply *is* and the other using *is sitting, is resting,* and the like. In prior D1 (THE MAN IS HOLDING A BALL) we had a +Human Animate entity and a −Animate entity in a stative relation, and the Naturalness prediction is that the former will be perceived as M_1 and the latter as M_2; the results are 24/1/1, with 17 (*is/was*) *holding* as the relations. D18–20 were three sentencings of the same stative relation involving three entities and two conjoined cognitions (A BALL IS ON THE TUBE AND THE TUBE IS ON THE PLATE—this following a tube-on-plate demonstration, hence the definite articles), and the question was whether there is a "natural" top-to-bottom

---

[7] We will usually report results in these sets of triples, where the first frequency (here, 25) is the number of speakers confirming the prediction, the second the number of "flubs" (here, 1—one subject who opened his eyes too soon and reported *the man holds his finger on a black ball!*), and the third frequency is the number of speakers going against the prediction.

ordering; the answer is clearly "yes"—for D18 there were 13 *ball–tube–plate* orderings, 7 *tube–(ball–plate/plate–ball)*, and only 3 sentences starting with the lowly *plate;* for D19 we find 12 *tube*-first, 7 *ball*-first, and 5 *plate*-first sentences; and for D20 (in desperation?) there are 10 *plate*-first (but always *plate–tube–ball,* never *plate–ball–tube*), 6 *tube*-first, and 6 *ball*-first sentences.

D3 (THE BALL/IS ROLLING ON/THE TABLE)[8] provides an interesting borderline case between Stative and Action relations—note that in D2 above we often got *is sitting (laying, resting,* etc.) *on* for verb phrases; the Naturalness principle predicts the mobile BALL as M_1 in either case, and the results are 22/4/0 (the 4 "flubs" being cases where the subject expressed the presupposed actor, *the man,* as NP_1). The immediately following D4 (THE BALL IS ROLLING SLOWLY ON THE TABLE) merely confirmed that information from the LEXICON (cognizing) will often be compared in the OPERATOR with information about the same topic drawn from the MEMORY (re-cognizing), creating in this case adverbial qualification *(slowly)*—19/3/4.

Action Relations. In perceived action relations (e.g., THE BOY KICKED THE CAN) it is assumed that the M_1s of cognitions will most naturally be the Actor (Agent, Instrument) and the M_2s the Recipients (either Animate or Inanimate); not only are the former nearly always more Mobile than the latter (and often +Animate, even +Human), but they are typically perceived slightly prior in time. D21 (THE ORANGE BALL HITS THE UPRIGHT TUBE) pits the Given-New principle (the TUBE having just been seen in D20, the BALL not having been seen since D14) against the Naturalness principle, and with direct perceptual-input support, Naturalness wins hands down, 21/0/5 (with the five countermands being passive constructions, of course). D7 (ONE SQUASH BALL ROLLS AND HITS ANOTHER), following several single-ball rollings, tested three predictions—(1) that the moving entity will appear as the subject NP, (2) that the second of the two conjoined COGs (HITS) will be the more salient, and (3) that the object NP will include some semireflexive form (because of the identity of the two entities): as for (1), the score of 21/5 "flubs"/0 demonstrates the natural salience of the moving entity (not a single passive sentence); as for (2), seven speakers expressed both COGs *(rolls and hits),* five expressed only one COG (and it was always *hits*), and nine fused the two-COG information into a single-clause sentence, *and always with COG 2 as the matrix,* for example, *a black ball rolled AGAINST (INTO) the other ball, one black ball COLLIDES WITH (STRIKES) another, a ROLLING black ball hits a stationary one;* as for (3), the score of 21/5/1 indicates that of the non-"flubs," 21 of 22 used some form of semireflexive.

---

[8] As suggested by the slashes, the theory claims that, in cognizing, prepositions may be parts of VPs (relations) rather than of NPs (entities); note the difference between *the astronaut chased the Martian with a stick/ the astronaut chased with a stick the Martian* (PP part of the VP relation) and *the astronaut chased the Martian with purple spots/*the astronaut chased with purple spots the Martian* (PP part of object NP).

D12–14 were three repetitions of a two-COG, three-entity action event (THE BLACK BALL HITS THE BLUE BALL AND THEN THE BLUE BALL HITS THE ORANGE BALL). Due to *the man's* performing difficulties—getting the three-ball carom shot to work for one subset of subjects on an uneven table!—there were a large number of "flubs," but the prediction (that the natural order in expression will be the order of cognizing) was clearly upheld for the crucial first demonstration (D12) in the series: 12 naturals, 13 "flubs," and only 1 passive (*the orange ball was struck by a smaller blue ball which was struck by an even smaller black ball*–note, "forced" by expressing the third entity first). But the passive is an available transform when an active has already been used: in D13 the score goes to 7/13/6, and for D14 it is the same (mixed clause-type sentences were counted in the passive category, for example, *the blue ball was hit by the black ball and it* (then) *hit the orange ball*). This series also provides a clear case of *explicit contrast* among entities in the same category (balls), in this case varying simultaneously in both size and color, generating modifying adjectives. D12 is typical of all three demonstrations in the series: 25 describers made explicit contrasts among the three NPs and only 1 did not—8 specifying both properties (*the large blue ball*), 15 just color (*the blue ball*), and only 2 just size (*the middle-size ball*); absolute color thus appears to be more salient than relative size when both are variable for the same objects.

D8 involved *three* conjoined COGs (THE MAN IS HOLDING TWO BLACK BALLS/HE BOUNCES ONE BALL ON THE TABLE/THAT BALL HITS THE PLATE) and was designed with the "malice aforethought" of producing center-embedding (THE BALL THE MAN BOUNCES HITS THE PLATE)—but nary a single center-embedded description was given, consistent with the very Un-naturalness of such sentencings. However, there are interesting predictions here: One is that the first, stative cognition (HOLDING), all "old" components, will be less likely to be expressed than the subsequent action cognitions (and we find only 10/26 describers expressing COG 1, but 23/26 expressing COG 2 and ditto for COG 3); another is that the two action COGs are more likely to be fused (*. . . bounced one ball onto the plate*) than the stative COG 1 with the action COG 2 (*one held ball was bounced . . .*), and there were 7 of the former and 0 of the latter; a third (and major) expectation is that the order of expressing the cognitions in sentencing will correspond to the order in perceptual experience (where all three COGs were expressed, there were 6 COG 1 → COG 2 → COG 3 and only two that changed this order in any way, and where only COGs 2 and 3 were expressed, there were 11 in the natural order and none in the unnatural).

Interactions of Motivation of Speaker/Vividness with Naturalness

Speaker Motivation and Vividness principles will only appear clearly when they override the dominant Naturalness principle. Although the Simply Describing study was not designed with these salience principles particularly in mind, a number of the demonstrations lend themselves to comparison of perceptual conditions (congruent) in which Motivation/Vividness yield the *same* ordering predictions as Naturalness with conditions (incongruent) where they predict different ordering than Naturalness.[9] Here we present a few comparisons of this sort.

Motivation/Vividness Congruent with Naturalness. In D17 (A CARDBOARD TUBE IS ON THE PLATE), a novel entity (the TUBE) is figural with respect to a familiar ground (or base, the PLATE), so all salience principles predict the same way; in the 26 sentencings we find 21 with TUBE expressed prior to PLATE and only 5 with the reverse order (none of which were passives, by the way, e.g., *the plate has a cardboard tube standing in its center*). In D26 (SOME POKER CHIPS ARE ON THE TABLE), the figural objects (POKER CHIPS) are very novel and the ground (TABLE) is very familiar, of course, by now; all 26 of the sentencings are in the predicted order (e.g., *ten white disks lay on the table*). Of course, both D17 and D26 are stative relations, and at least in the latter case it is rather hard to even conceive of an alternative construction—*the table is holding some poker chips*?

There were several demonstrations where an expression of Negation was the primary prediction (based upon implicit contrast with the immediately preceding demonstration, and hence cases of "denial of expectation"). One might argue that Naturalness would also move Negations "leftward." D16 (THE PLATE IS EMPTY) followed A BALL, A SPOON, AND A POKER CHIP ARE ON THE PLATE; there were 15 overt expressions of Negation, and in 8 of these the Neg was expressed prior to the entity noun, *plate* (typically as an adjectival modifier, *an empty plate . . .*), but there were other intriguing expressions—two cases of terminal adjectival displacement (with implied stress for the "new" information), *the plate was sitting on the table, empty,* and one lovely double Neg, *the man fooled us and placed nothing on the plate*! The final D32 (THERE IS NOTHING ON THE TABLE) yielded 25/26 expressions of Negation, and of these 17 expressed the Neg prior to the entity noun, *table;* examples: *there was nothing on the table, there were no disks . . . , no poker chips remain . . . , all objects have been removed from the table,* and *nothingness abounds*! For D24 (THE BALL MISSED THE TUBE) there were only 9 expressions of the experimenter-intended Negation (most sentencings being of the *rolled past, rolls to the side of* sort); it is interesting, however, that 8 of the 9 Negs involved *two COGs* (e.g., *the ball rolled toward the tube but did not hit it, the ball rolls toward the tube without hitting it*), suggesting that the Negs were produced by comparing the perceived "missing" event with many prior "hitting" events drawn from MEMORY.

---

[9] Since, with perceptual inputs, entities which have *high inherent semantic salience* (e.g., THE VERY BIG ORANGE BALL) are also likely to be those to which observers will *attribute motivational salience* (focus of attention, interest, etc.), no attempt will be made to differentiate Vividness and Motivation-of-Speaker principles here.

Motivation/Vividness Incongruent with Naturalness.   In most of the following cases, the novel, vivid, etc., entity is clearly in the Recipient or Ground (M_2) component, and therefore the Naturalness principle predicts one way of ordering and the other principles predict the opposite way. In D5 (THE MAN PUTS THE BALL ON A PLASTIC PLATE), the PLATE is the hitherto unseen entity; the results were 21/4/1 in favor of Naturalness, with the 4 "flubs" all being passives (*the ball was put on the plate*) and the one description favoring Motivation/ Vividness being *there is a plate with a small black ball which is later placed in it by the man* (!). In D6 (THE MAN IS HOLDING TWO BALLS), although the objects (SQUASH BALLS) were familiar, the presence to two of them at once was novel; the results were 22/1/3 favoring Naturalness, with all 3 reversals being the passives predicted by Motivation/Vividness. In D9 (THE MAN IS HOLDING A BIG BLUE BALL), this was the first presentation of other than squash balls; the results were 20/1/5 in favor of Naturalness, with 4 of the sentencings favoring Motivation/Vividness being the expected passives (the other counted as favoring M/V was *the man gazed at the blue ball*). D11 was a direct *attempt* to produce passives and therefore was phrased as A VERY BIG ORANGE BALL IS HIT BY A SMALL BLACK BALL, this also being the orange ball's first appearance; nevertheless, only 3 of the 26 speakers produced the expected passive sentences, the other sentences starting off with the familiar, but $^+$Motion, *little black ball.*

Although there is no question about the dominance of Naturalness over Motivation/Vividness in this Simply Describing situation, there is some evidence for interaction of principles in these incongruent cases. We should compare the 22/1/3 for D6, the 18/0/8 for D9, and the 23/0/3 for D11 with the first three demonstrations with only one little black ball—D1 24/1/1, D2 25/1/0, and D3 22/4/0: there does appear to be some effect of Motivation/Vividness here. As to the study of Simply Describing as a whole, there seems to be no doubt that there are intimate interrelations between perceptual and linguistic channels—in fact, that nonlinguistic inputs can literally "drive" the contents and forms of sentential outputs. This strongly suggests that, at some "deep" level of cognizing, nonlinguistic and linguistic processing must share the same system.

CONSTITUENT ORDERING IN SENTENCE RECONSTRUCTION: AN EXPERIMENTAL APPROACH

If the Vividness principle has any significance as a principle of sentence production, it should have some generality. Optional transformations would seem to provide a natural testing ground: there are many types of such transformations; one form can usually be identified as being more Natural than the alternative; and inherent semantic (affective) Vividness can be manipulated with relative ease. A sentence reconstruction task was devised—one that separates comprehension and production processes via the interpolation of making up a story in which each novel and complex sentence could be used and also minimizes the problem of "given information" that plagued many earlier studies. Here again the Vividness principle may be either congruent with the Naturalness principle (yielding the same predictions) or incongruent (yielding opposed predictions).

The Vividness principle extends beyond determination of the initial noun phrases of clauses to later constituents, so that *whenever* a grammatical option is available for reordering constituents of a clause and the constituents in question differ in Vividness, the more vivid should tend to occur prior to the less vivid (*ceteris paribus*). The principle should also apply to ordering of larger linguistic units, such as the conjoined clauses of complex sentences: more vivid clauses should be expressed earlier than less vivid (again, *ceteris paribus*). The experiment described below tested these hypotheses, using complex two-clause sentences in which each clause was one of several different types that admit optional transformations. Vividness of constituents was varied by interchanging words having either high or low inherent affective intensity (*Jackie Onassis/a wealthy woman, avalanche/snow, the Supreme Court/a judge,* and so forth); Naturalness was determined from the theory of cognizing and sentencing discussed earlier in this chapter, but was also checked by having additional subjects indicate their preferences for the alternative experimental clauses (the form assumed to be "natural" and its optional transform)—it not necessarily being the case, of course, that adult preference always corresponds to what seems "natural" from intuitions about prelinguistic cognizing.

Subjects

The subjects in the total study were 108 undergraduates at the University of Illinois. They participated in the several testings (the primary sentence reconstruction experiment and various rating and judgmental tasks) in partial fulfillment of a course requirement in introductory psychology.

Materials

Eight types of clauses were used in the experiment, five inversion types and three movement types. The inversion types, which admit optional transformations affecting two clause constituents, were Dative, Equative, Genitive, Passive, and Phrasal Conjunct Reversal. The movement types, Adverb Movement, Particle Movement, and Tough Movement, admit optional transformations affecting only one clause constituent.

Eight sets of clauses were written for each clause type. These are listed in Appendix A. For the five inversion types there were eight clauses in each set, and for the movement types there were four clauses. Each clause was written in the form of a complete sentence. The sets were designed to systematically vary, within a common frame, the vividness of the constituents affected by the optional transformation.

Vividness of constituents was first evaluated by two judges (the authors). This dimension of salience does not seem to correspond well to any factor tapped by published norms. It may be best thought of as the intersection of things high in meaningfulness, low in frequency, high in imageability, and highly polarized—very high *or* very low—on Evaluation and/or Dynamism (a fusion of Potency and Activity factors); needless to say, there are very few items in the high Vividness set when published norms of various types are culled for this intersection. Therefore, intuitive criteria were used in our evaluation. Whenever we disagreed about the relative salience of the constituents in a sentence, the sentence was rewritten and reevaluated.

As illustrated in Appendix B, with one base clause for each type of optional transformation, the within-set permutations were designed to systematically vary the Vividness of constituents in both untransformed and transformed structures. Thus, using a Dative example: in the untransformed (U) versions we have direct and indirect object constituents both high in vividness (U–H/H: *the nurse told a fairy tale to the orphans*); the first constituent high and the second low (U–H/L: *the nurse told a fairy tale to the children*); the first low and the second high (U–L/H: *the nurse told a story to the orphans*); and both constituents low in vividness (U–L/L: *the nurse told a story to the children*). Each of these four clauses was then transformed (T) to create the remaining four members of the set: T–H/H: *the nurse told the orphans a fairy tale;* T–L/H: *the nurse told the children a fairy tale*; T–H/L: *the nurse told the orphans a story*; and T–L/L: *the nurse told the children a story.* Using a Tough Movement example, movement sets contained one untransformed clause in which the affected constituent was judged to be high in vividness (U–H: *it was easy to hide the bomb*) and one in which a low Vividness word was substituted (U–L: *it was easy to hide the letter*); these two clauses were then transformed to create the transformed high (T–H: *the bomb was easy to hide*) and the transformed low (T–L: *the letter was easy to hide*).

Clauses from sets of different types were to be paired to produce the conjoined, two-clause sentences for the experiment. To accomplish this, each set of clauses was divided into two half-sets. For inversion types, one half-set consisted of two randomly-chosen, untransformed clauses and their corresponding transforms (e.g., *the nurse told a fairy tale to the children, the nurse told a story to the children, the nurse told the children a fairy tale, the nurse told the children a story*); the remaining four clauses from the same set (two untransformed clauses with their corresponding transforms) constituted the second half-set (*the nurse told a fairy tale to the orphans, the nurse told a story to the orphans, the nurse told the orphans a fairy tale, the nurse told the orphans a story*). Each half-set derived from the three movement types contained one of the untransformed clauses and its corresponding transform (e.g., *it was easy to hide the bomb, the bomb was easy to hide*). Each such half-set was coupled with a half-set *derived from a different clause type* to produce 64 couples. An example of a couple is: *the maharajah gave a rug to the queen, the maharajah gave a rug to the visitor, the maharajah gave the queen a rug, the maharajah gave the visitor a rug* (half-set 1); *tornados and high winds devastated many areas, storms and high winds devastated many areas, high winds and tornados devastated many areas, high winds and storms devastated many areas* (half-set 2).

Half-sets were *not* coupled randomly. The primary constraint was that each pair of clauses generated from the couple be unrelated but not completely bizarre. Thus, although there was in general no readily apparent relationship between the two clauses, it was at most only moderately difficult to think of a context in which the two clauses *might* be related in a complex sentence using a supplied conjoiner. An example of a pair meeting this constraint is

the maharajah gave the queen a rug
storms and earthquakes devastated many areas

where the supplied conjoiner was *after*. Couples producing pairs that were too closely related, for example,

it was easy to hide the bomb
the explosion destroyed the yacht

were avoided, as were combinations for which the authors felt contexts would be hard to find, such as

the pelican ate the fish
the proclamation freed the nobles' slaves

A second constraint was that all pairs generated from the couple could be used in either order.

Clause pairs were generated from each couple with the constraint that clauses from the same half-set within the couple were never paired with each other. All possible permutations of the clauses within each couple were used, except those subject to this constraint. This resulted in 32 pairs of clauses for each of the 34 couples in which both half-sets were inversion types, 16 pairs of clauses for each of the 28 couples of an inversion half-set with a movement half-set, and 8 pairs of clauses for each of the 2 couples in which both half-sets were movement types. There were thus 1552 unique pairs (when both clauses and order are taken into account). Table 1 gives a schematic description of pair generation from an inversion–inversion couple, an inversion–movement couple, and a movement–movement couple.

Design

Sixty-four subjects participated in the sentence reconstruction experiment. Items (clause pairs) were assigned to subjects in such a way that a subject never received more than one clause from the same original clause set. Since each

TABLE 1
Schema for Generating Clause Pairs from Couples

Half-sets contained in couple		Clauses in Half-set 1	Clauses in Half-set 2
Half-set 1	Half-set 2		
inversion	inversion	ABCD	1234
		pairs generated	
		A1, A2, A3, A4, 1A, 2A, 3A, 4A	
		B1, B2, B3, B4, 1B, 2B, 3B, 4B	
		C1, C2, C3, C4, 1C, 2C, 3C, 4C	
		D1, D2, D3, D4, 1D, 2D, 3D, 4D	
inversion	movement	ABCD	12
		pairs generated	
		A1, A2, 1A, 2A	
		B1, B2, 1B, 2B	
		C1, C2, 1C, 2C	
		D1, D2, 1D, 2D	
movement	movement	AB	12
		pairs generated	
		A1, A2, 1A, 2A	
		B1, B2, 1B, 2B	

original clause set was divided between two couples, each subject received items derived from 32 of the 64 couples. Half of the subjects received items derived from one set of 32 couples; the remaining 32 subjects received items derived from the other 32 couples.

Because each inversion–inversion couple generated 32 unique items, each item from such couples was assigned to only one subject. The 16 unique items derived from inversion–movement couples were given to two subjects, and the 8 unique items from movement–movement couples were given to four subjects. Each subject thus received a total of 32 items. Of the 1552 unique pairs, 1088 were administered once, 448 were administered twice, and 16 were administered four times. Because each clause appeared in more than one pair, each single clause was presented exactly eight times (to different subjects).

The pairs of clauses were typed on IBM cards. All of the pairs derived from a given couple were assigned one of the following conjoiners: *and, but, although, since, when, while, until, after, before, because, however.* The appropriate conjoiner for each item was also typed on an IBM card which was placed immediately after the card containing the clause pair in each subject deck. The 64 subject decks, consisting of the 32 items and conjoiners presented to each subject, were individually randomized.

Procedures

Main Sentence Reconstruction Experiment. Subjects were run individually. They were told that for each item they were to make up a sentence using the two clauses and the conjoiner, and that they could put the clauses in any order and use the conjoiner either between the two clauses or (for all except *and* and *but*) at the beginning of the sentence. The procedure is similar in this respect to that employed by Opačić (1973). The subjects were also told that they would then be asked to try to create a plausible context for each sentence they constructed, by describing a situation or sequence of events for which the sentence would be appropriate, *using the sentence as the last sentence in their description.* They were given one example of an item followed by a conjoiner, (for which the experimenter supplied a sentence and description), and then a second example, for which they were asked to make up a sentence and description. The instructions were slanted to give the impression that the descriptions were the major object of interest.

A pair of clauses, followed by the appropriate conjoiner, was read by the experimenter. Five seconds after the conjoiner was read, a tape recorder was started. Subjects first indicated whether they could describe a context by saying "yes" or "no." Then, regardless of their decision, they gave the sentence that they had constructed (Production 1), and followed it, if they had said yes, with their description, in which the sentence was used as the conclusion (Production 2). This procedure was repeated for each of the 32 items in the deck. No strict time limit was imposed: subjects could begin whenever they wished after the tape was started. However, if an item seemed to be causing unusual difficulty, the subject was asked just to construct a complex sentence from the clauses, and then the next item was read.

Clause Preference Rating. Four lists were used, with each of the four pairs of transformationally related alternatives from each inversion set assigned to one list, and each of the two pairs from the movement sets assigned to two lists. A transformationally related pair consisted of the transformed and untransformed versions of a clause, with lexical content held constant except for function words added or deleted in the transformation. For example, one Dative pair was *the archaeologist handed a tomahawk to the student* versus *the archaeologist handed the student a tomahawk.*

Pairs were assigned randomly to the four lists with the constraint that only one pair from each clause set was assigned to a given list. Each list was divided into eight pages containing eight pairs of clauses, one pair of each syntactic type. The pairs on each page were ordered randomly.

Half the pairs derived from each clause set were ordered with the transformed version of the clause following the untransformed version; the other half were in the opposite order. In addition, on each list half of the pairs of a given syntactic type were in the order untransformed–transformed, and the remaining half were in the opposite order.

There were 20 subjects, with 5 subjects receiving each of the four lists. Within each group, three subjects received one order of pages and two received the alternate order. They were instructed to indicate, for each pair, which of the two clauses "sounded better" or would be more likely to be spoken by them in a situation in which either clause was appropriate.

Constituent Vividness Rating. Eight lists were constructed from the clause sets, with one clause from each set appearing on each list. Clauses from inversion sets appeared on only one list, and each clause from a movement set appeared on two lists. Within each syntactic type, each vividness type (H/H, H/L, L/H, and L/L) was represented once in a transformed and once in an untransformed clause. There were thus equal numbers of clauses of each syntactic type in the transformed and untransformed versions, and equal numbers of clauses of each of the four Vividness types. However, since only one clause from each set appeared on a given list, there was no repetition of lexical item content within a list. The clauses on each list were ordered randomly, with the constraint that two clauses of different types intervened between occurrences of clauses of the same syntactic type. The mobile constituents in each clause were underlined and sequence numbers were printed below them. Each list of clauses was accompanied by a set of rating forms, containing one seven-point scale for each underlined constituent. The ends of the scale were labeled VIVID and DULL.

Twenty-four subjects participated, with three subjects being given one of the eight clause lists, a set of rating scales, and a page of printed instructions. They were told to print the sequence number in a blank preceding each scale, and then to rate the constituent on the scale. Their instructions for rating the constituents were as follows:

If you think that a word or phrase is extremely vivid, you should place a check in the blank closest to the VIVID end of the scale; if you think the word or phrase is extremely dull, you should place a check at the DULL end. The spaces in between can be used to indicate intermediate degrees of vividness. By "vivid" we do not mean imageable, although imageability may contribute to the vividness of a word. However, there are many other factors which add to a word's vividness. Thus, *demon,* although it is not very imageable, is very vivid; and *table*, while very imageable, is somewhat uninspiring. Vividness can be created by a word's novelty, or by its emotional overtones and connotations. A good way to go about rating a word's vividness might thus be to consider the degree to which it is an "attention-getter."

Two subjects in each group received lists in one order, and the remaining subjects received the list in the opposite order. Each mobile constituent received a rating from 12 subjects, as a consequence of the structure of the clauses and their assignments to lists.

Scoring. Only the data from Production 2 were employed in the analysis, the purpose of which was to test the prediction that the more salient (vivid) constituents within clauses should tend to precede the less salient. Clauses were scored as corrects, shifts, errors, or omits. The *correct* category allowed the following deviations from the input clause: (1) changes in number (singular/plural) and articles (definite/indefinite); (2) discrete synonym substitutions (one lexical item substituted for another near-synonymous lexical item, e.g., *lady* for *woman*); (3) deletions of redundant material which clearly did not change the intended meaning of the clause or affect crucial elements of the syntax, for example, a change from *the jockey rode the horse recklessly* to *the jockey rode recklessly;* (4) insertions of implied material which did not change the meaning of the clause or affect crucial elements of the syntax, for example, a change from *the driver* to *the driver of the car*. A *shift* was scored if the clause met all the criteria for correct, except that the clause was produced in its alternate syntactic form. All other productions were scored as *errors,* and if the subject failed to produce a clause, it was scored as an *omit.*

Results

Differences in the mean vividness ratings for constituents in each of the High/Low and Low/High clauses were compared with the a priori classifications of the constituents to determine if the subjects' ratings agreed with the authors' intuitions. Of the 104 clauses, the *direction* of the differences in the subjects' means agreed with the a priori classification in 94 cases. However, the *magnitude* of the differences between constituents was not reflected in the sentence production data: larger differences in rated vividness were not systematically associated with higher numbers of corrects for High/Low sentences or higher numbers of shifts for Low/High sentences. Since the Vividness ratings therefore had only directional validity, the all-or-nothing a priori classifications by the authors were employed throughout the analysis. High/High and Low/Low clauses were excluded from analysis, because such comparisons are irrelevant to the main purpose of the experiment (although it would be expected that H/H would be recalled better than L/L).

Although the *Movement Types* of optional transformation (Particle, Adverb, and Tough Movement) were included in the analyses, the results for neither corrects nor shifts were significant and are not reported here. In retrospect, it seems clear that movement clauses do not provide a very good test of the Vividness hypothesis—the Vividness of the *other constituents* within the clauses, around which the constituents affected by the transformation move, was not

TABLE 2
Percent Correct and Shift for High/Low and
Low/High Inversion Clauses

	Preferred		Nonpreferred	
	Correct	Shift	Correct	Shift
High/Low	47	7	41	9
Low/High	43	8	34	18

controlled relative to the vividness of the mobile constituent. In Inversion Types, the Vividness of one mobile constituent was manipulated *relative to* that of the other mobile constituent within the clause.

Similarly, although data on *Between Clause* production orders were analyzed in terms of Vividness predictions, the results are not reported here. For one thing, the main purpose of using complex (conjoined two-clause) sentential materials was methodological—to provide a reasonable means (creating a story context in which the complex sentence could be used) for dissociating comprehension and production phases. For another, the vividness judgments for whole clauses were absolute rather than comparative, and only the H/L and L/H members of sets are relevant to the Vividness hypothesis; thus *both* clauses in the relevant pairs contained both a High and a Low Vividness constituent (e.g., *the maharajah gave an elephant to the visitor* (H/L) conjoined with *high winds and tornados devastated many areas* (L/H) as a test item), and it is hard to see how valid Vividness judgments could be made under such conditions.[10]

Table 2 presents percentages of corrects and shifts for *Inversion Types* (summed), as simultaneous functions of High/Low versus Low/High Vividness and Preferred versus Nonpreferred clauses—the former based on the a priori classifications and the latter on the preference ratings by subjects. Analyses of variance treating both subjects and items as random effects (Clark, 1973) were carried out on these data. Separate analyses were performed for corrects and shifts, with Vividness and Preference as factors. F_1 refers to the test statistic with subjects as a random effect, F_2 to the test statistic with items as a random effect, and *min F'* to the lower bound of the appropriate quasi F ratio.

Vividness Effects. For *correct clause ordering*, the effect of Vividness was not significant $[F_1(1, 63) = 3.96, p < .10), F_2(1, 156 = 2.11, p < .25), min F'(1,$

---

[10] However, it must be reported that the results of the Between Clause analysis were—most bafflingly—*significantly in the wrong direction* (there were more shifts in order when the H/L clauses were presented first than when L/H were first). Whether this reflects some "end-focus" principle (cf. Quirk, Greenbaum, Leech, & Svartvik, 1972), completely *ad hoc* here, or merely the statistical fact that even a .005 probability result can happen by chance 5 times per 1000 (!), or some other confounding, we have no idea.

215) = 1.38, $p < .25$], but the results were in the predicted direction: there were more High/Low than Low/High correct in constituent ordering. The effect of vividness on *clause inversion shifts* was significant, however, and as predicted: there were more shifts in constituent ordering for Low/High clauses than for High/Low clauses [$F_1(1, 63) = 5.44$, $p < .05$, $F_2(1, 124) = 3.95$, $p < .05$]. Although the combined statistic did not reach significance [*min F'* (1, 201) = 2.29, $p < .25$], these results indicate that Vividness did affect production, such that more vivid constituents tended to occur earlier in the clause than less vivid constituents. Shifts from the order given are rather dramatic evidence for this, since the subject actually produces a clause whose surface structure is different from the one he heard.

The failure of corrects to reach significance is probably attributable to inflation of the correct category by rote memory effects. Despite instructions that their stories were more important than verbatim recall, most subjects gave evidence of trying to commit clauses to memory in order to be able to repeat them verbatim after telling their stories. When verbatim memory failed and shifts did occur, the effects of Vividness became more discernible. Verbatim memory effects were most striking when subjects occasionally employed clauses within their stories in their shifted form but then recited the correct forms at the end. For example, two subjects, given the Low/High clause *the ants and spiders were annoying,* twice in their stories spontaneously used the shift clause *the spiders and ants were annoying,* yet in their final production (Production 2) returned to *ants and spiders.*

Preference Effects. There was a relatively strong effect of clause preference on corrects and shifts for the Inversion-Type optional transformations, and they were in the predicted direction. For *correct clause ordering,* more preferreds were correctly produced than nonpreferreds, although the effect reaches an acceptable significance level only for subjects [$F_1(1, 63) = 9.53, p < .05$]; the items and combined statistics were $F_2(1, 156) = 3.58, p < .10$ and *min F'* (1, 218) = 2.60, $p < .25$, respectively. However, the greater number of *clause inversion shifts* for nonpreferred as against preferred was significant for both subjects and items [$F_1(1, 63) = 6.11, p < .05; F_2(1, 156) = 5.16, p < .05$]. The combined statistic just missed acceptable significance [*min F'*(1, 185) = 2.93, p < .10], but it should be kept in mind that the preference ratings were made by only five subjects per clause pair; it seems possible that the effect of preference was weakened by misclassification of sentences.

To investigate this possibility, the Production 2 data for all Inversion-Type sentences on which the raters divided 3/2 in their judgments were eliminated, leaving only the data for sentences with 4/1 or 5/0 splits. The results are shown in Table 3. The pattern which would be predicted if the "pruning" removed misclassified sentences is this: higher percentages of corrects for preferreds, lower percentages of shifts for preferreds, lower percentages of corrects for nonpreferreds, and higher percentages of shifts for nonpreferreds. Comparing the

TABLE 3

Percentage Corrects and Shifts for Preferred and Nonpreferred
Inversion Sentences with 3/2 Split Items Eliminated

	Vividness type	Correct	Shift
Preferred	High/Low	49 (47)[a]	9 (7)
	Low/High	47 (43)	7 (8)
Nonpreferred	High/Low	38 (41)	15 (9)
	Low/High	26 (34)	19 (18)

[a]Percentages in parentheses represent original values in each
category (see Table 2).

percentages for the selected (4/1, 5/0) items with the original percentages (in parentheses), it can be seen that, except for the shifts of preferreds for High/Low Vividness (1% in the wrong direction), the overall pattern of results is as would be expected from the "misclassification" hypothesis.

The problem of rote memorization also appeared to attenuate preference effects. In the correct category only the by-subjects analyses revealed significant differences; in the shift category there were significant differences in both by-subjects and by-items analyses (although not when combined). This suggests that, as in the Vividness analysis, the correct category contained many verbatim responses based on rote memorizing, and this tended to wash out other effects.

Naturalness/Preference Interactions. In the reanalysis of data from the Simply Describing study (Osgood, 1971), not only were Naturalness and Vividness/Motivation principles shown to interact but Naturalness was clearly the dominant variable. Can similar dynamics be shown to be operating in the present experiment with purely linguistic materials? Since Naturalness was not directly manipulated as a variable, we must first demonstrate that, where Naturalness predictions can be made, the preference ratings made by five subjects for each clause pair (but different sets of subjects—see Procedure) are in fact predictable from Naturalness. Given that this is the case to a reasonable degree, we can then see to what extent and for what optional transformation types Naturalness interacts with Vividness in determining correctness and shifts in sentence reconstruction.

Dative Inversion. Here the contrast is between SNP-V-DO-to-IO and SNP-V-IO-DO (e.g., *the boy tossed the frisbee to the St. Bernard/the boy tossed the St. Bernard the frisbee*). Although generative linguists have displayed little agreement on which of these constructions is the more basic, the Naturalness prediction is very clear: what has traditionally been termed the direct object (*the frisbee*) is obviously a part of the Action Relation (verb phrase) and hence is part of the incorporated (M) in the $- - (M) - \rightarrow$ component of the OPERATOR, while the so-called indirect object (*the St. Bernard*) is equally obviously the

TABLE 4
Percent Correct and Shift as Functions
of Preference (Naturalness) for Each Syntactic Type[a]

Sentence type	Preference type (Naturalness)	Vividness type	Corrects	Shifts
Inversion type	P	High/Low	54	19
		Low/High	48	20
Dative	(22/0/10) NP	High/Low	55	20
		Low/High	38	27
	P	High/Low	61	9
		Low/High	61	8
Passive	(20/0/12) NP	High/Low	48	22
		Low/High	38	27
	P	High/Low	42	6
		Low/High	46	11
Phrasal conjunct reversal	(no pred.'s) NP	High/Low	45	9
		Low/High	48	10
	P	High/Low	59	11
		Low/High	51	11
Equative	(21/2/9) NP	High/Low	61	8
		Low/High	54	25
	P	High/Low	54	7
		Low/High	42	3
Genitive	(27/0/5) NP	High/Low	43	10
		Low/High	36	21

[a] Abbreviations: P = preferred; NP = nonpreferred. Naturalness/Preference relations: for the parenthetical $(x/y/z)$s, x is the number of clause pairs for which preference ratings agree with predicted naturalness, y is the number of equal or ambiguous pairs (see text), and z is the number of pairs where preference goes against naturalness.

Recipient (M_2 component).[11] Table 4 gives the percentage of correct and percentage shift as functions of preference ratings (which we parenthetically in the table relate to Naturalness) for each syntactic type. For the 32 clause pairs of the Dative type, Naturalness predicted Preference for 22 pairs and failed for 10, this division being significant by the binomial expansion test at $p < .03$ (one-tail). This congruence should facilitate correctness for P (preferred) and

[11] We now have both cross-linguistic and experimental evidence supporting this analysis (see Osgood & Tanz, in press).

shifts for NP (nonpreferred); this is the case, with an average of 51% correct for P as against 46.5% for NP and an average of 23.5% shifts for NP as against 19.5% for P. That Vividness does interact with Naturalness is indicated by the fact that there are more corrects and fewer shifts for High/Lows (P and NP combined) than Low/Highs.

Passive Inversion. The contrast here is between SNP-V-ONP and SNP-be-V-by-ONP (e.g., *the bulldozer crushed the daffodils/the daffodils were crushed by the bulldozer*). Linguistic analysis and the Naturalness principle agree on the basic form in this case—the active construction. For the latter, the natural sequence is Actor—Action—Recipient in the OPERATOR, as elaborated earlier. For this type, as shown in Table 4, the Naturalness/Preference distribution was 20 right predictions as against 12 wrong predictions, significant at only the $p <$ .11 level. Although this significance level is lower than for the Dative type, the effect on sentence reconstruction appears to be greater—there are 61% corrects and only 8.5% shifts for P as against 42% corrects and 24.5% shifts for NP. On the other hand, perhaps because of lack of strong Naturalness support, there are Vividness differences (H/L versus L/H) for only the NP clauses.

Phrasal Conjunction Reversal. Here the contrast is between NP_1 —and—NP_2, where the conjoined NPs may be in either subject or object positions (for example, *the wasps and spiders were annoying/the spiders and wasps were annoying;* or *the cook prepared hotdogs and beans/the cook prepared beans and hotdogs*). Neither linguistic analysis nor Naturalness seem to have any differential predictions here. In the case of the latter, regardless of whether the conjoining is of two M_1 s or two M_2 s, whichever is first in order will be in the COG 1 and the other in the COG 2, since—at least in fresh cognizing as compared with re-cognizing from the MEMORY—these are complex 2-COG sentences. On the other hand, these forms should provide rather ideal testing ground for testing the Vividness principle, as well as the Cooper and Ross (1975) notions about ordering (although there is a real problem of the weights to give to their "salience" versus their N syllables, N words, and high/low formant principles). In any case, as can be seen in Table 4, only shifts favor the Vividness principle, and this by only small amounts.

Equative Inversion. In this type we compare SNP_1 —V—ONP_2 with SNP_2 —V—ONP_1 where the subscripts refer to NPs that are more namelike (NP_1 s) or more definite-description-like (NP_2 s), for example, *the priest was the murderer/the murderer was the priest.* The expectation was that the former would be preferred. After some puzzling over it, a possible Naturalness argument was arrived at: if we change the predicate from an NP to a predicative adjective, then what is more natural becomes quite clear (e.g., *the boy was ill/*ill was the boy,* except in special emphasis contexts); the reason, in part, seems to be that, relatively, the more stable categorization of an entity will more naturally be cognized prior to a relatively temporary qualification of it; extending this notion to the Equative type of clause, it would follow that the natural order would be [(rel. stable) $M_1 --(M) -\rightarrow$ (rel. temporary) M_2]. Thus, since being *a priest* is a relatively more permanent condition than being *a murderer* (or being *a clerk* is relatively more permanent than being *a guest*), the former should naturally be expressed prior to the latter.[12] Perhaps surprisingly, the predictions of preference ratings in this case proved to be very good (21/2/9), this distribution being significant at the $p < .03$ level. As shown in Table 4, although the average corrects for P (55%) versus NP (57.5%) go a bit the wrong way, the shifts are greater for NP (16.5%) than for P (11%); the Vividness effects are considerable, but mainly for the NP clauses (as would be expected).

Genitive Inversion. Here the contrast is between N—of—N and N(poss.)—N (e.g., *the powwow was held in the wigwam of Sitting Bull/the powwow was held in Sitting Bull's wigwam*), where the possessive NP may be in either subject or object positions. Linguistically speaking, the former is basic to the latter. Speaking naturalistically, the reverse should be true: Possessors are proto-typically ⁺Human and typically ⁺Animate whereas the Possesseds are proto-typically ⁻Animate and usually ⁻Human (notable exceptions being children, service people, and slaves, of course). In this connection, it is interesting that "Mommy shoe" and similar two-word expressions, contextually identified as possessive, appear to be much more frequent than the reverse order, "Shoe Mommy," for expressing the same relation—suggesting that the natural percep-tion-based COG is one in which the Possessor is the topic (M_1) and the Possessed is part of the commentary $(- \rightarrow M_2)$, thus MOMMY HAS SHOE/*SHOE BE-LONGS TO MOMMY. We therefore predict that the latter form (*. . . in Sitting Bull's wigwam*) will be preferred. The distribution of preference prediction bears out this analysis: 27 right and only 5 wrong, significant at beyond the .01 level. Table 4 shows that P has more corrects and many fewer shifts for the Genitive type, and for NPs shifting clause structure is twice as likely for Low/High Vividness as for High/Low vividness (21—10%).

Although the preference results for Movement Types are not given in Table 4—because the vividness of the constituents around which the mobile con-stituents move was neither measured nor controlled, as noted earlier—the predic-tive power of Naturalness to Preference was determined for these types. For Adverb Movement (e.g., *the fat lady ate the pie greedily/the fat lady greedily ate the pie*), linguistic analysis and Naturalness yield opposed views of what is basic: linguists speak of "adverb preposing," implying that the former is basic and the latter a transformation; under Naturalness analysis the adverb (as the term

[12] In preparing this chapter, one of the authors (CEO) reclassified the 32 Equative clause pairs so as to be consistent with this Naturalness interpretation before relating predictions to preference ratings.

implies, in this case!) obviously applies a semantic twist to the meaning of the verb, or, in cognizing terms, is a part of the (M) of the $- - (M) - \rightarrow$ relation. Predictiveness tends to support the Naturalness view, with an 18/4/10 distribution that is significant at the $p < .10$ level. For Particle Movement (e.g., *the admiral looked over the submarine/the admiral looked the submarine over*) linguistic and "naturalistic" analyses would seem to go the same way, the particle being clearly a part of the VP or, in our terms, the $- - (M) - \rightarrow$ relation again.[13] Preference predictions clearly support this analysis—13/3/0, which is significant at beyond the .01 level.

Finally, for Tough Movement (e.g., *it was impossible to open the coffin/the coffin was impossible to open*), linguistic and Naturalness arguments seem to lead to opposite conclusions: the use of the term "tough movement" by linguists itself suggests that the mobile material (here, *was impossible*) must be moved (transformed) from some location in the deep structure; a Naturalness argument starts with a search for basic Actor–Action–Object COGs, finds *someone tried-but-was-unable-to-open the coffin*, takes note of the fact that the second clause of the illustrative pair above is necessarily an "unnatural" passive (whereas the first clause is not), and opts for the first as the (somewhat!) more Natural. In any case, the preference prediction resulting is reasonably strong, considering the small number of clause pairs available (16)–9/5/2, which is significant at the $p < .05$ level.

DISCUSSION

Where do sentences come from? In a generative grammar the answer seems clear enough: the symbol S that tops every "tree" represents the set of all grammatical sentences in language L, the expansions of S by differential application of rewrite rules (e.g., NP $\rightarrow$ D + A + N) generating each possible member of the set—which is indefinitely large given recursive devices. This "answer" is most unsatisfying *psycho*linguistically (that is, for a theory of language performance); it fails to meet the pragmatic criterion that sentences produced be appropriate to contextual conditions—humans do not produce sentences *ad libitum*. There is also a problem with the linguistic definition of S: in most cases where one sentence is embedded in another, the superordinate S_1 obviously constrains the subordinate S_2 to some subset of all grammatical sentences in language L; thus, for example, *it is a fact (S_1) that . . .* permits . . . *the water is hot, the water has chlorine in it* (as S_2 s), but rules out sentences like . . . *we should put water in the tub, water the lawn!*, and *is the water hot?*

[13] This is in contrast to many prepositions, for example, **the admiral looked the submarine into;* note also this contrast: *the admiral looked over the submarine/the submarine over and gave it his OK*—but *the admiral looked over the submarine/*the submarine over and saw a full moon.*

This is not a criticism of linguistic methodology, of course: abstract *competence* grammars, providing post hoc descriptions of sentences, do not, *and need not*, provide any account of selection among the alternative rewrite rules possible at each node in a "tree." But this is precisely what an abstract *performance* grammar (i.e., a theory of cognizing and sentencing) would have to do. This becomes particularly clear in the case of factive, emotive, and many other types of illocutionary sentences: although the alternative factive verbs are "higher" in sentence generation linguistically (constituents of S_1), it is clear that a real speaker must have cognized the "lower" S_2 before he can select among *I (know, think, believe, doubt, pretend) that* in producing, for example, the sentence *I* (?) *that Mary has left John;* the same holds for emotive verbs like *I (hope, fear, regret,* etc.) *that*—the real speaker must have cognized, for example, *Mary will come back,* before he can select the appropriate feeling-verb to express.[14] This in itself would seem to be devastating to any claim that a linguistic competence grammar could be a theory of "how the mind works" in sentencing.

In the introduction to this chapter we analyzed the notion of "salience" into three distinguishable production principles: *Naturalness*—that the order of constituents in sentencing will tend to correspond to the order of components most frequently experienced in prelinguistic, perception-based cognizing; *Vividness*—that constituents representing cognitive components having inherent semantic features of high intensity (particularly affective) will tend to shift "leftward" (earlier) in expression; *Motivation-of-Speaker*—that constituents representing cognitive components to which the speaker attributes high motivation (interest, ego involvement, etc.) will tend to be expressed earlier in sentencing. It was also argued that all of these production principles are interrelated—reflecting an underlying multiplicative relation between meanings and motives (or habit strengths and drives in Hullian, 1943, terms)—and interact with each other, sometimes supportively and sometimes competitively.

The two studies reported here were designed primarily to get at Naturalness and Vividness, respectively—although attributed Motivation of Speaker was undoubtedly involved to some degree in both. Since these are *Speaker/Production* principles, rather than Listener/Comprehension principles, we must demonstrate that language comprehension variables have been eliminated or at least minimized. The first experiment on Simply Describing clearly meets this requirement—what was comprehended was the meanings of the *perceptual* signs of entities involved in various perceived action or stative relations. As to the second experiment on Constituent Ordering in Sentence Reconstruction, all we can claim is that comprehension variables were at least reduced by the interpolation

---

[14] Psycholinguistically, the "higher" S in such cases is a "commentary" on the embedded "lower" S, and it is not conceivable that one could comment on X before he knows what X is.

of "telling a story" between the presentation and reconstruction from memory of the complex experimental sentences. However, this experiment did provide an ideal testing ground for the Vividness principle by using sentential materials that allow optional transformations of diverse types.

Evidence for a Naturalness Principle

We have assumed that simple cognitions have a tripartite structure $[M_1 -- (M) - \rightarrow M_2]$, in which the M_1s will most naturally be the Actors or Instruments and the M_2s the Recipients or Objects in action relations and, in stative relations, the M_1s will most naturally be the Figures and the M_2s the Grounds. We say "most naturally" because our intuitions tell us that Actors, Instruments, and Figures characteristically have more salience for the prelinguistic child than Recipients, Objects, and Grounds; the former are typically $^+$Movement (or potential Movement), often $^+$Animate and even $^+$Human, and in many cases $^+$Palpable (graspable, feelable, etc.)—all properties that should be attention-getting and attention-holding in contrast to their opposites.[15]

Componential tests on concept pairs drawn from an *Atlas* of affective meanings (approximately 30 test pairs for each component), with comparable semantic differential measures for some 600 concepts across some 30 cultures around the world (see Osgood, May, & Miron, 1975), provide corroborative data: on a Stative Relations (Figure/Ground) component—illustrative pairs, EYES/FACE, NOISE/SILENCE, MY NAME/TALK, LAMP/ROOM, DOG/STREET)—Figural concepts are universally (in a statistical sense) more active, more intensely meaningful, and usually more highly evaluated than Ground concepts; on an Action Relations (Source/Recipient) component—for example, MOTHER/ BABY, PROFESSOR/STUDENT, LEADER/FOLLOWER, DOCTOR/PATIENT, KNIFE/APPLE, RAIN/FOREST, etc.—Actors and Instruments were similarly much more active and usually more potent; on an Animateness (Living/Non-living) component—for example, VOICE/SOUND, GRASS/SNOW, PEASANTS/ THE SOIL, HORSE/CART—the Living were obviously more active universally, but also more intensely meaningful as well as more highly evaluated; the same held for a Motility (Mobile/Immobile) component—for example, TONGUE/ TOOTH, BICYCLE/CHAIR, ANIMAL/VEGETABLE, FIRE/HEAT, SPHERE/ CUBE, FINGERS/FINGERNAILS; however, on a Palpability (Palpable/Inpalpable) component—for example, CUBE/SQUARE, BALL/SMOKE, STONE/ ROCK, EGG/A POINT, DICTIONARY/LIBRARY, PEN/WRITING—the Palpables were *not* significantly more active, potent, familiar, or intensely meaningful, contrary to our expectations.

---

[15] A considerable literature—too extensive to detail here—on research with infants supports this statement.

It is also a characteristic of semantic differential technique (cf. Osgood, May, & Miron, 1975, pp. 393–394) that concepts are rated (qualified) against their immediate superordinates *as implicit reference points.* Thus BABY is judged very small *(for a Human)* and TARANTULA is judged very large *(for a Spider),* even though the same speakers would obviously say "a baby is larger than a tarantula" if asked this relative-size question directly. Does this mean that, cognitively, subordinates (instances) should have Figural properties and their superordinates (categories) Ground properties? A cross-cultural Ordinateness (Subordinate/Superordinate) componential analysis—comparing, for example, SEPTEMBER/MONTH, BLUE/COLOR, DOG/ANIMAL, ROSE/FLOWER, BOX/THING, MY NAME/NAME—suggests that this may be the case; subordinates tended to be more potent and were much more intensely meaningful (affectively) than their superordinates, but they were not (surprisingly) more active or familiar. A recent paper by Eleanor Rosch (1975), entitled "Cognitive Reference Points," is highly relevant here: Given sentence frames of the "hedging" sort—for example, *X is (basically, essentially, roughly,* etc.) *Y*—subjects were presented pairs of stimuli in which one was an assumed reference point (a focal red, a vertical or horizontal line, a number being a multiple of 10) and the other was slightly deviant (an "off" red, an 80° line, the number 11), and asked to assign one of the nonlinguistic stimuli to each of the "slots" in the sentence. The prediction was that the "deviant" stimuli would tend toward the X (M_1) slot and the "reference" stimuli toward the Y (M_2) slot, and the results clearly bore this out.

It has been argued here that the basic functional unit in cognizing (perceptual or linguistic) is what we have called a simple COG having a tripartite structure, $[M_1 - - (M) - \rightarrow M_2]$, and that all complexes must be analyzed into such simplexes to be comprehended. Bever (1975) summarizes a considerable experimental literature that is generally consistent with this conception—for example, the shift in "perceptual" strategies[16] around age four from "in any ... NV sequence, the N is the Actor and the V is the Action" to the full-COG strategy "in any N_1VN_2, the N_1 is the Actor for the next inflected verb and the N_2 is the Object of the action" (accompanied by a temporary *increase* in errors for sentences like *it's the horse that the cow kisses,* incidentally). Perhaps most relevantly, Carroll and Tannenhaus (1975) present evidence that segmentation in processing complex, biclausal sentences (as indicated by shifts in the perceived locus of a tone toward versus away from the "processing zone" at clausal boundaries) is much stronger at the terminal boundaries of functionally *complete* clauses (our full COGs) than at the boundaries of functionally *incomplete* clauses. Thus the shift is greater for conjoined main clauses (*I felt sorry for the*

---

[16] Bever (and many others) use the term "perceptual" for cognizing processes which I am sure most psychologists would call "conceptual"—hence here, "conceptual strategies."

bum/so I gave him a dime) and complete subordinate clauses (*After the crook stole the woman's bag/he ran for safety*) than for headless nominalizations (*Meeting the pretty young girl/was the highlight of Peter's trip*) or noun phrases with modifiers (*The old painted wooden pipe/was on display at the local museum*).

Earlier we stated that Naturalness—given its prelinguistic base and its continuing role in the parallel processing of information in perceptual and linguistic channels—should be dominant over all other determinants of ordering. Reanalysis of the data from the Simply Describing study (Osgood, 1971) in terms of Naturalness (for either Stative or Action relations) clearly supports this expectation: not only were the sentencings for uncomplicated Statives (THE BALL IS ON THE TABLE) and Actions (A BLACK BALL ROLLS AND HITS THE BLUE BALL) overwhelmingly "natural," 25/1/0 and 22/1/3, respectively, for these examples, but even when Vividness/Motivation-of-Speaker were put in competition with Naturalness they had relatively little influence—for example, for THE MAN PUTS THE BALL ON A PLASTIC PLATE (the PLATE being novel), for THE MAN IS HOLDING A BIG BLUE BALL (BALL novel and contrastive), and even for A VERY BIG ORANGE BALL IS HIT BY A SMALL BLACK BALL (the statement of the demonstration in this case indicating our attempt to "force" a passive), the sentencings clearly reflect the dominance of Naturalness (21/4/1, 20/1/5, and 23/0/3, respectively).

Perhaps it could be argued that the instruction "to describe what you see with a sentence that a six-year-old just outside the door could understand" biased the subject-speakers toward the simplest (most "natural"?) constructions, but it should be kept in mind that the perceptual inputs constrained *only* the "what" (semantics) and not the "how" (syntax) of Simply Describing. Thus even stative D-2 (THE BALL IS ON THE TABLE) *could* have been linguistically paraphrased as *the table has the ball on it, there is a table with a ball on it, the table is now supporting the ball,* etc., but none such occurred; action D-21 (THE ORANGE BALL HITS THE TUBE), with the tube as immediately "given" information (in D-20), surely invited the passive transformation, but only 5 of 26 speaker-subjects utilized it; and although the three-COG potential of D-8 (THE MAN IS HOLDING TWO BALLS/and/HE BOUNCES ONE BALL/and/THAT BALL HITS THE PLATE) allowed for a wide variety of clause orders and embeddings, shifts from the natural clause order (sequence as perceived in time) only occurred twice and there was not a single instance of the efficient center-embedding we had been expecting (THE BALL THE MAN BOUNCED HIT THE PLATE).

The term *paraphrasing* literally refers to the process of comprehending one linguistic string and then producing another linguistic string which has the same meaning—thus *the swain courted the lass* might be paraphrased as *the young unmarried man tried to win the favor of marriage from the young unmarried woman.* Note that, if a string 1 is to be paraphrasable as some string 2, then string 1 must itself be meaningful as a whole—try paraphrasing *colorless furiously green sleep ideas*. The fact that, in our Simply Describing experiment, perceptual entity-event strings were "paraphrased" in interrelated sets of linguistic strings *that were both appropriate and paraphrases of each other* therefore implies that such entity-event strings are themselves meaningful.[17] More than this, such "paraphrasing" implies that the interacting cognitions in perceptual and linguistic channels must, at some deep level, share the same syntacto-semantic system. Finally, since linguistic constructs (NP, VP, etc., and S itself) have no relevance to—indeed, are completely inappropriate to—*pre*linguistic perceptuomotor understandings and expressings, it must follow that the deep cognitive system "where sentences go to and come from" is not itself linguistic in nature.

An everyday illustration of such "communicative competence" is the following: Two co-eds are walking together along a campus path and another co-ed with blond hair and a mini-mini-*mini*-skirt is approaching them. After she passes, one co-ed says to the other, "she also dyes her hair." Since *she* is a deictic pronoun, referring to some prior substantive, and since there was no relevant previous utterance, we must assume that the speaker's "she" refers to a prior *perceived* entity coded Human, Female; since the *also* anaphorically refers to an entire prior "sentence" (presumably something like *that girl/is wearing/a VERY short skirt/*), but since no such linguistic utterance occurred, again we must assume that the speaker is reacting to a *perceptually* induced prior cognition, assumed to be shared by speaker and hearer.

Evidence for a Vividness Principle

By deliberately manipulating the inherent semantic salience of constituents within clauses susceptible to optional order-inversion transformations, it was possible to test the effects of the Vividness principle. Thus for the Dative inversion we could compare, for example, *the boy tossed the frisbee* (High V) *to the dog* (Low V) with *the boy tossed the ball* (L) *to the St. Bernard* (H), as well as the H/L and L/H transformed versions, . . . *the St. Bernard the ball* and . . . *the dog the frisbee;* similarly, for the Passive inversion we could compare, for example, *the bulldozer crushed the flowers* with *the truck crushed the daffodils* as well as *the daffodils were crushed by the truck* with *the flowers were crushed by the bulldozer;* and so forth for the other transformation types. However, these tests of the Vividness principle involved two complications: (1) Given the expectations of "subject pool" subjects (apparently), despite instructions the segregation of production from comprehension variables was not as great as we had hoped—there was evidence that many subjects did attempt verbatim memo-

---

[17] Although not our prime concern here, it should be noted that the same argument applies to Simply Acting Out—where linguistic strings are "paraphrased" in obviously appropriate and meaningful behavior strings.

rization during the original presentation of the complex, biclausal sentences, prior to their "construction of contexts in which the sentences could be used." (2) For roughly half of the items contributing to the test for each transformation type, the Naturalness principle would be supportive of the Vividness principle (e.g., cases like *the bulldozer crushed the flowers*); but for the remainder of the items Naturalness would be competitive with Vividness (e.g., for cases like *the daffodils were crushed by the truck*).

These problems are evident in the results. As for complication (1), this showed up in the fact that the *correctness* measure (correct within-clause constituent ordering during reconstruction) was only significant for Preference effects (not for Vividness effects) for subjects across items and never significant for items across subjects; the *clause-inversion shifts* measure, however, was significant for both Vividness and Preference effects, and for both subjects and items as sources of variance in both cases. The second author attributes the attenuation of correctness-measure differences for both Vividness and Preference effects to the *verbatim/memory biases* that resulted in high correctness scores (and thus a *lack* of "reconstruction" in Production 2); in Table 4 it can be seen that the ratios of percentage correct versus percentage shifts run from at least 2/1 up to 5/1 or more.

The interaction of Naturalness with Vividness (complication (2) above) should have at least two effects in this experiment:

1. Being congruent with Vividness for about half the items, but incongruent for the other half, Naturalness effects would be expected to increase item variance; that this was the case is indicated by the fact that F_2 (the test statistic with items as a random effect) was only significant for the shifts measure, and *min F'* (taking into account subject/item interaction variance) never reached the $p < .05$ level of significance.

2. Predicted effects should be stronger when Naturalness is congruent with Vividness than when it is not; this was generally the case for the analyses by types of transformations reported under Naturalness/Preference interactions in the Results section. Here we report a summary over all transformation types combined, in terms of the four interaction predictions that can be made[18]:

(a) *Natural* (preferred) *forms should be recalled correctly more frequently than Unnatural* (nonpreferred); although the difference here in absolute magnitude is small, 54% versus 47%, only one of the four transformational types goes against the trend (Equatives, 55% versus 58%).

(b) *Natural forms should yield constituent shifts within clauses less frequently than Unnatural;* there were roughly half as many shifts for Natural as for Unnatural forms presented in items (11% versus 20%).

(c) *The Vividness effect/(%H/L minus %L/H) upon correct recall should be*

---

[18] Since no Naturalness predictions could be made for the Phrasal Conjunct type of transformation, only the other four types are combined here.

greater for Natural than for Unnatural given forms; this prediction does not hold up, the H/L minus L/H difference being + 6.5% for Natural forms given, but + 10.25% for Unnatural.

(d) *The Vividness effect (%H/L minus %L/H) upon shifts should be less for Natural than for Unnatural given forms;* this prediction does hold up, the H/L minus L/H difference being + 1.0% for Naturals but −10.0% for Unnaturals (that is, as predicted, given the Unnatural form, the percentage shift from L/H to H/L in Vividness is greater than that from H/L to L/H), and this holds for all four transformation types. The confounding with rote memorizing effects is also apparent in this summary analysis: shift predictions hold up much better than correctness predictions.

This experiment has demonstrated that salience effects in sentence production are not restricted to the passive but rather appear to be general for optional transformations. Nevertheless, the effects were considerable for the much studied passive.[19] One possible reason for this may be the relative infrequency of the passive alternative; Svartvik (1966), in a frequency count based on texts totaling 320,000 words, found that the passive voice was only one-seventh as frequent as the active, and over 70% of this one-seventh were of the truncated (agentless) form. The latter fact itself testifies to the uninteresting (indeed, often redundant in communication situations) nature of the logical subject when passive transforms are employed. In this connection, psycholinguist H. Clark (1965, p. 369) says "... people put what they want to talk about (usually animate things of little uncertainty) in the beginning of the sentence," the logical object in the case of passives. A recent paper by linguist Evelyn Ransom (1975) carries this argument further by describing both a *Definiteness–Specificity Hierarchy* (the more definite and specific the surface subject of a passive sentence relative to its surface agent, the more acceptable the sentence) and a *Humanness–Animacy Hierarchy* (the more animate and particularly human the surface subject relative to the surface agent, the more acceptable the passive transform), which combine into what she calls an *Importance Hierarchy* that appears to perfectly parallel our "salience" continuum (Naturalness, Vividness, and Speaker-Motivation combined).

Is There Cognitive Primacy of Stative Relations?

In the theory of cognizing developed by the first author (C.E.O.) Naturalness considerations dictated that, in stative relations, M_1 and M_2 are coded for

---

[19] In an earlier (1974) and unpublished study on the comprehension and recall of sentences permitting the same types of optional transformation as used here, the second author found that, although Vividness served to significantly enhance correct recall of all types, it only influenced the syntactic form of the recalled sentences (i.e., shifts in the predicted direction) for the passive transformation.

"figure of state" and "ground of state," respectively, and, in action relations, M_1 and M_2 are coded for "source of action" and "recipient/object of action," respectively—but no claim has been made for any primacy in development of one type of relation (action or state) over the other. The second author (J.K.B.) has argued convincingly (to C.E.O.) that stative relations have primacy, and we give the essence of the argument here.

Both Bates (in press) and MacWhinney (1975) have suggested a developmental priority for Figure/Ground semantic coding. It might be further hypothesized that Source/Recipient codings, as they develop, have a simultaneous Figure/Ground coding, with Sources of actions generally having more figural properties and Recipients/Objects of actions generally having more ground properties. Thus, such semantic distinctions should often overlap, but with Figure/Ground codings (simple existential relations often expressed by the verb *to be*) originally, and always potentially, independent of Source/Recipient codings—but never the reverse. When the action-related and state-related codings conflict—as when the recipient of an action takes on figural properties by virtue of increased salience—the speaker reverts to the more "primitive" Figure/Ground coding, and a passive is produced. Many examples of topicalization reflect pure Figure/Ground distinctions that violate the usual subject/predicate order of things—even producing ungrammatical utterances such as the real-life "Garlic I taste!" example in the *Psycholinguistics Monograph* (Osgood, 1954, p. 170).

On this account, there is an ordered (developmentally) set of three possible coding patterns for basic ("natural") cognitions:

1. *Ordinary stative.* This is the minimal basic cognitive structure, presumably the one with which very young children operate prelinguistically (perceptually) and later linguistically as well,

$$[M_1\ (^+Fig) -- (M) - \rightarrow M_2\ (^-Fig)]\ ,$$

which for older children and adults operating with action-related features as well would be

$$[M_1\ (^+Fig,\ ^0Source) -- (M) - \rightarrow M_2\ (^-Fig,\ ^0Source)]\ ,$$

and this would underlie ordinary stative cognitions, such as *the flowers are on the table.*

2. *Ordinary action.* This requires additional differentiation of Source/Recipient semantic coding and presumably would be acquired somewhat later by children—how much later depending, as Bates suggests, on the language being learned. The basic coding for both children and adults would be

$$[M_1\ (^+Fig,\ ^+Source) -- (M) - \rightarrow M_2\ (^-Fig,^-Source)]$$

and would underlie the comprehension of perceived events like THE CAT JUMPED ON THE PILLOW and production of sentences like *the bulldozer ran into the fence.*

3. *Extraordinary action.*   As noted above, when Figure and Source codings are incongruent, it is assumed that Figure coding takes priority, being more basic or "primitive," and, as exemplified by the passive construction, the component coded as ⁻Source (Recipient/object) is topicalized as M_1, thus

$$[M_1 \ (^+Fig, ^-Source) - - (M) - \to M_2 \ (^-Fig, ^+Source)]$$

with the shift in what we have called the OPERATOR being determined by the greater salience of the Recipient/Object in this case relative to the Actor/Instrument involved in the perceiving or sentencing.

Presumably a similar analysis could be made of optional transformations other than the passive, but this remains to be done. What about *extraordinary statives?* These seem hard to come by intuitively (viz., ?*the field is around the cow,* ?*the pillow is under the cat*). Perhaps the perceptual phenomena of ambiguous figures will give a hint of the answer: reversible figure/ground patterns are ones in which two "figures" are about equally salient for the same visual pattern (like the reversible cube or Boring's Mother in law versus Wife) and they are characterized by having no neutral condition where both stative relations are simultaneously being cognized—rather, perception "flips" in all-or-nothing fashion from one Figure/Ground relation to the reverse. In other words, there can be no ⁰Figure feature coding; furthermore, the Figure/Ground codings of the two entities, M_1 and M_2, in stative relations *are always relative to each other,* never absolute— thus THE PILLOW is ⁺Figure with respect to THE FLOOR but ⁻Figure with respect to THE CAT. Again, it would seem that linguistic and nonlinguistic (perceptual) cognitive processes are intimately interrelated.

Are Naturalness Ordering Principles Universals of Human Languages?

It is obvious that we believe Naturalness of constituent ordering in terms of Figure/Ground and Source/Recipient—Object to be human universals, based as they are upon prelinguistic perceptuosemantic information processing. However, the basic cognitions for "ordinary" stative and action relations we have intuited have a Subject—Verb—Object structure—and the authors are native speakers of American English, an SVO-type language. What must be shown is that the same underlying order in cognizing holds for speakers of languages whose dominant orders for SAAD (simple active affirmative declarative) sentences are SOV or VSO. There are at least two sorts of evidence that can be brought to bear—first, the relative frequencies of these three basic types in the languages of the world, and, second, consistent SVO ordering in language development regardless of type—but we can only make a small beginning in offering such evidence.

Relative Frequencies of SAAD Language Types.   In one of the earliest papers on language typology, Greenberg (1963) presents data on 30 human languages;

of these, 43% were identified as SVO, 37% as SOV, and 20% as VSO. As the Stanford University Language Universals Project has developed over the past decade, the samples used by researchers have expanded: Sedlak (1975) utilized a sample of 44 languages, of which 61% are identified as SVO, 32% as SOV, and only 7% as VSO; Blansitt (1973), also in a study of bitransitive constructions, used a much larger sample of 92 languages, with 54% identified as SVO, 30% as SOV, and 16% as VSO. As far as we are aware, no one has as yet provided such identifications for all languages available in the Stanford project. But the trend is pretty clear—something more than 50% SVO, about 35% SOV, and only about 12% or so VSO. When Sedlak divides his sample of 44 languages into Fixed Order (one order of Direct and Indirect Objects predominate, as in Russian) versus Variable Order (no one order predominates), we also note the following interesting fact: whereas SVO languages are about equally likely to be Fixed (13) or Variable (14) in ordering, the less frequent types are relatively Fixed in ordering (12 to 3 for SOV and VSO combined)—suggesting that SVO languages offer greater flexibility.

SVO Ordering in Development Regardless of Language Type. There have been comparatively few cross-linguistic studies of language development with particular reference to word order (really, constituent order, but with the limitations of two- and three-word production capacities!). A number of such studies is now underway, particularly under the aegis of the Language–Behavior Research Laboratory of the University of California (see Slobin, 1973). In this paper Slobin gives first place among his "suggested universals in the ontogenesis of grammar" to word (and morpheme) order, and suggests that order in child language preserves the order in the input adult language—a proposition we shall momentarily see reason to question.

One of the completed investigations in this program, a doctoral thesis by Ljubica Radulović (1975, under Slobin's direction), is particularly cogent for our question of the universality of Naturalness in word ordering. The thesis reports two intensive longitudinal studies and one extensive cross-sectional (checking) study of language development in Serbo-Croatian (research conducted in Dubrovnik, Yugoslavia). What makes the comparison with English (where there is much data) highly significant is the fact that, while both are SVO languages, Serbo-Croatian (SC) is highly inflected and, compared with English, word order in adult speech is extremely variable. This variability is very much under the control of what we have called Salience principles:

> Hence, in SC, if I choose to say a sentence in an order such as "I go to school" the focus of attention is upon the actor. By contrast, if I choose to say "To school I go" the focus is upon . . . my destination point. Finally if I choose to say "Go to school I" the action of going receives the greatest attentional focus [p. 101].

Radulović's major conclusion is that "contrary to the adult model, which is relatively unconstrained in word order, children's spontaneous utterances are found to follow *a fairly inflexible word-order pattern of subject–verb–object* ... a theoretical proposition is advanced that children learning languages that differ widely in certain aspects of their structure, for example an order language such as English versus a heavily inflectional language such as Serbo-Croatian, *exhibit identical strategies in respect to the development of the word order patterns* [Abstract, p. 1, italics added]."

It might also be noted that, as the inflectional (affixing) system develops, it first gets established in the SVO order and only then does freedom in word ordering begin to appear. Radulović (1975, p. 31) emphasizes that this SVO pattern is almost identical for the two longitudinally and the 48 cross-sectionally studied children; furthermore, although the verb may shift about somewhat (thus, VSO and SOV as well as SVO), utterances with O before S (thus, VOS, OSV, or OVS) are practically nonexistent in the data; and although VS is a frequent exception to the rule at the youngest ages (2:0–2:4), then decreasing, Radulović attributes this (contextually) to be perceptual situations in which the action is changing rather than constant, hence to salience effects—"the child's early constructions appear to be primarily perception-based [Abstract, p. 4]."

Given Slobin's suggested universal above—that "word order in child speech reflects word order in the input language [1973, p. 197]"—and given the extreme variability of word order in ordinary adult Serbo-Croatian, the question naturally arises: do adults reduce their utterances to simple SVO orders when talking with children? The answer (Radulović, 1975, pp. 81–82) is a clear "no"! She selected random samples of the mothers' talk to their children (longitudinally studied) and found word orders to be extremely variable; "for example, there are 88 different word orders in one hundred sentences spoken by Damir's mother ... (and) 87 ... in one hundred sentences of Ana's mother." Although these findings for a highly inflected language are entirely consistent with our Naturalness hypothesis, what we need still is evidence for SVO ordering in the course of development for inflected languages with highly variable word order and, particularly, uninflected languages with relatively fixed word orders—*of the SOV and VSO types.*

APPENDIX A: SENTENCE SETS FOR EXPERIMENT

(First terms in parentheses are High and second Low Vividness)

1. Dative
   1-1. The nurse told a (fairy tale/story) to the (orphans/children).
   1-2. The duke rented his (castle/house) to a (vampire/teacher).
   1-3. The art gallery sold a (Picasso/painting) to (Jackie Onassis/a wealthy woman).
   1-4. The businessman bought a (martini/drink) for (a senator/his son).

1-5. The maharajah gave an (elephant/rug) to the (queen/visitor).

1-6. The boy tossed the (frisbee/ball) to the (St. Bernard/dog).

1-7. The archaeologist handed a (tomahawk/pencil) to the (nun/student).

1-8. The acrobat loaned his (trampoline/watch) to a (juggler/schoolboy).

2. Equative

2-1. The (cheerleader/ringleader) was the (hero/injured one).

2-2. The (blacksmith/owner) was the (sheriff/contractor).

2-3. The (priest/clerk) was the (murderer/guest).

2-4. The (gypsy/driver) was the (king/singer).

2-5. The (gambler/janitor) was the (pilot/observer).

2-6. The (hunter/speaker) was the (heavyweight champion/author).

2-7. The (rapist/go-between) was a (drag-racer/salesman).

2-8. The (champion/buyer) was a (butcher/woman).

3. Genitive

3-1. The (courage/attitude) of the (quarterback/team) was responsible for the victory.

3-2. The proclamation freed the (slaves/property) of the (nobles/land-owners).

3-3. The (windshield/fender) of the (hearse/car) was smashed.

3-4. The bullet was fired from the (rifle/gun) of the (FBI agent/guard).

3-5. The (painfulness/size) of the (blister/cut) made it impossible to wear a shoe.

3-6. Columbo wanted to exhume the (corpse/body) of the (actress/victim).

3-7. The (godmother/mother) of the (gourmet/children) had been a witch.

3-8. The pow-wow was held in the (wigwam/tent) of (Sitting Bull/the chief).

4. Passive

4-1. The (avalanche/snow) covered the (circus/town).

4-2. A young (astronaut/student) found a (new galaxy/dollar).

4-3. The (Supreme Court/judge) upheld the (death sentence/verdict).

4-4. The (explosion/accident) destroyed the (yacht/car).

4-5. The (gangster/wife) shot the (mistress/storekeeper).

4-6. The (bulldozer/truck) crushed the (daffodils/flowers).

4-7. (A world famous architect/an alumnus of the university) designed the (Assembly Hall/building).

4-8. The (pelican/bird) ate the (snake/fish).

5. Phrasal Conjunction Reversal

5-1. The police arrested the (head coach/rookie) and the (star player/scout).

5-2. The (prince/lawyer) and the (millionaire/doctor) both loved the model.

5-3. The major crops in Spain are (oranges/corn) and (olives/rice).

5-4. The (wasps/ants) and (spiders/flies) were annoying.

5-5. The cook prepared (oxtail/beans) and (hot dogs/rice).

5-6. (Tornados/storms) and (earthquakes/high winds) devastated many areas.

5-7. The secretary returned from vacation with (V.D./a headache) and a (sunburn/cold).

5-8. (Stagecoaches/horses) and (covered wagons/carts) were used to tour the old Western town.

6. Adverb Preposing

6-1a. The fat lady ate the pie (greedily/contentedly).

   b. The fat lady (greedily/contentedly) ate the pie.

6-2a. The butler picked up the china (awkwardly/carefully).

   b. The butler (awkwardly/carefully) picked up the china.

6-3a. The policeman pulled out his gun (nervously/carefully).

   b. The policeman (nervously/carefully) pulled out his gun.

6-4a. The burglar entered the mansion (stealthily/quietly).

   b. The burglar (stealthily/quietly) entered the mansion.

6-5a. The mugger attacked his victim (viciously/unexpectedly).

   b. The mugger (viciously/unexpectedly) attacked his victim.

6-6a. The jockey rode the horse (recklessly/skillfully).

   b. The jockey (recklessly/skillfully) rode the horse.

6-7a. The wolves howled (eerily/softly) in the distance.

   b. The wolves (eerily/softly) howled in the distance.

6-8a. The crippled caterpillar crawled across the patio (painfully/slowly).

   b. The crippled caterpillar (painfully/slowly) crawled across the patio.

7. Particle Movement

7-1a. A guide pointed out the (palace/sights).

   b. A guide pointed the (palace/sights) out.

7-2a. The musician picked up his (tuba/instrument).

   b. The musician picked his (tuba/instrument) up.

7-3a. The admiral looked over the (submarine/report).

   b. The admiral looked the (submarine/report) over.

7-4a. The chef threw out the (spoiled venison/leftover sauce).

   b. The chef threw the (spoiled venison/leftover sauce) out.

7-5a. The museum threw away (a priceless painting/all of their guidebooks) by mistake.

   b. The museum threw (a priceless painting/all of their guidebooks) away by mistake.

7-6a. The lumberjack cut down the (giant redwood/old tree).
    b. The lumberjack cut the (giant redwood/old tree) down.
7-7a. The husband took out the (dog/trash).
    b. The husband took the (dog/trash) out.
7-8a. The woman took off her (bra/coat).
    b. The woman took her (bra/coat) off.

8. Tough Movement
    8-1a. It was hard to climb the (cliff/stairs).
        b. The (cliff/stairs) was hard to climb.
    8-2a. It was fun to ride the (merry-go-round/train).
        b. The (merry-go-round/train) was fun to ride.
    8-3a. It was easy to hide the (bomb/letter).
        b. The (bomb/letter) was easy to hide.
    8-4a. It took ten years to build the (tomb/house).
        b. The (tomb/house) took ten years to build.
    8-5a. It was impossible to open the (coffin/door).
        b. The (coffin/door) was impossible to open.
    8-6a. It was interesting to watch the (chimps/crew).
        b. The (chimps/crew) was interesting to watch.
    8-7a. It was frightening to hear the (mob/noise).
        b. The (mob/noise) was frightening to hear.
    8-8a. It was considered dangerous to eat unfamiliar (mushrooms/foods).
        b. Unfamiliar (mushrooms/foods) were considered dangerous to eat.

APPENDIX B: EXAMPLES OF SETS OF CLAUSES
OF EACH SYNTACTIC TYPE

Syntactic type	Clause type	Set
Dative	U–H/H[a]	the boy tossed the frisbee to the St. Bernard
	U–H/L	the boy tossed the frisbee to the dog
	U–L/H	the boy tossed the ball to the St. Bernard
	U–L/L	the boy tossed the ball to the dog
	T–H/H	the boy tossed the St. Bernard the frisbee
	T–L/H	the boy tossed the dog the frisbee
	T–H/L	the boy tossed the St. Bernard the ball
	T–L/L	the boy tossed the dog the ball
Equative	U–H/H	the priest was the murderer
	U–H/L	the priest was the guest

	U–L/H	the clerk was the murderer
	U–L/L	the clerk was the guest
	T–H/H	the murderer was the priest
	T–L/H	the guest was the priest
	T–H/L	the murderer was the clerk
	T–L/L	the guest was the clerk
Genitive	U–H/H	the powwow was held in the wigwam of Sitting Bull
	U–H/L	the powwow was held in the wigwam of the chief
	U–L/H	the powwow was held in the tent of Sitting Bull
	U–L/L	the powwow was held in the tent of the chief
	T–H/H	the powwow was held in Sitting Bull's wigwam
	T–L/H	the powwow was held in the chief's wigwam
	T–H/L	the powwow was held in Sitting Bull's tent
	T–L/L	the powwow was held in the chief's tent
Passive	U–H/H	the bulldozer crushed the daffodils
	U–H/L	the bulldozer crushed the flowers
	U–L/H	the truck crushed the daffodils
	U–L/L	the truck crushed the flowers
	T–H/H	the daffodils were crushed by the bulldozer
	T–L/H	the flowers were crushed by the bulldozer
	T–H/L	the daffodils were crushed by the truck
	T–L/L	the flowers were crushed by the truck
Phrasal conjunct reversal	U–H/H	the wasps and spiders were annoying
	U–H/L	the wasps and flies were annoying
	U–L/H	the ants and spiders were annoying
	U–L/L	the ants and flies were annoying
	T–H/H	the spiders and wasps were annoying
	T–L/H	the flies and wasps were annoying
	T–H/L	the spiders and ants were annoying
	T–L/L	the flies and ants were annoying
Adverb movement	U–H	the fat lady ate the pie greedily
	U–L	the fat lady ate the pie contentedly
	T–H	the fat lady greedily ate the pie
	T–L	the fat lady contentedly ate the pie
Particle movement	U–H	the admiral looked over the submarine
	U–L	the admiral looked over the report
	T–H	the admiral looked the submarine over
	T–L	the admiral looked the report over
Tough movement	U–H	it was impossible to open the coffin
	U–L	it was impossible to open the door
	T–H	the coffin was impossible to open
	T–L	the door was impossible to open

[a]Abbreviations: U = untransformed clause; T = transformed clause; H = high salience; L = low salience.

ACKNOWLEDGMENTS

Parts of this chapter are based on portions of a dissertation directed by the first author and submitted by the second author to the Graduate College of the University of Illinois at Urbana-Champaign in partial fulfillment of the requirements for the Ph.D. degree. We would like to especially thank Ellen Brewer and Edward Shoben for their assistance in programming and data analysis, and William F. Brewer for advice, criticism, and general helpfulness.

REFERENCES

Baroni, A., Fava, E., & Tirandola, G. *L'ordine delle parole nel linguaggio infantile*. Unpublished manuscript, University of Padova, 1973.

Bates, E. *Language and context: Studies in the acquisition of pragmatics*. Unpublished doctoral dissertation, University of Chicago, 1974.

Bates, E. Pragmatics and sociolinguistics in child language. In D. Morehead & A. Morehead (Eds.), *Language deficiency in children: Selected readings*. University Park, Maryland: University of Maryland Press, in press.

Bever, T. G. Functional explanations require independently motivated functional theories. Psycholinguistics Program, Columbia University, 1975 (mimeo).

Blansitt, E. L. Bitransitive clauses. In *Working papers on language universals*. Committee on Linguistics, Stanford University, 1973.

Bloom, L. *Language development: Form and function in emerging grammars*. Cambridge, Massachusetts: MIT Press, 1970.

Bloomfield, L. *An introduction to the study of language*. New York: Holt, 1914.

Bock, J. K. *Given-new and salience: The effects of two sentence production principles on syntactic structure*. Unpublished doctoral dissertation, University of Illinois at Urbana-Champaign, 1975.

Bowerman, M. *Early syntactic development*. Cambridge, England: Cambridge University Press, 1973.

Carroll, J. B. Process and content in psycholinguistics. In R. Glaser (Ed.), *Current trends in the description and analysis of behavior*. Pittsburgh: University of Pittsburgh Press, 1958.

Carroll, J. M., & Tannenhaus, M. K. Functional clauses are the primary units of sentences segmentation. Psycholinguistics Program, Columbia University, 1975 (mimeo).

Chafe, W. L. *Meaning and the structure of language*. Chicago: University of Chicago Press, 1970.

Chomsky, N. *Aspects of the theory of syntax*. Cambridge, Massachusetts: MIT Press, 1965.

Clark, H. H. Some structural properties of simple active and passive sentences. *Journal of Verbal Learning and Verbal Behavior*, 1965, 5, 99–106.

Clark, H. H. The language-as-fixed-effect fallacy: A critique of language statistics in psychological research. *Journal of Verbal Learning and Verbal Behavior*, 1973, 12, 335–359.

Cooper, W. E., & Ross, J. R. World order. In *Papers from the parasession on functionalism*. Chicago: Chicago Linguistics Society, 1975.

Ertel, S. *Words, sentences, and the ego*. Unpublished manuscript, University of Göttingen, 1971.

Flores d'Arcais, G. B. *Some perceptual determinants of sentence construction*. Unpublished manuscript, University of Padova, 1974.

Fodor, J. A., Bever, T. G., & Garrett, M. F. *The psychology of language*. New York: McGraw-Hill, 1974.

Greenberg, J. H. Some universals of grammar. In J. H. Greenberg (Ed.), *Language universals.* Cambridge, Massachusetts: MIT Press, 1963. Chapter 5.

Greenfield, P. M., & Smith, J. *Language before syntax: The development of semantic structure.* New York: Academic Press, in press.

Gruber, J. S. Topicalization in child language. In D. A. Reibel & S. A. Schane (Eds.), *Modern studies in English.* Englewood Cliffs, New Jersey: Prentice-Hall, 1969.

Hebb, D. O. *The organization of behavior: a neurophysiological theory.* New York: Wiley, 1949.

Hull, C. L. *Principles of behavior.* New York: Appleton-Century-Crofts, 1943.

James, C. T., Thompson, J. G., & Baldwin, J. M. The reconstructive process in sentence memory. *Journal of Verbal Learning and Verbal Behavior,* 1973, **12,** 51–63.

Jesperson, O. *The philosophy of grammar.* London: Allen & Unwin, 1924.

Johnson, M. G. Syntactic position and rated meaning. *Journal of Verbal Learning and Verbal Behavior,* 1967, **6,** 240–246.

Johnson-Laird, P. N. The interpretation of the passive voice. *Quarterly Journal of Experimental Psychology,* 1968, **20,** 69–73.

Johnson-Laird, P. N. Experimental psycholinguistics. *Annual Review of Psychology,* 1974, **25,** 135–160.

Lashley, K. S. The problem of serial order in behavior. In L. A. Jeffress (Ed.), *Cerebral mechanisms in behavior* (The Hixon Symposium). New York: Wiley, 1951.

Lindsley, J. R. Producing simple utterances: How far ahead do we plan? *Cognitive Psychology,* 1975, **7,** 1–19.

McWhinney, B. Pragmatic patterns in child syntax. *Papers and Reports on Child Language Development,* 1975, No. 10, 153–165.

Olson, D. R. Language and thought: Aspects of a cognitive theory of semantics. *Psychological Review,* 1970, **77,** 257–273.

Opačić, G. *Natural order in cognizing and clause order in the sentencing of conjoined expressions.* Unpublished doctoral dissertation, University of Illinois at Urbana-Champaign, 1973.

Osgood, C. E. Effects of motivational states upon decoding and encoding. In C. E. Osgood & T. A. Sebeok (Eds.), *Psycholinguistics: A survey of theory and research problems.* Indiana University Publications in Anthropology and Linguistics, Memoir 10, 1954. (Also issued as a supplement to *Journal of Abnormal and Social Psychology,* 1954, **49.**)

Osgood, C. E. A behavioristic analysis of perception and language as cognitive phenomena. In J. Bruner (Ed.), *Contemporary approaches to cognition.* Cambridge, Massachusetts: Harvard University Press, 1957. (a)

Osgood, C. E. Motivational dynamics of language behavior. In M. R. Jones (Ed.), *Current theory and research in motivation.* Lincoln, Nebraska: University of Nebraska Press, 1957. (b)

Osgood, C. E. On understanding and creating sentences. *American Psychologist,* 1963, **18,** 735–751.

Osgood, C. E. Where do sentences come from? In D. D. Steinberg & L. A. Jakobovits (Eds.), *Semantics: An interdisciplinary reader in philosophy, linguistics, and psychology.* London: Cambridge University Press, 1971.

Osgood, C. E. *Focus on meaning: III. Cognizing and sentencing.* The Hague: Mouton, 1976 (in press).

Osgood, C. E., & Hoosain, R. Salience of the word as a unit in the perception of language, *Perception and Psychophysics,* 1974, **15,** No. 1, 168–192.

Osgood, C. E., May, W. H., & Miron, M. *Cross-cultural universals of affective meaning.* Urbana, Illinois: The University of Illinois Press, 1975.

Osgood, C. E., & Tanz, C. Will the real direct object in bitransitives please stand up? In *Linguistic studies in honor of Joseph Greenberg.* Stanford: Stanford University Press, 1976, in press.

Paivio, A. Mental imagery in associative learning and memory. *Psychological Review,* 1969, **76,** 241–263.

Paivio, A., Yuille, J. C., & Madigan, S. Concreteness, imagery, and meaningfulness values for 925 nouns. *Journal of Experimental Psychology Monograph Supplement,* 1968, **76** (1, pt. 2).

Pillsbury, W. B. The mental antecedents of speech. *Journal of Philosophy, Psychology, and Scientific Methods,* 1915, **12,** 116–127.

Prentice, J. L. Response strength of single words as an influence in sentence behavior. *Journal of Verbal Learning and Verbal Behavior,* 1966, **5,** 429–433.

Prentice, J. L. Effects of cuing actor versus cuing object on word order in sentence production. *Psychonomic Science,* 1967, **8,** 163–164.

Quirk, R., Greenbaum, S., Leech, G., & Svartvik, J. *A grammar of contemporary English.* New York: Seminar Press, 1972.

Radulović, L. Acquisition of language: Studies of Dubrovnik children. Unpublished doctoral dissertation, University of California at Berkeley, 1975.

Ransom, E. N. Constraints between passive subjects and agents. Paper presented at the Mid-America Linguistics Conference, 1975.

Rommetveit, R. *Words, meanings and messages.* New York: Academic Press, 1968.

Rosch, E. Cognitive reference points. *Cognitive Psychology,* 1975, **7,** 532–547.

Schlesinger, I. M. *Sentence structure and the reading process.* The Hague: Mouton, 1968.

Sedlak, P. A. S. Direct/Indirect object word order: A cross-linguistic analysis. In *Working papers on language universals.* Committee on Linguistics, Stanford University, 1975.

Segal, E. M., & Martin, D. R. The influence of transformational history on the importance of words in sentences. Paper presented at the meeting of the Psychonomic Society, October, 1966.

Slobin, D. I. Cognitive prerequisites for the development of grammar. In C. A. Ferguson & D. I. Slobin (Eds.), *Studies of child language development.* New York: Holt, Rinehart, & Winston, 1973.

Stern, G. *Meaning and change of meaning.* Bloomington: Indiana University Press, 1965. (First published, 1931).

Svartvik, J. *On voice in the English verb.* The Hague: Mouton, 1966.

Tannenbaum, P. H., & Williams, F. Generation of active and passive sentences as a function of subject or object focus. *Journal of Verbal Learning and Verbal Behavior,* 1968, **7,** 246–250.

Turner, E. A., & Rommetveit, R. Experimental manipulation of the production of active and passive voice in children. *Language and Speech,* 1967, **10,** 169–180.

Turner, E. A., & Rommetveit, R. Focus of attention in recall of active and passive sentences. *Journal of Verbal Learning and Verbal Behavior,* 1968, **7,** 543–548.

Wundt, W. Die Sprache. In A. L. Blumenthal (trans.), *Language and psychology: Historical aspects of psycholinguistics.* New York: Wiley, 1970. (First published 1900.) Sections from Chapter 7.

7
Where Do the Subjects
of Sentences Come from?[1]

Suitbert Ertel

Institut Für Psychologie
Universität Göttingen

According to traditional grammars a nuclear sentence consists of two major parts, the subject and the predicate. A constituent structure grammar tells us the same story in different terms: There are two immediate constituents of a sentence, a noun phrase (NP) and a verb phrase (VP). Generative grammarians also hold this doctrine. The sentence (S) is generated by expanding (S) to (NP)+(VP). As a matter of fact, the binary partitioning of the sentences satis-fies—or at least does not violate—naive linguistic intuition.

This intuition has, however, resisted every attempt at explanation. In what follows the problem and some attempts to solve it will first be discussed. Then a new theoretical attempt will be suggested and research testing this approach will be reported.

I. THE PROBLEM

A structural analysis of Sentence (1) illustrates the difficulty

(1)   Paul met Mary.

under question. In this sentence two noun phrases can be distinguished: NP_1 (Paul) and NP_2 (Mary). Note that a tree diagram of the sentence (see Fig. 1) shows that the noun phrase symbols are located at two different node levels:

[1] Based on an invited lecture given at places in the United States and in Poland. For writing the present text I had help from colleagues and native English speakers: Barry McLaughlin and Robert J. Jarvella. Charles E. Osgood gave helpful comments on an earlier version.

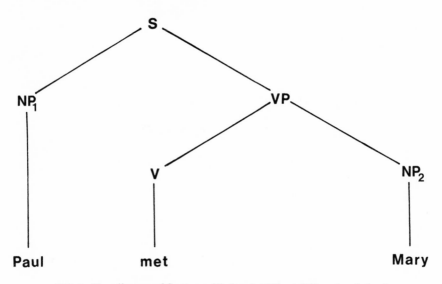

FIG. 1   Tree diagram of Sentence (1) showing NPs at different node levels.

NP_1 is immediately dominated by S, while NP_2 is immediately dominated by VP, VP being at the same node level as NP_1. This, of course, is the result of the binary partitioning of the sentence, which, as was mentioned before, is intuitively justified. However, does this intuition make sense theoretically?

The example suggests that an answer can hardly be expected from the semantics of the sentence. The meaning of the verb *meet* denotes a social event whose participants are involved symmetrically, that is, Sentence (1) says that Paul and Mary came together. What is said about Paul does not differ from what is said about Mary. The syntactic asymmetry between NP_1 and NP_2 is obviously not motivated by the sentence meaning. If we take into account additional evidence, which we cannot go into at this point (Ertel, 1974), we reach the general conclusion that any attempt to base the category of the subject on semantic considerations (subject=actor, or similar) is futile.

II. VARIOUS APPROACHES

Having realized this, some linguists looked for so-called functional aspects of sentence structure. In doing this, however, they departed, more or less, from the traditional approach. The subject–predicate partitioning of the sentence was supplemented by different binary divisions called *topic–comment* or *theme– rheme*.

One might expect that this new emphasis on the communicative function of sentence componenets would throw light on the function of the traditional sentence subject. This question will be dealt with by examining first the concept pair *topic–comment,* which is American in origin (Hockett, 1958), second the *theme–rheme* approach, which is of Czech origin (Prague school, Mathesius, 1929). Finally, the pertinent views of Halliday (1970), a British linguist, will be presented.

2.1 Topic–Comment

Hockett's *topic* is that part of the sentence denoting the person or thing about which something is said. The *comment* is that part of the sentence presenting the statement made about the person or thing. This sounds reasonable as a first approximation. Sapir already said (after Lyons, 1968, p. 334) "There must be something to talk about and something must be said about this subject of discourse."

But Hockett's topic–comment distinction does not help solve the problem of how to make sense of the grammatical subject. In fact, Hockett did not seriously try to make sense of it. He wanted to abandon the intricate concepts of subject and predicate and replace them with his own concepts which are more clearly, that is, operationally, defined. According to him the *topic* is always the initial part of the sentence ("the speaker announces a topic"); the *comment* is always the rest of the sentence (having announced a topic the speaker "then says something about it."). If we partition English sentences on the basis of this simple definition we find that the grammatical subject coincides with the topic of a sentence in most, but not in all, cases. In Sentence (1), for example, *Paul* is announced as the topic of the sentence, and *Paul* is also the grammatical subject. But in Sentence (2) the object noun *this book* is announced as

(2)   This book John has never read.

the topic, while the grammatical subject *John* is, according to Hockett's definition, part of the comment. Sentence (2) shows that topic and subject are different. Hockett himself realized this: "In English and the familiar languages of Europe, topics are usually also subjects and comments are predicates. But this identification fails sometimes in colloquial English, regularly in certain special situations in formal English, and more generally in some non-European languages" (Lyons, 1968, p. 335). To sum up, Hockett's "topic" does not yield an answer to the present question.

2.2 Theme–Rheme

Another approach stems from Mathesius, the founder of the Linguistic Circle of Prague, the "Prague School." According to the Prague linguists' theory on the "functional sentence perspective" (FSP) the sentence is also divided into two parts, the *theme* and the *rheme.* Firbas (1964), a younger member of this group, defines *theme* and *rheme* as follows: "Very roughly speaking, *thematic* elements are such as convey facts known from verbal or situational context, whereas *rhematic* elements are such as convey new, unknown facts, [p. 112]." Note that Mathesius' theme–rheme is similar to Hockett's topic–comment, insofar as in general the element about which something is said (topic) is the "given" or the "known" element (theme), while what is said about this element (comment) is generally "new" (rheme). Nevertheless, *theme–rheme* is conceived of as a unique category, and there are sentences, for example, Sentence (3), which show that theme is different from topic, and rheme different from comment.

    (3)   Unexpectedly, a young lady entered the room.

In (3), a young lady is in first position (topic), but is a "new" element (rheme), while *the room* is in a succeeding position (part of the comment), but is contextually "given" (theme). It is true that the theme, just like the topic, is *statistically* related to the grammatical subject: the theme coincides with the subject more often than the rheme. However, there are many cases where subject and theme do not coincide, as in Sentence (3). Thus, FSP theory does not provide functional meaning for the grammatical subject.

2.3 Halliday's Interpretation

An extensive discussion of the phenomena of sentence structure has been presented by Halliday (1967, 1970). This author tries to do justice to various theoretical contributions by considering the different aspects one by one within a broader conceptual taxonomy. Fortunately, he also considers explicitly the grammatical subject, which Hockett and the FSP-theorists had more or less neglected. His conclusion is: "The notion 'grammatical subject' by itself is strange, since it implies a structural function whose only purpose is to define a structural function. Actually . . . the 'grammatical subject' is a function defined by mood . . . [1970, p. 160]." What does Halliday mean? If one compares the following Sentences (4), a declarative sentence, and (5), a question, and (6), a command, one finds that the three sentence moods are indicated with the help of the grammatical subject: Its presence preceding the verb, as in (4), indicates a declaration; its presence following the verb, as in (5), indicates a question; and its absence, as in (6), indicates a command: "The function of the grammatical subject is thus a meaningful function in the clause, since it defines the communication role adopted by the speaker [p. 160]."

    (4)   You can climb trees.
    (5)   Can you climb trees?
    (6)   Climb trees.

It is not necessary here to summarize Halliday's total conceptual taxonomy of sentence structure; suffice it to note that he has dealt with almost every semantic and every functional aspect brought to bear in discussions of sentence structure, Hockett's topic and Mathesius' rheme included. If, for him, the grammatical subject is meaningful only as a mood indicator—a view which, according to Lyons, he seems to have adopted from Fillmore (Fillmore from Tesnière)—one may at least conclude that the range of possible interpretations of the subject must be quite narrow. Looking more closely at Halliday's interpretation one gets the impression that even this last resort to the idea that the subject is a mood indicator is doomed to failure. It is true that the presence or absence of the subject and the position of the subject with respect to the verb may indicate the sentence mood, for example, in English or German. But this is an incidental and an optional function of the subject allowing for many exceptions (see Sentences 7–9).

(7)   Du gehst jetzt ins Bett (You go to bed now)
(8)   Jetzt geht er ins Bett (German word order: Now goes he to bed)
(9)   Er geht schon ins Bett? (He goes to bed already?)

Sentence (7) is a command without deletion of the subject—according to Halliday it should be deleted; in (8), a declarative sentence, the subject *succeeds* the verb—it should precede it; in (9), a question, the subject *precedes* the verb—it should succeed it. In sum, Halliday's function of the subject quite often does not work. Moreover, in certain languages, like Latin, the grammatical subject lacks these functions altogether. The subject—obviously a linguistic universal—can hardly be based on a sporadic side effect such as that which Halliday proposes.

Chomsky, after having taken up the question of grammatical function (subject–predicate) states in his "Aspects" book (1965): "Whatever the force of such observations may be, it seems that they lie beyond the scope of any existing theory of language structure or language use [p. 163]." His somewhat pessimistic conclusion is "that the syntactic and semantic structure of natural languages evidently offers many mysteries, both of fact and of principle, and that any attempt to delimit the boundaries of these domains must certainly be quite tentative [p. 163]."

III. A PSYCHOLOGICAL INTERPRETATION OF THE GRAMMATICAL SUBJECT

One must agree with Chomsky that speculations in this area are at this time necessarily tentative. The present speculations are no exception. Hopefully, however, the research to be reported lends these speculations some empirical support.

A sentence is the product of an active mental construction. This construction occurs within the phenomenal field, or the "life space" (Lewin), of the speaker. Note that when I say "phenomenal field of the speaker" I refer to "phenomenal field" as something that is given to the speaker: the totality of the world as it appears to him. But in the same phrase I refer to "the speaker" as a human being as given to me or to everybody else. It was Gestalt psychology that emphasized the often neglected fact that the human being himself is part of his own phenomenal field. He has a percept and a concept of himself just as he has percepts and concepts of his mother, his city, and society. Henceforth the term *ego* is used when referring to the speaker as part of the speaker's own phenomenal field. Thus one may say: Sentence construction occurs within the phenomenal field of the speaker, which includes an ego.[2]

To say "The sentence is the product of an active mental construction" deliberately presupposes that there are different kinds of active mental constructions, linguistic constructions being only one subset. This presupposition implies that linguistic mental constructions are regarded as comparable to nonlinguistic mental constructions, for example, to manual constructions of physical objects that are governed by mental images or plans (Miller, Galanter, & Pribram, 1960). Indeed, it is deliberately implied that sentence construction is comparable to manual construction at some basic level of abstraction. This idea might seem strange, hence a brief explication is in order.

Let us take it for granted, at present, that there are such things as cognitive units in the phenomenal field which may be referred to by uttering linguistic units called nominal phrases. *Paul* is a nominal phrase which might denote something that is a cognitive unit within my phenomenal field. Now, a brief inspection of one's mental processes would reveal that the sections of the phenomenal field attended to at a given moment abound with cognitive units. For example, the unit *Paul* may be just one element of a structured group of elements that may be referred to by enumerating *Mary, friend, telephone call, appointment, dinner,* etc. A person seems to be able to think of or attend to a great number of such interrelated units nearly simultaneously. However, the person cannot and usually does not want to communicate all of what is present in his phenomenal field at one time. Linguistic production is dependent upon the speaker's selective communicative intention, and it is constrained by the necessity of linear chaining of verbal units.

It is assumed here that one of the basic mental operations underlying sentence construction is a certain manner of selection that may be called *nominal seizing.* The speaker seizes one and only one of the cognitive units that offer themselves as nominal candidates within the realm of what is going to be uttered. The cognitive unit that has been seized is the primary reference point of the sentential construction. Once the reference point is decided upon, the rest of the sentence—the other nominal units included—will be set in relation to this point. Its main role, thus, is to serve as a kind of cognitive device for fixing the sentential construction. As a rule, it will be represented linguistically as a noun

---

[2] For a further application of Gestalt principles to linguistic phenomena see Ertel, 1975.

phrase preceding the verb and nonsubject noun phrases. Apparently we are dealing here with the noun phrase that has traditionally been classified as the grammatical subject.

Before considering the consequences of these contentions a closer look at the hypothetical operation called nominal seizing is required. Following the argument above one may say that nominal seizing, on a more general level of abstraction, is structurally similar to the mental operation governing overt manual grasping: taking hold of something with one's hand. Suppose I take hold of a toy from among several toys within my reach. The toy in my hand differs from the rest of the toys within my phenomenal field in one respect: it is closer to my phenomenal ego. Therefore, if the subject of a sentence represents a cognitive unit that has been mentally seized by the speaker one should expect symptoms of relative closeness between the subject element and the speaker's ego. In the next section, some empirical tests of this prediction will be reviewed. To illustrate this discussion a visual scheme is presented, showing the relative ego distance of the nominal units of Sentence (1), as well as of Sentences (10) and (11) (see Fig. 2). Note that Sentences (1), (10), and (11) are logical paraphrases of each other. The difference lies only in the choice of the subject, and the

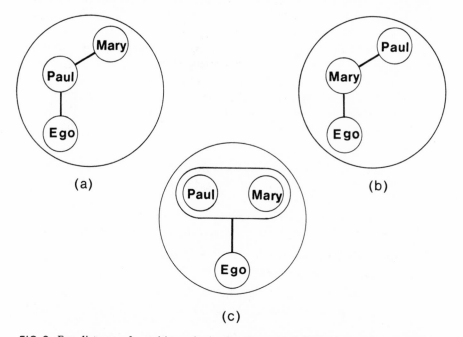

FIG. 2 Ego distance of cognitive units in the phenomenal field of a speaker. (a) Corresponding to "Paul met Mary"; (b) corresponding to "Mary met Paul"; (c) corresponding to "Paul and Mary met."

resulting asymmetrical distances between NP_1, NP_2 on the one hand and the speaker's ego on the other.

(1)   Paul met Mary.
(10)   Mary met Paul.
(11)   Paul and Mary met.

IV. EMPIRICAL EVIDENCE

A number of empirical studies has been undertaken to test the general assumptions about the sentence subject. The strategy of research was to look for evidence in different areas of cognitive behavior: in sentence interpretation, problem solving, as well as in speech production under laboratory and nonlaboratory conditions.

4.1 Sentence Interpretation

Two pictures depicting a communication situation were presented to the subjects (see Figure 3). The subjects were instructed that the speaker (see balloon) uttered a sentence to his neighbor, referring to one of the girls at the fence, either to Inge on the left or to Gisela on the right. The subject's task was to find out to which girl the speaker apparently refers. The four boys standing in a row were also referred to individually in various sentences.

Six different sentences were used, three sentences containing the preposition *in front of* and three sentences containing the preposition *behind.* Within each subgroup of sentences the grammatical subjects varied (compare Sentences 12, 13, and 14).

(12)   I am watching the girl standing in front of a fence.
        (The German original: Ich beobachte gerade das Mädchen, das vor einem Zaun steht.)
(13)   Hans is watching the girl standing in front of a fence.
        (Hans beobachtet gerade das Mädchen, das vor einem Zaun steht.)

The names of the four boys (Hans, Uwe, Karl, Otto) were used alternatively and randomly within the list of sentences.

(14)   It is Hans whom the girl standing in front of a fence is watching.
        (Den Hans beobachtet gerade das Mädchen, das vor einem Zaun steht.)

The sentence with the preposition *behind* corresponding to (12) is (15).

(15)   I am watching the girl standing behind a fence.
        (Ich beobachte gerade das Mädchen, das hinter einem Zaun steht.)

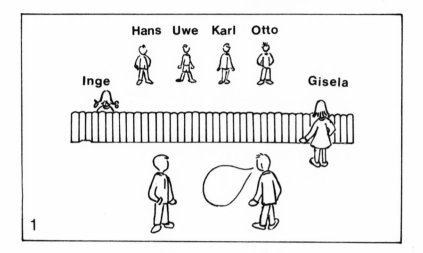

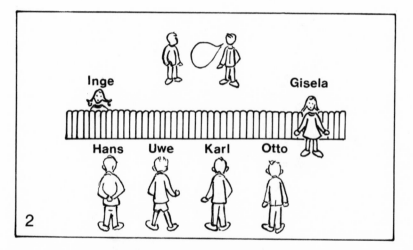

FIG. 3 Picture material used for the sentence interpretation experiment. The speaker (see balloon) refers in a sentence to one of the girls at the fence. To which girl does he refer?

In addition, two sentences with *behind* corresponding to (13) and (14) were used. Two pictures paired with 6 sentences yield 12 picture/sentence combinations. The material was arranged in a booklet for each subject in an individual random order.

The reader trying to perform the task of the subjects will note that the prepositions *in front of* and *behind* may be interpreted from different perspectives; as viewed by the speaker, as viewed by the boys, as viewed by the girls, and

TABLE 1
Number of Subjects Choosing the Girl Who Is Standing "In Front of the Fence" or "Behind the Fence" from the Perspective of the Speaker[a]

Subject of sentence	Picture 1			Picture 2			$f_{p_1} + f_{p_2}$
	"In front of"	"Behind"	f_{p_1}	"In front of"	"Behind"	f_{p_2}	
"I"	24	25	49	24	25	49	98
"Hans" etc.	11	13	24	14	11	25	49
"Girl"	16	18	34	16	20	36	70
	51	56	107	54	56	110	217

[a]Speaker perspective interpretations (SPI). $N = 26$.

even perhaps as viewed by the subject looking at the picture. The present theory predicted that the subjects would tend to choose the perspective of the person being referred to in the subject position of the sentence. For Sentence (12), in which the pictured speaker refers to himself in the subject position (I am watching . . .), the subjects would interpret the prepositions from the perspective of the speaker. However, for Sentence (13), in which the pictured speaker refers to Hans in the subject position (Hans is watching . . .), the subjects would tend to interpret the prepositions from the perspective of Hans.

Table 1 shows the number of subjects who chose the girl who is standing *in front of the fence* and *behind the fence* as viewed by the pictured speaker. First it should be noted that there is no considerable difference in frequencies between *in front of* sentences and *behind* sentences (see sum total of columns). Therefore, the polarity of the prepositions does not seem to have an effect.

The two picture orientations in Fig. 3 were used to control for an effect due to the subjects' own ego location. It will be seen from Table 1 that there is no considerable difference in frequencies between picture 1 and picture 2 (see sum totals f_{p1} and f_{p2} of the rows). The result indicates that the perspective of the subject looking at the picture apparently does not influence his interpretation of the pictured speaker's sentences.

The main result may be seen if the sum total $(f_{p1} + f_{p2})$ (see last column of Table 1) of the "I-subject" sentence (first row) is compared with the sum total $(f_{p1} + f_{p2})$ of the "Hans-subject" sentence (second row). If the pictured speaker refers to himself in the subject position the great majority of the subjects interpret the prepositions from the perspective of the speaker $(f_{p1} + f_{p2}$, first row). For picture 1, the girl *in front of* the fence is Gisela, the girl *behind* the fence is Inge, for picture 2 vice versa. However, if the pictured speaker refers to Hans in the subject position (Hans being always on the opposite side of the fence as viewed from the pictured speaker), the number of subjects who chose the pictured speaker's perspective is considerably fewer, that is, many subjects chose the perspective of Hans in this case $(f_{p1} + f_{p2}$, second row). A test of significance considers the subjects as independent units, and the number of speaker perspective interpretations (SPI) per S as the dependent variable (range: 0–4). The mean number of SPIs for "I-subject" sentences is 3.77, for "Hans-subject" sentences, 1.89. This difference is very significant ($p < .001$, sign test).

One could argue, however, that the fact that for Sentence (13) so many subjects chose *Hans* as the point of reference for interpreting the prepositions need not be due to the subject role of Hans in this sentence. Speakers generally may tend to select the *first noun phrase* in a sentence as a reference point, whether it is the subject of the sentence or not. In order to control for a possible position effect, Sentence (14) was used in this task. In Sentence (14), as compared with Sentence (13), *Hans* and *the girl* have exchanged their grammatical categories, not their positions in the sentence. If the prepositions in the sentence are interpreted from the perspective of the person who is referred to in the *first noun phrase,* no difference in frequency of SPI between Sentence (13) (second row) and Sentence (14) (third row) would result. On the other hand, if the interpretation of the prepositions tends to use the perspective of the person being referred to in the *subject position,* the frequency of SPI for Sentence (14) (third row) would exceed the frequency of SPI for Sentence (13) (second row), perhaps approaching that of Sentence 12 (first row).

What are the subjects' responses? The third row frequencies in the table show that a majority of subjects interpreted the preposition from the perspective of the speaker, whereas the second row frequencies are considerably lower ($p <$ .001). This result is in accord with expectation. However, the frequencies in the third row are less than in the first row. The difference of the means: 3.77 first row, 2.69 third row, is statistically significant (p = .002, sign test). This could in fact mean that the position of a noun phrase in a sentence has an additional effect.

In sum, the results lend support to the assumption that the cognitive unit underlying the subject noun phrase of a sentence is closer to the speaker's ego than that underlying an object noun phrase. A speaker may give up his egocentric perspective and shift to the perspective of the person to whom he is referring in subject position. This tendency is not found with respect to persons to whom the speaker refers as grammatical objects in a sentence.

4.2 An Experiment on Kinship Reasoning

In an experiment on reasoning with kinship relations the subjects were presented sentences like (16) and (17):

(16)   My sister is your daughter.
(17)   My nephew is your brother.

Note that these sentences represent miniature reasoning problems insofar as each sentence presupposes certain speakers and hearers that may be identified after pondering on the sentence for a while. This was precisely the subjects' task. For each sentence they had to find out "Who can say this sentence to whom?" and to give the answer as soon as they found one. The subject needed to give only 1 out of 4 (sometimes 2) alternative correct answers to each sentence. The time between the presentation of the sentence and the onset of an answer was the dependent measure.

For example, the possible correct answers to Sentence (16) are:

(a)   a son to his father
(b)   a son to his mother
(c)   a daughter to her father
(d)   a daughter to her mother

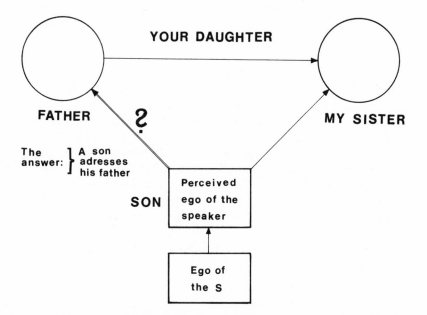

FIG. 4 Schematized cognitive relations between the speaker's ego and the kinship roles involved in comprehending Sentence (16).

Solution (a) may be schematized as in Figure 4. The subject (see lower box) is likely to identify with the ego of the fictitious speaker (see upper box) and take on his role. He will probably first attend to the relation "my sister" (oblique arrow to the right) asking himself how the person to whom his sister is related as daughter (horizontal arrow to the right) is related to himself (oblique arrow to the left).

So far the task is not yet informative. But compare Sentences (16) with (18) and (17) with (19):

(18)   Your daughter is my sister.
(19)   Your brother is my nephew.

Sentence (18) is synonymous with Sentence (16), and Sentence (19) with Sentence (17). Only the subject noun phrase and the predicate noun phrase have been interchanged. Logically, this makes no difference. For our theory, however, there is a difference. If it is true that the subject noun phrase is the one that the ego of the speaker takes hold of as the primary referential unit, then Sentence (16) with *my sister* as the subject would be more consistent than Sentence (18) with *your daughter* as the subject.

In Sentence (16) the syntactic role and the semantic content of the subject are congruent. The "ego-near" phrase *my sister* is in the "ego-near" subject position.

In Sentence (18) the syntactic role and the semantic content of the subject are incongruous. The "ego-distant" phrase *your daughter* is in the "ego-near" subject position. The prediction is that tasks with kinship relations conveyed by congruent sentences (C), like (16), would be easier to solve than tasks with kinship relations conveyed by incongruent sentences (IC), like (18).

The experiment was run with 32 psychology students individually, 16 male and 16 female. Eighty sentences were presented as tasks, 40 congruent (C) and 40 incongruent (IC) sentences, but logically synonymous with the C sentences.

Each of the following 20 pairs of kinship terms occurred four times in the sentences: brother–son, daughter–niece, father–brother, husband–son, son-in-law–brother-in-law, husband–father, wife–sister-in-law, mother–aunt, mother-in-law–wife, granddaughter–daughter, nephew–cousin, cousin–daughter, father–son, sister–granddaughter, brother–cousin, daughter–cousin, wife–sister, grand-daughter–niece, uncle–son, sister–sister-in-law. The pair of kinship terms *daughter–sister*, for example, was used in Sentences (16) and (18) (see above), as well as in Sentences (20) and (21):

(20)   My daughter is your sister.
(21)   Your sister is my daughter.

The four sentence items were distributed within the total series in such a way that several other items were presented in between. In fact no subject noticed that during the experiment logically identical problems were repeated: the subject was told to find the answer as soon as the problem card was handed to him. If an answer came to his mind he should first very briefly check whether it was correct in order to respond only with an appreciable degree of certainty about the correctness of the answer. Then he should say *yes* as a signal for the experimenter to press the stopwatch. After this signal he was instructed to give the answer phrase. The subject was told that the problems would vary greatly in difficulty. He was also given a list with all possible kinship terms in order to refresh this part of his subjective lexicon. The list did not contain kinship terms without sex feature (e.g., parents), and the subject was not allowed to use them.

For each sentence pair the difference in solution time (IC − C) was calculated. Each positive difference in solution time for a subject was marked as (+), that is, in accord with expectation, and each negative difference for a subject was marked as (−). The number of positive differences yielded the final index for a subject.

Out of the 32 subjects, the indices of 25 subjects were positive, as compared with only 5 subjects whose indices were negative. (For one subject the index was 0.) This result would be expected by chance with a probability of less than .001 (one-tailed binomial test).

The overall mean solution time for the total of 20 × 4 problems was 13.1 sec ($\sigma = 5.3$, range 1.9–198.5 sec). The mean solution time for the easiest problem (father–son) was 8.1 ($\sigma = 5.8$), and for the most difficult problem (nephew–

TABLE 2
Mean Number of Male and Female Speakers
and Hearers Occurring in the Responses
of Male and Female Subjects

Sex of the speaker and hearer in the subjects' responses		Sex of the subjects	
		Male	Female
Male	Speaker	59	23
	Hearer	57	24
Female	Speaker	7	43
	Hearer	10	41

grandson) the mean solution time was 26.1 (σ = 32.8). The mean number of errors was 9.8 (=12% of the tasks). As the solution times for errors did not significantly differ from the solution times for correct responses they were included in the total score.

An additional test of our model—although a less rigorous one—may be made with the present data. As noted above, for a sentence like (16), four correct answers are possible. For Sentence (16), for example, the subject may select a male or a female speaker (son or daughter) and he may select a male or female hearer (father or mother). This allows for four permutations, and therefore four answers are correct. Comparing the total answers of the male subjects with those of the female subjects one finds a striking difference.

As can be seen in Table 2, on the average, male subjects selected male speakers and male hearers much more frequently than female speakers and female hearers. Female subjects, however, selected female speakers more frequently than male speakers and female hearers more frequently than male hearers. Thus, one of the features of the subject's ego, sex, imposes itself on the sentence interpretation process. The process is influenced by a general readiness on the part of the subject to identify with the persons or roles to which he is referring. And the main result, the difference in difficulty of interpretation between C and IC sentences, suggests that the subject position is the natural locus for such identification.[3] (For more details see Ertel, 1974.)

[3] However, as the subject noun is always in first position and the predicative noun in second position, one cannot rule out an alternative explanation: the effect might be due to word order alone, not to the subject function of the head noun. Clark (personal communication, 1975) suggested an experiment in which an experimenter A addresses a subject B by saying sentences like *My daughter is your sister,* adding the question *Who am I for you?* In this case the pronoun *my* refers to A and *you* to B, that is, B might solve the problem

4.3 A Content Analysis of Soccer Reports

Among the spectators of league soccer matches there are usually newspaper reporters. One of them will be residentially close to team A and will write an article for the Monday edition of the local newspaper in city A. Another reporter will be residentially close to team B and will write an article for the Monday edition of the local newspaper in city B about the same soccer match.

As material for a content analysis 40 soccer reports were collected from various newspaper editors upon request. Each report used was matched with another report from the opposing team's reporter about the same match. Thus the views of the writers, which may be biased individually, would be counterbalanced by a view from a reporter colleague from the other team's city.

From the sentences of each report all those were selected in which the reporter referred to one member of the A-team as well as to one member of the B-team. Possible examples of such sentences are (22)–(27):

(22)   Müller clearly dominated Overrath.

(23)   Ovarrath had great difficulties with Müller.

(24)   Overrath was put to the test·by Müller.

(25)   Overrath was powerless against Müller's brilliant shooting.

(26)   Overrath lost the ball to Müller.

(27)   Müller and Overrath dueled to no advantage.

The names of the players in a sentence are noun phrases, and their grammatical function is either subject or object, the latter a direct, dative, or a prepositional object. The noun phrases of the sentences referring to two opposing players were classified, and the frequencies of occurrence of each syntactic function were tabulated separately for the players of the reporter's home team and for the players of the opposing team.

The theory predicts a difference in frequency between the syntactic positions of members of the reporter's home team and of members of the opposing team. The members of the reporter's home team are, in general, psychologically closer to the reporter's ego than the members of an opposing team. Therefore the members of the reporter's home team should be referred to linguistically and more frequently in the subject position than the members of the opposing team, and less frequently in the object position. The results may be seen in Table 3.[4] For all reports the mean number of sentences consistent with expectation (see

---

sentences with *you* in subject position faster than the problem sentences with *my* in subject position. In fact, this is to be expected, since in this case the reference of *you* uttered by A is identical to the reference of *my* uttered by B or by a person with whom B identifies.

[4] The other two logical cases—both the home team and opposing team players in the subject position or both in the object position—are not relevant for us and, besides, they are very rare: out of 40 reports not more than five sentences of each kind were observed. An example of the first kind of sentence is (27).

TABLE 3
The Mean Number of Sentences in a Soccer Report Having
in Subject Position Home Team Players While
Opposing Team Players are in Object Position (Consistent
with Expectation (+)); or Home Team Players in Object Position
While Opposing Team Players Are in Subject Position
(Inconsistent with Expectation (−))

		$\bar{X}$	σ	Number of reports
Home team players in subject	All matches	2.92	2.75	40
position (+)	Home team lost	3.13	3.13	20
	Home team won	2.68	2.28	20
Opposing team players in subject	All matches	1.21	1.42	40
position (−)	Home team lost	1.09	1.37	20
	Home team won	1.36	1.49	20

mean first row) exceeds considerably the mean number of sentences inconsistent with expectation (see mean fourth row). In order to apply nonparametric statistical inference, for each report the number of sentences regarded as consistent minus the number of sentences regarded as inconsistent was calculated. Every report was marked "+" if this difference was positive, and it was marked "−" if the difference was negative; one report with no difference and 7 reports having no sentence in which players of both teams were mentioned were neglected. Out of the 32 reports used, 26 were marked "+," and only 6 reports were marked "−." For this event the binomial test indicates a chance probability of $p < .0001$.

One could argue that reporters generally might tend to overestimate the strength and activity of their home players. As perceived instigators of activities are more likely than perceived respondents to be given the subject position, other conditions being equal (Ertel, 1974), the relatively great number of sentences with *home players* referred to in the subject position might reflect this bias in social perception. If this were true one could perhaps do without the ego-perspective hypothesis to explain the above result.

In order to see whether this conjecture holds the statistical analysis was done separately for the games lost and the games won by the home team of the reporters. The bias in perception hypothesis would predict, for the reports on games lost, a considerably smaller mean number of sentences having in the subject position a home team player (+) and a greater mean number of sentences having in the subject position an opposing team player (−) as compared with the games won. However, as Table 3 shows, this prediction is not supported. The difference in frequencies between matches lost and matches won is in fact in the opposite direction. Out of 15 reports on *matches lost* having a difference in the number of plus and minus sentences, 14 had more plus than minus cases, while out of 17 reports on *matches won* 12 had more plus and 5 more minus cases.

In fact, language offers many ways to refer in the subject position to a player who is acted upon by an opponent or who is only reacting to his attacks (see Sentences 23–26); the passive construction (24) is only one of several alternatives for this purpose. If a writer identifies with a player intensely enough he may take his perspective even more when this player is perceived as being attacked than when he is perceived as attacking. However this may be, one may conclude that the data, if viewed from the ego-perspective hypothesis of the grammatical subject, make sense.

4.4 An Experiment on Sentence Production with Artificial Names[5]

The primary purpose of this experiment was to test the assumption that the choice of the subject of a sentence can be elicited by the affective meaning properties of the underlying units referred to.

In order to have optimal control of affective meaning (the independent variable, see Osgood, Suci, & Tannenbaum, 1957), the materials used in the study consisted of artificial strings of phonemes whose affective meaning had been already obtained (Ertel, 1969). In this earlier study, the subjects were given 28 bipolar eight-point scales with artificial phonetic qualifiers such as OKAR-ELIN, FANGO-MNUHF, together with three meaningful substantival scales, *harmony–disharmony,* representing "evaluation," *strength–delicacy,* representing "potency," and *movement–quiescence,* representing "activity." Twenty concepts were judged on these 28 + 3 scales in the usual Semantic Differential fashion. A factor analysis of the 31 scales yielded the E, P, and A factors, as expected. Eighteen pairs of phonetic qualifiers were selected, six for every factor, as representative for E, P, or A, respectively. "Representative for a factor" means high loadings on this factor and low loadings on the other two factors. The results are shown in Table 4. The rationale of the experiment was as follows: The artificial phonetic strings have no lexical meaning; however, they have affective quality. Further, they may be used as proper names for persons in a sentence production task. Subjects were asked to write down a sentence about two persons whose "names" were presented. The names contrasted with regard to the polarity of one affective meaning dimension (e.g., OKAR–ELIN). No constraints for sentence production were imposed except that both names should be used in a sentence. In most sentences one of the names was expected to take the subject position, while the other was expected to take the position of

[5] This study was carried out under the guidance of the author by Hanna Jordan in fulfillment of the requirements of the Vordiplom für Psychologen at the University of Münster.

TABLE 4
Factor Loadings of 18 Artificial Phonetic Scales and Three
Substantival Scales on Evaluation, Potency, and Activity[a]

	Evaluation	Potency	Activity
1. LINGA–SCHNIEM	.73	−.02	−.01
2. LOMAR–GRÄMU	.55	.03	−.21
3. BENTO–CHÜER	.56	−.17	−.02
4. TENDO–QUAUNG	.68	−.24	−.09
5. LEGEM–AAFS	.63	−.22	.06
6. FANGO–MNUHF	.70	−.17	.25
7. *Wohlklang–Missklang* (harmony–disharmony)	.62	.11	−.04
8. OKAR–ELIN	.04	.77	−.09
9. AKANT–ENEGI	−.09	.57	−.14
10. TAKAM–MEILEM	.05	.79	−.13
11. KARNO–LELI	−.07	.78	−.02
12. RAMAT–NEILEE	.04	.80	−.07
13. TAMOS–LINDO	−.14	.77	−.07
14. *Stärke–Zartheit* (strength–delicacy)	.16	.42	.18
15. DONDONELL–TELOMO	−.01	−.15	.45
16. HELLELLO–SONEM	.12	−.13	.77
17. FOLLANEM–FALEE	.05	.13	.60
18. ONDENNEL–SOOM	−.02	−.17	.78
19. LODENNO–LOTO	.10	−.12	.70
20. MALLANO–PAHL	.21	−.20	.62
21. *Bewegung–Ruhe* (movement–quietude)	.10	.00	.49

[a]Communalities of these factors: 28%, 25%, 29%. Two additional factors (10%, 6%) have been omitted. The order of scales and left–right arrangement of the poles were random on the testing sheet.

a predicative complement. If affective meaning has an influence on subject selection, E^+ names, P^+ names, and A^+ names should be more frequently selected as the subject of a sentence than E^-, P^-, and A^- names, respectively.

Ninety-eight students served as subjects: 64 male students from the Gymnasium (mean age 16:5), and 34 university students (mean age 20:9), 19 male and 16 female. The Gymnasium and university students were tested in two independent groups. Each pair of artificial names was recorded on tape and one presentation consisted of ten repetitions (A–B–A–B–A–B, etc.). The pauses between names were the same between and within pairs (about 1 sec). The sound intensity was very low in the beginning of the presentation, increased gradually, and dropped again at the end. This was done in order to reduce possible order effects of presentation (primacy–recency) which might influence name selection. The order of pairs with respect to affective meaning dimensions was random. The main part of the instruction was as follows:

> This is an experiment on sound symbolism. Two artificial sound complexes will be presented to you from tape. Consider them as names of male persons.
> These names are different in impressional quality. Try to imagine two persons whose characters are similar to their names. Furthermore, imagine a situation in which these two persons somehow interact in a manner congruent with their characters. Write down just one simple sentence to describe the social interaction of the persons. For example: "A invites B for a luxurious dinner. A is trying to outwit B in a game, or whatever you may imagine. Feel free to write what you like. No restriction is made as to the order of occurence of the names in the sentence. The sentences may be short. Please avoid complex constructions with subordinate clauses."

The data were treated as follows: Only those sentences were scored in which one name had been used in the subject position, the other name in an object position. Some subjects showed many sentence constructions with both names in the subject position, for example, "OKAR and ELIN are hitch-hiking around the world," or both in the object position. Subjects with more than nine sentences of this kind were discarded, together with those who (1) did not follow instructions, (2) put down the name as a memory aid before writing the sentence, and (3) had more than 30% omissions. In all, 26% of the subjects were not considered in the data analysis.

A sentence was marked as "+" if the name with "positive" affective quality (E^+, P^+, A^+) had been used as the subject and the name with "negative" affective quality (E^-, P^-, A^-) as an object. A sentence was marked as "−" if the position of the names in the sentence was the reverse.

For every subject, the number of "+" and "−" scores was computed separately for each dimension, E, P, and A. If the number of "+" sentences of a subject in one dimension category was greater than the number of "−" sentences, he was classified as "+"; if the proportion of "+" and "−" sentences was the reverse, he was classified as "−"; if the number of sentence categories was equal, the subject was classified as "=", for each dimension separately.

TABLE 5

Number of Subjects Who Produced More (+ > −) and Fewer (− > +) Sentences with "Positive" Names in Subject Position than in Object Position, and an Intermediate Category (+ = −)

	All subjects			Gymnasium subjects			University subjects		
	+	=	−	+	=	−	+	=	−
Evaluation	42	12	19	28	5	9	14	7	10
Potency	39	19	15	26	5	11	13	14	4
Activity	36	10	27	17	5	20	19	5	7

Table 5 shows the number of subjects in each category for each dimension. As expected, for E, P, and A the number of subjects in the "+" group is greater than the number in the "−" group. However, the difference is significant for E and P only. The Gymnasium students differed markedly from the university students with respect to A, for no apparent reason. Overall, the hypothesis of this experiment was confirmed. The subjects preferred to choose the E$^+$ names, the P$^+$ names, and, with the exception of the Gymnasium students, the A$^+$ names as the subjects of the sentences. It is very unlikely that the subjects were aware of what the experimenter expected in this experiment. Therefore, the general assumption that affective meaning can be a determinant of the choice of subject perspective is substantiated.

V. DISCUSSION

The theoretical background against which the results of the four empirical studies will be discussed requires more elaboration. One of the main theoretical assumptions is that there exists a distance relation between a speaker ego and the nominal units that are being referred to in a sentence. In fact, the empirical data made sense on the basis of this assumption: The distance relations between the ego of the speaker and various nominal units within his cognitive field appeared to be unequal. A unit having the grammatical role of a subject seemingly was closer to the ego than a unit having the grammatical role of an object.

The asymmetry between nominal units of a sentence with respect to ego-distance is thought to be the result of a general feature of sentence construction: the speaker seizes one of the nominal units among a range of nominal candidates in order to give his sentence a primary reference point. Having seized this unit, the speaker will set the other units of the sentence in relation to his reference unit. The linguistic construction called a sentence is thus anchored to its grammatical subject—analogous to a village that is built around a church. The anchoring of a sentence is signaled on the surface level by its linguistic form (case inflection, word order, etc.). Anchoring is achieved by the speaker as part of his encoding activity and by the hearer as part of his decoding activity. Anchoring the sentence means seizing a nominal unit and setting it in primary (close) relation to the cognizing ego.

5.1 Interpreting the Studies

The results of the first experiment exemplify one of the possible concomitants of the hypothetical asymmetry between nominal units in a sentence. It was shown that the interpretation of *in front of* and *behind* may vary. A speaker tends to interpret these prepositions from his own perspective. But he may also shift his perspective to another person. The results of the experiment supported the hypothesis that if such a shift of perspective occurs this shift will be toward the person who is being referred to as the subject of the sentence—the subject being the grammatical category in which the speaker anchors his cognitive construction.

The second experiment was an attempt to bring syntax and semantics together in a somewhat different way. The first and the second person pronouns were used in noun phrases of sentences that stated various kinship relations. To manipulate these pronouns is a semantic affair. However, to interchange the *my* and *you* noun phrases in sentences like *my brother is your son* is also a syntactic affair which, fortunately, does not affect the sentences' logical content. Now it turned out that comprehending a kinship sentence of this format was easier when the *my* noun phrase was the grammatical subject and the *you* noun phrase was the predicate complement. If the pairing of grammatical categories on the one hand and first/second person pronouns on the other shows a facilitating or inhibiting effect—such as was observed—there must be a common level where syntax and semantics meet.

The fact that A "loves" B is not a linguistic fact, nor does the fact that a newspaper reporter from Munich "identifies with" the players of Bayern München have any linguistic basis. The content analysis of soccer reports, however, showed that such facts may affect sentence generation in a nonexperimental setting: If players X and Y are going to be referred to in one sentence, and if within the writer's phenomenal field X is closer to his ego than Y, then X is more likely to be referred to as the grammatical subject of the sentence. Note that in this study the grammatical subject was treated as a dependent variable, while in the first two studies it was treated as an independent variable.

The fourth experiment resembles the third study in this respect. Again, the study centered on the *antecedents* of subject selection. This time, however, no preestablished cognitive—emotional bonds came into play (liking, identifying, etc.) but rather affective features of novel objects, that is, nonsense and sound strings. The subject's task was to use the sound strings as names of persons in a sentence. Boucher and Osgood (1969) have postulated a "Polyanna hypothesis," according to which there is a universal tendency to encode affectively positive elements more readily than affectively negative elements. Other things being equal, good ($^+$evaluation), strong ($^+$potency), and moving ($^+$activity) units will be attended to to a greater extent than bad ($^-$evaluation), weak ($^-$potency), and quiet ($^-$activity) units.[6] Whenever an ego attends to something, however, it is psychologically near to, sometimes even absorbed by that object. The Polyanna hypothesis, linked with the ego-distance hypothesis, predicted that positive

---

[6] These basic and primitive tendencies have been discussed at length in Ertel (1972). The linguistic and psychological asymmetry of polar terms was interpreted as basically affective in nature (see also French, 1974). Affect was conceived as a term denoting a phenomenal relation between two cognitive units, one of which is the ego.

names would be preferred to negative names in the subject position. Again this prediction was supported.

5.2 Relating the Theory to Its Predecessors

The four studies that have been reported are not the first to emphasize relations between psychological processes and grammatical categories (subject, object). A brief glimpse at earlier attempts, however, will show the difference between previous work in this area and the present approach.

Most previous research dealt with the grammatical subject in connection with voice. It was generally claimed that the choice of the subject determines the encoding decision between active or passive sentence forms. And the choice of the subject, the authors contended, may have psychological antecedents.

There was also wide agreement on what kind of determinants might be relevant, although there is some divergence in nomenclature. Carroll (1958) referred to "focus of attention"; Tannenbaum and Williams (1968) called the same thing "conceptual focus"; Turner and Rommetveit (1968) talked about properties like "salience" and "importance" in addition to "focus of attention." Another label is Johnson-Laird's "emphasis" (1968). Flores D'Arcais (1973) borrowed the term "topic" from linguistics using it in a psychological sense: Topic according to him is the "principal feature," the "center" or "theme" of a situation, and the "emergence" of such a center or theme he calls "topicalization." "The choice of the voice, thus, is in part dependent on the topicalization of some object [p. 9]."

A variety of experimental paradigms has been applied in order to test these general models. Carroll (1958) presented his subjects with a short active event and asked them to simply describe the event. Four types of questions were used to direct the focus of attention to the object of the action or to the agent (e.g., "What happened to the [acted upon]? What did the [actor] do?"). When attention was directed to the object of the action, the first sentence in the subjects' descriptions of the situation tended to be in the passive voice; when the question directed attention to the agent, subjects tended to respond with active sentences.

Tannenbaum and Williams (1968) controlled "conceptual focus" in a different manner. The subjects read a small passage in which a central element (theme) was described from one of two points of view: the element was elaborated on either as an actor or as an acted upon element. The investigators thereby intended to induce a generalized set to attend either to the agents of events or to the recipients of events. After this treatment the subjects were presented pictures—unrelated to the content of the passage—which they were asked to describe using either an active or a passive sentence. The latencies for active and passive sentences differed between the experimental groups as expected. Those subjects having read the passage with an emphasis on the theme as agent had shorter latencies for actives and longer latencies for passives when compared to subjects who had read the passage with an emphasis on the theme as recipient.

Turner and Rommetveit (1968) used a different technique to manipulate the "focus of attention." Children were shown pictures depicting, for example, a rabbit eating a carrot. The picture was gradually drawn past a window in a cardboard frame. However, either the actor or the acted upon object appeared first. The task of the child was to start describing the picture as soon as possible. The results showed that if the acted upon element appeared first, there was a tendency to use passive constructions, although active constructions generally prevailed. But when the actor was shown first, only active constructions were used.

The above studies attempted to manipulate the subjects' attention by asking appropriate questions (Carroll), by inducing a generalized set (Tannenbaum & Williams), or by presenting sequentially parts of pictures the subjects had to describe (Turner and Rommetveit). The experiments reported by Flores D'Arcais (1973) dealt less with attention and more with perception. While the previous authors attempted to influence subject selection by inducing a set or controlling the sequence of perceptual input, Flores D'Arcais assumed that subject selection in a sentence describing a picture may be controlled by inherent properties of the picture itself—without resorting to extraneous attention control. The author claimed that pictures could be devised that have an internal representation corresponding to the way in which the sentences describing the pictures are organized. In the experiment the subject was shown a picture of a big truck followed by a small car. In his description of the picture, the subject tended to prefer *the big truck* as the subject of his sentence ("The truck is followed by the car" or "The truck precedes the car"), presumably because one of the perceptual elements was "topicalized" by its *size.* Next to size, the left–right position of the elements and the direction of the action were shown to be determinants of "topicalization."

5.3 Concluding Remarks

How does the present approach compare with its predecessors? Previous authors thought of the grammatical subject as a formal *linguistic* category assigned to lexical units in a way that could be influenced by psychological, that is, attentional–perceptual processes.

The present study holds that the problem in question is basically psychological. The subject category is conceived of as part of a *cognitive construction* generated by a speaker who wants to express by linguistic signs what he has in mind. The features of the subject are thus part of the process of active "sentencing" (Osgood, 1975; see also Ertel and Bloemer, 1975).

Nominal seizing and anchoring are contended to be invariant features of the subject. What may vary are its determinants. Probably only two determinant factors are involved, a *dynamism* factor—the phenomenon that has also been called salience, importance, emphasis, center, topic, Polyanna effect[7]—and a *primacy* factor which refers to givenness. Thus, a nominal unit may be seized as a subject because it has already been brought to the stage. For example, as part of a situational context, an animate object A may be perceived as initiating an event as agent and become prominent because of its primitive "dynamism." Also it may be attended to earlier than another animate object B involved in this event. For two reasons, then, A is more likely than B to be seized as the primary reference point. And once A has been selected as the subject its role as reference point is likely to be maintained for subsequent sentences until it is displaced by another nominal unit, which then becomes the new reference point.

If this model is valid it might account for facts that have long since puzzled students of language: The fact that grammatical subjects are typically—but not always—agents; the fact that the subject typically—but not always—represents the given; the fact that the subject typically—but not always—represents the topic (the unit about which the speaker talks) than the comment; the fact that the subject noun typically—but not always—precedes the object noun. According to this model the grammatical subject may have *different* antecedents: one antecedent factor may call for a nominal unit as subject while a rivaling factor would at the same time call for a different nominal unit. The selection of the subject will then depend upon the relative strength of the rivaling factors.

Sentences (28a)—(28e) illustrate the point. Proceeding from Sentence (28a) to (28d) one finds that the factor calling for subject selection in (28a), that is, "dynamism" of the agent, gradually decreases while the primacy factor (knowness) connected with *my friend* gradually becomes dominant. Given finally the context of (28d), a subject selection as in (28e), and consequently a different verb selection, would be preferred to that of (28d).

(28a)   When I returned to the bazaar, a cunning merchant had just sold my friend an expensive watch. (The story may continue: I knew at once that we would have serious money problems for the rest of our tour.)

(28b)   When I returned to the bazaar, a merchant had just sold my friend an expensive watch.

(28c)   When I returned to the bazaar, a merchant had just sold my friend a watch.

(28d)   When I returned to the bazaar, a merchant had just sold my friend a nice souvenir.

---

[7] Osgood's Polyanna process (Boucher & Osgood, 1969) refers primarily to an evaluative salience; dynamism, also Osgood's term, refers to affective potency and activity. Osgood and Richards (1973) extend these types of salience to generalized Positiveness (Yang) and Negativeness (Yin).

(28e)   When I returned to the bazaar, my friend had just bought a nice souvenir (from a merchant).

Examples like these show that none of the antecedent factors is a *necessary* condition for subject choice. But this does not mean that the subject has no invariant feature. If it had none it would in fact remain a mystery, as Chomsky (1965) put it.

The "mystery" of the subject is only one of a great number of problems implicated in the comprehensive programme developed by Osgood in a chapter devoted to the question "Where do sentences come from?" (1971). He was able to give "quite ample reason to believe that many properties of grammar are present in some form in pre-linguistic perceptuo-motor behavior [p. 527]." The present study has tried to add one more argument in support of this psycholinguistic assumption.

POSTSCRIPT

After completion of this chapter the author received a theoretical paper of McWhinney (1975) which is relevant for the present discussion. This author generates a theoretical construct ("logical focus") that is nearly identical to the one elaborated above. The basic difference, however, is that "logical focus," according to McWhinney, is not an invariant feature of a grammatical category, nor is the psychological basis of the grammatical subject discussed. Nevertheless, the conceptual similarity between our "primary reference point," "ego-anchoring activity" on the one hand and "logical focus" on the other, is striking. McWhinney's logical focus is a "reference point for predication"; it "provides a perspective for the interpretation of the sentence"; the speaker "assumes the perspective of the logical focus"; this "is facilitated when the perspective is active, dominant, animate, and potent [p. 21]."

Strangely enough, the author seems to believe that he is dealing with the pragmatic "periphery" of language, whereas from this author's point of view he is concerned with facts and phenomena that are central to syntactic structure.

REFERENCES

Boucher, J., & Osgood, C. E. The Polyanna hypothesis. *Journal of Verbal Learning and Verbal Behavior*, 1969, 8, 1–8.
Carroll, J. B. Process and content in psycholinguistics. In R. Glaser (Ed.), *Current trends in description and analysis of behavior*. Pittsburgh: University of Pittsburgh Press, 1958.
Chomsky, N. *Aspects of a theory of syntax*. Cambridge, Massachusetts: MIT Press, 1965.
Ertel, S. *Psychophonetik. Untersuchungen über Lautsymbolik und Motivation*. Göttingen: Hogrefe, 1969.

Ertel, S. *Words, sentences, and the ego.* Unpublished manuscript. Institute of Psychology, University of Göttingen, 1972.

Ertel, S. Satzsubjekt und Ich-Perspektive. In L. H. Eckensberger and U. S. Eckensberger (Eds.), *Bericht über den 28.Kongress der Deutschen Gesellschaft für Psychologie.* Göttingen: Hogrefe, 1974.

Ertel, S. Gestaltpsychologische Denkmodelle für die Struktur der Sprache. In S. Ertel, L. Kemmler, & M. Stadler (Eds.), *Gestalttheorie in der modernen Psychologie.* Darmstadt: Steinkopf, 1975.

Ertel, S., & Bloemer, W. D. Affirmation and negation as constructive action. *Psychological Research,* 1975, 37, 335–342.

Firbas, J. On defining the theme in functional sentence analysis. *Travaux de Cercle Linguistique de Prague,* 1964, 1, 267–280.

Flores D'Arcais, G. B. *Some perceptual determinants of sentence construction.* Report No. EO36-73. Psychological Institute, University of Leiden, 1973.

French, P. L. *Logical and psycho-logical theories of semantic coding in reasoning.* Unpublished doctoral dissertation, University of Illinois, 1974.

Halliday, M. A. K. Notes on transitivity and theme in English. *Journal of Linguistics,* 1967, 3, 177–274.

Halliday, M. A. K. Language structure and language function. In J. Lyons (Ed.), *New horizons in linguistics.* Harmondsworth: Penguin Books, 1970.

Hockett, C. F. *A course in modern linguistics.* New York: Macmillan, 1958.

Johnson-Laird, P. N. The choice of the passive voice in a communicative task. *British Journal of Psychology,* 1968, 59, 7–15.

Lyons, J. *Introduction to theoretical linguistics.* Cambridge, England: Cambridge University Press, 1968.

Mathesius, V. Zur Satzperspektive im modernen Englisch. *Archiv für das Studium der neueren Sprachen,* 1929, 155, 202–210.

McWhinney, B. *A psycholinguistic approach to pragmatic focussing.* Manuscript submitted for publication, 1975.

Miller, G. A., Galanter, E., & Pribram, K. H. *Plans and the structure of behavior.* New York: Holt, 1960.

Osgood, C. E. Where do sentences come from? In D. D. Steinberg & L. A. Jakobovits (Eds.), *Semantics: An interdisciplinary reader in philosophy, linguistics, and psychology.* London: Cambridge University Press, 1971.

Osgood, C. E. *Focus on meaning.* Psycholinguistic Papers, Vol. 3: Cognizing, and Sentencing. Book in preparation, 1975.

Osgood, C. E., & Richards, M. M. From Yang and Yin to *and* or *but. Language,* 1973, 49, 380–412.

Osgood, C. E., Suci, G. J., & Tannenbaum, P. H. *The measurement of meaning.* Urbana, Illinois: University of Illinois Press, 1957.

Tannenbaum, P. H., & Williams, F. Generation of active and passive sentences as a function of subject and object focus. *Journal of Verbal Learning and Verbal Behavior,* 1968, 7, 246–250.

Turner, E. A., & Rommetveit, R. Focus of attention in recall of active and passive sentences. *Journal of Verbal Learning and Verbal Behavior,* 1968, 7, 543–548.

8

Components of a Production Model

I. M. Schlesinger

Hebrew University, Jerusalem
and
Israel Institute of Applied Social Research

There are several ways to approach the construction of a production model. One might take generative grammar as one's starting point, assume that it has been internalized by the speaker, and wonder what kind of mechanism is required to make use of this internalized knowledge in speaking and comprehending speech. Another approach is to concentrate on writing computer programs that can analyze or produce at least a small subset of natural language sentences. It is also possible to be skeptical regarding both these approaches. As for generative grammar, it is becoming more and more clear that its relation to the speaker–hearer's performance is much less straightforward than was once fondly hoped. Current formulations of generative grammar have turned out to not adequately predict the complexity of processing sentences. Moreover, there are a priori reasons why the rules according to which a performance model operates are not likely to be identical to those formulated by the linguist (Fodor, 1971; Watt, 1970). One may have similar misgivings regarding attempts to model the human speaker by computer programs. The routines which seem most appropriate for the computer may turn out to differ from the processes occurring in the speaker–hearer, who after all operates under quite different constraints and has different resources at his disposal (see, e.g., Keyser & Petrick, 1967). While admitting that work in artificial intelligence may in principle lead to a valid model, one may feel that recent attempts at simulation were premature.

Where does this skepticism lead to? Unless he is willing to abandon all attempts at model building, the skeptic is left with no choice but to lean back and do some hard thinking on his own. Though he will not rely too much on work in linguistics and in programming, he will not be left high and dry. The findings of current linguistic theory are such that no psycholinguist, skeptic or otherwise, can afford to disregard them. Computer simulation will have a place in testing a theory of production and in further refining it. But with linguistics at the back of his mind and with the prospect of simulation in front of him, our theorist will have to concern himself very seriously with the little that is known about human processing of language and the little that one may plausibly assume about it. He will gain perspective by considering not only normal processing but also cases where something goes wrong, as, for example, in speech errors. And, finally, he has an additional set of considerations to guide him: how does the child learn to be an adult user of language?

In this chapter I present a concise presentation of a model that resulted from a recent attempt to follow such an approach (see Schlesinger, in press, for a fuller treatment). It is not a fully spelled out theory and for the most part makes few predictions which, if tested, would constitute a serious corroboration of the model. It is a sketch with the details remaining to be filled in, but it is hoped that it will be helpful in future work.

I. INPUT MARKERS

My description of the production model begins with the component containing the semantic representation underlying the utterance. The semantic representation is formalized as an *input marker*, or *I-marker* for short. The latter is the input to *realization rules*, which map it into the utterance.

The I-marker is an expression consisting of elements and relations between them. Consider the sentence

(1)   Mary had a little lamb.

Mary is the possessor of the lamb, and "little" is an attribute of the lamb. (Of interest here are not the relations between the entities denoted by the words, nor the relations between the words themselves, but rather the relations in the I-marker.) The I-marker underlying (1) may be presented, with some simplification, as

(2)   (POSSESSOR–POSSESSED Mary, (ATTRIBUTE little, lamb)).

Here POSSESSOR–POSSESSED is a relation with two arguments. The second argument (the "possessed") is itself a relation with two arguments. An embedded expression like (ATTRIBUTE little, lamb) in (2) may be called *I-marker constituent*. Realization rules convert the I-marker (2) into the utterance (1).

Another example of an I-marker, again with some simplification, would be

(3)   (GOAL-ACTION log, (INSTRUMENT-ACTION axe, cut)).

Into which sentence can this I-marker be converted? Is the sentence to be in the past tense, or in the present tense? Is it *the* log or just *a* log which is (or was, or will be) cut? Here it becomes apparent what the simplification consists of. Tense, definiteness, and several other aspects of verbs and of nouns must also figure in the I-marker. They are represented there by relations having a single argument instead of the two-argument relations in (2) and (3). For example,

(4)   (GOAL-ACTION (PLURALITY log), (FUTURE cut)).

PLURALITY is a one-argument relation, and so is FUTURE. This I-marker may be realized as follows (assuming that, unless indicated otherwise, in the I-marker, the indefinite is always intended):

(5)   Logs will be cut.

To summarize, I-marker relations have the form of either (6) or (7),

(6) $(R\ a,\ b)$
(7) $(R\ a)$

where R stands for any relations and a and b are variables substitutable by elements or by other relations. Relations can be recursively embedded within each other, for example,

(8) $(R_i\ (R_j\ a,\ (R_k\ (R_l\ a,\ b), R_m\ a)),\ b)$

In principle there may also be relations with more than two arguments. In the following we will simply speak of "relations" irrespective of the number of their arguments.

Realization rules, the nature of which will be discussed in Section IV, convert I-markers into utterances. To a given I-marker different realization rules may be applicable. Thus, an I-marker may be realized as (1) by one set of realization rules, and as (9) by a different set, the choice between rules being determined by various considerations.

(9)   It is Mary who had a little lamb.

The elements between which I-marker relations hold are not words. Words appear in utterances, and the I-marker contains the concepts which lie "behind" words and are ultimately expressed by them. Often we begin uttering a sentence without being clear about the exact words to use for naming the concept we have in mind. What is known about the nature of these concepts? Attempts have been made recently to treat words, or what they denote, formally by decomposing them into semantic features (e.g., Katz, 1972). Evaluations of these attempts vary from regarding them as insufficient to viewing them as simply misguided (cf., e.g., Lyons, 1968, paragraph 10.5, for a discussion). In the present context it seems preferable to view these concepts as given and to consider only how they operate in the production model. So as to eschew a term previously used in many contexts and with many quite different meanings we shall call the concepts in I-markers *protoverbal elements,* a term which indicates the aspect which is relevant here, namely, that they are the precursors of words. Realization of the I-marker involves also *lexicalization,* that is, the substitution of appropriate words for protoverbal elements (see Section IV.D). In the case of synonyms two or more lexicalizations of the same protoverbal element are possible.

To return to the relations appearing in I-markers, the above examples suggest that these are of the kind appearing in semantically based grammars (e.g., Fillmore, 1968). No detailed proposal for the relations appearing in I-markers given in this chapter should be regarded as more than tentative. As a general principle it may be stated that the list of I-marker relations should include those and only those relations that are needed if the system of realization rules is to produce every possible utterance in the language. In other words, I-markers and realization rules should be investigated as parts of an interdependent system.

Here the following objection might be raised. After all, notions like "goal," "instrument," and "attribute," which figure in the above examples, seem to relate to the way we perceive the world. So why should a theory of production take its lead from the "grammar" of realization rules and not from Cognitive Psychology? The answer is that it seems to be by no means obvious that such notions figure in our cognitions independently of language. The production process does not start with the I-marker, but rather at a level beyond it: that of *cognitive structures.* The cognitive structure of the speaker at the time of the speech act leads to the formation of an I-marker. The latter is therefore on the one hand the *in*put to realization rules, and on the other hand an *in*termediary between cognitive structures and utterances.

I-markers, then, are theoretical constructs and do not correspond simply to such notions as "message," "meaning," or "intention." These pretheoretical notions are not contained in any one component of the model but rather are distributed between the I-marker component, the cognitive structure component (see the next section), and a third component: that of *communicative considerations,* which determines the choice between realization rules and about which more will be said in Section III. Only by considering all three components will the nature of I-markers become clear.

II.   COGNITIVE STRUCTURES

An utterance originates in the cognitive structure of a speaker on the occasion of speaking. This cognitive structure is prelinguistic and directs the formation of an I-marker. The present section shows what motivates this differentiation between two levels underlying the utterance and discusses the nature of cognitive structures.

A. Selection of I-Markers

Suppose we intend to report on an event we have just seen happening. It will usually be quite impossible to describe the event in all its details as we remember it, nor will we try to do so. Instead, a selection will have to be made regarding what to include in the description and what may be left unsaid. At the time of speaking, or slightly prior to it, there will thus be more in the cognitive structure than in the I-marker. The same holds true when we describe an object, and in fact in many, perhaps most, cases in which statements are made.

What are the determinants of selection? Evidently there are details of an event or an object which seem more marginal and less important relative to others; this will of course depend largely on the context in which the utterance is made. Olson (1970) has shown that the choice of an attribute by which we refer to an object depends on the set of objects from which it is to be distinguished. Thus, if these objects differ in color, the intended object may be referred to by its color, whereas its shape will be mentioned if it is singled out from like-colored objects differing in shape. Individual variations in describing events were revealed in an informal experiment carried out by Osgood (1971), who asked subjects to describe simple events like a ball rolling on the table and hitting a larger ball of a different color. Some subjects would mention size in their description and others only color; and while some would mention in their description that the ball was rolling, others might just report on the ball hitting the other ball, apparently taking it for granted that the ball had been rolling before hitting the other one. Evidently, people differ in the degree to which they want to be specific in a given situation.

The speaker's cognitive structure, then, will generally contain more than the I-marker which underlies his utterance. This raises the question whether the I-marker should be viewed simply as a proper part of the "material" which appears in the cognitive structure. In other words, are cognitive structures constituted of the same relations and elements as I-markers, or are they structurally different? This problem will be dealt with in the following sections, but first some additional reasons will be discussed for postulating a level of cognitive structures as distinct from the I-marker level.

B. Changes of Mind and Speech Errors

Frequently we have only a very general idea of what we are going to say and make up our minds about details as we are talking. This may lead to hesitation in speaking, but more often it may go unnoticed. A subject of Osgood's experiment mentioned in the preceding section may have decided in the course of making the utterance to refer to the size of the rolling ball or to omit this detail. Further, he may have changed his mind in the course of talking as to whether size should be mentioned. His cognitive structure did not change; rather, a different selection was decided on and this resulted in another I-marker.

Sometimes the change of mind affects the way things are said. When the originally intended utterance and the one finally emitted are synonymous, the change of mind involves merely a choice of different realization rules for the I-marker. This is the situation described in Fig. 1. However, when nonsynony-

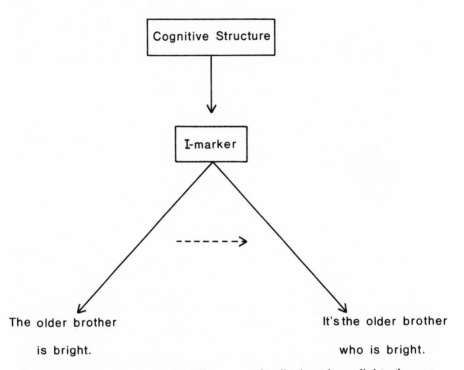

FIG. 1   A change of mind involving different sets of realization rules applied to the same I-Marker.

mous utterances are involved, there must have been a change in I-marker. If I am about to say about one of two brothers that he is stupid, and then attenuate this to the statement that he is not quite as bright as his older brother, then I have obviously switched to a different I-marker; see Figure 2. But the cognitive structure which led to the utterance has probably not changed.

Different kinds of speech errors have been described in the literature and these cannot be discussed in detail here. For the present issue it is sufficient to point out that some types of errors, such as sound exchanges (e.g., *flay the pictor;* Fromkin, 1971), are merely due to faulty operation of realization rules, whereas others involve in addition a competition between I-markers. Thus, the two words *verge* and *fringe* are not synonymous; they are lexicalizations of different protoverbal elements (compare Section I). The following self-correction (quoted in Garrett, 1975) must therefore have been due to the intrusion of a slightly different I-marker:

(10)   I'm chronically on the fringe... on the verge of making a break.

But no change takes place in the message to be conveyed, and hence both I-markers involved here represent the same cognitive structure.

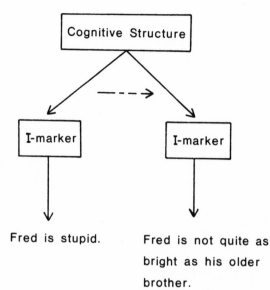

FIG. 2   A change of mind involving two different I-markers.

In (10) competition between I-markers led to uttering a word, that was subsequently replaced by another one. In other cases "bottlenecks" occur:

(11)   I don't want to intervere.

Evidently, *interfere* and *intervene* are competing here, resulting in both words being blended. Each of these words may have been fairly appropriate in the situation in which (11) was uttered, but note that they are not synonymous: they belong to different protoverbal elements. This situation is as described in Fig. 3.

Closely allied to the above treatment of changes of I-markers is the issue of paraphrases which will be taken up in the next section.

C. Paraphrases

Paraphrases have motivated many formulations of rules in transformational grammar. It has been assumed that if different sentences have the same meaning they must have the same deep structure. This is feasible as long as a certain regularity is exhibited by the paraphrases in question. Thus, for any sentence NP_i *likes* NP_j there is a synonymous sentence NP_j *pleases* NP_i (and a similar relationship holds for *buy* and *sell*), and this may be taken by some linguists as evidence that these sentences have the same deep structure. Often however, no such regularity is to be found and the paraphrastic relationship is limited instead

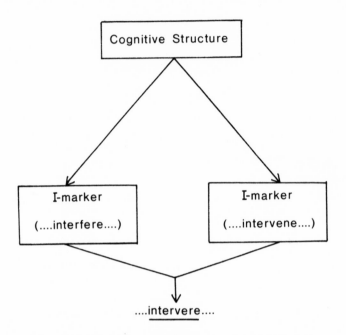

FIG. 3   A blend of two words belonging to different I-markers.

to a single type of sentence pair. For instance, sentence (12) means the same as (13), but it seems that there are no other verbs besides *rain, hail,* and *snow* for which such paraphrases can be constructed.

(12)   Rain is falling.
(13)   It is raining.

Postulating identical deep structures for (12) and (13) would necessitate introducing transformational rules that are valid only for these few particular words. It seems preferable therefore to view these sentences as coextensive without insisting that they have the same deep structure (cf. Chafe, 1970, pp. 88–90).

To return to our production model, in certain situations both (12) and (13) seem to be appropriate; a cognitive structure which led to uttering the one could equally well have led to uttering the other. But, on pain of introducing a great number of ad hoc realization rules for this and similar cases, we must conclude that these two utterances result from different I-markers. We see again, as in the preceding section, that one cognitive structure may be associated with different I-markers (cf. Fig. 2).

A similar argument shows that different I-markers must underlie any two utterances which mean the same to the interlocutors, not because of any linguistic regularity but by dint of factual knowledge, for example,

(14)   Look at that bird flying with one of its wings broken!
(15)   Look at that bird flying with one whole wing!

Apart from its slight awkwardness there is nothing in (15) that bars its being said in the situation which is appropriate for saying (14); hence identical cognitive structures may be involved. Note, however, what would follow if we were to assume also that the same I-marker is involved in (14) and (15). Then the two sets of realization rules which convert this I-marker into (14) and (15) should also be applicable when "airplane" is substituted for "bird" in the I-marker. But the utterances which would result are not interchangeable, because four-winged planes may have been referred to. Let us assume for the sake of the argument that the realization rules leading to (14) could be applied to an I-marker of a quite similar structure, resulting in

(16)   Look at that horse running with one of its legs broken!

When the realization rules resulting in (15) are applied to this I-marker, we get

(17)   Look at that horse running with one whole leg!

But (16) and (17) will obviously not be interchangeable when referring to the same horse, and therefore they cannot have the same I-marker underlying them. The only way out of this contradiction would be to limit those realization rules required for (14) and (15) to birds' wings, but then we would have to introduce different rules for wings of various types of planes, for horses' legs (when *three whole legs* is substituted in (17), the sentence means the same as (16)), as well as for legs of cows, bees, and centipedes. The system of realization rules would thus have to include an indefinitely large number of parallel rules, and even these would do justice only to the coextensiveness of sentences like (14) and (15).

And it is not only the knowledge of the world shared by the speakers of the language that would have to be systematized in this manner. In a given situation a speaker may have the choice of different utterances, which, though they certainly may not mean the same, convey the same message to the hearer. Suppose I say to someone that only one of the engines of the airplane is still working. If he knows what particular plane I am talking about—but only then—I might say instead that three of its engines have stopped. To accommodate this within the system of realization rules, one would have to incorporate into it information specific to the situation and the speaker's assumptions about what the hearer knows.

It appears therefore that such fact-dependent and situation-dependent "paraphrases" should not be accorded identical I-markers. Rather, given a certain cognitive structure, there may be a choice between different I-markers [e.g., between (14) and (15)]. This means that the production mechanism requires a two-stage rule system: from cognitive structures to I-markers and from

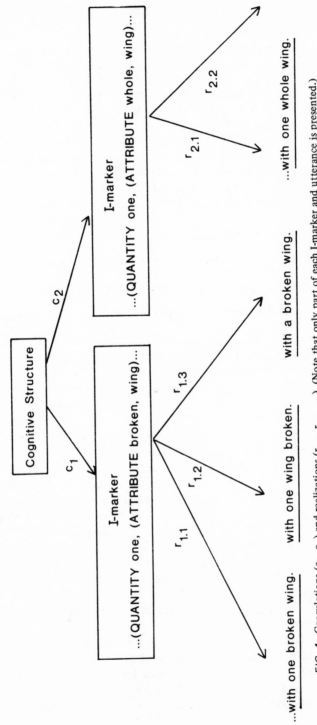

FIG. 4 Coagulations (c_1, c_2) and realizations ($r_{1.1}$, $r_{1.2}$ . . .). (Note that only part of each I-marker and utterance is presented.)

I-markers to utterances.[1] Cognitive structures have to be *coagulated* into I-markers, and I-markers have to be realized as utterances. The mapping of cognitive structures into I-markers is one-to-many, just as the mapping of I-markers into utterances is one-to-many; compare Fig. 4. A direct, one-stage mapping into utterances is not feasible because, as shown above, it would entail an endless duplication of rules so as to take into account the nature of the world we live in, as well as indefinitely many situationally contingent facts. A reasonably limited "grammar" of rules is possible only for the mapping of I-markers into utterances, and only such a limited rule system can be learned.

Admittedly, such a proposal only pushes the problem one step further back. We still do not know how to formulate those rules by which cognitive structures are coagulated into I-markers. The diversity of factual knowledge and situational factors which these rules would have to take into account makes such a formulation appear a formidable task. But at any rate the conclusion arrived at above that there can be no one-stage rules leading from cognitive structures to utterances is inescapable. In other words, one level of "deep" structure is not enough.

So far there is very little that can be said with any degree of certainty about cognitive structures, and only some very schematic remarks seem to be justified about the nature of these structures. First, there is no a priori reason why cognitive structures should involve the same elements and relations as those which appear in I-markers. Introspectively, our attempts at communication seem to be preceded by something much vaguer and more amorphous than the clearly defined relations and elements that are assumed to figure in I-markers (hence the term "coagulation"). Another claim that can be made about cognitive structures is that they must be of a form sufficiently general to permit a given cognitive structure to coagulate into different paraphrastic I-markers [cf. (14) and (15)]. This suggests that cognitive structures are organized in a way which differs from the organization of I-markers. It seems that no attention has been paid to these considerations by those researchers who have attempted to describe the stuff of which our cognitions are made.

A few experimental studies have been carried out which bear on the determinants of choice between coagulations. Wason (1965) and Greene (1970a, b) have investigated the preference for positive versus negative formulations of the same message content, and have shown that the negative form is used to correct a mistaken expectancy or to state something in relation to a prior assertion or unstated presupposition. A production model must include the components that make the choice between alternative coagulations on the basis of such considerations. I shall call this component *I-marker selector.*

The conclusion that there is a prelinguistic level distinct from the I-marker

---

[1] Strictly speaking, more than two stages, if we take into account the successive stages of realization rules; compare Section IV.D.

level is arrived at not only by considering phenomena like changes of mind, speech errors, and paraphrases. It also accords with our experience of groping for the expression of thoughts which seem quite clear to us but difficult to convey to others. Frequently it is not a single word we are looking for or a particular syntactic construction that causes trouble, that is, the difficulty does not seem to lie with the application of the realization rules. Rather, we are muddled by the more general problem of how the thought should be formulated, that is, how to coagulate. That this should happen frequently is to be expected under the assumption that the form of cognitive structures differs from that of I-markers.

D. Cross-Linguistic Comparisons

One of the ways in which cognitive structures apparently differ from I-markers is that the former include a much vaster array of relations. There seems to be no reason why our thinking should be limited to the list of relations that appear in the grammar of our language. There is much plausibility to the opposite claim that any two events or situations are perceived of in terms of different relations. This vast number of possible relations perceived in the world is categorized into a reasonably small number of classes, and it is these which figure in I-markers. Such categorization is absolutely necessary, because the number of realization rules operating on I-marker relations must be kept within reasonable limits. Too large a number of relations would make the system of realization rules too complicated to learn (cf., also, Schlesinger, 1974).

Support for this view comes from the many studies that have shown a great divergence between languages of the world in regard to the relations they express. Take, for example, various aspects of the verb. Outside the Indo-European family one finds that the verb may be inflected in various languages to express repetition and duration of the action, an "inferential" modality to refer to nonwitnessed events (the latter has been reported, from first-hand experience, by Slobin (in press), and many others as well). Primitive languages, as Jespersen (1964, p. 427) has remarked, may be "capable of expressing a multiplicity of *nuances* which in other languages must be expressed by clumsy circumlocutions." On the other hand, some notions which appear in Indo-European are not represented in the grammar of certain other languages. Speakers of many languages do not express temporal notions, which are realized in English and other languages by tense. And Cassirer (1953, p. 235) reports that "a great number of languages lack forms by which to designate the antithesis between singular and plural."

How are these differences to be accounted for? One certainly can not claim that speakers of different languages are limited in their thinking to certain relations. No empirical evidence has been forthcoming for such an extreme version of linguistic determinism, which also seems to be utterly implausible. The speakers of a language that does not mark nouns for number are evidently quite aware of the distinction between one and many of the same thing. Similarly, deaf people in Israel, communicating in a sign language that makes no distinction between the agent and goal of an action, are not thereby befuddled in their interpretation of everyday events: they are quite well aware of who does what to whom (Schlesinger, 1971a). The differences between languages, then, can not all be explained by differences in the cognitive structures of their speakers. So how should these divergencies be described in theoretical terms?

One possible answer to this question would be that languages differ only in their systems of realization rules, whereas the I-marker relations are universal. When someone intends to communicate about an event or a state of affairs in a given situation, his I-markers will be of a particular form, whatever the language he speaks; that is, it will include any relation which appears in any language of the world (number, as well as temporal and every other aspect of the action expressible in the grammar of any language, etc.). The realization rules of his language, however, operate only on a subset of these relations, and relations not included in this subset are left unexpressed. The differences between languages, accordingly, are differences in the subsets of linguistically expressed relations.

It seems preferable, however, to locate these crosslinguistic differences in the I-markers themselves. Only that subset of relations which is operated on by realization rules appears in the I-markers of a given language. Other relations may figure in the speakers' cognitive structures but not in their I-markers. Remember that the motivation for introducing an I-marker component is to provide an input to the "grammatical" mechanism of realization rules. There is thus no point in transporting the relations from cognitive structures into I-markers unless they are operated on by realization rules.

Support for this solution comes from the fact that languages not only differ in the subset of relations expressed by their respective grammars, but also in the way a given event is coded: speakers of different languages may apparently select different relations in referring to a given situation. The cognitive structures of the English and of the Nootka speakers are probably similar when it comes to describing, for example, a boat grounded on the beach. However, the Nootka speaker says something to the effect of "it is on the beach moving canoewise" (Carroll, 1956, p. 236). Despite his way of speaking, one cannot deny that the Nootka speaker recognizes the canoe as being an object (unless one is hopelessly addicted to an extreme form of Whorfianism). The Nootka speaker differs from the English speaker in the way he coagulates the cognitive structure pertaining to this event. Another example comes from Japanese. The Japanese coagulate their experience of seeing a tree in a manner differing from that of the English speaker: for them seeing resides in the thing seen (Weisgerber, 1962, p. 311).

It is proposed, then, that I-markers are language specific, whereas cognitive structures are largely universal. (Whether one should accept a weak version of linguistic relativity admitting some predisposing effect of language on cognitive structures, need not concern us here.) I-markers are language specific not only in regard to relations but also in regard to protoverbal elements. It is well known that words of different languages slice up reality in different ways. While in English the words referring to different types of "use" include, *use, employ, utilize,* and *avail oneself of,* quite different conceptual distinctions are made in German, namely (inter alia): *verwenden,* for use of raw materials (like flour for baking); *gebrauchen,* for use of objects, usually those belonging to the speaker (e.g., use of soap and brush for washing); *benutzen,* for the use of the resources of others (e.g., use of the street or the bus); and *einsetzen* for use of one's own resources to attain one's aims (Weisgerber, 1962, pp. 190–191).

The fact that a given language has no grammatical means for expressing a certain relation or no words for referring to a certain concept of course does not mean that the speaker of the language is doomed to silence as far as these notions are concerned. If no word is available, he can employ various ways of circumlocution. The lack of a realization rule for a certain relation may result either in his omitting mention of this relation (e.g., in speaking English we often do not make it explicit whether an event was witnessed or not) or else he may add a phrase to indicate the relation intended (e.g., "I heard that . . . ," and a similar phrase for the "inferential"). Often there are standard ways of expressing such notions. For instance, in Lithuanian one can if one chooses to, and occasionally one does, use the word for "this" to do the job of the definite article, which is lacking in that language. In general, it seems true that anything that can be said in one language can be expressed in any other language, with the possible exception of the finest nuances and of emotional effects and associations aroused. The question is only what price has to be paid in terms of length of the expression and its cumbersomeness. This of course is another way of saying that speakers of different languages do not differ in their cognitive structures so much as in their I-markers.

E. Semantic Assimilation

All the multifarious connections perceived in reality which can appear in cognitive structures are categorized into a reasonably short list of I-marker relations. As pointed out in Section II.D, without such a categorization the system of realization rules would be so complicated as to be quite unmanageable for any speaker. One of the ways in which this categorization proceeds is to collapse two cognitively distinct relations into one on the basis of some similarity between them. John's car belongs to him and John's nose also "belongs" to him, but in a different sense. Yet for all this, both alienable and inalienable possession are treated in English (and many other languages) in the same way, that is, they belong to the same I-marker relation and consequently the same realization rules apply to them. The child first tends to use a certain construction (e.g., *daddy chair*) for alienable possession and even this only in a certain context, and only gradually does he extend the use of the same construction to other kinds of possession (Edwards, in press). The adult speaker may or may not be conscious of the fact that two distinguishable notions are merged in his language. I shall call this merging of relations *semantic assimilation.*

This process seems to be quite common in the languages of the world. The notion of an instrument, for instance, seems to be an easy one to apprehend, and there appears to be no reason why it should be confused with others. But many languages express the instrument via a different I-marker relation: by the locative marker in Japanese, Finnish, and Semitic languages, and by the comitative marker in English (*with*) and Malay (Brown, 1973; Hetzron, 1974). In English there is also the option to treat the instrument as if it were an agent:

(18)   The axe cut logs.

That this is not merely a different surface realization for an underlying instrumental relation has been shown elsewhere (Schlesinger, in press). The evidence rests mainly on the fact that a construction like (18) is unacceptable for other than rather routine actions; for instance, the following sounds odd:

(19)   *The chisel carved the statue.

The reason is that in (18) the instrument can be treated as if it were an agent, whereas such a metaphor jars our sensibility when a more creative action is referred to, as in (19). It must be concluded, therefore, that in cognitive structure the instrument may be distinct from the agent, but in the I-marker it often is assimilated to the agent (in many English sentences) or to other relations (in other languages).

Note that one consequence of postulating a semantic assimilation process is that I-markers are much closer to surface structures than are the underlying structures of certain semantically based linguistic theories. In Fillmore's case grammar it is the "instrumental" case which underlies (18), and the "subject" position of *axe* is a surface phenomenon. By contrast, according to the present model, the agent in the I-marker of (18) is closer to the surface than Fillmore's "instrument." Being closer to the surface involves a simplification of realization rules. This is one of the advantages of introducing I-markers as an intermediate level between cognitive structures and the surface.

The principle of semantic assimilation is apparently a much more pervasive one than the above examples seem to indicate. As stated, the relations in cognitive structures are indefinitely many, and they have to be somehow classified into a small number of categories: the I-marker relations. Such a classification will be guided of course by similarity perceived between the relations in cognitive structures, but similarity is multidimensional and in itself is not sufficient to cause classification to occur. A case can be made for the claim that relations in cognitive structures are uncategorized. Instead, each occurrence of a situation or an event is perceived in a unique way and involves relations unique to this occurrence: categorization of these relations takes place mainly in the I-marker, when one intends to talk (to others or to oneself); see Schlesinger (in press) for a detailed argument to this effect.

III. COMMUNICATIVE CONSIDERATIONS

There will usually be several different ways of expressing a given I-marker. Thus the following are alternative expressions of what is presumably the same I-marker, differing in respect to focus and emphasis:

(20)   The logs were cut by the axe.
(21)   It is the logs that were cut by the axe.
(22)   The axe cut the logs.
(23)   It is the axe that cut the logs.
(24)   It is the logs that the axe cut.

There are other alternatives, too, differing in stress and intonation contour from the above, that are also effected by realization rules.

A production model must include a component of *communicative considerations* that chooses between these different realizations. This component bases its decision on factors such as the required emphasis and focus, the intended presuppositions, and stylistic considerations, like avoidance of monotony and euphony. Further, it may opt for a colloquial or a formal "level" of style. The component chooses not only among possible ways of expressing relations, but also among alternative lexical items. Thus, it decides whether to speak in a polite or vulgar manner, to use an easy or a more difficult vocabulary, etc. A more detailed discussion of these factors is to be found in Schlesinger (in press).

This component operates on realization rules in the following manner. Each communicative consideration has a *shunting marker* associated with it. The same shunting marker tags the realization rules whose application conforms to the communicative consideration in question. In this manner a communicative consideration selects among the available realization rules those which are appropriate. For instance, if for a given speech act there is a communicative consideration which demands that the goal term be in focus, the shunting marker will select those realization rules that put the goal term first. There may be several sets of such realization rules, as shown in (20), (21), and (24) above, and the choice among these will be made on the basis of additional communicative considerations. Sentences (22) and (23), on the other hand, will result from a different shunting marker.

There may of course also be instances when the speaker applies no specific communicative considerations (i.e., it does not matter to him which of two alternatives is chosen). In these cases the realization rule which happens to have the greatest response strength at the moment will be applied. Often this will be that rule which is used more frequently.

The form of the utterance, then, is determined jointly by the I-marker and communicative considerations, with the latter determining how the former is to be realized. The question may be raised now how these two components divide between them the material to be converted into the utterance. The proposal made elsewhere (Schlesinger, in press) is that the I-marker contains only the "propositional content" of the utterance. Its "illocutionary force"—that is, whether the speaker intends to assert or to promise, or even whether he asks a question or makes a statement—is contained in the component of communicative considerations, and so are considerations as to style, presupposition, and other factors mentioned above. It should be noted, however, that not everything that might be called "communicative consideration" in the intuitive sense of the term belongs in this component: some such considerations may affect the coagulation of a particular I-marker and hence belong in the I-marker selector (Section II.C).

The components of the proposed model are presented schematically in Fig. 5. There are two rule systems: coagulation rules which convert cognitive structures into I-markers and about which very little is known (see Section II.C) and realization rules converting I-markers into utterances, which will be discussed in the following section.

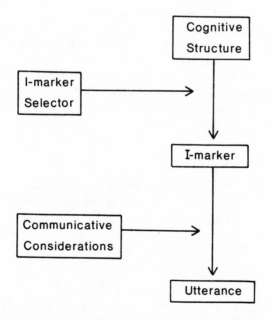

FIG. 5 Components of the production model.

IV. REALIZATION RULES

A. Types of Realization Rules

Our final sections deal with the question of what operations have to be performed on the I-marker in order to convert it into an utterance, or in other words, what realization rules have to be applied. In the most general terms one might say that realization rules select an appropriate linguistic expression for

1. the relations in the I-marker, and
2. the protoverbal elements in the I-marker
3. in accordance with the communicative considerations of the speaker.

To do so they must achieve at least the following:

(a) find an appropriate lexical item for each protoverbal element;
(b) accord a grammatical category to each protoverbal element;
(c) assign a relative position to each protoverbal element;
(d) introduce inflectional affixes and grammatical formatives (function words);
(e) impose an appropriate intonation contour;
(f) convert the string obtained by the operation of (a)–(d) into proper phonological form.

After this, the articulatory apparatus can take over.

The conversion of protoverbal elements into words, (a), is called *lexicalization*. This is performed by means of a *lexicon* which lists lexical items for each protoverbal element. Rules which perform operations (b)–(d) will be called *relation rules*. (d) is in part also achieved by *concord rules*, which take care of grammatical agreement and are applied after relation rules. *Intonation rules* are responsible for (e). Last to operate are *phonological rules*, which prepare the output of the above rules for articulation, (f).

B. The Form of Relation Rules

The following are examples of relation rules required in the production of simple active declarative sentences. For other sentence structures, different relation rules will be required. The choice between the alternative sets of rules is made by the component of communicative considerations by means of shunting markers (Section III).

(25)   GOAL–ACTION $a, b \rightarrow (\text{GOAL } b^V + a^N)^V$
(26)   AGENT–ACTION $a, b \rightarrow (\text{AGENT } a^N + b^V)^S$
(27)   INSTRUMENT–ACTION $a, b \rightarrow (\text{INST } b^V + \text{with} + a^N)^V$
(28)   POSSESSOR–POSSESSED $a, b \rightarrow (\text{POSS } a^N + s + b^N)^N$

(29)   POSSESSOR–POSSESSED a, $b \rightarrow$ (POSS b^N + of + a^N)^N

(30)   PLURALITY $a \rightarrow$ (PLUR a^N + s)^N

In each formula the left-hand side presents a relation which may appear in an I-marker (cf. Section I). The arrow stands for "is realized as" and the expression to the right of the arrow is the *realizate*. The latter contains the information specified under (b), (c), and (d) in the preceding section. Specifically, relation rules achieve the following:

1. They supply a grammatical category for each element of the relation. For instance, in (25) the first argument of the GOAL–ACTION relation—that is, the "goal"—is marked as a noun by the superscript N, and the second argument as a verb by the superscript V.

2. In addition to rule 1, relation rules assign a category marker for each realizate as a whole. For instance, in (25) the realizate is marked V, which means that it functions as a verb in the context of other relation rules. This is necessary for the operation of these rules, as will be seen below. The superscript S in (26) means, of course, "sentence."

3. Relative position is assigned to the two (or more) arguments. Thus, in (25), the second argument precedes the first (and this results in a realizate *cuts logs*, for instance). The plus sign is used to indicate relative position; note that the expression left of the arrow contains commas and not plus signs.

4. Affixes are introduced, as in (28) and (30). These are in roman type here to distinguish them from the variables a and b.

5. Function words are introduced, as in (27) and (29) (also in roman type).

The information as to the relation realized is retained in the realizate for reasons that will become clear below when we discuss how these rules operate.

Note that (25)–(29) are rules for two-argument relations, and (30) is a rule for a one-argument relation. Formulas (28) and (29) are examples of two alternative rules applying to the same relation.

The above rules are, of course, only appropriate for the production of English sentences. Relation rules of other languages may differ considerably from these. In uninflected languages relation rules introduce affixes—compare (30)—and, possibly, do not assign a relative position.

The relation rules presented here differ from the transformational rules in current versions of generative grammar in various ways. One crucial difference worth considering here is that transformations apply to underlying structures as a whole, whereas relation rules apply to individual relations. The latter form of rule seems to be more appropriate for a performance model. A speaker does not have to plan a whole sentence ahead, but can process it as he talks. Often he changes his mind in midspeech. This would present difficulties for an account based on rules converting an I-marker as a whole into a complete utterance. It is suggested therefore that relation rules apply to smaller sections of the I-marker;

compare (25)–(30). A further reason for having rules of this form is that the rules which figure in a comprehension model are best conceived of as the inverse of realization rules, so as to avoid the necessity of learning two entirely different sets of rules. Now, comprehension requires that the input to the rules should not be the utterance as a whole but a smaller segment of it (Schlesinger, in press), and consequently relation rules should convert segments of the I-marker into utterance segments.

So that the production process does not run into difficulties, relation rules should not operate independently of each other. A given realization of a relation may often be admissible only within a certain sentence structure; that is, it may be dependent on the application of other realization rules. There are two mechanisms that take care of this problem. First, communicative considerations select a subset of relation rules which "go together." Thus, if these considerations require that the utterance be a simple active sentence, they select (25) and (26), whereas if it is to be a passive sentence, they select two different rules: the agent term in the passive sentence does not precede the action term, as in (26), but rather succeeds it and is introduced by *by*, and—unlike (25)–the goal term preceds the action term. Second, as shown in the following section, the category markers applying to whole realizates prevent certain faulty constructions.

C. The Operation of Relation Rules

To illustrate how relation rules of the form specified in the preceding section operate, let us take the following I-marker, simplified for convenience of exposition.

(31)   (AGENT-ACTION *David*, (INSTRUMENT-ACTION (POSSESSOR-
POSSESSED *Robin, brush*), *paint*))

The simplification consists in the omission of, inter alia, the time the action took place and other aspects of the action. Thus, either (32) or a similar sentence in a different tense may be the result of realizing the full I-marker.

(32)   David was painting with Robin's brush.

Other sentences (for example, the passive form) are also possible realizations; but for the purpose of this example we assume that the communicative consider-ations component has selected those relation rules that result in (32). The appropriate relation rules are given as (25)–(30) in Section IV.B. Comparing these with (31) we find that only (26), (27), and (28) have to be applied. (As an alternative to (28), (29) would have been possible, but the construction *the brush of Robin* is awkward; so let us assume that the communicative considera-tions component has selected (28).) In which sequence do we apply these three rules? Let us try the INSTRUMENT–ACTION relation first:

Step 1. I-marker relation realized: INSTRUMENT–ACTION

Result of applying relation rule (27) to I-marker (31):

(AGENT–ACTION *David*, (INST *paint*^{V} + with + (POSSESSOR–POSSESSED *Robin*, *brush*)^N)^V)

Note that in this step only part of the I-marker is realized. For the INSTRU-MENT–ACTION relation grammatical categories are introduced and relative positions are accorded to the term (by plus signs). On the other hand, the POSSESSOR–POSSESSED and AGENT–ACTION relations remain as in (31).

Suppose now that the POSSESSOR–POSSESSED relation is realized in the next step.

Step 2. I-marker relation realized: POSSESSOR–POSSESSED
Result of applying relation rule (28) to the output of Step 1:

(AGENT–ACTION *David*, (INST *paint*^{V} + with + (POSS *Robin*^{N} + s + *brush*^{N})^N)^V)

The remaining relation is now realized:

Step 3. I-marker relation realized: AGENT–ACTION
Result of applying relation rule (26) to the output of Step 2:

(AGENT *David*^{N} + (INST *paint*^{V} + with + (POSS *Robin*^{N} + s + *brush*^{N})^N)^V)^S

This completes the application of relation rules. Every one of the elements has now been accorded its position and a grammatical category, and the function words necessary for expressing relations have been introduced.

Note that the output of Step 3 does not contain words—except for the function word "with"—but rather protoverbal elements. Remember that I-markers contain protoverbal elements (Section I), and it is these on which the relation rules in Steps 1–3 have operated. To turn these into words, a look-up of the lexicon has to be performed. Further, concord rules, intonation rules, and phonological rules must be applied; more of this in the next section.

In Section IV.B it was noted that relation rules accord category markers not only to every element in the realizate, but also to the realizate as a whole; compare (25)–(30). The last two steps show how this affects the operation of realization rules. For example, the output of Step 1 specifies that the third element in the realizate, INST, must be marked by the category marker N. The realizate of relation rule (28) is an expression marked N (besides including two elements with this category marker), and it therefore satisfies the above condition. The fact that category markers are assigned to realizations as a whole serves to avoid faulty constructions. For instance, application of realization rules may result in

(33)   The trumpet's sound broke the windowpanes.

Here the *trumpet's sound* is the agent term, and since it is realized from an expression marked N, it satisfies the condition of rule (26): the first (agent) term must be marked N. By contrast, *the trumpet sounded* does not result from a realizate marked N (presumably it results from one marked S) and hence can not appear in (33) in place of *the trumpet's sound.*

The above example illustrates only one of the possible sequences. The reader can easily prove to himself that any other sequence is also possible. Relation rules are so formulated that they can be applied independently of each other. This fact about the formal apparatus, however, leaves open the question of what actually happens in production. Conceivably, speakers use only a certain sequence or a certain subset of all possible sequences of relation rules. But in the absence of any empirical evidence to this effect there seems to be no reason why the production mechanism should thus be limited. Rather, it seems plausible that there should be several alternative routes to the production of an utterance, since this enables the mechanism to combat "noise."

Which of the possible permutations is actually employed in a given speech act may depend on a variety of factors (such as saliency of relations, learned preference, etc.), about which practically nothing is known at present.[2] It should be noted that the sequence may affect the point at which actual utterance of words becomes permissible. In the above example all three steps must take place before any words can be uttered. After Step 1 it has not been determined yet which word is to be uttered first, because the AGENT–ACTION relation has not yet been realized, and hence *David* has not yet been accorded its position. Once the latter relation is realized, the output begins with "AGENT *David*^{N} . . . ," and actual uttering of the sentence can begin (after the necessary lexical look-up is performed and after concord rules, phonological rules, and intonation rules have been applied).

4. Other Realization Rules

The protoverbal elements in Steps 1–4 above must be lexicalized, that is, replaced by appropriate words. This involves a look-up of the lexicon, which lists for every protoverbal element those words by which it can be expressed and the category marker of each of these words. For a word to be insertable in a realizate its category marker must agree with that of the protoverbal element in the realizate. Under a protoverbal element in the lexicon, words differing only in grammatical categories may be listed, for example,

(33)   *good*^{A}
      well^{ADV}

---

[2] Fodor, Bever, and Garrett (1974) argue that processing is left to right and that this is not only true (trivially) as far as the uttering of words is concerned, but also at higher levels of processing. This may be a predominant tendency of the processing mechanism, but there is no evidence that this is its only available strategy.

The category markers then specify that *good* is insertable if the protoverbal element in the realizate is marked A, and *well*, if it is marked ADV.

Two or more synonyms may be listed in the lexicon under the same protoverbal element. Some words listed in the lexicon will have shunting markers associated with them (compare Section III), which constrain the contexts in which they may be used (formal, vulgar, literary, etc.). Further, the lexicon may list for a protoverbal element a string of words by which it may be expressed. Thus, the protoverbal element which lists $save^V$ will also list the string (*put by for a rainy day*)^V. The structure of the lexicon is discussed in greater detail elsewhere (Schlesinger, in press, Chapter 2).

At what point in the production process does lexicalization take place? One obvious possibility is that lexicalization is performed after all relation rules have been applied (e.g., in Section IV.C only the output of Step 3 is lexicalized). But apparently this is not always the case. We often know what words we are going to use without being quite clear yet about the structure of the sentence we are going to utter. The way the realization process has been formalized in Section IV.3 actually leaves room for lexicalizing elements at any point. When a protoverbal element in a realizate is lexicalized, this does not affect the operation of the relation rules in any way. But even a protoverbal element in an I-marker constituent may be lexicalized—for example, *brush* in Step 1—provided we permit relation rules to operate on words as they do on elements. For instance, we postulate that a rule like (28) can operate not only on the protoverbal elements *a* and *b* but also on the words *a* and *b*, with the result of (POSS $a^N + s + b^N)^N$. Lexicalization of elements in I-marker constituents, however, may necessitate a revision of the process, namely, when a word is chosen which subsequently turns out to have a category marker differing from the one required by the relation rule.

A few comments on speech errors are in order here. A rather frequent type of error is one where two words in the sentence are exchanged. Such errors apparently occur when two protoverbal elements in a realizate are lexicalized simultaneously and the words are interchanged and replace the wrong protoverbal element. Thus, instead of saying (32) a speaker might utter

(34)   David was brushing with Robin's paint.

when *brush* and *paint* are lexicalized in Step 2 (or in Step 3). The relations in the realizate are not affected by such an exchange, and consequently the inflectional affixes and function words are left "stranded" (as Garrett, 1975, has observed; cf., also, Fromkin, 1971); only *paint* is transposed in the above fictitious example, whereas — -*ing* is left in its place.

Concord rules are responsible for grammatical agreement; in (32), for instance, *was painting* is appropriate rather than *were painting*. These rules presumably operate after relation rules and after lexicalization. Finally, intonation rules and phonological rules are applied. The former operate on the complete string of words, imposing an intonation contour appropriate to the relation expressed therein, and the latter convert the string of words and affixes into the appropriate sounds. There is quite a substantial body of knowledge pertinent to these two kinds of rules and nothing of interest can be added here to what is already known.

This completes my survey of the components of a production model. As already pointed out at the beginning of the chapter, most of the statements made are programmatic. They are based on the little that is known and on a priori considerations. Tighter formulations will become possible once more research findings are available. It is hoped that the proposed model may serve as a framework for such research, providing it with a sharper focus.

REFERENCES

Brown, R. *A first language: The early stages.* Cambridge, Massachusetts: Harvard University Press, 1973.

Cassirer, E. *The philosophy of symbolic forms. Vol. 1: Language.* New Haven, Connecticut: Yale University Press, 1953.

Carroll, J. B. (Ed.), *Language thought and reality: Selected writings of Benjamin Lee Whorf.* Cambridge, Massachusetts: MIT Press, 1956.

Chafe, W. L. *Meaning and the structure of language.* Chicago, Illinois: University of Chicago Press, 1970.

Edwards, D. Constraints on actions: A source of early meanings in child language. Unpublished manuscript.

Fillmore, C. J. The case for case. In E. Bach & R. T. Harms (Eds.), *Universals in linguistic theory.* New York: Holt, Rinehart, & Winston, 1968. Pp. 1–90.

Fodor, J. A. Current approaches to syntax recognition. In D. L. Horton & J. J. Jenkins (Eds.), *Perception of language.* Columbus, Ohio: Merrill, 1971. Pp. 120–139.

Fodor, J. A., Bever, T. G., & Garrett, M. F. *The psychology of language.* New York: McGraw-Hill, 1974.

Fromkin, V. A. The non-anomalous nature of anomalous utterances. *Language,* 1971, **47**, 27–52.

Garrett, M. F. The analysis of sentence production. Massachusetts Institute of Technology, 1975.

Greene, J. M. Syntactic form and semantic function. *Quarterly Journal of Experimental Psychology,* 1970, **22**, 14–27. (a)

Greene, J. M. The semantic function of negatives and positives. *British Journal of Psychology,* 1970, **61**, 17–22. (b)

Hetzron, R. A synthetical-generative approach to language. *Linguistics,* 1974, **138**, 29–62.

Jesperson, D. *Language: Its nature, development and origin.* New York: Norton, 1964.

Katz, J. J. *Semantic theory.* New York: Harper & Row, 1972.

Keyser, S. J., & Petrick, S. R. Syntactic analysis. Physical Sciences Research Papers, No. 324, Air Force Cambridge Research Laboratories, 1967.

Lyons, J. *Introduction to theoretical linguistics.* Cambridge, England: Cambridge University Press, 1968.

Olson, D. R. Language and thought: Aspects of a cognitive theory of semantics. *Psychological Review,* 1970, **4**, 257–273.

Osgood, C. E. Where do sentences come from? In D. D. Steinberg & L. A. Jakobovits (Eds.),

Semantics: An interdisciplinary reader in Philosophy, linguistics and psychology. Cambridge, England: Cambridge University Press, 1971. Pp. 497–529.

Schlesinger, I. M. The grammar of sign language and the problem of language universals. In J. Morton (Ed.), *Biological and social factors in psycholinguistics.* London: Logos Press, 1971. Pp. 98–121.

Schlesinger, I. M. Relational concepts underlying language. In R. L. Schiefelbusch & L. L. Lloyd (Eds.), *Language prospectives–Acquisition, retardation and intervention.* Baltimore, Maryland: University Park Press, 1974. Pp. 129–151.

Schlesinger, I. M. *Production and comprehension of utterances.* Hillsdale, New Jersey: Lawrence Erlbaum Associates, in press.

Slobin, D. I. The more it changes . . . On understanding language by watching it move over time. In J. Macnamara (Ed.), *Language learning and thought,* New York: Academic Press, in press.

Wason, P. C. The contexts of plausible denial. *Journal of Verbal Language and Verbal Behavior,* 1965, **4,** 7–11.

Watt, W. C. Two hypotheses concerning psycholinguistics. In S. R. Hayes (Ed.), *Cognition and development of language.* New York: Wiley, 1970. Pp. 137–220.

Weisgerber, L. *Von den Kräften der deutschen Sprache.* Vol. 1: *Grundzüge das inhaltsbezogenen Grammatik.* Düsseldorf: Schwann, 1962.

9
Semantic Constraints on Sentence Production: An Experimental Approach[1]

Sheldon Rosenberg

University of Illinois at Chicago Circle

INTRODUCTION

It is curious to note that while the analytic–experimental approach has dominated the methodology of research on speech perception and comprehension, students of sentence production, with not many exceptions, have shown a preference for essentially correlative investigations of large stretches of so-called spontaneous connected discourse (i.e., speech sampled naturalistically or under simulated naturalistic conditions), on the basis of which attempts have been made to infer functional relations. Clearly, the emphasis in these studies of speech production has been on generalizability to whatever is meant by the phrase "everyday speech behavior." However, while they may lead to some important speculations, correlative studies of connected discourse are of limited value in answering questions concerning the determinants and organization of the speech production process. For one thing, the regularities they reveal are normative rather than being indicative of the mature language user's capacity for speech production, and for another, the number of determining variables is such as to produce a degree of confounding which from the standpoint of interpretation is usually hopeless. Too, as discourse proceeds it becomes increasingly more difficult to identify the ideational input to the speech production process.

[1] Experiments 1 and 2 were first discussed in a paper presented at the Symposium on Sentence Production, Midwestern Psychological Association Meetings, Cleveland, May, 1972. Experiment 3 was presented at the Psychonomic Society Meetings, Denver, November, 1975.

195

The sort of thing which worries me here can be shown with reference to the research on the significance of pauses in spontaneous speech (e.g., Goldman-Eisler, 1968, 1972; Hawkins, 1971; and Rochester's 1973 review). Pauses, which are generally unfilled, tend to be assigned to the following categories: phonation (produced by the articulatory gestures required for certain sound segments), breath (air intake), juncture (grammatical-constituent boundary markers), and hesitation, with pause length increasing (roughly) in the order given. Juncture pauses are thought by some to be nonfunctional for the speaker but possibly functional for the listener, while hesitations are generally thought to mark either points of uncertainty in lexical (content-word) choices or, more importantly, where the speaker is planning the next clausal or sentential segment in his or her discourse. In actual practice, however, it is frequently difficult if not impossible to distinguish operationally between juncture and hesitation pauses.

As I see it, there are three very serious problems with this account. First, everything we know about human information-processing capabilities makes it impossible, I believe, to dispense with the assumption that planning can take place at any point in a monologue or dialogue, including during stretches which contain no detectable periods of silence. Second, a given pause may be associated with a number of functions simultaneously. Third, the long pauses which are called hesitations and typically attributed to clausal or sentential planning could be associated with other information-processing functions as well. Thus, a pause between such units may occur, for example, (a) when it is necessary to review the segment just uttered, (b) when there is a need to rehearse what one has said, (c) in the process of retrieving from immediate memory a previously created plan (or portion thereof) for the next segment in a discourse, and so on.

In general, then, the longer pauses in connected speech might be associated with one or some combination of the following: (a) the speaker's desire to take into account the constraints under which the listener is operating, (b) information-processing load, (c) the monitoring process which detects and corrects errors, (d) lexical uncertainty, and (e) clausal or sentential planning.

It should be noted here in passing that I have chosen to exclude from consideration pausal phenomena that might be associated with affective reactions and states such as anxiety (Murray, 1971).

It should be clear by now that questions about the determinants and organization of the speech production process are not likely to be resolved unless we turn our attention toward the development of manipulative research paradigms which (a) insure adequate control over input, (b) limit information-processing demands, and (c) constrain the speaker's responding. The main purpose of the present paper is to describe the efforts along these lines in which I have been involved, but before doing so, it will be necessary to take a close look at the work of others in order to see what it suggests concerning the workings of the sentence production process. The review that follows is selective and organized under the headings Correlational Studies of Pausal Phenomena, Experimental Investigations, and Speech Errors.

Correlational Studies of Pausal Phenomena

The bulk of Goldman-Eisler's extensive program of research on pausal phenomena in spontaneous speech (as well as some related work by others) was presented in detail in her 1968 book (see Boomer, 1970, for a critical review). Briefly, Goldman-Eisler claims that in preparing for overt speech the language user first chooses a semantic content, and sometimes along with it (i.e., in parallel) some lexical items (key content words), then selects an appropriate syntactic structure, and finally selects words appropriate to semantic content and syntactic structure. With respect to this last notion, what Goldman-Eisler is saying is that not all words are selected prior to speech initiation. She proposes, further, that the three basic decisions will delay the initiation of overt speech; that speech planning ". . . must be accompanied by an arrest of the speech act, i.e., by pausing [p. 33]." In addition, Goldman-Eisler appears to feel that hesitation pauses occurring prior to utterance initiation should be attributed mainly to semantic and syntactic decisions, while hesitations occurring within a sentence should indicate that lexical choices are being made among possible alternatives.

The general comments I made earlier on the interpretation of pausal phenomena in spontaneous speech are, of course, relevant here. In addition, it should be pointed out that the methodology of the research which Goldman-Eisler interprets as being supportive of the view that hesitations within a sentence mark points of lexical uncertainty has been found (Boomer, 1970) to be highly questionable. However, methodology aside, it is doubtful whether there exists in the literature any really convincing evidence for Goldman-Eisler's proposal concerning the relationship between lexical uncertainty and within-sentence hesitations (see, for example, the study by Tannenbaum, Williams, & Hillier, 1965).

Problems of interpretation notwithstanding, Goldman-Eisler presents some interesting findings which I have summarized below. It is to be noted that she adopted the convention of discarding periods of silence of less than .25 sec on the assumption that they marked breaks due to phonation.

1. While the total rate of speech production (which was based on vocalizing plus pausing) was, of course, highly dependent on the length and frequency of pausing, articulation rate (which was based on vocalizing only) appeared to be independent of the length and frequency of pausing.

2. A finding which could have been produced by any number of factors was that repetitions of (i.e., practice on) the same production task tended to increase articulation rate and decrease pause rate.

3. Spontaneous speech was characterized more by nonbreath than by breath pauses, whereas reading was characterized more by breath than by nonbreath pauses. Thus, pauses of at least .25 sec that were not associated with air intake (some of which undoubtedly contained a component of phonation pause) tended to disappear during reading. However, although it is impossible to avoid the suggestion that such pauses are indicative of cognitive activity, it is not possible to identify that activity from correlational observations, nor to reject the notion that what takes place during such pauses may frequently take place during periods of continuous vocalization as well.

4. Although breath pauses tended to occur relatively more frequently at grammatical (primarily clausal) than at other junctures during both spontaneous speech and reading, the difference in question was greatest for reading. Indeed, during reading *all* breaths were taken at grammatical junctures. Unfortunately, the data on the location of nonbreath pauses during spontaneous speech and reading were not presented.

Boomer (1965) was concerned with the question of the nature of the grammatical encoding units in speech and was guided in his research by the assumption ". . . that hesitations in spontaneous speech occur at points where decisions and choices are being made [p. 148]." Briefly, it was assumed that the size and nature of encoding units could be inferred from patterns of hesitations. Further, his biases led him to adopt the phonemic clause of Trager and Smith (1951) ". . . as a provisional encoding unit [p. 149]." The phonemic clause is supposedly a phonologically-defined utterance segment, unrelated to hesitations, that ends in one of the terminal junctures (pitch contours) and contains one and only one primary stress (highly stressed word).

There are problems with the concept of the phonemic clause, however, as Valian (1971) and others have pointed out. First, in actual practice the linguist uses nonphonological (i.e., nonintonational) information in determining phonemic clauses. Second, the phonemic clause corresponds generally to the surface structure clause (basically, a subject and its predicate, including any embeddings or compounds they might contain). Third, both primary stress and terminal juncture appear to be semantically motivated. Primary stress, for example, appears to make an important contribution to the expression of the topic—comment (old information—new information) relation in utterances (Hornby, 1972).

Boomer had recordings of spontaneous speech marked for successive phonemic clauses, unfilled pauses longer than 200 msec, and all filled pauses. The phonemic clauses varied appreciably in length, and virtually all the hesitations occurred, as is usually the case, at word boundaries. As anticipated, the hesitations tended to occur most often early in the phonemic clauses but, contrary to expectation, not before the first word but before the second. Similar findings were reported for a breakdown in terms of unfilled and filled pauses.

It seems clear that the main finding here was due to the decision not to include in the analysis what were classified as juncture pauses—certain filled pauses occurring before the first word of a phonemic clause. Had these pauses been included, the hypothesis that hesitations tend to occur most often prior to the first word of a phonemic clause would have been strongly supported.

Thus, it appears that when speakers hesitated they tended to do so most often prior to initiating a phonemic clause. I say "when speakers hesitated" because *over 50% of the phonemic clauses in Boomer's corpus did not contain any hesitations,* that is, they were uttered fluently. How long were these fluent segments? How many phonemic clauses did they contain on the average? How were they structured syntactically and semantically? Unfortunately, none of these questions was raised by Boomer, so it is curious to find that he interprets his results as indicating that the phonemic clause is "the molar encoding unit of speech." And in order to preserve the phonemic clause as *the* encoding unit, he proposes that in the case of the fluencies, planning for the next clause was going on while the previous one was being uttered. The logical alternatives to this view, of course, are that there are instances in which hesitations are associated with planning for more than one phonemic clause, or planning for segments which transcend the phonemic clause boundary, or both. However, this is all beside the point, since we have no way of telling *from this kind of investigation* what speakers are doing when they do or do not hesitate before uttering a phonemic clause. The phonemic clause might be an encoding unit, a monitoring unit, a storage unit, a unit which serves the needs of the listener, etc., or all of these simultaneously.

Hawkins (1971) examined the frequency and length of pauses (filled and unfilled) occurring before a variety of syntactic units in the spontaneous speech of children aged 6.5–7.0 years. Thus, Hawkins, like many other investigators in this area, did not look at pauses in relation to both the segments they precede and the segments they *follow.* Hawkins made .3 sec the shortest pause to be considered, and he took the surface structure clause to be the highest unit in spontaneous speech. The next highest units were the word group (phrase) and the word, in that order.

Hawkins' subjects paused most frequently and longest before clauses, with phrases and words running second and third, respectively. These results are complemented by a recent observation of Goldman-Eisler (1972) to the effect that pausing before linguistic units in spontaneous speech increases in the order words within (surface structure) clauses, relative subordinate clauses, subordinate clauses initiated by a subordinator (e.g., *because, if*), coordinate clauses, and sentences (structures which can contain more than one surface structure clause), with the largest adjacent increase occurring between coordinate clauses and sentences. This pattern is modified, however, when subjects are asked to read the spontaneous discourse.

Thus, what Goldman-Eisler's findings indicate is that one needs to specify more systematically the type of syntactic unit associated with hesitations. This conclusion is further enhanced by the results of an investigation by Rochester and Gill (1973) in which speech disruptions were examined in relation to syntactic structure (noun phrase complements versus relative clauses) and situational context (monologues versus dialogues).

Experimental Investigations

One reasonable expectation about the speech production process is that speakers in planning their utterances will take into account what they know about the constraints under which speech is perceived by listeners. Lieberman (1963) has observed that in a compensatory fashion words from low redundancy contexts are given greater stress by the speaker than words from high redundancy contexts. Unfortunately, there are two problems with this experiment, one methodological and the other interpretive. First, the sentences produced were not created by the speakers but read by them, and second, the tendency to stress words from nonredundant contexts more than words from redundant contexts could have been the result of an attempt to mark the nonredundant lexical information as being *new* rather than *old*.

Speakers asked to describe TAT pictures in a single sentence were judged to have hesitated relatively more than yoked listeners asked to repeat the speakers' descriptions in an experiment by Martin (1967). In addition, Martin found that speakers hesitated relatively more frequently before content words than listeners. These general findings were confirmed in a second experiment (Martin & Strange, 1968) that included a condition in which speakers were primed with content words given by nonprimed speakers. Although primed speakers also hesitated relatively more frequently than listeners, they tended to behave like listeners with respect to the content–word/function–word contrast.

Martin's overall findings for speakers' versus listeners' hesitations are consistent with observations by Goldman-Eisler (1968) of the relative frequency of hesitations in speaking and reading. However, a number of considerations make interpretation of his experiments difficult. First, the hesitation rate overall was quite low (only approximately 11% before the words produced). Thus, most of the words in the descriptions were *not* preceded by a hesitation. Related to this is the fact that the absolute size of the significant differences tended to be quite small. Second, the task itself produced utterances that were ungrammatical, short, and fragmentary, thus making the identification of possible within-sentence clausal boundaries very difficult. Third, the contribution of input encoding time to hesitancy was not controlled for, a fact that is particularly important given the built-in ambiguity of TAT pictures. Fourth, what *preceded* the judged hesitations was not examined. Fifth, the period between picture presentation and sentence initiation, a period presumably of substantial planning given that the speakers were asked to describe each picture in a single sentence, was not examined separately. Sixth, the use of judgments of hesitation in the category of unfilled pauses rather than a direct measure of silence probably resulted in a failure to detect many of the shorter pauses associated with sentence processing activities, or possibly some tendency to perceive pauses where there were none. And last of all, the procedure did not supply any really convincing evidence from which to infer what the subjects were actually doing during the judged hesitations. It is to Martin's credit, however, that he is aware of, and has attempted to deal with, some of these problems (Martin, 1968).

Johnson (1966), following Yngve's (1960) lead, has attempted to evaluate a way in which the organization of surface structure clauses might be related to sentence initiation time. Briefly, he has proposed that the operational schema for controlling the sentence production process is the hierarchic surface phrase structure tree with encoding units for nodes and decoding units for the node expansions. Thus, in initiating a sentence such as *The boy kicked the ball* the speaker retrieves from memory a cognitive representation of the sentence as a whole that is decoded in two steps into cognitive representations of its immediate constituents, in this instance a subject and a predicate. The predicate is then stored in short-term memory and the subject decoded in two steps to produce representations of its two immediate constituents. Next, the second of these constituents is stored in short-term memory while the first is decoded into *The* and the sentence initiated. The process continues as the speaker retrieves from short-term memory the last encoding unit stored and decodes it. Thus, between the activation of this process and the production of *The* the number of decoding operations (Johnson's measure of sentence initiation complexity) is four.

It is to be noted that every nonterminal-node expansion is associated with not only two decoding operations but one memory storage entry as well. Therefore, there is a perfect correlation between number of decoding operations prior to sentence initiation and the amount of information that has to be held in short-term memory. Yngve (1960, 1961) has emphasized the latter while Johnson has chosen the former as his measure of sentential processing complexity. Either decision seems arbitrary, however, and perhaps it is best, therefore, to consider that number of decoding operations and memory load jointly determine processing complexity.

For the case in which all operations are performed and the time to perform each operation is the same, one would predict a positive linear relationship between number of decoding operations to produce the first word in a sentence and sentence initiation time. This expectation was evaluated by Johnson using a repeated-measures design in which subjects learned to criterion and then overlearned mixed lists of digit–sentence paired associates. Each list contained sentences at two levels of hypothetical operational decoding complexity plus a digit paired with *The* and a digit paired with *The patient.* The predicates of the two sentence types were equated on decoding complexity. Latencies between digit presentation and response initiation were measured on the overlearning trials.

Johnson's findings were as anticipated; sentence initiation time was significantly longer for the sentences associated with the greater number of hypothetical decoding operations, and there was some indication that the relationship between number of decoding operations and sentence initiation time was linear. Although, as anticipated, it took longer to learn the more complex sentences, there were some data which persuaded Johnson that the latency results were not due to differences in degree of original learning. However, the latency results would be more convincing, I believe, if more trials to criterion had been required, if a homogeneous-list/independent-groups design had been used, and if there were available comparable results for a wider range of sentence initiation complexities, for a variety of sentence continuation (predicate) complexities, and for high complexity sentences less awkward syntactically and semantically than the ones Johnson used.

Some problems with the model itself should be mentioned here also. First, it does not allow for recoding or chunking, that is, for the possibility that the decoding unit for a fully planned and completely accessible sentence might be the contents of the entire subject or predicate or the string of words as a whole. Second, it does not address itself to the problem of nonbinary expansions of surface structure constituents (e.g., *John and Mary*. . .). Third, it appears in general to make predictions only under highly circumscribed conditions. And last, its implications appear to be inconsistent with certain of the empirical phenomena of spontaneous speech; for example, that speakers tend to pause more and longer before clausal and sentential structures than they do at subject–predicate boundaries, that over 50% of the clausal transitions in spontaneous speech are fluent, and that there are errors in speech which transcend subject–predicate boundaries (e.g., *The old mashes were shoveled by the cold men* instead of *The cold ashes were shoveled by the old men*).

In a series of experiments on sentence completion carried out under a variety of conditions, Forster (e.g., 1966, 1967, 1968) found that right-deleted sentences were completed at a faster rate than left-deleted sentences. He tends to interpret his finding in the context of Yngve's model in terms of the constraints established by the necessity for left-to-right processing at some level in sentence planning and execution. He is aware, however, that there are alternative explanations for such a phenomenon, and has attempted to eliminate some of the more obvious ones (e.g., differential semantic constraint, differential encoding time, length restrictions on responses).

It is still not clear, however, what we are to make of Forster's observations, except perhaps that since the mature speaker–listener has had little experience in a predominantly right-branching language such as English in planning, executing, and perceiving the second half of a surface structure clause or sentence prior to the first half, he or she does not have available efficient strategies for doing so.

In an experiment by Tannenbaum and Williams (1968), exposure to a short printed passage in an active or passive voice format, with a semantic focus on either the actor or the object or neither, was followed by presentation of a line drawing involving an actor as subject and an acted-upon object. Subsequently, speakers were cued to describe the drawing in either an active or a passive sentence. The dependent variable was the time that elapsed between the cue and the completion of the sentence. Thus, these authors decided not to analyze sentence initiation time and sentence execution time separately, a decision that makes interpretation of their findings difficult given the fact that passives are longer than actives.

Actives were produced faster than passives, with the largest differences between them occurring under neutral and actor focus. The shortest production times for the active sentences occurred when the focus was on the actor, while for the passive sentences it was the object focus that resulted in the shortest production times. There was no effect of initial voice format.

The best guess is that the difference in the pattern of results for actives and passives was associated primarily with factors operating prior to sentence initiation, but we cannot be sure without looking at sentence initiation and execution times separately.

Description and interpretation of cartoon pictures were compared by Goldman-Eisler (1968) who found, among other things, that speakers pause more during interpretation than they do during description. Her subjects were presented with cartoon pictures and asked to describe and then interpret them after having indicated that they had gotten their point. Unfortunately, there are some serious confoundings in this experiment. For example, description always preceded interpretation, the speaker knew during description that the cartoon had to be interpreted later on, and description was preceded by a requirement (the instruction to say "got it" as soon as a subject had perceived the point of the cartoon series) that clearly involved more than the encoding of picture contents.

To take just the first problem mentioned, it is obvious that description and interpretation should have been manipulated in the following manner (along with fixed response periods and appropriate controls for prior knowledge of the second task).

Condition A: Describe then interpret.
Condition B: Interpret then describe.
Condition C: Describe then continue describing.
Condition D: Interpret then continue interpreting.

Thus, the subjects in Condition C might pause as much during the second period of description as the subjects in Condition A during interpretation because they are running out of things to describe; subjects who interpret before describing are likely to pause more than subjects who interpret after describing because the initial interpretation is likely to be accompanied or preceded by covert description, and so on.

Intuition suggests that the sentence production process is aroused by any encodable input, whether the input be internal or external; in other words, that the sentence production process is initiated by an act of perception. Thus, with this view it becomes important to attempt to determine or control for the contribution of input encoding time to sentence initiation time in experiments on semantic and other planning activities in speech production. In everyday speech encoding time might be the time it takes to comprehend, or to draw an appropriate inference from, something another speaker has said, or the time it takes to recognize the contents of a picture or activities in the immediate environment, or the time it takes to recognize a word picked up during a noisy cocktail party, and so on.

Some observations on differential encoding times are available from an experiment by Reynolds and Paivio (1968). These investigators presented subjects visually with a series of abstract and concrete words, one at a time, and had them *define* each of them for 30 sec. Thus, with the present view, given the nature of the subject's task, the time between word presentation and the beginning of a definition could be taken as a measure of input encoding time. Presumably, the word recognition process is complete (or nearly so) prior to definition initiation. What was observed here was that (a) abstract words took significantly longer to encode than concrete words; (b) subjects paused relatively less during the concrete than they did during the abstract definitions; (c) the concrete definitions were judged to be more adequate than the abstract definitions; and that (d) the concrete definitions were longer than the abstract definitions. This last finding could have been the result of the constraint of 30 sec; however, it does suggest that it takes more time to complete an abstract definition than it does to complete a concrete one. Thus, taken together, findings (b), (c), and (d) suggest that encoding of the abstract words continued after definition initiation.

I hope I have not given the impression in this discussion of input encoding time that what I am proposing is that speakers *always* delay sentence planning and initiation until input encoding is completed and, more importantly, that input encoding and sentence planning are *always* independent activities. We should want to examine, for example, the possibility that in many situations in which the intention of the speaker is to describe the input, the dominant strategy is as follows: partial input encoding → partial utterance planning → execution of part of a clause → more input encoding, and so on. However, in the special case of input describing in which the semantic organization (but not necessarily the specific content) of the input is known beforehand and also seriously constrains the type of sentence that can be created to describe it, a more-or-less direct mapping of the output of input encoding onto sentence execution may be possible. In other words, in this special case the output of input encoding *is* the plan for the utterance.

The conditions of this special case were in general met in a series of carefully controlled experiments by Lindsley (1975) in which practiced speakers were constrained to describe simple pictures, each of which involved an actor, an action, and an object, with part or all of a previously specified type of simple active sentence. The dependent variable was sentence initiation time. In brief, what Lindsley found was that in this type of situation, speech is initiated prior to full input encoding and that the speech encoding unit involves the subject and some degree of verb selection.

Taylor (1969) attempted to study the relationship between sentence content difficulty and sentence processing time as well as structural complexity in an experiment in which subjects were presented a long list of "topic" words (nouns, verbs, and adjectives) varying in concreteness and familiarity (frequency), one word at a time, and asked to use each of them in a complete sentence. This investigator, like many others, assumed that latency (sentence initiation time) and hesitation (filled and unfilled pauses within a sentence) reflected planning activities. It is important to note here also that topic familiarity was confounded with length, and that there was apparently no attempt to equate the words in the various conditions on such attributes as mass versus count (for the nouns), animate versus inanimate (for the nouns), and process versus state (for the verbs). Taylor's measure of the structural complexity of the produced sentences was the one devised by Johnson (1966), which we have already discussed, and Taylor also looked at sentence type (e.g., simple declarative, passive, negative), but I will have nothing to say about this variable.

A Wilcoxon test across subjects indicated that hesitations in the categories of pauses and repeats occurred significantly more frequently on unfamiliar topics than on familiar topics (presumably for both abstract and concrete words but this is impossible to determine from the way in which these results were reported). In addition, there was significantly greater pausing on frequent abstract words than on frequent concrete words. Thus, when word frequency was low, concreteness had no effect on hesitancy. The results for the comparisons involving frequent concrete words are questionable, however, since the sentences in this condition were consistently shorter than the sentences in the other conditions, and Taylor apparently did not correct for this in determining hesitancy scores.

According to Johnson's formula, most of the sentences required only two or four operations to initiate, but the unfamiliar topics contributed more sentences to the category of six or eight operations than the familiar topics.

Taylor's design called for, and the data appeared to permit, a 2 X 2 repeated-measures factorial analysis of variance (although today we would probably insist on a multivariate analysis) of the latency scores, but only the result of a simple analysis of variance was reported. The value of F was significant, and the order of sentence initiation mean latencies, from longest to shortest, was for unfamiliar abstract (3.76 sec), unfamiliar concrete (3.49 sec), familiar abstract (2.71 sec), and familiar concrete (2.27 sec). Collapsing over conditions, we find means of 3.63 and 2.49 for unfamiliar versus familiar, and 3.24 and 2.88 for abstract versus concrete. Thus, since the difference associated with word frequency was appreciably larger than the difference associated with word concreteness, it should be clear that the overall F test has not given us all the information we need to interpret the cell means. However, it should be obvious in the light of our discussion of encoding time and the results of Reynolds and Paivio's (1968) study, that any attempt to relate latency differences associated with input complexity to speech planning activities must take into account the contribution of input encoding time to sentence initiation time.

Unfortunately, the interpretation of Taylor's latency findings is further complicated by the fact that Kintsch (1974) has failed to find a significant effect of single-word lexical complexity on sentence initiation time, a fact which at present I am unable to account for.

As a final item, Taylor found no evidence of a significant relationship between latency and sentence length or between latency and the number of hypothetical operations required to initiate a sentence.

Osgood (1971), in an extensive informal investigation, has shown how particular linguistic forms and structures are cued by environmental manipulations (demonstrations). However, since he was not interested in examining sentence processing time, I will not attempt to discuss his work here.

It should be clear that with the exception perhaps of the studies by Reynolds and Paivio (1968) and Lindsley (1975) on input encoding, the experimental literature on speech production has been plagued by problems of method, analysis, and interpretation. Most of the problems of method and analysis cited could be corrected, but the interpretive problems are another matter. These, I believe, are a reflection mainly of the fact that most investigators in this area have adopted a rather oversimplified model of the sentence production process.

Speech Errors

Observations of regularities in the organization of speech errors have been the source of some speculations (e.g., Boomer & Laver, 1968; Fromkin, 1971, 1973)[2] about the planning process for error-free speech, but unfortunately, these speculations have been plagued by questions about, for example, data sampling, the classification of particular errors, the rationale for assuming that speech which contains errors is planned in the same manner as error-free speech,

---

[2] See also Foss and Fay (1976). These authors propose that there are error data which indicate that certain linguistic transformations describe operations performed in the sentence production process.

the specific linguistic and information-processing mechanisms responsible for particular errors, parallel versus serial processing, and the contribution of heuristic shortcutting strategies (Bever, 1970) to speech planning. But let us look (briefly) at a few of these observations and speculations.

One observation which has been made (e.g., Fromkin, 1971) is that the linguistic segment most commonly involved in a speech error is not the morpheme, or the word, or the phrase, or the clause; in other words, it is not one which is likely to be associated with semantic, syntactic, or possibly lexical decisions, but the phone. However, what is interesting here is that there appears to have been no serious attempt to interpret *this particular fact.* Does it say something about the complexity of articulatory programming, or articulation itself, or monitoring, that is, about the final stages in the speech production process? Or does it say something about the way in which information at this level is stored after it has been generated, or the degree of similarity between segments at this level, or how these segments are planned to begin with? We simply do not know.

Two other observations, namely, that most speech errors are errors of anticipation, that is, involve segments not yet uttered, and that speech errors typically involve segments from the same surface structure (or phonemic) clause, have suggested that speech is typically not planned one segment at a time but in units the size of a single surface structure clause. An equally plausible interpretation of these observations, however, and therefore one which also has to be evaluated experimentally, is that it is not the planning strategy *per se* that is responsible for these regularities, but rather the possibility that the outputs of planning are *stored* together prior to speech execution and thus can interact with each other.

When two words in an utterance are reversed (e.g., *The wall was pushed up against the table* instead of *The table was pushed up against the wall*) and when an incorrect word is substituted for the intended one (e.g., *John elected to leave yesterday* instead of *John expected to leave yesterday*), syntactic form class constraints are typically not violated. Thus, it has been suggested (Fromkin, 1971; Nooteboom, 1969) on the basis of these observations that syntactic structuring typically precedes lexical selection in speech planning. However, it is to be noted that if we take the view that the reversals in question are the result of a failure to order constituents of underlying semantic role relations properly, this category of errors would have to be classified as syntactic. In addition, if we add to this the fact of errors in which form classes *are* reversed, as well as the fact of errors in which whole phrases and clauses are reversed, we conclude that there are some different possibilities: for example, that some lexical selection precedes syntactic structuring, or that syntactic and lexical decisions are made in parallel.

There are a number of other kinds of speech errors whose characteristics are thought to have implications for how error-free speech is planned, but I will not be able to take the time to discuss them here. It should be clear, however, on the basis of the examples given above that if speech error phenomena are to make some contribution to our understanding of error-free speech, then psycholinguists will have to become interested in evaluating experimentally the alternative hypotheses as to their origin, as well as the alternative possibilities they raise concerning the organization of planning processes for error-free speech. That there is already some recognition of the advantages of such an approach is clear in the work of MacKay (1972, 1974) and Baars, Motley, and MacKay (1975).[3]

CONCLUSIONS

What this review of research literature has indicated is that there are only a small number of empirical generalizations that can be made at present about speech production. Thus, it seems that major syntactic units (e.g., single clauses, conjoined clauses) in connected discourse are sometimes preceded by pauses, that under constrained input—output conditions input encoding may be mapped directly onto articulatory programming, that under constrained input—output conditions only a portion of a sentence is planned prior to speech initiation, and that the time between input presentation and sentence initiation is not related to sentence length. Not much to go on, as the reader can readily see.

However, on the basis of our discussion of this literature, and related considerations, a number of empirical hypotheses emerge which, I believe, are worth attempting to evaluate in the laboratory. A partial list of these hypotheses follows.

1. Speech planning can take place prior to and during speech execution, including during continuous vocalization, breath intake, and silence, the only limitations on where and when it can occur being those associated with information processing load.

2. There is flexibility in regard to the decisions which need to be made and the manner in which they are made (e.g., serially versus in parallel) during planning for a given utterance. This is not to say, however, that certain of the decisions the speaker makes do not *obligate* him or her linguistically at the next stage of speech planning. Indeed, it may be the study of just these conditions of obligation that will lead us to identify the specific operations which, for example, convert semantic representations into syntactic structures, or assign intonation patterns to syntactically organized semantic representations.

3. A pause during speech may be occasioned by speech planning, speech execution, or information-processing activities either singly or in combination with each other.

---

[3] But see also Garrett (1975). This author offers some alternative interpretations of the data of speech errors.

4. Any linguistic unit from the word to connected discourse is a potential terminal unit in speech production. By terminal unit I mean one that is planned to be expressive of semantic intentions. Thus, with this view it is incorrect to speak of *the* encoding unit of speech planning; we should be concerned, rather, with questions of how the unitization process in speech planning is influenced by considerations of communicative effectiveness (e.g., disambiguation), information-processing load, environmental constraints, audience factors, and individual difference factors.

5. It is likely, on the expectation of decisional and terminal-unit flexibility, that speakers have acquired, and utilize regularly, strategies for shortcutting the speech planning and execution processes which involve omitting, combining, or reordering certain operations. Thus, among the candidate strategies that come to mind are the following: (a) generate semantic propositions and their syntactic structures simultaneously; (b) begin lexical selection prior to syntactic structuring; (c) begin executing an utterance prior to completing its planning and allow the constraints created by what was executed to determine the remainder of the utterance; and (d) delete wherever possible repeated elements in the underlying semantic propositions and omit from execution terminal elements which listeners can themselves generate on the basis of linguistic and nonlinguistic contextual cues.

6. Speakers come by some semantic propositions more easily than others and so a difference between individual sentences (or clauses) in ease of semantic planning in the case in which planning is not taking place during execution of a previous utterance should be associated with a difference in sentence initiation time but not necessarily in syntactic complexity. Thus, in the case, for example, of pictorial and other environmental input, in which the speaker's intent is to describe the input, differences in speech planning time may reflect differences in the ease of encoding the relations which obtain between persons, objects, and events, or, in the case of other types of intent (e.g., interpersonal, expository, rhetorical) differences in planning time may reflect differences in the ease of creating (or perhaps retrieving from memory) whole semantic propositions.

It will be recalled that Goldman-Eisler (1968) and Taylor (1969) were concerned with the effects of semantic-content difficulty on speech processing time, but that the results of their studies were inconclusive.

This Introduction, then, constitutes the background for the series of experiments presented in the next section, experiments which were concerned primarily with the evaluation of Hypothesis 6. It should be mentioned here as a final item, however, that throughout this Introduction I have assumed that in the case in which mature speakers are not utilizing shortcutting strategies which involve omitting certain activities, the speech production process involves (a) input encoding, (b) semantic proposition generation, (c) syntactic structuring of (b) including the selection of most functors, (d) more-or-less automatic intonational patterning of the syntactically structured semantic proposition, (e) lexical (primarily content–word) selection, (f) inflectional selection, (g) automatic phonetic structuring of the syntactically ordered phonological and syllabic outputs of lexical and inflectional decisions, (h) generation of a hierarchically organized neuromotor-command program for the articulators, (i) articulation, and (j) monitoring on the basis of stored representations of the semantic, formal, and information-processing decisions of both planning and execution. These assumptions, of course, have the status of empirical hypotheses and, as such, are open to revision and/or elaboration if and when observation requires that we do so.

THE EXPERIMENTS

The paradigm employed in the present experiments had the following general characteristics.

1. The input consisted of sets of two, and in one case four, familiar (according to the 1944 norms of Thorndike and Lorge) concrete nouns varying in normative semantic relatedness (e.g., in semantic categorial overlap) but not, as far as could be determined linguistically, in semantic selectional restrictions (e.g., animacy), semantic role potentialities (e.g., agent, instrument), syntactic subcategorial features (e.g., number), or syntactic role potentialities (e.g., subject, direct object).

2. The speaker was required to use each set of lexical items in a single sentence, with no restrictions being placed on the length, content, or grammatical complexity of the sentence.

3. The main dependent variables were latency (the time from the end of the last word in a set to the beginning of a sentence), sentence length (in words), and certain aspects of the semantic and syntactic structure of the sentences produced. In two instances, however, pause (silence within a sentence) and duration (vocalization time) were also examined.

It was the case, then, that what were termed related (REL) and unrelated (UNREL) items did not differ in regard to their general semantic and syntactic relational potentialities, but rather in the likelihood that the speaker had available in long-term memory semantic propositions for which they would be appropriate. Thus, it was anticipated that speakers would be less likely to have to *compute* an appropriate semantic proposition for a REL set than for an UNREL set, and would therefore require less time to initiate a sentence containing REL items than they would a sentence containing UNREL items.

Input encoding time, it should be mentioned here, was controlled for in the present experiments by only using, in both the REL and UNREL conditions, nouns which were concrete and familiar.

Experiment 1 (Sheldon Rosenberg and Michael S. Zolno)

Method. The subjects were 20 undergraduate native English speakers who participated in this study as part of a course requirement. Twelve REL and 12 UNREL pairs of familiar concrete nouns were selected with the assistance of college free association norms and combined to produce two mixed lists of six REL (e.g., *uncle aunt, street road*) and six UNREL pairs (e.g., *queen clerk, city lake*) each. The REL sets contained high strength associative pairs while the UNREL sets contained low strength associative pairs. The REL and UNREL words within each list were balanced both between and within pairs as indicated above, and on length and animacy. There were three animate–animate and three inanimate–inanimate REL and UNREL pairs. Also, no word occurred more than once in a given list.

The subjects were tested individually in a sound-insulated room. Each pair was printed on a different index card and the order of the words within the pairs was counterbalanced. In addition, the pairs within the lists were presented in a different random order to each subject. The experimenter read the words within each of the pairs out loud at a rate (roughly) of one word per second, and the subjects responded orally. The reading of the pairs and the subject's sentence productions were recorded on the same tape for analysis later. The subject's task was to use the words in each pair of nouns once in a single sentence in any order, the only other restriction being that they had to be used as nouns. The subjects were urged in the instructions to start talking when they had thought of a sentence for a given pair. The experimenter allowed a few seconds to pass after each sentence was produced before presenting the next pair in a list.

Results. The error (e.g., stimulus word not used, noun used as a verb) rate was very low for both conditions as were the rates for filled pauses prior to sentence initiation and false starts, so we will not concern ourselves here with these measures. All analyses reported are for correct responses. The processing time measures were obtained by playing the taped sentence productions into a voice operated relay to which were attached two timers calibrated in milliseconds. Table 1 contains the group means and standard deviations for the two REL and UNREL lists combined. The N for each list was 10. Included in Table 1 are the means and standard deviations for median latency, median pause, median duration, and mean length, as well as for certain other measures which we will discuss presently. The statistical test performed on each of these measures was the normal curve approximation for the Wilcoxon matched-pairs signed-ranks test across subjects. Thus, each subject received two scores for each measure, one for the REL items and one for the UNREL items. The measures of processing time are reported in seconds, and because the experimental conditions did not differ in sentence length, the figures reported for duration and pause are based on the absolute values for these dependent variables summed over the full sentences.

TABLE 1
Means and Standard Deviations (SD) for
Measures of Experiment 1

	Condition			
	REL		UNREL	
Measure	Mean	SD	Mean	SD
Median latency (sec)	1.94	1.01	2.63	1.95
Median pause (sec)	.12	.22	.29	.66
Median duration (sec)	2.12	.84	2.33	1.21
Mean length (words)	8.74	2.18	9.22	2.51
SPC	1.8	.6	1.7	.6
IPC	2.1	.8	2.2	1.1
SC	1.1	.1	1.2	.1
LC (Proportion)	.27	.05	.27	.08

As anticipated, the sentence initiation latencies for the REL items were shorter than they were for the UNREL items, and significantly so; p = .0239, one tailed. However, when the statistical analysis was carried out on the two lists separately, the difference in question, while it was in the predicted direction for both lists, reached significance at the .05 level, one tailed, on only one of them. Thus, the generality of the results for latency across lists is questioned. The REL and UNREL conditions did not differ significantly for the two lists combined for either pause or duration. Indeed, if we were to compute the pause rates per word or syllable for the REL and UNREL items we would find that the sentences once initiated were in general uttered fluently. This is precisely what we had anticipated we would find, given the limited information-processing demands of the present task.

We wanted to determine next whether the two experimental conditions were associated with sentences varying in semantic, lexical, or syntactic complexity, but discovered almost immediately that there was no solution available to the question of complexity measures which was not objectionable for reasons of semantic–syntactic confounding, lack of independence generally, uncertainty of linguistic analysis, questionable psychological reality, and uncertainty of scaling attributes. We decided, therefore, that for present purposes it would be advisable to concentrate on possible measures which were (a) consistent with our intuitions about the sentence production process, (b) linguistically relatively uncontroversial, and (c) easy to score. We decided, therefore, on the following set of tentative complexity measures for use in the noun–noun situation, with our major linguistic source being the model summarized in Jacobs and Rosenbaum's (1968) book on English transformational grammar.

SPC (semantic propositional complexity). This was our measure of the number of elementary underlying semantic propositions (i.e., single subject–predicate relations) in a sentence, and it was determined by simply counting the number of elementary underlying subject–predicate clauses in the deep structure of a sentence. Note that content overlap between semantic propositions is not considered in determining this measure, and that its use requires the wholly indefensible assumption that different types of semantic propositional structures should be weighted equally.

IPC (input propositional complexity). A scale was developed to represent the "fate" of the REL and UNREL nouns in the underlying semantic structure of the subject's sentence productions with points being assigned as follows:

1, for the case in which the two nouns appeared in the same elementary underlying semantic proposition (e.g., *The LAKE was near the CITY*);

2, for the case in which the two nouns played identical semantic roles in identical elementary underlying semantic prositions (e.g., *My UNCLE and AUNT are visiting next week*);

3, for the case in which the two nouns played identical semantic roles in identical elementary underlying semantic propositions (e.g., *My UNCLE and AUNT are visiting* were integrated by a subordinator (e.g., *I painted the TABLE before I painted the DOOR*);

4, for the case in which the nouns played identical semantic roles in underlying semantic propositions which displayed some content overlap (e.g., *A STUDENT works in the school and a FARMER works on the farm*);

5, for the case in which the nouns played identical semantic roles in different underlying semantic propositions (e.g., *A CLERK works in a store and a QUEEN rules*);

6, for the case in which the nouns played different semantic roles in underlying semantic propositions which displayed some content overlap (e.g., *As a little girl I always wanted to be a QUEEN and live with a KING*); and

7, for the case in which the nouns played different semantic roles in different elementary underlying semantic propositions (e.g., *There was a great PEACE in the city after the SICKNESS was cured*).

The nouns that are capitalized in the above examples are instances of either REL or UNREL items. The value .5 was added to each of the above scale scores in all instances in which one of the nouns in a pair occurred in an additional elementary underlying semantic proposition. This occurred when a noun appeared more frequently in the underlying structure of a sentence than in its surface structure. Thus, in general, what we tried to capture with this complexity metric were the degree of semantic propositional integration and the degree of content overlap for the nouns in each pair.

SC (syntactic complexity). Although there does not seem to be any evidence to support the view that the surface structure clause is *the* syntactic planning unit of speech or even *one of the principle* syntactic planning units of speech, we were unable to come up with any less objectionable candidates for a measure of syntactic complexity. Thus, we decided arbitrarily to use for this purpose the number of surface structure clauses (subject–predicate constructions) in each of the sentences the subjects produced. In determining this measure, type of surface structure clause was not considered, nor was the number of deep structure clauses each surface structure clause might have contained embedded in it.

Each subject received two scores for the above measures, one was the mean for the REL-item sentences and the other the mean for the UNREL-item sentences.

LC (lexical complexity). This was the proportion of the total number of words (contentives plus functors) in the sentences which were content items (adjectives, nouns, verbs, and certain adverbs), with scoring being determined by the table of functors listed in the article by Miller, Newman, and Friedman (1958). The rationale for this measure was the assumption that content-word selection involves more time and effort than function-word selection.

The group means and standard deviations for these measures for the REL and UNREL conditions can be found in Table 1. Note that the differences on these measures between REL and UNREL pairs were negligible and in one instance (LC) there was no difference. The normal curve Wilcoxon test results over subjects for both lists combined were all nonsignificant at $p = .05$, two tailed. Thus, there was no indication in the present experiment that the REL and UNREL conditions led to the production of sentences that differed in semantic, lexical, or syntactic complexity as herein defined.

Since our main interest was in determining possible differences between the REL and UNREL conditions, no attempt was made to examine the dependent variables in the experiment in terms of an overall regression analysis. Besides, the small number of subjects used, the possibility that subjects used different strategies under the REL and UNREL conditions, the fact that there were only two levels of semantic relatedness, the range-of-talent problem, plus all of the problems associated with the individual complexity measures would have made such an analysis of questionable value at this time.

Discussion. Thus, the predicted results for latency were found but they turned out to be limited to only one of the two experimental lists. It seemed advisable, therefore, to replicate Experiment 1 using different lists (and different subjects as well).

Experiment 2 (Sheldon Rosenberg)

Method. Experiment 2 was not an exact replication of Experiment 1 because I felt that some methodological refinements were required. First of all, each subject received practice on the production task prior to testing. Second, the instructions were modified so as to facilitate determining the processing time measures. Third, the instructions were modified so as to reduce the likelihood that subjects would rehearse their sentence productions covertly prior to overt execution. And last, the REL and UNREL noun pairs were constructed from category norms (Battig & Montague, 1969; Shapiro & Palermo, 1970) rather than free association norms. Category norms contain lexical concept instances varying in frequency. The REL pairs (e.g., *lion tiger, car truck, tulip rose*) contained high frequency instances of the same concept while the UNREL pairs (e.g., *dog owl, spoon book, coat lamp*) contained instances of different concepts. All of the controls exerted in selecting items were the same as they were in Experiment 1. Two comparable lists of REL and UNREL pairs were constructed with appropriate controls for within-pair and within-list order.

The subjects were 20 undergraduate native English speakers who participated in the study as part of a course requirement. They were assigned alternately to the two lists as they appeared in the laboratory, and the procedure they followed is indicated in the instructions they received, which are reproduced below.

This is a study in sentence production. In it you will be read 12 pairs of nouns, one pair at a time. Your task for each pair is simply this: Make up a sentence that contains the nouns from the pair. Start saying your sentence out loud into the microphone here as soon after you hear the two nouns as you can. Your sentences will be recorded on tape for analysis later. As soon as you complete a sentence, raise your hand up and down like this (the experimenter demonstrates). Once we begin there will be no additional instructions except the signal to get ready for the next pair. The procedure then that we will follow throughout is this:

1. I will say GET READY.
2. Then I will say a pair of nouns.
3. Then you will produce out loud a sentence that contains the nouns you've just heard.
4. And as soon as you've finished saying your sentence, you will signal me by raising your hand up and down.

Please follow these additional instructions in performing your task:

1. The words you are given must be used as nouns.
2. Use each noun only once in the sentence that you make up.
3. Where the two nouns appear in a given sentence and in what order is up to you. For example, whether they appear close together or a number of words apart is up to you.
4. The content, length, and grammatical complexity of your sentence is up to you.
5. Try to work continuously during your task.

Are there any questions? Let's try a pair for practice then.
GET READY: ACTOR LAWYER.

Note that in the first experiment the subjects were asked to start talking *after they had thought of a sentence for a given pair,* whereas in the present experiment the instructions were "Start saying your sentence out loud into the microphone here as soon after you hear the two nouns as you can." It was felt that this change would reduce the likelihood that the subjects would say their sentences to themselves in their entirety prior to uttering them out loud.

Results. Errors, filled pauses, and false starts were again rare occurrences. The summary statistics for this experiment can be found in Table 2 where it will be noted that sentences tended to be initiated fastest under the REL condition. The difference between conditions when analyzed across subjects was significant for the two lists combined; $p < .0007$, one tailed. The trends were in the same direction for the two experimental lists and also highly significant; $p = .0082$, one tailed and $p = .0162$, one tailed.

The only other measure to produce a significant ($p = .0160$, two tailed) difference overall between the REL and UNREL conditions across subjects was SPC, with the REL items tending to be associated with *more* elementary underlying semantic propositions than the UNREL items. However, the analyses for individual lists revealed that SPC was significantly higher for the REL items on only one of the lists.

Discussion. Thus, the expectation that an increase in semantic relatedness in the input to sentence production would result in a decrease in sentence initiation time was clearly supported by the results of Experiment 2. In addition, it was clear that the UNREL condition did not lead to the production of sentences which were linguistically more complex than those which were produced under the REL condition. However, because it seemed evident that our confidence in these findings would be enhanced if they were to be confirmed under conditions of increased constraint on the semantic and syntactic role relational structures of the sentences produced under REL and UNREL lexical input, a third study was carried out.

TABLE 2
Means and Standard Deviations (SD) for
Measures of Experiment 2

| | Condition | | | |
| | REL | | UNREL | |
Measure	Mean	SD	Mean	SD
Median latency (sec)	2.13	1.07	2.97	2.16
Median pause (sec)	.70	.72	.70	.58
Median duration (sec)	2.07	.62	2.08	.66
Mean length (words)	10.44	2.74	10.83	2.29
SPC	2.2	.5	2.0	.5
IPC	2.2	.5	2.3	.9
SC	1.2	.3	1.3	.3
LC (proportion)	.30	.05	.29	.06

Experiment 3 (Sheldon Rosenberg and Richard Hamilton)

Method. Twenty undergraduate native English speakers participated in this study as part of a course requirement and were assigned alternately to the two mixed lists of REL and UNREL noun pairs which were used. Each list contained 11 REL pairs, 11 UNREL pairs, and 8 pairs of neutral filler nouns. The filler items were the same for the two lists. Unlike the previous investigation, the noun pairs used here were selected from norms (Rosenberg & Koen, 1968) of lexical dependencies in active declarative sentences. Participants in the normative study were required to respond to each of a series of animate nouns with the verb and noun that they most frequently associated with it. The animate nouns all served as grammatical subjects in simple active affirmative declarative sentence frames (e.g., The thief ____ the ____.).

In the present study each REL pair consisted of an animate noun and one of its high frequency inanimate-noun associates (e.g., *farmer field, Indian arrow, artist picture, student test*), while each UNREL pair contained an animate noun and one of its low frequency inanimate-noun associates (e.g., *editor basket, lawyer town, baby dust, rabbit dollar*). The filler items consisted of four REL and four UNREL noun pairs, half of which were inanimate–inanimate pairs and half inanimate–animate pairs. Within each list the animate nouns from the REL and UNREL pairs as well as the inanimate nouns from the REL and UNREL pairs were balanced on Thorndike and Lorge (1944) frequency, length (in letters and in syllables), concreteness, syntactic features, syntactic and semantic role potentialities, and so on, so that they would have identical semantic and syntactic structural potentialities.

The nouns in each pair were read out loud by the experimenter in the order animate noun–inanimate noun, using a different list order for each subject, and the subjects responded orally as before. However, in the present experiment the subjects were required to use the nouns in each of the pairs *in the order in which they were presented.* In all other respects, however, the instructions and procedure of the present experiment were identical to those of Experiment 2.

Thus, it should be clear to the reader by now that what we hoped to accomplish by (a) using REL and UNREL pairs which contained an animate and an inanimate noun selected from simple sentential norms, (b) presenting the nouns in each of the REL and UNREL pairs in the order animate–inanimate, and (c) requiring the subjects to use the nouns in each pair in the order given was to constrain the subjects to structure the REL and UNREL items in a similar manner in terms of both underlying semantic propositions and surface syntax.

Results. The means and standard deviations for the measures of interest in Experiment 3 can be found in Table 3. It will be noted that duration and pause were not examined in the present study. If the procedures of the present study did in fact reduce the semantic complexity of the sentences produced under the

TABLE 3
Means and Standard Deviations (SD) for
Measures of Experiment 3

| | Condition | | | |
| | REL | | UNREL | |
Measure	Mean	SD	Mean	SD
Median latency (sec)	1.52	.91	2.05	1.07
Mean length (words)	7.32	1.84	9.24	2.84
SPC	1.4	.4	1.6	.6
IPC	1.2	.3	1.4	.5
SC	1.0	.03	1.1	.2
LC (proportion)	.34	.04	.33	.06

REL and UNREL conditions, then the means for SPC and IPC in Table 3 should be lower than the corresponding means in Table 2. Inspection of Tables 2 and 3 will show that this was indeed the case. Also, if the constraints of the present procedure reduced the syntactic complexity of the sentences produced as well, then the means for SC, and possibly length also, should be smaller in Experiment 3 than the corresponding means for Experiment 2. Inspection of Tables 2 and 3 will show that this was the case for both the REL and the UNREL conditions. It should be noted, finally, that under the conditions of Experiment 3 the means for median latency were smaller for both the REL and the UNREL items than they were in Experiment 2. However, it remains to be determined whether these last findings were the result of complexity reductions or a general reduction in semantic proposition generation time or both.

We have made no mention of the differences between Experiments 2 and 3 in LC, but this is because we could find no basis for making a prediction. And, of course, the statistical reliability of the differences we have noted here between Experiments 2 and 3 will have to be determined in a separate experiment in which the independent variable is represented by the materials and procedural differences between the two experiments. To return to the results of Experiment 3, it can be seen in Table 3 that there was a tendency for sentences to be initiated faster under the REL condition than under the UNREL condition. This difference was significant for both lists combined ($p = .0022$, one tailed) as well as for each list separately ($p = .0329$, one tailed and $p = .0143$, one tailed), with the direction of the difference being the same for both lists.

Thus, it is clear that even under the increased semantic and syntactic constraints of the present task, a high degree of semantic relatedness in the input facilitated sentence initiation latency.

With the exception of LC, the means for all of the measures in Table 3 were higher for UNREL items than they were for REL items. The difference was significant overall ($p = .0548$, two tailed) for SPC and in the same direction for both lists, but significant ($p = .0500$, two tailed) for only one of them. The experimental conditions did not differ significantly for the two lists combined on IPC, LC, or SC. The length difference, however, was significant overall ($p = .0003$, two tailed), and for each list separately as well ($p = .0214$, two tailed and $p = .0050$, two tailed), and in the same direction for both. Inspection of the sentences produced under the REL and UNREL conditions suggested that the results for length were due to differences in the use of optional constituents such as prepositional phrases, but, unfortunately, we have no explanation for why such differences should have occurred.

Responsibility for the differences in average sentence length lay with statistically significant differences in both the average number of content words and the average number of function words per sentence overall and for the two lists separately. However, the difference between the overall group means for the REL and UNREL conditions on average number of content words per sentence was less than 1.00 (.63 to be exact).

Discussion. It seems to have been the case, then, that the pattern of results for the complexity measures in Experiment 3 tended to confirm the findings of Experiment 2, namely, that the UNREL condition did not lead to the production of sentences that were more complex linguistically than the sentences produced under the REL condition. It would seem reasonable to conclude, therefore, on the basis of the results of all three experiments, that when input encoding reveals strong preestablished semantic relations between the elements or constituents of the input, semantic proposition generation is facilitated and as a result sentence initiation time is reduced.

The present research paradigm, of course, does not constitute a direct test of the claim that semantic proposition generation involves mainly retrieval from long-term memory in the case of REL input and mainly computation in the case of UNREL input. In addition, a question must be raised concerning the generality of the results of Experiments 1, 2, and 3 for the case in which the encoded input to sentence planning contains more semantic elements than can be modeled by a pair of nouns. The last experiment we conducted, which is described below, was an attempt to evaluate the generality of the findings of the previous studies for the case in which the REL and UNREL input consists of four rather than two nouns selected from semantic category norms (Battig & Montague, 1969; Shapiro & Palermo, 1970).

Experiment 4 (Sheldon Rosenberg and Richard S. Fink)

Method. The subjects were 24 undergraduate native English speakers who participated in the experiment as part of a course requirement. When they

TABLE 4
REL and UNREL Input Sets Used
in Experiment 4

REL	UNREL
apple pear banana peach	onion desk ticket shoe
rifle bomb sword pistol	hotel dime card girdle
beer whiskey gin wine	dirt jello snow wood
hammer saw chisel wrench	crayon rug wallet stream
piano drum trumpet violin	bottle ball pillow wagon
rose tulip carnation orchid	rock cigar umbrella raisin
broom mop sponge brush	coat net spoon lamp
stove refrigerator toaster sink	boat calculator doughnut tree
magazine book newspaper pamphlet	handkerchief clock window saddle
car bus train truck	cup pin hill chair

appeared for the experiment they were assigned in rotation to four different left-to-right orders of a single mixed list of 10 REL and 10 UNREL sets, with each set containing four nouns. Each REL set with its corresponding UNREL set can be found in Table 4. As in Experiment 2, the REL set contained high frequency instances of the same concept while the UNREL set contained instances of different concepts. However, unlike Experiment 2, where the REL and UNREL lists were balanced *overall* on word length and Thorndike and Lorge (1944) frequency, in the present instance for each REL set there was a specific UNREL set which was matched with it as closely as possible on a word-to-word basis on length (in letters and syllables) and Thorndike–Lorge frequency. Note in Table 4 that all of the sets contained concrete inanimate nouns, that very few mass nouns were used, and that all the count nouns were singular. Thus, in general, it will be seen that each REL set and its UNREL counterpart were matched as closely as possible on those linguistic features and roles which would give them very similar or identical semantic and syntactic structural potentialities.

Each of the four orders for a given set was printed on an index card. Thus, there were four decks of cards each of which contained the same list of 10 REL and 10 UNREL sets.

The instructions from Experiment 2 were modified to accord with the fact that four nouns had to be used in a single sentence. In addition, simultaneously with reading a set of four nouns (at a rate of approximately one per second) the card on which it was printed was placed on a stand in front of the subject so that he or she would not have the additional load of trying to remember the four nouns during sentence planning. The noun sets in the lists were presented in a different random order to each of the subjects. The subjects' task was again to produce a single sentence for each set of nouns, with no constraints being placed on order of use or on sentence length, content, or grammatical complexity. All subjects received a single practice set prior to being presented with the experimental list. Thus, with the exception of the modifications mentioned, the instructions and procedures of Experiment 4 were identical to those of Experiment 2.

Results. The subjects made on the average approximately one error on the REL sets and one error on the UNREL sets. The summary statistics for this experiment for correct responses can be found in Table 5. It is to be noted there that we abandoned our measure of lexical complexity and did not examine pause or duration. In addition, the measure of input propositional complexity (IPC) had to be modified for the four-noun case. For this purpose we extracted from each of the sentences a subject produced the elementary underlying sentences in which the four stimulus nouns appeared, and then computed the proportion of these in which more than one of the stimulus nouns appeared in the same elementary underlying sentence and/or shared essentially the same propositional content in the different elementary underlying sentences in which they appeared. Let us examine a concrete example of what we are talking about. The following sentence was one which occurred for the UNREL set *wallet crayon stream rug.*

As I lie on my rug by the stream I noticed that the crayon that was in my wallet was missing.

The elementary underlying sentences which we extracted from it were

I lie on my rug by the stream
I noticed . . .
The crayon was missing
The crayon was in my wallet.

TABLE 5
Means and Standard Deviations (SD) for
Measures of Experiment 4

| | Condition | | | |
| | REL | | UNREL | |
Measure	Mean	SD	Mean	SD
Median latency (sec)	5.04	6.98	10.33	10.55
Mean length (words)	18.36	4.86	22.31	7.06
SPC	5.2	.9	4.1	1.5
IPC (proportion)	.73	.14	.54	.20
SC	1.6	.6	1.9	.7

Thus, since there are four elementary sentences underlying the surface form produced, and two of them contain more than one of the stimulus nouns, the IPC score for this item is .50.

To take another example, a response such as *I bought a shoe, a desk, a ticket, and an onion* for the UNREL set *shoe desk ticket onion* would receive an IPC score of 1.00, because each of the stimulus nouns is associated with the same propositional content.

Means were computed for each subject over the IPC scores for the responses to the REL and UNREL sets, and SPC, SC, and length were scored as they were in the previous studies. Latency and complexity scores were also determined for each REL set and its UNREL counterpart so that the results could be analyzed across items as well.

It will be noted in Table 5 that there was an increase in the size of the means and standard deviations under the REL and UNREL conditions over what they were in the previous experiments for the measures that were comparable to those used earlier. Notice in particular the very considerable variability in latency for both REL and UNREL inputs. One possible explanation for the increases in latency is that they were due to increased input encoding time, but this is an unlikely possibility since the measurement of latency (as in the other experiments) did not begin until the end of the vocalization of the last noun in a set. Thus, the increases in latency must have been associated in some way with the increase in the amount of information that had to be integrated into the utterances the subjects were required to produce.

The large intersubject variability observed for both REL and UNREL inputs under the four-noun condition may very well have been related to individual differences in conceptual ability, but I made no attempt to examine this possibility.

Latency, as was to be expected, was significantly longer under the UNREL condition across both subjects ($p = .0009$, one tailed) and items ($p = .0025$, one tailed). Also, for 50% of the subjects median latency for UNREL items was more than twice what it was for REL items. Thus, it is likely that computational demands under the UNREL condition were considerable.

Surprisingly, the sentences of the REL condition tended to be associated with *more* elementary underlying semantic propositions (the SPC measure) than the sentences of the UNREL condition, and this effect was reliable both for subjects ($p < .0005$, two tailed) and items ($p = .0050$, two tailed). However, it will be recalled that this also occurred in Experiment 2—the noun–noun counterpart of the present one—and was significant overall and for only one of the two experimental lists. However, in spite of the present findings for SPC, the REL condition was significantly lower than the UNREL condition on IPC. Thus, semantic propositional integration and overlap tended to be highest for the sentences produced under the REL condition of Experiment 4. These findings were significant for subjects ($p < .0001$, two tailed) and items ($p = .0050$, two tailed).

The increase in SPC for the REL condition was also not accompanied by an increase in SC or length, as can be seen in Table 5. Indeed, the means for the measures in question were both higher for the UNREL items. No attempt was made to determine quantitatively why the higher level of SPC under the REL condition was not associated with an increase in SC or in length. However, an informal examination of the sentences produced suggested that this finding was due to differences between the REL and UNREL conditions in the incidence of deletions of identical constituents as well as in the use of optional phrasal constituents in elementary sentences.

The difference between conditions for SC was significant when tested across subjects (p = .0156, two tailed) and items (p = .0094, two tailed). Similarly, the effect observed for length was significant across subjects (p = .0003, two tailed) and items (p = .0050, two tailed).

Discussion. It seems clear, then, that even though the REL and UNREL items were selected so as to have very similar or identical semantic and syntactic structural potentialities, when their number was increased, the difference between them in sentence initiation time was associated with differences in (a) the complexity of the semantic propositions the items were mapped onto (IPC), (b) the syntactic complexity of the sentences the items appeared in, and (c) length. There was also an association with number of elementary underlying semantic propositions, but the direction of the association was the reverse of what it was for the other complexity measures. Thus, since we obtained discrepant results on only one of the complexity measures, we cannot in the present instance reject the possibility that differences in semantic and syntactic complexity (and perhaps lexical selection load as well) contributed something to the difference we found between the REL and UNREL conditions in sentence initiation time.

GENERAL DISCUSSION

I tried to show in the Introduction that there is little to be learned about the speech production process from the results of large-scale correlative studies of pausal phenomena in spontaneous connected speech or from studies of speech errors, and that although experimental methods hold more promise of helping us identify the organization and operation of the speech production process, most of the available experimental literature suffers from serious methodological and conceptual problems. The discussion of the literature, however, did lead to some hypotheses which I suggested would be worth attempting to evaluate in the laboratory, and the one I became involved with concerned the relationship between ease of semantic planning and sentence initiation time and complexity.

It was assumed in the present research that the semantic propositions occasioned by input encoding could be either retrieved from memory or computed, and that computation takes more time than retrieval. Thus, on the expectation that speakers would be more likely to have available in long-term memory propositions for which semantically related lexical input would be appropriate than semantically unrelated lexical input, it was anticipated that sentences occasioned by the former type of input would be initiated faster than sentences occasioned by the latter type of input. This prediction was strongly supported by the results of the present research. However, only in the case of lexical input that consisted of two nouns did it seem reasonable to conclude that the facilitation of sentence initiation time under semantically related input is associated mainly with ease of semantic proposition generation. The results of Experiment 4 raised the possibility that the complexity of semantic and syntactic structural decisions (and possibly lexical decisions as well) contributes to sentence initiation time when the amount of information in the input to the sentence production process is increased.

The foregoing statements concerning the relationship between sentence complexity and sentence initiation time, however, must be seen for what they are, namely, tentative working hypotheses, since they are based upon results obtained using measures of undetermined validity. For the measure SPC it was assumed that the amount of information processed during semantic proposition generation is equivalent to the number of elementary semantic propositions retrieved or computed, while for the measures designated IPC it was assumed that certain sets or configurations of semantic propositions for which the lexical input would be appropriate would make greater demands on the immediate (i.e., working) memory component of the sentence production process than certain other sets. In brief, on this measure low input propositional complexity is associated with instances in which the input items appear in the same elementary underlying semantic proposition or play identical semantic roles in identical elementary underlying semantic propositions. The measure of syntactic complexity (SC) for a given sentence production was the number of surface structure clauses it contained, and in using it, it was assumed that each surface structure clause a speaker chooses, or is obligated, to encode adds an increment to sentence planning time. A measure of lexical selection complexity was used in the first three experiments but abandoned after it was found to be relatively stable for a wide variety of sentence lengths and sentence types that our subjects were producing. Finally, length was included among the complexity measures because it represents directly the number of content and function words a speaker has to select for inclusion in the final execution program for a sentence.

How are we to proceed with the investigation of the validity of measures of processing complexity in sentence production? Clearly, what are needed for this purpose are not regression analyses but experimental procedures that will permit us to hold input and ease of proposition generation constant while we manipulate syntactic and other linguistic obligations, and procedures that will permit us to hold all else constant while we manipulate input or ease of proposition generation. Unfortunately, given the degree of confounding that characterizes most if not all candidate measures of processing complexity in sentence production, it may be that all we will be able to do is approximate such procedures.

Of course, the methods of measuring sentence processing complexity in the present research paradigm were based upon the assumption that outside of differences in the way in which semantic proposition generation takes place, sentence planning proceeds in the same fashion for the REL and UNREL conditions. There is an alternative to this assumption, however, which we cannot reject on a priori grounds (or on the available evidence), namely, that mature speakers have available overlearned linguistic programs for talking about *both* semantically related and semantically unrelated input *which differ in just the sorts of features that are being detected by the present sentence complexity measures when the amount of information in the input increases.* Thus, with this view a linguistic program that is simple for dealing with multielement REL input becomes complex when multielement UNREL input is encountered and, conversely, a linguistic program that is simple for dealing with multielement UNREL input becomes complex when multielement REL input is encountered.

It should be pointed out here that the foregoing view does not mean that a given type of input will be associated with only one type of surface structure "frame," or that a given linguistic program cannot be realized using a variety of surface structure frames. Thus, the sorts of linguistic programs I am talking about might result in REL items being used as compounds, but whether they are used as a compound subject, a compound direct object, etc., can vary from sentence to sentence. Similarly, a program which requires that UNREL items serve different functions in different elementary sentences could be realized using any number of different single- or multiple-clause surface sentential structures.

Obviously, any attempt to evaluate a view of sentence complexity that talks in terms of differential linguistic programming strategies rather than number of operations and the like must begin with an attempt to identify the sorts of strategies mature speakers might be using. With this purpose in mind, I decided to examine all of the sentences subjects produced in the main free-responding studies, Experiments 2 and 4, and upon doing so noted, first of all, that there was simply no indication in either study for both the REL and the UNREL conditions that the subjects were using the same surface sentential frames over and over again. In Experiment 2, for example, there were only 15 instances out of a total of 476 correct responses in which a subject used a given sentence frame more than once. Second, although the subjects in Experiment 2 received similar mean scores for the REL and UNREL conditions on IPC, there were some interesting differences between the two input conditions that were being masked by the effect of averaging over the numerical scale values which had been assigned to the various response categories. The most common fate for the nouns in a REL pair was for them to appear as a compound of some sort, whereas the most common fate for the nouns in an UNREL pair was for them to appear in the same elementary sentence. In addition, there was a greater tendency for the UNREL items to play different semantic and syntactic roles in different elementary sentences than the REL items. Last, I noted that the subjects in Experiment 4 showed an appreciable dependence under the REL condition on structures in which the nouns served identical semantic and syntactic functions in identical elementary sentences, as well as an appreciable dependence under the UNREL condition on structures in which the nouns served different semantic and syntactic functions in different elementary sentences, and on structures in which two or more of the nouns could appear in the same elementary sentence.

These trends do not tell the whole story of the sentences produced by the subjects in Experiments 2 and 4, but they should lead us to consider seriously the following possibilities.

1. Even under the two-noun condition, subjects use differential linguistic programming strategies for REL and UNREL items.

2. There may be only a small number of overlearned linguistic programming strategies associated with talking about REL and UNREL input.

3. An increase in the amount of information in a given type of input does not necessarily lead to changes in linguistic programming strategies.

4. The strategies in question do not constrain speakers to output the same surface sentential structure over and over again when the nature of the input remains constant.

One hypothesis that is raised indirectly by the possibility of overlearned linguistic programming strategies which we are now attempting to evaluate in the laboratory is that the strategies speakers use for processing UNREL input under conditions of increased information content (as in the case of four nouns) operate best when the "use in a single sentence" constraint is removed. Briefly, what we expect to find under these circumstances for the UNREL condition are a reduction in sentence initiation time and increases in sentence complexity as measured by the dependent variables mean IPC, mean number of surface structure clauses, and mean length.

In addition to attempting to evaluate the validity of alternative representations of sentential complexity, it will be necessary to attack directly the question of differential processing time for retrieval as contrasted with computation of semantic propositions, and one approach I am exploring at present involves comparing retrieval latencies (sentence initiation times) for laboratory-acquired sentential associates of noun sets with production latencies for the same sets.

Finally, I want to mention that throughout these investigations it was assumed that the experimental procedures employed would insure that most if not all of the planning would take place prior to sentence initiation. However, in retrospect, while this still seems to be a reasonable assumption in the case of the noun–noun paradigm, I feel uncomfortable making it in the case of the four-noun paradigm and want, therefore, to attempt to evaluate this claim directly in future research.

REFERENCES

Baars, B. J., Motley, M. T., & MacKay, D. G. Output editing of artificially elicited slips of the tongue. Paper presented at the Midwestern Psychological Association meetings, Chicago, May, 1975.

Battig, W. F., & Montague, W. E. Category norms for verbal items in 56 categories: A replication of the Connecticut category norms. *Journal of Experimental Psychology Monograph,* 1969, 80, No. 3, Part 2.

Bever, T. G. The cognitive basis for linguistic structures. In J. R. Hayes (Ed.), *Cognition and the development of language.* New York: Wiley, 1970. Pp. 279–362.

Boomer, D. S. Hesitation and grammatical encoding. *Language and speech,* 1965, 8, 148–158.

Boomer, D. S. Review of F. Goldman-Eisler, Psycholinguistics: Experiments in spontaneous speech. *Lingua,* 1970, 25, 152–164.

Boomer, D. S., & Laver, J. D. M. Slips of the tongue. *The British Journal of Disorders of Communication,* 1968, 3, 2–11.

Forster, K. I. Left-to-right processes in the construction of sentences. *Journal of Verbal Learning and Verbal Behavior,* 1966, 5, 285–291.

Forster, K. I. Sentence completion latencies as a function of constituent structure. *Journal of Verbal Learning and Verbal Behavior,* 1967, 6, 878–883.

Forster, K. I. The effect of removal of length constraint on sentence completion times. *Journal of Verbal Learning and Verbal Behavior,* 1968, 7, 253–254.

Foss, D. J., & Fay, D. Linguistic theory and performance models. In J. Worth & D. Cohen (Eds.), *Testing linguistic hypotheses.* New York: Hemisphere Press, 1976.

Fromkin, V. A. The non-anomalous nature of anomalous utterances. *Language,* 1971, 47, 27–52.

Fromkin, V. A. (Ed.), *Speech errors as linguistic evidence.* The Hague: Mouton, 1973.

Garrett, M. F. The analysis of sentence production. In G. Bower (Ed.), *Advances in learning theory and motivation.* Vol. 9. New York: Academic Press, 1975.

Goldman-Eisler, F. *Psycholinguistics: Experiments in spontaneous speech.* New York: Academic Press, 1968.

Goldman-Eisler, F. Pauses, clauses, sentences. *Language and Speech,* 1972, 15, 103–113.

Hawkins, P. R. The syntactic location of hesitation pauses. *Language and Speech,* 1971, 14, 277–288.

Hornby, P. A. The psychological subject and predicate. *Cognitive Psychology,* 1972, 3, 632–642.

Jacobs, R. A., & Rosenbaum, P. S. *English transformational grammar.* Waltham, Massachusetts: Blaisdell, 1968.

Johnson, N. F. On the relationship between sentence structure and the latency in generating the sentence. *Journal of Verbal Learning and Verbal Behavior,* 1966, 5, 375–380.

Kintsch, W. *The representation of meaning in memory.* Hillsdale, New Jersey: Lawrence Erlbaum Associates, 1974.

Lieberman, P. Some effects of semantic and grammatical context on the production and perception of speech. *Language and Speech,* 1963, 6, 172–179.

Lindsley, J. R. Producing simple utterances: How far ahead do we plan? *Cognitive Psychology,* 1975, 7, 1–19.

MacKay, D. G. The structure of words and syllables: Evidence from errors in speech. *Cognitive Psychology*, 1972, 3, 210–227.

MacKay, D. G. Aspects of the syntax of behavior: Syllable structure and speech rate. *Quarterly Journal of Experimental Psychology*, 1974, 26, 642–657.

Martin, J. G. Hesitations in the speaker's production and the listener's reproduction of utterances. *Journal of Verbal Learning and Verbal Behavior*, 1967, 6, 903–909.

Martin, J. G. Some acoustic and grammatical features of spontaneous speech. Paper presented at the Pittsburgh Conference on the Perception of Language, 1968.

Martin, J. G., & Strange, W. Determinants of hesitations in spontaneous speech. *Journal of Experimental Psychology*, 1968, 76, 474–479.

Miller, G. A., Newman, E. B., & Friedman, E. A. Length–frequency statistics for written English. *Information and Control*, 1958, 1, 370–389.

Murray, D. C. Talk, silence, and anxiety. *Psychological Bulletin*, 1971, 75, 244–260.

Nooteboom, S. G. The tongue slips into patterns. *Leyden studies in Linguistics and Phonetics*. The Hague: Mouton, 1969.

Osgood, C. E. Where do sentences come from? In D. D. Steinberg & L. A. Jakobovits (Eds.), *Semantics*. Cambridge, England: Cambridge University Press, 1971. Pp. 497–529.

Reynolds, A., & Paivio, A. Cognitive and emotional determinants of speech. *Canadian Journal of Psychology*, 1968, 22, 164–175.

Rochester, S. R. The significance of pauses in spontaneous speech. *Journal of Psycholinguistic Research*, 1973, 2, 51–81.

Rochester, S. R., & Gill, J. Production of complex sentences in monologues and dialogues. *Journal of Verbal Learning and Verbal Behavior*, 1973, 12, 203–210.

Rosenberg, S., & Koen, M. J. Norms of sequential associative dependencies in active declarative sentences. In J. C. Catford (Ed.), *Studies in language and language behavior, supplement to Progress Report VI*. Ann Arbor, Michigan: University of Michigan, Center for Research on Language and Language Behavior, February 1, 1968.

Shapiro, S. I., & Palermo, D. S. Conceptual organization and class membership: Normative data for representatives of 100 categories. *Psychonomic Monograph Supplements*, 1970, 3, No. 11(Whole No. 43), 107–127.

Tannenbaum, P. H., & Williams, F. Generation of active and passive sentences as a function of subject or object focus. *Journal of Verbal Learning and Verbal Behavior*, 1968, 7, 246–250.

Tannenbaum, P. H., Williams, F., & Hillier, C. S. Word predictability in the environment of hesitations. *Journal of Verbal Learning and Verbal Behavior*, 1965, 4, 134–140.

Taylor, I. Content and structure in sentence production. *Journal of Verbal Learning and Verbal Behavior*, 1969, 8, 170–175.

Thorndike, E. L., & Lorge, I. *The teacher's word book of 30,000 words*. New York: Columbia University Teachers College, 1944.

Trager, G. L., & Smith, H. L. *Outline of English structure*. Norman, Oklahoma: Battenburg Press, 1951.

Valian, V. V. Talking, listening, and linguistic structure. Unpublished doctoral dissertation, Northeastern University, Boston, Massachusetts, 1971.

Yngve, V. H. A model and an hypothesis for language structure. *Proceedings of the American Philosophical Society*, 1960, 104, 444–466.

Yngve, V. H. The depth hypothesis. In R. Jakobsen (Ed.), *Structure of language and its mathematical aspects: Proceedings, 12th symposium in applied mathematics*. Providence, Rhode Island: American Mathematical Society, 1961.

10
Producing Ideas and Sentences

Joseph H. Danks

Kent State University

> *Speaker A:* ...
> *Speaker B:* I don't understand what you mean.
> *Speaker A:* You know what I mean even if I didn't say it right.
> *Speaker B:* No, I don't.
> *Speaker A:* I know what I want to say but I can't think how to say it.

In spite of their lack of communication at one level, these speakers share a common assumption, namely, that thought, language, and speech are separated from each other. First we have an idea; then we compose the sentence expressing that idea; then we speak the sentence. This conceptual division is shared not only by persons-in-the-street but also by psychologists and linguists investigating speech production (and speech comprehension as well). One way to illustrate this discrete processing sequence is by analogy with a computer program as in Fig. 1. The three stages are represented as subroutines of a main executive program that controls the flow of information between the subroutines. Control returns to the executive for a decision whether to continue production after execution of each subroutine.

First, there is a thinking stage. Speakers usually talk about something and that something is an idea to be encoded in a specific language form. Except for the radical behaviorists, many investigators assume that the thinking stage is relatively independent of the process of constructing a sentence. There are ideas that we want to express but, like Speaker A, we are unable to find the proper words to convey the meaning. We recognize thoughts that should or do remain unexpressed, although to our embarrassment that recognition occasionally comes too late. The return of control to the executive following idea generation represents this decision, that is, whether the idea should be encoded in a sentence or not. Social, interpersonal, and conceptual factors influence the decision to continue.

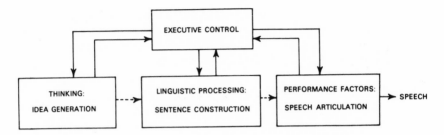

FIG. 1   A discrete processing model of sentence production.

The second stage encodes the intended idea in linguistic form. The syntactic structure is determined and the particular lexical items are selected. Although one need not be limited to a formal model derived from linguistic theory, several models of sentence production have incorporated rules derived from transformational–generative grammar (e.g., Fodor, Bever, & Garrett, 1974; Katz, 1964). For psycholinguists this section of the sentence production program holds the greatest interest because here we see the workings of specific linguistic mechanisms. After the sentence is constructed, it is evaluated for communicative effectiveness in terms of social criteria. What is the probability that the listener will interpret the utterance as intended by the speaker? If this probability is too low, the utterance may be edited to increase its communicativeness.

The last step in the sentence production process involves the conversion of the underlying sentence into speech. Here the abstract representations constructed in stage two are encoded in articulatory commands and the motor movements are executed. As argued by Liberman (1970), there is not a one-to-one mapping between the phonological code of the abstract representation and the movements of the articulators. The conversion involves a complex coding operation to determine the proper instructions to the articulatory apparatus. In addition, nonlinguistic performance factors, such as memory limitations, distractions, interruptions, etc., can modify the speech output from this last stage.

The discrete processing model introduced thus far and developed in the next section is based on a faulty notion of how mental processes are organized. Even though it matches our intuitions of how we speak and has been accepted by several theorists, sentences are not produced in discrete stages. Idea generation is not separable from sentence construction, indeed the whole notion of fixed subroutines corresponding to psychological processing is false. In typical speech production situations, sentences and ideas are produced simultaneously in an abstract code corresponding to speech. That is to say, our response mode determines the symbolic code used in thinking and influences the direction and structure of thought. Thought is possible in several modes, but one of the most common is speech.

In this chapter I will be concerned with the theoretical and empirical separation of idea generation from sentence construction. In the next section, theoretical proposals that assume a discrete processing model of sentence production are presented. To test the assumption that ideas are generated before sentences are constructed, two experiments are reported representing empirical attempts to effect that separation. Both studies used methodologically different, though conceptually related, approaches. The results were not consistent with the assumption of discrete processing stages although regular, consistent relationships were obtained in both studies. The results lead to a discussion of an alternative conception in the final section, namely, that idea generation and sentence production represent the same functional process. This conception is developed in more detail as well as extended to cover sentence comprehension and language processing in general.

SEPARATING IDEAS AND SENTENCES

Conceptual Separation

Psycholinguists have been most efficient in compartmentalizing the problems and issues that they study. Although foreshadowed in earlier work (Saussure, 1916), Chomsky's (1965) competence–performance dichotomy firmly walled off performance variables such as limited memory capacities, distractions, slips of the tongue, etc., from the core of linguistic processing. In its simplest form this distinction was incorporated into a production model by postulating that a grammar (competence) constructed a sentence in toto which was then degraded by a variety of performance factors. Competence had to be fully explored and specified before work could reasonably begin on building a performance model for which competence would supply the core. Thus were linguistic rules and representations separated from speech behavior.

To complete the isolation of language, a demarcation was needed on the deep side of language as well to separate it from cognition. That is, language and thought are different. Although the separation of language from thought was not formalized by Chomsky, the cleavage was implicit in his assertions that semantics was to be excluded from the proper study of linguistics. Semantics later was gathered into the linguistic fold, but there was a residual implication that there was a still deeper component which was beyond the pale of linguistics. Undifferentiated thought was assumed to supply the content on which the linguistic forms could operate.

These divisions are easily discerned in a speculative model of sentence production proposed by Fodor, Bever, and Garrett (1974). They described a central linguistic core composed of a base structure, lexicon, transformational component, semantic component, and phonology. This core constructs a sentence corresponding to a message source. On the other side of the linguistic components are performance devices that introduce minor perturbations in the acoustic signal. Among these are an output buffer, which introduces memory limitations, and an articulatory apparatus.

The Fodor *et al.* (1974) model has much in common with Katz's speculations ten years earlier. Katz (1964) explicitly stated that the speaker first selects an idea to communicate, then applies formal linguistic rules to generate the sentence and ultimately the speech:

> The speaker . . . chooses some message he wants to convey to the hearer. He selects some thought he wishes to express to him, some command he wants to give him, or some question he needs to ask him. This message is, we may assume, in whatever form the semantic component of this linguistic description uses to represent the meaning content of thoughts, commands, questions, or the like. The speaker then uses the sentence production procedure to obtain an abstract syntactic structure having the proper conceptualization of this thought, command, or question as its semantic interpretation. This procedure helps him find a sentence that is suitable to the circumstances by rejecting all syntactic structures which, though they bear the proper semantic interpretation, are for sentences that are too long, syntactically too complicated, too pedantic, etc. After he has a suitable syntactic structure, the speaker utilizes the phonological component of his linguistic description to produce a phonetic shape for it. This phonetic shape is encoded into a signal that causes the speaker's articulatory system to vocalize an utterance of the sentence [p. 132].

Lest the reader think that Katz is speaking only metaphorically, he continues his discussion by postulating neural mechanisms in the brain corresponding to the linguistic components.

> The linguistic description and the procedures of sentence production and recognition must correspond to independent mechanisms in the brain. Componential distinctions between the syntactic, phonological, and semantic components must rest on relevant differences between three neural submechanisms of the mechanism which stores the linguistic description [Katz, 1964, p. 133].

Katz confused the cognitive program with the neuroanatomical mechanism (cf. Glucksberg & Danks, 1975; Sutherland, 1966), but the critical point for this discussion is that the separation of idea selection from sentence generation is complete.

Both the Fodor *et al.* (1974) and Katz (1964) proposals depend on formal linguistic rules for their sentence construction stage and leave idea generation as an amorphous, undefined input to the sentence construction process. The implication is that idea generation is whatever remains after one explains as much as possible via linguistic rules—both syntactic and semantic. In fact, the linguistic rules constrain explicitly the form of the ideational representation to a semantic (linguistic) format.

Dependence on linguistic formalisms may be neither necessary nor desirable because formal grammars were written for purposes other than as a description of how speakers and listeners produce and comprehend speech (McNeill, 1975a). Both Schlesinger (1971) and Carroll (1974) explicitly reject linguistic formalisms although both introduce new formalisms of their own. The Schlesinger and Carroll proposals are quite similar in their overall orientation, but the specifics of the representations and processes differ. Both Schlesinger and Carroll postulate an intentive component that contains a representation of the intentions and meanings that are actually expressed by the speaker in an utterance. The intention stage is followed by a process component in which a surface-level sentence is derived from the intentional representation.

Schlesinger calls the speaker's intention an "*input marker,* or *I marker,* [which is] the formalized representation of those of the speaker's intentions which are expressed in linguistic output [1971, p. 65, italics in the original]." Input markers contain "concepts." These are neither words nor lexical items, but the precise form of a concept is left unstated. The input marker is structured as a hierarchy of concept pairs joined by relations such as attribution, agency, possession, and instrumentality.

In the second phase of sentence production, *realization rules* convert the input marker into a word string that can be realized as speech. The realization rules fulfill two functions: to assign each concept (which later becomes a lexical item) both its grammatical class and its position within the sentence string. Realization rules have the same functional power as transformations do in generative grammars. The input marker represents the way speakers encode their ideas—not a logical formalism—and the realization rules correspond to the processes speakers actually use in sentence construction and not to linguistic descriptions.

Carroll (1974) has written a performance grammar as an operational computer program that generates a fairly large set of sentences, albeit still a limited set. The intentive component, containing intention markers, is "a collection of elements and values of variables that express the basic meaning of the utterance that is to be output by the grammar [p. 33]." The elements are concepts representing categories like "deep subject," "deep verb," and "deep object." The variables, which take on the elements as values, are "theme," "mode," "query," and "emphasis," among other sentential characterizations. A code component then receives the intention marker as input and constructs a grammatical sentence from it. "The code component... [consists] essentially of a series of performance rules that represent what the speaker has learned about how to talk, i.e., how to transform the contents of any given I-marker [intention marker] into verbal output that will satisfy the conventions of the language system [p. 40]." The code component is a real time process that outputs a left-to-right string of words.

In summary, the proposals of both Schlesinger and Carroll describe an intention state followed by a production process. An idea and a speaker's wish to express that idea is represented as an intention in a form compatible with the production stage. The latter stage constructs the sentence corresponding to the intention via rules representing the speaker's cognitive processes. Basic to both proposals are assumptions that the thought component must be separate from the language component and that language is a transducer of ideas.

Methodological Separation

Research in sentence production has lagged behind research in comprehension, except in the case of young children where investigators have attempted to write grammars to account for children's productions. The apparent reason for this bias—in both cases—has been the seduction of psycholinguists by the "bright-light" fallacy. Just as the drunk hunted for his lost wallet under the street light, investigators have restricted their studies to easily constrained phenomena and to the methods that constrain them.

Comprehension appears to be easily constrained. The input to the subject is completely under the control of the experimenter. The experimenter may not have identified all the relevant variables in advance, but once identified they are potentially accessible to control or manipulation. The output side has presented a few more difficulties because the result of real interest is a mental representation rather than overt behavior. However, a wide variety of tasks—learning, memory, matching, verification, and paraphrase, among others—have been devised to converge on that mental representation.

Why has the study of production processes in adult speakers lagged? The problems of experimental control in production are the reverse of those in comprehension. If the experimenter attempts to control the input to the speaker, any stimulus—picture, word, sentence, or symbol—presented to the subject for him to respond to verbally must first be comprehended by the subject before responding. Since the investigator is interested in production and not comprehension, this comprehension phase represents contamination, just as response production is contamination in comprehension studies. One investigator's object of study is another's "error." To the extent that time spent generating an idea—in response either to the experimenter's stimulus or to internal plans and goals—is independent of the construction of a sentence to express that idea, then it should be excluded when one attempts to model sentence production processes. In addition, control over the input restricts the range of productions available to the subject. In this case, the subject may alter this production process from the usual to meet the restrictions imposed by the input. Thus, input should be left relatively uncontrolled in production tasks.

What about output? Here also one would like to leave the subject free to produce utterances as he constructs them rather than imposing some artificial limitation on the form, structure, or content. The investigator of production processes is left in a tenuous position. The optimal strategy would be to leave both the input and output sides of the procedure relatively unconstrained. But this means that establishing a functional relation between ideas and the speech expressing those ideas is difficult indeed. "Getting the data we need (e.g., on the relative production complexity of sentences of different syntactic types) would involve somehow getting the subject spontaneously to produce sentences of an antecedently specified message or form, and there is no very satisfactory procedure for doing this [Fodor *et al.,* 1974, p. 397]." Thus, the methodological problems involved in studying sentence production appear more formidable than those involved in studying comprehension.

EXPERIMENTAL SEPARATION OF IDEAS AND SENTENCES

Because of the theoretical pervasiveness of discrete processing models, two experiments were designed to isolate the idea-generation stage from the sentence-construction stage. If the two stages are called and executed as successive subroutines, then we should be able to find variables that act on one but not the other and vice versa. If we cannot discover such independently acting variables, then a discrete processing model may be incorrect and alternatives should be considered. The time required for a subject to produce a sentence was taken as a measure of the complete sentence production process. Then we searched for other variables that would reflect either variation in the time to generate an idea (stage one) or variation in the time to construct a sentence (stage two). Identification of variables that differentially correlate with the two stages should provide insight into the processing of each stage as well as empirical support for discrete stages.

The basic task was the same in both experiments. The subjects produced a sentence using one, two, or three concepts, either nouns or verbs. No restrictions were placed on the content or structure of the sentence. The basic dependent variable was the time needed by the subject to compose the sentence (*production latency*) and was defined as the time for the subject to initiate writing the sentence. The subject was instructed not to begin writing until the sentence was completely formulated in his mind. In previous research using similar instructions in a paraphrasing task, the sentence initiation latency was highly correlated ($rs = .80$) with latencies from two other comprehension tasks (Danks, 1970).

In the first experiment, the conceptual relatedness of stimulus word pairs was postulated to reflect the time to generate an idea and the syntactic complexity of the produced sentence to the time to construct that sentence. The sentence production latencies were decomposed by multiply correlating them with these two variables. If the stages are indeed distinct and if they are reflected by conceptual relatedness and syntactic complexity, then we can isolate statistically two components of the sentence production latency.

In a second experiment, the sentence production time was decomposed procedurally by giving the subjects two successive tasks. First they generated an idea to a concept set; later they produced the sentence corresponding to that idea. If there are separate stages and if this procedure isolates them, then the idea generation latency should be most highly correlated with the conceptual complexity of the produced sentences and sentence production latency should be correlated with the sentential complexity of those sentences.

Experiment I: Statistical Separation[1]

Method. Pairs of related and unrelated nouns were selected from Rosenberg's Associative Sentence Norms II (1966). Rosenberg obtained his norms by presenting sentence frames of the form "The $Noun_1$ $Verb_t$ the $Noun_2$," where $Noun_1$ was given and $Verb_t$ and $Noun_2$ were blanks to be filled in by the subject. The norms are tabulations of the $Verb_t$ and $Noun_2$ responses. We selected 60 $Noun_1$ (base) words along with a high and low frequency $Noun_2$ response to each. For example, *animal* was paired with *food* and *tent* for high and low frequency, respectively, and *mother* with *child* and *ring*. The high frequency nouns were usually the most frequent response, although sometimes the second or third most frequent response was selected to avoid repetitions of words. The high frequency pairs had a mean response probability of .27 (range: .08– .76). The low frequency words were arbitrarily selected from the set of words with a response probability of .02.

All subjects were undergraduate women at Kent State University who were fulfilling an introductory course requirement and who were native English speakers. Two groups of 12 subjects were presented with 60 word pairs consisting of the 60 base words paired with complementary sets of high- and low-frequency response words. Each group received 30 high- and 30 low-frequency words arranged in a single random order for all subjects. The subject was instructed that she would see a series of word pairs, that she was to write a sentence containing both words, and that there were no other restrictions on the sentence. The visual presentation of each pair of words started a clock that was stopped by a switch closure in a special ball-point pen when the subject started writing the sentence.

Results and discussion. The sentence production latencies were transformed into log scores to correct for skewed distributions. The geometric mean latencies for high and low pairs were 5.90 sec and 6.39 sec, respectively, a significant difference, $F(1, 20) = 6.41, p < .02$. Not unexpectedly, the high-frequency pairs were easier to combine in a single sentence than were the low-frequency pairs. Had they not been easier, we would have been skeptical indeed as to the validity of our procedure, since relatedness was defined in terms of norms obtained in a

---

[1] This experiment was originally reported by myself and Linda Ohlweiler (1972) at a Symposium on Sentence Production chaired by Sheldon Rosenberg at the Midwestern Psychological Association meeting in Cleveland.

production task. These results are primarily a manipulation check and they agree with Rosenberg's (1972) results in which oral production latency was also a function of the semantic relatedness of two stimulus nouns.

The main purpose of this experiment was to decompose the production latencies by multiply correlating them with measures of idea generation and sentence construction. For the time to generate the idea, *ratings of relatedness* should reflect both a cognitive and a linguistic judgment of the difficulty of generating an idea to relate the word pairs. The ease with which the subject generated an idea relating two concepts probably is a function of the frequency of experiencing the two concepts together in the past and this frequency should be a major contribution to the ratings. The word pairs were given to an independent sample of 100 subjects who were asked to rate the relatedness of the two nouns on a scale from one to ten. They were given examples of *salt–pepper* (10), *salt–dirt* (4), and *salt–microphone* (1). Other examples of possible bases of relatedness were provided, such as concepts found together, similarity of objects, opposites, similar functions, and shared category or class membership. The mean rating for high frequency pairs was 9.03 and 5.32 for low frequency pairs. This difference was highly significant, $F(1, 98) = 411.27, p < .001$, providing validity to the rating procedure.

The second stage is in large measure a function of the complexity of the syntactic relation that is needed to realize the particular cognitive relationship involved. The complexity of the syntactic relation between the presented pairs of words was measured with a structural index. Specifically, the sentences which the subjects produced were analyzed into their base structure clauses. The *structural index* was derived from the extent to which the word pairs were included in the same base structure clauses and their relation within those clauses. For example, two nouns that were related as a noun and an object of a prepositional phrase modifying that noun were in a less complex relationship than if the nouns were related as subject of the sentence and an object of a prepositional phrase modifying the indirect object. However, since subjects were actually writing surface structure sentences, not base structures, a measure of the relationship between the base structure clauses as realized in the surface structure was also included in the scale. If both nouns were included in the same surface and same base structure clause, then this was considered a lower level of complexity than if the nouns were separated in two different base and/or surface structure clauses. There were 12 sentences for each pair of words (one from each subject). The structural index was defined as the mean score for each pair. A sign test across the 60 base words contrasting the high frequency pairs with the low frequency pairs was significant, $z = 4.07, p < .001$, providing some validation for the structural index.

The mean ratings of relatedness and the structural index were then multiply correlated with the mean latency for each word pair in order to separate the idea-generation and sentence-construction stages. When other variables, such as the frequency of the individual words (Kučera & Francis, 1967) and the strength of association between the base word and the high frequency word, were included in the analysis, only trivial increases in the multiple correlation were obtained. Hence, we shall consider further only the three major variables.

The mean production latency correlated − .33 with the ratings of relatedness and + .22 with the structural index; the ratings and structural index correlated − .38. All of these Pearson product-moment correlations were significant, all ts (118) > 2.40, $p < .01$. The multiple correlation of these variables using ratings and the structural index as predictors and the latency as the dependent variable was + .35. This is a moderate, but significant, correlation, $F(2, 117) = 8.17, p < .001$.

There was some support for the statistical decomposition of the response latencies corresponding to two stages of sentence production. That suport was weak, however, since the multiple correlation accounted for only 12% of the variance. There must have been considerably more to this sentence production task than was measured by the ratings of relatedness and the structural index. The largest simple correlation was between the ratings and structural indices themselves. This correlation could arise for either of two reasons. First, one or both of the variables could be impure measures of the underlying processes they were intended to reflect. The impurity could result from either the structural index reflecting idea generation or the ratings reflecting part of the sentence construction process or both. The structural index was based on the relations between the word pairs in the produced sentences and may have been overly sensitive to the semantic relatedness presumed to contribute to idea generation. Second, a discrete processing model may be incorrect in any reasonable sense of separate stages. Perhaps the separation is only a figment of the speaker's intuition that theorists have accepted too readily. Before expanding on this second conclusion, a different procedure to separate the two stages was devised.

Experiment II: Procedural Separation[2]

The same basic sentence production paradigm was retained from the first experiment, but an idea-generation task was added to the procedure. The first time a subject saw a list of concepts, he was to think of an idea relating the concepts. The subject did not have to express his idea nor did he expect he would have to do so later. The time for him to think of the idea was called *idea latency* and was assumed to be a relatively direct reflection of idea generation. The subject was shown the concept list again and he wrote a sentence incorporating all the concepts. He was encouraged to write a sentence corresponding to the idea produced in the first phase, but this was not required. Only sentences

[2] I thank Tim Jay for his assistance in collecting and analyzing the data reported in this experiment.

which subjects indicated matched the earlier idea were included in subsequent analyses. The time to begin writing the sentence was called *production latency*. The sentences produced were analyzed according to several different linguistic indices of both surface structure and base structure variables.

Even if the two stages are mechanically independent of each other, idea generation has a direct influence on the sentence-construction stage because more complex ideas would require more complex sentences to express them. In spite of that influence, indices of base structure complexity should be more related to the semantic intentions or the idea behind the sentence than surface structure indices would be. In contrast, the surface structure indices would be more related to the complexity of producing a particular sentence, given a particular base structure, than would the base structure indices per se. Hence, a discrete processing model predicts that idea latencies would correlate more highly with base structure indices than surface structure indices, and that the correlations of production latencies with the indices would show the reverse relationship.

Method. The stimulus words were taken from populations of 100 verbs and 180 nouns that had been collected to cover as completely as possible the syntactic and semantic properties of those parts of speech. Seven trial types defined stimulus presentation conditions: a single noun (N), a single verb (V), two nouns (NN), two verbs (VV), a noun and a verb (NV), two nouns and a verb (NNV), and a noun and two verbs (NVV). Each trial type was randomly assigned to one of seven positions within each of seven blocks of trials. A list was then constructed by randomly selecting words, without replacement from the populations of nouns and verbs, to fill each trial type. Twenty such lists were formed. While the order of trial types was identical for all 20 lists, the stimulus words representing those types were different. The order of nouns and verbs within each of the mixed part of speech trial types, NV, NNV, and NVV, was counterbalanced.

Each subject, tested individually, was first instructed to think of an idea incorporating each set of concepts as they were presented. When he had done so, he placed a check mark on an answer sheet. The subject was told explicitly that he did not have to tell the experimenter what his idea was, only to respond when he had an idea. Nothing was mentioned about any additional tasks. Following this first round of testing, the subject was instructed that he would be presented with the sets of words a second time, and for each set he was to write a sentence corresponding to the idea he thought of earlier. If he could not remember his idea, he was to indicate such and think up a new sentence. As in the first experiment, a clock was started upon presentation of the words and was stopped when the subject began writing.

The subjects were 10 male and 10 female undergraduates at Kent State University who volunteered to participate in exchange for points convertible to course credit in a general psychology course. All were native speakers of English. Each subject was presented with one of the 20 unique lists.

The latency obtained in the first half of testing was called the *idea latency* and that obtained during the second run through the list was the *production latency*. Three indices reflecting surface properties of the sentences were computed—number of *surface structure clauses*, number of *surface structure roles*, and *number of words*. A clause was defined as a subject plus a verb, so complement constructions were not counted separately. The roles were closely related to cases as in Fillmore's (1968) case grammar, but were not completely identical with them. The roles scored were agent, object, instrument, result, experiencer, source, goal, location, time, method, and cause. All the sentences were then analyzed into the base structure sentences that contributed to the final sentence. Adjectives and other modifiers were derived from separate base structure sentences. Two base structure indices were counted—the number of *base structure sentences* and the number of *base structure roles*. The base structure roles were the same as the surface structure roles. Six other linguistic indices were computed including the number of content and function words, the number of base structure sentences containing at least one stimulus word, and the number of base structure sentences and roles when modifiers were not derived from separate sentences. Correlations among all 11 measures indicated that the five presented here adequately characterized the complexity of the sentences.

The first block of seven trials was considered practice and was not scored. Sentences for which the subject indicated that the sentence did not relate directly to his earlier idea were excluded from analysis, as were sentences that did not include all of the stimulus words. For the former sentences the interpretation and comparison of the latencies would be clouded because the idea latency and the production latency would reflect two unrelated cognitive events. The mean number of such sentences discarded was 7.9. The *percentage of "no's"* reported for trial types reflects this rate. The elimination of sentences from the data led to missing data for some subjects in some conditions. Where this occurred, that subject's mean was inserted and the number of subjects with complete data is indicated.

Results and discussion. For each subject on each trial type, the mean was computed for each measure. Means across subjects are presented in Fig. 2 for each of the latencies and in Fig. 3 for each of the five structural indices, in addition to the percentage of "no's." All subjects had complete data on all trial types save one subject on NVV. Pairwise tests showed that the means on most of the variables clustered in three groups as a function of whether one, two, or three stimulus words were presented. Increased number of stimulus words produced longer latencies, more clauses, roles, and words at both the base and surface structure levels, and increased instances where the idea and sentence did not match, all χ^2s (6) > 60, ps < .001, according to Friedman's two-way

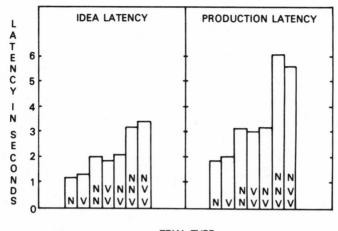

FIG. 2   Mean idea-generation latency and mean sentence-production latency as a function of the stimulus set.

analyses of variance. Although there were some significant differences within these groups, the effects did not seem to fall into any consistent pattern.

Because of large between-subject variation, Pearson product-moment correlations across sentences were computed separately for each subject among the latencies and for each structural index with each latency, ignoring classification by trial types. The mean correlation across subjects was then calculated. If the two stages are in fact independent, then idea latency and production latency should not be correlated. The mean correlation of idea and production latency across subjects was .56, which is significantly different from zero, $t(19) = 12.20$, $p < .001$. This sizable correlation does not bode well for a discrete processing model.

A discrete processing model predicts that surface structure indices would have higher correlations with the production latency and that base structure indices would have higher correlations with the idea latency. As can be seen from the mean correlations in Table 1, these predictions were not borne out. There was not any hint of an interaction between the two types of structural indices and the two latencies. Further, multiple correlations computed separately for each subject using the structural indices as predictors of the two latencies also failed to show any differential effects consistently across subjects.

In order to explore further a possible relation between the latencies and the structural indices, the latter were converted to quasi-independent variables. Continuing to ignore the trial types, the values of the five structural indices were combined into the largest number of groups such that all or most subjects had at least one sentence assigned to each group. Consider base structure roles as an

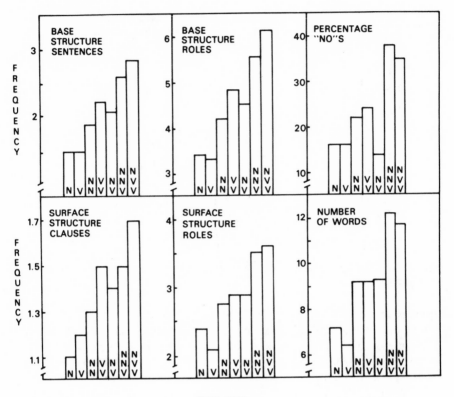

TRIAL TYPE

FIG. 3 Means of the various structural measures of the produced sentences as a function of the stimulus set.

TABLE 1
Mean Correlations between Structural Indices
and Response Latencies across Subjects[a]

	Structural index				
	Base structure		Surface structure		
Response latency	Sentences	Roles	Clauses	Roles	Words
Idea	.31	.36	.26	.36	.41
	(.15)	(.17)	(.36)	(.14)	(.17)
Production	.32	.34	.20	.30	.43
	(.14)	(.15)	(.19)	(.16)	(.14)

[a]Standard deviations are indicated in parentheses.

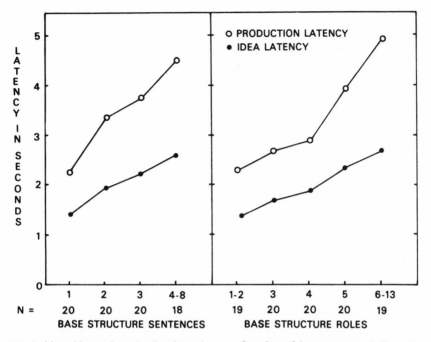

FIG. 4 Mean idea and production latencies as a function of base structure indices. The numbers of subjects with complete data for each level of the structural variables are indicated below the abscissas.

example. The number of base structure roles ranged from one to eight. However, many subjects did not have at least one sentence with each of the values four through eight. The values of the base structure sentence variable were redefined as one, two, three, and four–eight. All subjects had at least one sentence falling in each of the first three categories. This grouping procedure was performed on all five structural indices. At each of the new levels of each structural variable, the means for the latencies were computed for each subject across as many sentences as he had in that category. The means were then calculated across subjects and are shown in Figs. 4 and 5. Those few cases of missing entries were filled by that subject's overall mean. The number of subjects with complete data is indicated below each abscissa.

Ideal results for a discrete processing model would be for idea latency to increase with increases in the base structure indices while production latency remained flat. In contrast for the surface structure indices, the production latency should increase while the idea latency remained flat. Realistically, however, we would accept as support for a discrete processing model an interaction between the idea and production latency curves, with the idea latency curve having a steeper slope for the base structure indices and the sentence latency curve having a steeper slope for the surface structure ones.

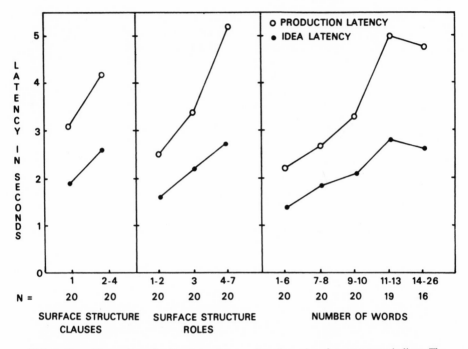

FIG. 5 Mean idea and production latencies as a function of surface structure indices. The numbers of subjects with complete data for each level of the structural variables are indicated below the abscissas.

Difference scores between idea and production latencies were significant for base structure roles, surface structure roles, and number of words (see Table 2 for F values).[3] All three interactions resulted from production latency increasing faster than idea latency as a function of the structural variables. Although three of the interactions (difference score analysis) were significant, the pattern was not as predicted by a discrete processing model. Such an interaction was predicted for surface structure variables; the opposite was predicted for base structure variables. When subjects follow the sentence production process through to completion, they need relatively more time to fill in the details for the longer sentences.

For both latency measures on all five structural variables, there was a significant increase in latency as an increasing function of linguistic complexity (see the left half of Table 2 for F-values). It took more time to think of the idea for

[3] Because of large differences in variances for idea and production latencies, separate one-way analyses of variance were computed. The interaction between idea and production latencies was tested by a one-way analysis of variance on difference scores, a procedure that is statistically equivalent to testing the interaction term in an overall analysis of variance (Huck & McLean, 1975).

TABLE 2
F-Values of the Relation of Idea and Production Latencies to the Linguistic Indices

Structural variables	Degrees of freedom	Original latencies			Residual latencies		
		Idea	Production	Difference	Idea	Production	Difference
Base structure:							
Sentences	3,57	12.66*	7.24*	1.98	5.78*	1.57	0.41
Roles	4,76	7.81*	8.51*	4.11*	3.70*	7.27*	1.58
Surface structure:							
Clauses	1,19	9.72*	7.84*	1.21	9.55*	4.90*	0.08
Roles	2,38	9.82*	13.94*	4.77*	2.83	4.42*	0.80
Words	4,76	14.03*	6.29*	2.51*	3.41*	3.68*	0.84

$*p < .05.$

longer, more complex sentences and to construct those sentences when requested. The idea generation occurred 10 to 15 min prior to the sentence production, yet there was a strong relationship between the idea latency and the linguistic structure of the sentence.

One alternative explanation of these results remains to be tested before rejecting a discrete processing model. Perhaps the latency measures were not pure measures of their respective stages. The idea latency may have been contaminated by the inclination of subjects to follow through with an implicit sentence. The production latency might have been contaminated by idea generation because the subject first had to *re*generate his idea before the sentence could be constructed. The significant correlation between idea and production latencies ($r = .56$) indicated these possibilities may be true. In a further effort to tease out differential effects, the idea latencies were regressed against the production latencies separately for each subject, and the production latencies in turn were regressed against the idea latencies. Both idea and production latencies were separated into predicted and residual components based on these regressions. Analyses of variance then were conducted on the residual latencies as a function of the linguistic indices.[4] If the failure to find support for a discrete processing model in the original latencies was caused by cross-contamination of the two measures, the residual latencies should show purer idea generation and sentence construction effects following the partialing of production and idea latency variance, respectively.

A discrete processing model predicted the same set of interactions for the residual latencies as for the original latencies. In contrast to these predictions, there were no interactions between the two residuals on any of the linguistic variables (see Residual latencies—Difference in Table 2). None of the difference score analyses even approached significance. Both the idea latency residuals and the production latency residuals did increase as a function of the linguistic variables even though the common variance had been removed by the regression analysis. The idea latency residuals increased significantly on all linguistic indices except surface structure roles, and production latency residuals showed significant increases on all linguistic indices except base structure sentences (see the right half of Table 2). Out of 38 points there were only 4 reversals in the regular increases and only one of these reversals was greater than .10 sec. It is striking that the residual latencies were not random, but were nearly as strongly related to the linguistic variables as were the original latencies. The analysis of the residual latencies lent even less support for a discrete processing model than did analysis of the original latencies. The safest conclusion, especially in light of the

---

[4] This procedure is analogous to an analysis of covariance in which idea latency is the covariate for production latency and then production latency is the covariate for idea latency. The principal difference is that since all of the variables were within subject, the regression was computed separately for each subject.

powerful main effects for original and residual data, is that idea and production latencies reflect basically the same process.

Increases in production latency as a function of increasing sentential complexity has not been an unequivocal finding, however. In a paradigm similar to this one (Taylor, 1969), speakers orally produced sentences in response to single nouns that varied in frequency and abstractness. Abstract and infrequent words resulted in the speaker taking longer to begin his sentence, but latency did not vary with either sentence length or syntactic complexity. The latter variable was measured both in number of simple transformations (Chomsky, 1957) and in terms of the surface structure complexity of the subject noun phrase (Yngve, 1960). Taylor concluded that conceptual complexity (a result of the input word properties) influenced production latency, but that syntactic complexity did not. Speakers planned the conception of the whole utterance before starting to speak, but constructed the particular sentence as they went along. In contrast to Taylor's results, when speakers orally produced well-learned sentences in response to numerical stimuli in a paired-associate task, increased syntactic complexity of the subject noun phrase increased the response latency (Johnson, 1966). In fact, the increase in response latency was approximately linear with the increase in complexity as measured by number of surface structure operations (Yngve, 1960). Since Johnson's effects of syntactic complexity were on the order of .05 sec, Taylor's recording method (accurate to ±1 sec) may not have been sufficiently sensitive to pick them up.

In sum, production latency was a function of syntactic complexity as well as the complexity of the input stimulus and the output sentence length. However, the idea latencies and production latencies did not appear to be measuring different processes, at least with respect to the sentences actually produced. Perhaps these measures were inappropriate for assessing sentence production, but such a conclusion seems a bit unreasonable, given the large number of significant and consistent effects across both experiments. Except for the predicted effects relative to the separation of the two stages, the data were quite reliable and the effects interpretable.

A more reasonable conclusion is to reject a discrete model for an integrated processing interpretation. When the subject conceived his idea in the first phase of the experiment, he did so in linguistic terms rather than in abstract concepts. That is, he actually constructed the sentence in the first phase, and in the second phase he simply recalled the sentence and wrote it down. The longer and more complex the sentence in the idea stage, the longer it took to recall or regenerate it, therefore increasing production latency. The implication of this explanation is that idea generation and sentence construction are not discrete stages. The regularities, both in the original latencies and in the residuals, combined with the continuing failure to obtain an interaction, strongly suggests that sentence production is a unitary, integrated process. In the mind of a real speaker, producing ideas and sentences are one and the same process. Let us explore this notion in more detail.

IDEA GENERATION AND SENTENCE CONSTRUCTION
ARE THE SAME PROCESS

The crucial fault with a discrete processing model lies in the assumption that thought, linguistic processes, and production apparatus, especially the former two, are distinct subroutines, in which only the specific values (content) carried in the variables at the time of execution provide a connection. The solution to this flaw is to recognize that these processes are not discrete subroutines, but that the process of sentence construction is the same process as generating the idea (the thinking process itself), at least for those tasks in which a verbal response is required. The conception of sentence production suggested here develops from the same contextualist approach that Jenkins (1974) applied to studies of memory and sentence comprehension. Since the data on comprehension are more plentiful and reliable, let us briefly review them.

Sentence Comprehension as a Constructive, Task-Oriented Process

Sentence comprehension research has focused on studying sentences in isolation. The guiding model was simple. Upon presentation of a sentence, subjects called in a sentence comprehension subroutine to analyze the sentence and to derive a mental representation that encoded the meaning of the sentence. A variety of tasks then could be used to tap that representation. It became evident, however, that the representation was affected by prior verbal material as well as by physical and social contexts. So the subroutine was reprogrammed to accept new and different sources of data as input, but the necessity for a separate subroutine was not questioned.

Devising a task that would veridically tap that representation was viewed only as a methodological problem, not a substantive one. However, the search for The Task became a search for the Holy Grail. Following on from the verbal learning and memory tradition, tasks from those fields were first used, but they were found to bias the representation (Fillenbaum, 1973). "Purer" measures of comprehension were then devised that purported to be free of contamination from "memory factors" (Carroll, 1972; Danks, 1969). Yet in retrospect these pure measures were also influenced by the particular demands placed on the subject. The subject did not process linguistic material in isolation of his anticipation of what the experimenter might later ask of him any more than he processed sentences in isolation of prior context.

Nowhere was the effect of task demands more obvious than in a series of investigations using a picture–sentence verification task with simple active and passive sentences (see Glucksberg & Danks, 1975, for a summary). Previous studies (McMahon, 1963; Slobin, 1966) had shown passives more difficult to verify against pictures; presumably because they involved more complex processing to comprehend. Olson and Filby (1972) found that in appropriate contexts—focus on actor for actives and focus on patient for passives—the difference in verification latency was markedly attenuated. However, Glucksberg, Trabasso, and Wald (1973) extended these studies and concluded that a single verification model to account for all the data was impossible to construct. Subjects varied their encodings as well as their comparison strategies as a function of the particular verification task they were engaged in. Some of the critical variations were the amount of material to be held in memory simultaneously, the temporal schedule for information input, and the relation of negative foils to positive instances. In other words, comprehension and encoding differences resulted from the use to which people put those encodings.

The practical solution is not to continue searching for the one pure measure of comprehension, but to accept task effects as being an intrinsic part of comprehension. The use of language to fulfill the task demands *is* the comprehension process. In the real world we are always comprehending something for some purpose, and that purpose affects the depth of processing and the type of representation generated and maintained (Mistler-Lachman, 1972, 1975). We do not call a subroutine labeled sentence comprehension, then use the result of that processing in a variety of tasks. We do not even have a single subroutine with multiple exit points. Rather we have certain automatic routines corresponding to those demands that we face frequently, but there is not one process that is comprehension. The comprehension model proposed by Carpenter and Just (1975) accounts for verification tasks quite well even though they do not discuss *how* the initial encoding is formed. The encoding is derived specifically to fulfill the processing demands of a verification task. But their model will explain only verification tasks and other closely related tasks, and not the full range of comprehension. There is no single comprehension subroutine and there are no language-specific comprehension strategies, but there are general purpose information-processing strategies that construct a representation appropriate to meet the task demands. If the task were somewhat different, say to remember a story line or to continue a conversation, the representation would undoubtedly be different. In sum, task demands do not simply introduce perturbations into a relatively fixed comprehension process. Instead, the task-related processing is the comprehension process.

Integration of Thought and Speech

Sentence production also cannot be viewed as a succession of fixed processing stages that are relatively invariant across situations and tasks. For any given utterance, there is a single process that leads from some vague intention to communicate to the actual articulation of speech. Unless we adopt the position that thought is only the speech itself, a totally unacceptable position, some mental processing must precede the speech articulation. But this is not to say that there is a lock-step succession of qualitatively different processing stages such as depicted by a discrete processing model. As a speaker thinks of what he wants to say, he simultaneously plans how he is going to say it. He begins constructing an utterance from the first glint of an intention to speak and the construction of a sentence is just another aspect of the thinking that generates the idea.

The intimate coordination between thought and language has led Kozhevnikov and Chistovich (1965) to postulate that analysis of articulation (speech) cannot be studied in isolation from its meaning. Their unit of analysis is the *syntagma*, which is defined as "a sentence or a part of a sentence distinguished by meaning... [that] is clearly connected with articulation and must definitely be pronounced at one output [p. 74]." Note that a syntagma has two sides. One represents the organization of the motor performance in such terms as phonemic clauses, syllables, and articulation of phonemic sequences (e.g., Boomer, 1965; Fromkin, 1968, 1971). The other side of a syntagma is the schema of the idea and its semantic representation in the sentence. A syntagma is the integration of these two aspects into a coherent process that represents the organizational schema of speech production (Lashly, 1951).

A common procedure for the investigation of how speech production proceeds has been an analysis of the temporal characteristics of spontaneous speech and how these characteristics correlate with various linguistic indices. For example, Boomer (1965) found that hesitations were relatively more probable between the first and second words of a phonemic clause. A phonemic clause is "a phonologically marked macrosegment which... contains one and only one primary stress and ends in one of the terminal junctures" (Boomer, 1965, p. 150). Because the speaker is permitted free reign over his potential utterances, the analysis is reduced to a strictly correlational one. That is, what linguistic structures are associated with the speaker's hesitations, pauses, breathing points? Even where a correlation is established, the investigator can never be certain that there is not some other linguistic variable that would correlate better with the temporal parameters. A good example of this phenomenon is illustrated below by McNeill's (1974) interpretation of syntagmas instead of syntactic structure as determining hesitations. The two experiments reported in this paper were also correlational and the difficulty in knowing which linguistic variable was most appropriate was evident in the inclusion of several different ones in the analyses. Various competing theoretical interpretations frequently cannot be separated easily. Particularly if the points at which the competing explanations differ are few, the correlations for both will always be similar. But the most important difficulty with this approach to studying speech production is the failure to consider the coordination of conceptual organization with performance. Goldman-Eisler (1968) carries this failure to the opposite extreme when she claims that conceptual structure actually interferes with articulatory organization. "Cognitive processes accompanying speech seem to interfere with the orderly integration of such extra-linguistic phenomena as hesitations and breathing into the linguistic process. . . . The cognitive processes seem from this to be out of phase with the motor and peripheral processes of speech utterance and breathing" (Goldman-Eisler, 1968, pp. 98–99).

McNeill (1974, 1975b) has attempted to redress the imbalance by explicitly investigating the coordination between the two aspects of the syntagma, particularly from the conceptual side. "For many speakers, normal speech seems to be uttered *as* it is organized. The conceptual arrangements behind speech can be worked out at nearly the same time the sentence is produced, certainly not always a phrase or sentence in advance" (McNeill, 1975b, p. 356). McNeill marshalls three sources of evidence in support of his claim.

First, the coordination of thought and action is much tighter in the young child. Beginning with sensorimotor schemata, the child's thought is organized around the actions he performs on the world (Piaget, 1962). The interiorization of the action schemas provides the organization for the child's limited speech production as well as for this thought. Word order in the child's reduced speech is dominated not only by adult word order, as expected, but also by a conceptual organization isomorphic with the child's action schemas, thus forming a direct link between speech and schema. The data presented in several diary studies of children's speech supports this interpretation (McNeill, 1975b).

Second, McNeill (1974) has analyzed adult speech in terms of conceptual relations such as "is agent of," "has object," "is consequence of," "is constituted by," "is property of," and "at location of." These conceptual relations combine to form syntagmas as expressed in the surface structure. About 70% of the surface morpheme sequences can be predicted by the underlying conceptual structure. Most of the remaining 30% result from obligatory syntactic procedures. Surface features of the speech stream, for example, hesitations, pauses, are largely accounted for by major shifts in the conceptual structure. Many of these shifts occur at grammatical boundaries to be sure, but some do not. Further, the shifts in conceptual structure are better predictors of hesitations and pauses than is grammatical structure. The syntagma is defined not only in terms of articulation features as originally proposed by Kozhevnikov and Chistovich (1965), but simultaneously in terms of the conceptual structure underlying the utterance.

Third, gestures are viewed not as extraneous embellishments to speech, but as vestiges of the action schemas acquired as children. Adults were asked to perform certain simple actions, such as tying a bow knot, and to describe their action while doing so (McNeill, 1975b). The overt actions correlated directly with the syntagmas used to describe them and not with individual words. With speech on relatively abstract topics, the coordination with syntagmas was preserved in gestures although the gestures were not as iconic.

McNeill's analyses have demonstrated the power of the syntagma to coordinate thinking and speaking. Unfortunately, because the current methodology is largely correlational, causal relations are difficult to establish. What is needed now is to investigate the mechanism of the coordination. An on-line technique to reflect the temporal course of sentence construction during spontaneous speech that avoids the problem of correlational analyses implicit in the studies of hesitation phenomena would be especially valuable. How the conceptual structure is integrated with speech through time then could be determined.

If generation of an idea coincides with constructing a sentence that expresses that idea, then the syntactic and semantic structure of language presumably influences the structure of thinking (Whorf, 1956). The generation of new thoughts, ideas, and conceptions resulting from reorganizing old experiences as well as immediate experience is interpreted in linguistic categories. The assumption of a discrete processing model permitted the separation of thought from the influence of language. Humans were postulated to think in "mentalese," a universal human symbol system that is independent of specific languages yet is readily translatable into spoken language (Fodor et al., 1974).

What a "thinker" needs is not one mentalese, but many mental languages to fit the variety of output demands on his thought. We are able to think in modes other than verbal, the most obvious one being visual. When there are demands for a visual output (e.g., Brooks, 1968) or a visual comparison (e.g., Tversky, 1969), then processing appears to rely on visual codes. There is no reason to believe that internal "languages" are limited to one or two. It would be more efficient to have several mental languages that are individually adapted to our typical performance modes—one of which is speech. When action corresponding to our thought is speech, thought tends toward a language-based mentalese. However, thought can be separated from the influence of language by switching to a mentalese associated with a different response system.

Representation of Objects and Events

One way of representing our experiences is to code them in language forms. Particularly if the overt response expected is verbal, whether in or out of the laboratory, then the experiencer will represent the event in a symbolic form that is at minimum highly compatible with sentence construction. That representation may not be implicit speech, but it is a form like that used to represent linguistic information. The flexibility of representation is the result of the subject's expectancy of what he will have to do with the information. And the representation can vary as a function of this expectancy.

Studies of both comprehension and production demonstrate this coding flexibility. For example, when listeners verify active and passive sentences against pictures, verification time was considerably faster if the comprehender's attention had been focused on the surface subject of the sentence by prior context (Olson & Filby, 1972). Speakers required to produce an active sentence that describes a picture did so faster if the previous paragraph had been about the actor (the surface subject of the active sentence) rather than the patient of the action (Tannenbaum & Williams, 1968). In contrast, if required to produce a passive sentence, the response was faster following a paragraph focusing on the patient rather than the actor. Overall, active sentences were produced faster than passive ones, but since the latencies were measured to the end of the sentence, the fact that the passives contain more words may explain this difference. The relative availability of active and passive sentences—and presumably the mental representation of the picture to which they correspond—was strongly affected by the preceding context which defined the topic as well as the task demands.

If the relative accessibility of actives and passives is influenced by topic, so is the probability with which speakers produce them. When the topic has been defined as the patient by prior context, the speaker is more likely to produce a passive sentence (which makes the patient the surface subject) than an active one. The reverse is the case when the topic is the actor (Prentice, 1967). Perhaps in the absence of other constraints, a rule of conversation is to give the "old" information first—as the surface subject—and then follow it with "new" information about that topic (Halliday, 1967). If speakers tended to follow such general rules, it would certainly ease the burden of comprehension for the listener. A pragmatic-communication rule, based on similar reasoning, has been suggested to explain why speakers sometimes prefer to reorder prenominal adjectives and why such inversion of adjective order facilitates comprehension by a listener (Danks & Schwenk, 1972, 1974).

Several theoretical proposals have been advanced for the symbolic representation of events and complex information (Anderson & Bower, 1973; Kintsch, 1974; Norman & Rumelhart, 1975; Reid, 1974). That these representations can be applied equally well to live events, drawings, and sentences implies that the form of the representation may be a critical indication of the simultaneous integration of ideas and sentences. If so, a potentially useful task would be to have speakers describe various sorts of pictorial events—live skits, movies, cartoons, still photographs, or line drawings—in which the events, as well as the context in which they are presented, are varied in systematic ways (Olson, 1970; Osgood, 1971). Using pictorial events as convenient stimuli (e.g., Goldman-Eisler, 1968) is not sufficient; the systematic manipulation of events is crucial for this approach to be of value. By comparing the effect of variation in the pictures on variation in the descriptions, a representation can be constructed to mediate between conceptual structure and language form. Under what pictorial depictions and what contexts do speakers explicitly code actors, patients, instruments, intentions? In some recently initiated research, Nancy Frost and I have found that relatively small differences in how events were pictorially depicted markedly affected their description. Not only was the surface word order (identification of the subject–actor) affected, but the basic semantic specification of the verb was also.

How does the "syntax" of the picture control the mental representation as well as the subsequent linguistic description? The studies mentioned have been quite limited as far as the features of representation and the sentential elements investigated. The extension to other aspects, such as other case roles, intentions, presuppositions, and implications, would permit the formulation of a more generally applicable representational format.

The problem with most of these conceptions for the arguments developed here is that the units encoded by a single representation are often of sentence size, or at least the size of an underlying sentence or clause. The claim here has been that the planning units of speech production are syntagmas, units that are defined by the conceptual structure and may be much smaller than a whole sentence. Lindsley (1975) focused a microscope on a minute, but important, aspect of sentence production—whether verb selection occurs prior to, during, or following the initiation of the utterance. Across several experiments, speakers were required to produce only the subject (actor), only the verb (action), or a short sentence containing both subject and verb, as quickly as possible in response to a single picture. In some blocks of trials, the actor or action or both were held constant. When the actor or action was held constant, the speaker did not have to spend time selecting the subject or verb, respectively. There were three principal findings:

1. Verb selection was initiated before the speaker began his utterance.

2. Verb selection was not completed until after the speaker had begun to speak.

3. When speakers were required to produce utterances containing not only the subject and verb, but also the direct object (patient of the action), they were no slower in initiating their utterance than when they produced only the subject and verb.

Hence, the speakers were not planning the whole sentence completely in advance because the object selection must have occurred while they were actually uttering the subject and verb. Although these data were obtained in an extremely limited, artificial context, they are consistent with the position being presented here, namely, that the picture is not completely encoded (at least, linguistically) before an utterance is initiated, but neither does the speaker progress by producing one word at a time.

CONCLUSIONS

This paper began with a discrete processing model of sentence production (cf. Fig. 1). Linguistic processing was viewed as analogous to a subroutine that could be called by the main program to construct a sentence once the idea had been generated to serve as an input variable to the subroutine. The results of the sentence construction subroutine were then transferred to an output device that performed the sentence as speech. Although several writers have conceptualized sentence production (and sentence comprehension) in terms of such discrete components, the two experiments reported in this paper as well as others in the literature indicate that the walls isolating these components be dismantled. The experiments suggested that the thinking processes, at least those that result in speech, are completely integrated with the process of sentence production. Our ideas come into being as we select the words and construct the sentences we utter. On the other side of the hypothetical sentence construction subroutine, the separation of linguistic processing from performance devices has deteriorated. The lack of distinction between linguistic and performance variables has been well documented in comprehension tasks and the extension to production tasks may well be appropriate.

An analogous approach to the study of linguistic phenomena currently is being developed in sociolinguistics. This movement—called ethnography of speaking or ethnolinguistics by Dell Hymes (1974a, b)—asserts that speaking (and listening) cannot be understood outside the sociocultural matrix within which it occurs. The speaker's intentions result from an understanding of the function of the utterances. Decisions about intention and sociocultural function by the speaker are just as central to his speech production as are decisions about word order and lexical items. Stylistic variation is not something that speakers impose on their utterances after the basic grammatical form has been constructed by a sentence construction device, but the influence of sociocultural context and style acts simultaneously with grammatical construction.

The most profitable course for sentence production research to steer is toward the representations and processes that coordinate thought and speech. Unfortunately for us investigators, these processes will vary considerably over the particular tasks that we set for our subjects. The differences in representations and processing strategies resulting from task demands probably far outweigh the commonalities. If that is so, then the postulation of isolated subroutines specific for linguistic inputs and outputs, but general for all such linguistic interfaces, is of dubious value. Rather, we will need to analyze the processing of each task separately to ferret out overriding information-processing strategies that are sufficiently general and flexible to apply to a wide spectrum of inputs, outputs, and situations.

ACKNOWLEDGMENTS

This contribution was written while on leave at Princeton University. I gratefully acknowledge the support of the Department of Psychology there as well as the support of Grant Nos. MH-20137 and MH-21230 from NIMH. The conceptions developed in this paper benefited from discussions with Jim Dooling, Tim Jay, Linda Ohlweiler, and Christine Riley. I thank John Carroll, Jim Dooling, Sam Glucksberg, and David McNeill for their critical comments on an earlier draft of this chapter.

REFERENCES

Anderson, J. R., & Bower, G. H. *Human associative memory.* Washington, D.C.: Winston, 1973.

Boomer, D. S. Hesitations and grammatical encoding. *Language and Speech,* 1965, **8,** 148–158.

Brooks, L. R.. Spatial and verbal components of the act of recall. *Canadian Journal of Psychology,* 1968, **22,** 349–368.

Carpenter, P. A., & Just, M. A. Sentence comprehension: A psycholinguistic model of verification. *Psychological Review,* 1975, **82,** 45–73.

Carroll, J. B. Defining language comprehension: Some speculations. In J. B. Carroll & R. O. Freedle (Eds.), *Language comprehension and the acquisition of knowledge.* Washington, D. C.: Winston, 1972.

Carroll, J. B. Towards a performance grammar of core sentences in spoken and written English. *International Review of Applied Linguistics,* 1974, **12** (Special Festschrift issue in honor of B. Malmberg; G. Nickel, Ed.), 29–49.

Chomsky, N. *Syntactic structures.* The Hague: Mouton, 1957.

Chomsky, N. *Aspects of the theory of syntax.* Cambridge, Massachusetts: MIT Press, 1965.

Danks, J. H. Grammaticalness and meaningfulness in the comprehension of sentences. *Journal of Verbal Learning and Verbal Behavior,* 1969, **8,** 687–696.

Danks, J. H. The verb–object relation and sentence comprehension. Midwestern Psychological Association, Cincinnati, 1970.

Danks, J. H., & Ohlweiler, L. S. How are semantic relations realized in sentence production? Midwestern Psychological Association, Cleveland, 1972.

Danks, J. H., & Schwenk, M. A. Prenominal adjective order and communication context. *Journal of Verbal Learning and Verbal Behavior,* 1972, **11,** 183–187.

Danks, J. H., & Schwenk, M. A. Comprehension of prenominal adjective orders. *Memory and Cognition,* 1974, **2,** 34–38.

Fillenbaum, S. *Syntactic factors in memory?* The Hague: Mouton, 1973.

Fillmore, C. J. The case for case. In E. Bach & R. T. Harms (Eds.), *Universals in linguistic theory.* New York: Holt, Rinehart & Winston, 1968.

Fodor, J. A., Bever, T. G., & Garrett, M. F. *The psychology of language.* New York: McGraw-Hill, 1974.

Fromkin, V. A. Speculations on performance models. *Journal of Linguistics,* 1968, **4,** 47–68.

Fromkin, V. A. The non-anomalous nature of anomalous utterances. *Language,* 1971, **47,** 27–52.

Glucksberg, S., & Danks, J. H. *Experimental psycholinguistics.* Hillsdale, New Jersey: Lawrence Erlbaum Associates, 1975.

Glucksberg, S., Trabasso, T., & Wald, J. Linguistic structures and mental operations. *Cognitive Psychology,* 1973, **5,** 338–370.

Goldman-Eisler, F. *Psycholinguistics: Experiments in spontaneous speech.* New York: Academic Press, 1968.

Halliday, M. A. K. Notes on transitivity and theme in English: II. *Journal of Linguistics,* 1967, **3,** 199–244.

Huck, S. W., & McLean, R. A. Using a repeated measures ANOVA to analyze the data from a pretest-posttest design: A potentially confusing task. *Psychological Bulletin,* 1975, **82,** 511–518.

Hymes, D. Linguistic theory and functions in speech. In D. Hymes, *Foundations in sociolinguistics.* Philadelphia: University of Pennsylvania Press, 1974. (a)

Hymes, D. Ways of speaking. In R. Bauman & J. Sherzer (Eds.), *Explorations in the ethnography of speaking.* London: Cambridge University Press, 1974. (b)

Jenkins, J. J. Remember that old theory of memory? Well, forget it! *American Psychologist,* 1974, **29,** 785–795.

Johnson, N. F. On the relationship between sentence structure and the latency in generating a sentence. *Journal of Verbal Learning and Verbal Behavior,* 1966, **5,** 375–380.

Katz, J. J. Mentalism in linguistics. *Language,* 1964, **40,** 124–137.

Kintsch, W. *The representation of meaning in memory.* Hillsdale, New Jersey: Lawrence Erlbaum Associates, 1974.

Kozhevnikov, V. A., & Chistovich, L. A. *Speech: Articulation and perception.* Washington, D.C.: U. S. Department of Commerce, Joint Publications Research Service, 1965.

Kučera, H., & Francis, W. N. *Computational analysis of present-day American English.* Providence, Rhode Island: Brown University Press, 1967.

Lashley, K. S. The problem of serial order in behavior. In L. A. Jeffress (Ed.), *Cerebral mechanisms in behavior.* New York: Hafner, 1951.

Liberman, A. M. The grammars of speech and language. *Cognitive Psychology,* 1970, **1,** 301–323.

Lindsley, J. R. Producing simple utterances: How far ahead do we plan? *Cognitive Psychology,* 1975, 7, 1–19.

McMahon, L. E. Grammatical analysis as part of understanding a sentence. Unpublished doctoral dissertation, Harvard University, 1963.

McNeill, D. "New" conceptual basis for speech production. Lectures given at the Interdisciplinary Institute on Reading and Child Development, University of Delaware, 1974.

McNeill, D. The place of grammar in a theory of performance. Paper presented at the New York Academy of Sciences symposium on Developmental Psycholinguistics, 1975. (a)

McNeill, D. Semiotic extension. In R. L. Solso (Ed.), *Information processing and cognition.* Hillsdale, New Jersey: Lawrence Erlbaum Associates, 1975. (b)

Mistler-Lachman, J. Levels of comprehension in processing of normal and ambiguous sentences. *Journal of Verbal Learning and Verbal Behavior,* 1972, **11,** 614–623.

Mistler-Lachman, J. Queer sentences, ambiguity, and levels of processing. *Memory & Cognition,* 1975, **3,** 395–400.

Norman, D. A., & Rumelhart, D. E. *Explorations in cognition.* San Francisco: Freeman, 1975.

Olson, D. R. Language and thought: Aspects of a cognitive theory of semantics. *Psychological Review,* 1970, **77,** 257–273.

Olson, D. R., & Filby, N. On the comprehension of active and passive sentences. *Cognitive Psychology,* 1972, **3,** 361–381.

Osgood, C. E. Where do sentences come from? In D. D. Steinberg & L. A. Jakobovitz (Eds.), *Semantics.* Cambridge, England: Cambridge University Press, 1971.

Piaget, J. *Play, dreams, and imitation in childhood.* New York: Norton, 1962.

Prentice, J. L. Effects of cuing actor vs. cuing object on word order in sentence production. *Psychonomic Science,* 1967, 8, 163–164.

Reid, L. S. Toward a grammar of the image. *Psychological Bulletin,* 1974, 81, 319–334.

Rosenberg, S. Associative sentence norms II: Simple declarative sentence. NIMH Technical Report No. 6, George Peabody College for Teachers, 1966.

Rosenberg, S. Semantic constraints on sentence production. Midwestern Psychological Association, Cleveland, 1972.

Saussure, F. de. *Cours de linguistique generale.* (1st ed., 1916.) English translation by W. Baskin, *Course in general linguistics.* New York: McGraw-Hill, 1966.

Schlesinger, I. M. Production of utterances and language acquisition. In D. I. Slobin (Ed.), *The ontogenesis of grammar.* New York: Academic Press, 1971.

Slobin, D. I. Grammatical transformations and sentence comprehension in childhood and adulthood. *Journal of Verbal Learning and Verbal Behavior,* 1966, 5, 219–227.

Sutherland, N. S. Discussion of paper by Fodor and Garrett. In J. Lyons & R. J. Wales (Eds.), *Psycholinguistic papers.* Edinburgh: Edinburgh University Press, 1966.

Tannenbaum, P. H., & Williams, F. Generation of active and passive sentences as a function of subject or object focus. *Journal of Verbal Learning and Verbal Behavior,* 1968, 7, 246–250.

Taylor, I. Content and structure in sentence production. *Journal of Verbal Learning and Verbal Behavior,* 1969, 8, 170–175.

Tversky, B. Pictorial and verbal encoding in a short-term memory task. *Perception and Psychophysics,* 1969, 6, 225–233.

Whorf, B. L. *Language, thought and reality.* Edited by J. B. Carroll. Cambridge, Massachusetts: MIT Press, 1956.

Yngve, V. H. A model and an hypothesis for language structure. *Proceedings of the American Philosophical Society,* 1960, 104, 444–466.

11
Conceptualizing and Formulating in Sentence Production

Gerard Kempen

University of Nijmegen, The Netherlands

The study of the psychological process of generating acoustic language utterances has to cover three aspects. First, there is the problem of content selection: how does the speaker decide which conceptual structures (thoughts, perceived events) he will convert into natural language utterances? Goldman (1974) calls this the what-to-say problem. The second aspect is syntactic form selection: mapping a conceptual structure into a string of morphemes or, rather, morphs. Actually, two issues are at stake here. One is form determination: which procedure carries out the conversion of conceptual structures into morpheme strings? The other is paraphrase selection. A conceptual structure usually can be phrased many ways; this raises the question of how the speaker chooses between alternative paraphrases. Third, morpheme strings are phonetically realized as sound sequences. These three aspects I will call the processes of conceptualizing, formulating, and speaking, respectively.

This paper concentrates on conceptualization and formulation. It is commonly presupposed that they are processes which take place in temporal succession, without overlap in time. Put differently, the content of an utterance is thought to have been selected before the formulation process starts. I will present evidence that runs counter to this assumption and exposes the conceptualization process as being strongly dependent upon the formulation process. Furthermore, I will put forward an idea that might contribute to the solution of both the content and paraphrase selection problems. The key notions I will use here are syntactic constructions (Kempen, in press) and scripts (Schank & Abelson, 1975).

The experimental part of the paper deals with tasks where subjects had to memorize and reproduce sentences. If certain precautions are exercised, sentence reproduction may be considered a genuine form of sentence production that is experimentally very tractable. I will report an experiment that puts to test a prediction from the syntactic construction concept. Finally, in reviewing a line of experimentation that focused on the lexical structure of verbs, I will show that syntactic constructions provide a better explanation of the published data than lexical structures do.

I. OBSERVATIONS ON THE DEPENDENCE
OF CONCEPTUALIZATION ON FORMULATION

That we must assume some sort of dependence of content selection upon formulation is indicated by a variety of linguistic and psychological observations. Here, I list four of them.

1. *Content revision.* Every skilled speaker of a language will have had experiences of the following kind. While in the middle of planning or pronouncing a sentence he notices that the syntax of the utterance built thus far does not allow him to express the content he intended for the remainder of the utterance. The mismatch between conceptual intentions and syntactic possibilities that arises here is resolvable in two ways: either by revising the content selection for the remaining utterance part, or by abandoning the attempted fragment and making a restart. The former choice implies that syntactic decisions are given priority over conceptual ones.

2. *Syntactic morphology.* Languages differ considerably with respect to the elaborateness of their syntactic morphology. As examples I take tense, number, and addressing systems. Japanese does not distinguish between singular and plural as does English, Dutch, etc. Nouns of Bahasa Indonesia have an unmarked form that may serve both singular and plural function, and a special form marked as plural. Thus, speakers of Dutch or English who wish to use a count noun always have to think about the number of objects this noun refers to: one or more; unlike speakers of Japanese or Bahasa Indonesia who need not worry about this. Analogous contrasts exist between the way a language keeps track of the social relation between speaker and addressee. English only has the second personal pronoun *you*, Dutch distinguishes between *je/jij* and the polite form *U*; Japanese has a complicated system. In the area of verb tenses languages vary widely, too. Compare English and Dutch, which differentiate between past (perfect, imperfect), present, and future, with Bahasa Indonesia. This language has no tense system at all and marks tense (by special words) only if the situation asks for it.

Often it is assumed that conceptual structures ("deep structures") underlying sentences are universal, that is, invariant over languages. This would imply, for example, that the conceptual structures underlying Japanese, Indonesian, and English sentences contain information about number, tense, and speaker/ addressee relationship respectively. All this information would be thrown away during the formulation processes in the respective languages. More economical and efficient seems the assumption that the syntactic morphology determines which of the conceptual dimensions (numbers, temporal and social relations) make part of the "deep structures" in these languages.

3. *Lexicon.* Most systems that have been proposed for representing word and sentence meanings posit a distinction between words and concepts. More specifically, the meaning of a single word is often represented by a structure of several concepts. For example, Schank (1972) proposes that one sense of the verb *throw* is represented by a conceptual structure where, among other things, the primitive acts PTRANS, PROPEL, and GRASP have their place. PTRANS indicates change of location of the thrown object; PROPEL and GRASP have to do with the way the location change is effected. If the conceptualization process generates a conception that contains these three concepts, the formulation process will consult the lexicon and find the word *throw* to be applicable. But suppose the formulation process starts with a conceptual structure that only contains the primitive acts PTRANS and PROPEL. The verb *throw* is too specific now. In English, the transitive *move* would do, but Dutch does not have a verb which is neither too specific nor too general (Kempen, 1975). A speaker of Dutch would have to make a choice here. Either he resorts to a long and cumbersome circumscription (something like "to propel NP so that NP moves to . . .") or he revises the selection of primitive acts in such a way that a more specific or a more general Dutch verb fits. The latter choice implies that the lexicon, the list of (frequent) words of the language, becomes one of the determinants of the conceptualization process.

To this I may add a suggestion put forward by Goldman (1974). Perhaps, the formulation process always tries to be maximally specific. For instance, if the conceptual acts that together correspond to the English verb *give* are offered to the formulation process, then the lexicon might suggest *return* as a more specific alternative. This might initiate a search within the memory: did the receiver own the given object at some earlier time? If so, then this information is added to the current conceptual structure.

4. *Syntactic constructions.* Often the speaker need not plan all the details of the sentence that is going to express the intended content. He may use prefabricated sentence frames or phrases that he knows will accommodate his intentions. An important aspect of such phraseology is that it partly takes over the content selection job. If I reserve the term *theme* for the general topic the speaker wishes to communicate to his audience (e.g., the event he perceives, an idea that occurred to him), then the sentence frames determine which parts of the theme will be overtly expressed. On the one hand, only a limited range of aspects fits into a selected frame, while on the other, for each slot in the selected frame the speaker is forced to find an appropriate filling.

The first to notice that sentence frames are able to support the conceptualization process was Selz (1922). His example is the phraseology of definition sentences. He observed that subjects who attempted to define difficult words utilized sentence frames such as *An X is a Y that . . .* or *An X is a . . . Y* to guide the process of retrieving the logically required memory information.

In the next section I will introduce the notion of a *syntactic construction* which, as defined there, is more adequate than sentence frame or phrase. I will argue that the utilization of syntactic constructions for guiding the conceptualization process is a widespread phenomenon, one calling for a special type of sentence production mechanism.

II. SYNTACTIC CONSTRUCTIONS

The arguments reviewed in Section I suggest the following general design of the human sentence production mechanism (cf. Fig. 1). From the theme the speaker wishes to communicate to his audience, the Conceptualizer selects a part as the content of the next sentence to be uttered (Arrow 1). The selected conceptual structure is input to the Formulator (Arrow 2) that fabricates a syntactically organized word string. The syntactic decisions taken during the formulation process may call for a revision of the initial conception offered to the Formulator (Arrow 3). The end result is a sequence of words generated from left to right (cf. Observation 1 of Section I).

In what way can such a sentence production mechanism incorporate the sentence frame phenomena of the previous section? Let me first define the notion of a syntactic construction. A syntactic construction is a pair consisting of (a) a conceptual pattern and (b) a syntactic frame. Borrowing from Schank's (1972) conceptual dependency theory I define a conceptual pattern as a combination of conceptual relations (actor, object, instrument, etc.) and, possibly, concepts. A syntactic frame is a sequence of word categories or words. Word categories may be defined in syntactic terms (e.g., parts of speech, such as noun, intransitive verb, preposition) or in terms of meaning (e.g., words denoting a time interval). The concrete words may be function words (e.g., *by* in the passive construction) as well as content words (e.g., *is a* or *consists of* in definition sentences; cf. Section I).

The syntactic frame of a syntactic construction is said to *express* the conceptual pattern. In English, for example, the syntactic frame N1VN2 (noun + finite

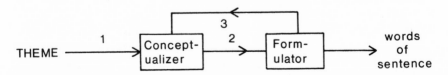

FIG. 1   Global design of the human sentence production mechanism according to the present theory. For explanation see text.

verb + noun) expresses the conceptual pattern "actor ⇔ primitive act ← object." Thus, *John threw stones* and John⇐actor⇒PTRANS←object–stones are concrete embodiments of, respectively, the syntactic frame and the conceptual pattern of this construction. A syntactic frame may belong to more than one syntactic construction, and so can a conceptual pattern.

I will assume that, associated with each frequently occurring syntactic construction, speakers of a language have available a program which does the following two things:

1. It searches through the conceptual network that previously has been designated as the theme, looking for an instance of the conceptual pattern.

2. It casts the retrieved conceptual information in the form of the syntactic frame.

These programs I will call Search-and-Formulate programs.

Under circumstances that I will describe in Section III, the formulating process starts with two types of input: not only a conception but also a syntactic construction. The associated Search-and-Formulate program is called, then, and maps the conception, or a revision of it, into a word sequence embodying that syntactic construction.

III. WHERE DO SYNTACTIC CONSTRUCTIONS COME FROM?

How does the speaker find a syntactic construction that guarantees a quick and successful wording of his communicative intentions? As yet, I have identified two probable sources of syntactic constructions.

First there are numerous instances of what I will call repetitive speech situations. The radio reporter who reads out a series of sporting results might use the same syntactic construction for each match. In situations like these, both the content and a suitable sentence frame are known to the speaker before he initiates his next utterance.

That the conceptualization process can be affected by such prevailing syntactic constructions is easy to demonstrate. Suppose a person is presented with cards depicting geometrical figures such as squares, circles, triangles. On each card, one figure has been underlined. The person has to indicate the identity of the underlined figure to a second person who cannot see the drawings on the card, in as few words as possible. Looking at a card containing the figures

the person might say "the triangle." But if the same triangle is underlined in

△ □ △ ◯

a longer phrase would be called for, for example, "the big triangle." In the latter case, size as well as form have to be considered. Making the appropriate selections is a task of the conceptualization process. Under normal circumstances, people are very efficient in building a description sentence which contains just enough information to single out the underlined figure (cf. Osgood, 1971). Now prepare a deck of, say, 20 cards in such a way that the first 15 of them require the longer construction. But from the 16th card onward the shorter construction (without adjective) will suffice. Will the subjects, after 15 repetitions of the longer construction, immediately switch over to the shorter construction? It is my experience that many subjects, adults as well as children, are fooled and persevere in the long construction for one or more cards. In the opposite condition, too, subjects make errors or hesitate: after 15 short-construction cards they often fail to mention the adjective required by the 16th card. Thus, the prevailing syntactic construction seems capable of guiding the conceptualization process.

The second source of syntactic constructions, I hypothesize, is linked to nonrepetitive but nevertheless standard situations. Schank and Abelson (1975) introduce the notion of a *situational script,* a "predetermined and stereotyped sequence of actions that define a well-known situation [p. 3]." The sequence can often be divided into *scenes,* and each scene contains certain *players* who take specific *roles.* Schank and Abelson's example is the restaurant script with its entering, ordering, eating, and exiting scenes, and with roles played by the customer, waiter, and cashier. From the customer's point of view the ordering scene looks as follows.

ATRANS—customer receives menu
MTRANS—customer reads menu
MBUILD—customer decides what he wants
MTRANS—customer gives his order to waiter

Knowledge of situational scripts helps a person to plan his own behavior as well as to understand (texts describing) other people's actions.

The aspect of scripts which is of interest here in the MTRANSes where players talk to each other (e.g., customer delivering his order to waiter). I put forward the idea that, within a person's knowledge base, such MTRANSes may have a syntactic construction associated with them. If somebody finds himself playing a role in a situational script, these constructions help him to shape the utterances he is going to produce. The constructions need not have interindividual generality: different persons may have different constructions for a given speak–MTRANS. And the same person may even have different preferred constructions in different periods of time. The important point is that the association between a speak–MTRANS in a situational script and a syntactic construction resides in the speaker's memory for some period, and is activated during each staging of the script within that period.

I do not know of any published empirical data that support or undermine this idea. So I decided to obtain some—rather informal—observations on spontaneous speech during a standard situation. A Dutch speaking girl of 3 years and 8 months, my daughter Jessica, played an assembly game on five consecutive days, together with her mother. Each day the game—making a little doll out of Lego pieces—was repeated twice. Thus, I collected 10 samples of tape-recorded speech of about 10 minutes each. The game always began with the Lego pieces (not only blocks but also heads, arms, wigs, etc.) lying on a table. Jessica chose one of the models (a boy, a girl, a grandma) as the doll she wanted to make. Then she started constructing the doll—always in the same fashion, from the feet upward to the wig. Jessica's mother was around for giving help, answering questions, redirecting her to the game after interruptions, distractions, etc.

Without going so far as to write a complete script for the game, I looked for "scenes" that satisfied the following three conditions:

1. Jessica often produced an utterance during the scene.
2. The scene occurred in most repetitions of the game.
3. The scene is easy to identify. I selected these: "Choosing the model," "Doll finished," and "Which wig?" (Jessica found it difficult to tell apart the various wigs.)

Table 1 gives the utterances recorded during these scenes. It also presents the sentence frame that seems to have been active during each scene. Since only a small proportion of the utterances does not fit into those frames, I take these observations as, at least, an encouragement to pursue further the idea of syntactic constructions hooked up with scripts. Indeed, apart from trivial cases such as the phraseology of buying train tickets, this or a similar principle seems necessary for explaining such remarkable feats of sentence production as are displayed by, for instance, radio reporters doing running commentaries of soccer matches or horse races.

A second aspect of the doll-assembly observations is worth stressing, too. Only a minority of Jessica's utterances were directly instrumental to attaining her goal. For instance, the "Which wig?" questions were likely to elicit help in overcoming an obstacle to finishing off the doll. But the purpose of both other utterance groups in Table 1 is much less clear. Nonetheless, they had a stable position in the doll-assembly script. On the other hand, MTRANSes that would have been judged perfectly relevant just never occurred. For instance, Jessica never commented on how she liked the doll she had made. Generalizing away from these observations, scripts might contain speak—MTRANSes at fixed places. Some of them bear no direct relationship to the goal of the script or are even adverse to it. Such "superfluous" speak—MTRANSes together with the "essential" ones described by Schank and Abelson become important determinants of the conceptualization process in that they control when and about what kind of things persons talk in script-like situations.

TABLE 1
Utterances and Sentence Frames for
Three Scenes of the Doll-Assembly Game Described
in Section 3[a]

Utterances	Sentence frames
Scene 1: Choosing the model	
3 Ik ga oma maken	
4 En nou ga ik 't jongetje maken	
5 En nou maak ik deze	(en) nou ga ik (DET) N maken
6 Dit meisje	
7 Nou ga ik dit meisje maken	
8 En nou ga ik dit meisje maken	
9 En nou oma	
10 Nou ga ik dit meisje maken	
Scene 2: Which wig?	
1 Welke moet ie dan op?	
5 Welke muts moet ie dan op?	
6 Welk mutsje moet ie hebben?	welke (N) moet ie (ADV) V
8 Welke moet ie nou op?	
9 Welke moet ie op?	
Scene 3: Doll finished	
1 Nou is 't meisje klaar	
2 Klaar	
3 Daar is oma	
4 Nou is 't meisje klaar	(zo) nou is (DET) N klaar
5 Nou is dit klaar	
7 Zo, nou is ie klaar	
8 Zo, nou is ie klaar	
9 Nou is oma klaar	
10 Zo	

Vocabulary

daar = there	klaar = finished
dan = then	maken = make
deze = this	moet = have to
dit = this	muts(je) = cap (here also: wig)
en = and	nou = now
ga = go	oma = grandma
hebben = have	op = (put) on
ie = he (here also: she)	't = the
ik = I	welk(e) = which (one)
is = is	zo = so
jongetje = boy	

[a]Numbers refer to repetitions of the game.

A final remark. Throughout this section I have emphasized the stereotyped sides of human sentence production. Of course, there is more to it; see Section VI.

IV. AN EXPERIMENT ON PARAPHRASTIC REPRODUCTION OF SENTENCES

The first experimental support for the idea of Search-and-Formulate programs associated with syntactic constructions was obtained by means of the paraphrastic reproduction method (Kempen, 1973, in press; Levelt & Kempen, 1975). Contrary to what is often thought, literal reproduction of a memorized sentence does not imply that the subject has stored it in a literal format. It is possible for literal reproduction to start from a genuine conceptual representation of the meaning of the sentence, provided the subject knows the syntactic construction of the memorized sentence. The Search-and-Formulate program belonging to that construction will then take care of the exact wording. An accurate memory for the individual words (irrespective of order) does not seem necessary for this to be possible. The subject only needs to remember words if, for some slot in the syntactic frame, the language offers a set of synonyms that would all be fitting. It seems justified to consider sentence reproduction a special case of sentence production, as long as this description is valid.

The experiment to be reported here applies the paraphrastic reproduction method. After having memorized a number of sentences the subject has to recall them not only literally but also in the form of a paraphrase prescribed by the experimenter. If the reproduction sentence (or phrase) contains the total content of the memorized sentence, then it is called a full paraphrase. It is a partial paraphrase if it expresses only part of the memorized sentence. By way of example, (1) and (2) are full paraphrases, (3) is a partial paraphrase of (1) and (2):

		notation
(1)	... omdat die waakse honden fietsers bijten	S2
	(... because those watchful dogs bite cyclists)	
(2)	... want die waakse honden bijten fietsers	M2
	(... for those watchful dogs bite cyclists)	
(3)	... want die waakse honden bijten	M1
	(... for those watchful dogs bite)	
(4)	... omdat die waakse honden fietsers	S1
	(... because those watchful dogs cyclists)	

Notice the word order reversal within the predicates of the Dutch sentences. Coordinate clauses like (2) have the order verb–object; in subordinate clauses such as (1) the obligatory order is object–verb. Now also consider (4) which is a truncation of (1). Unlike (3) which, in a sense, is a truncation of (2), (4) is ungrammatical. Quartets such as (1) through (4) provide the opportunity to test a prediction from the Search-and-Formulate programs proposed in Section II.

As for notation, clauses (1) through (3) consist of a conjunction, a subject phrase, and a predicate phrase. In (1) and (2), the predicate phrase contains two words; in (3) only one word. Since the predicate phrases of (2) and (3) have the word order of a main clause, I will refer to the constructions they instantiate by M2 and M1, respectively. The word order of the two-word predicate of (1) is that of a subordinate clause: S2. Although (4) does not contain a full predicate, I will refer to sentences of this type by S1.

The Search-and-Formulate programs associated with predicate phrases M1, M2, and S2 may be expected to take different execution times. The M1 program can presumably be executed faster than the M2 and S2 programs, for the latter have to engage in a more extensive search through the theme and in more complex response planning. Since no Search-and-Formulate program is available for ungrammatical "predicate phrases" of type S1, the subjects have to follow a different course. They might first execute the S2 program. Then, since this program delivers a word pair as a result, they curtail this result in such a way that only the first word is actually uttered. The latter operation requires extra time. Taken together, the execution times are expected to assume the rank order M1 < (M2, S2) < S1. At the end of this section I will explain why this prediction is, indeed, crucial.

In order to obtain data that reflect the execution times of the programs I devised a special probe latency procedure. Each subject first learned 12 sentences which all embodied the same syntactic construction. The stimuli to be presented during probe latency measurement were assembled this way. The first word was a conjunction (*want* or *omdat*). Then followed the subject phrase of one of the memorized sentences. Latencies (reaction times) were measured under four conditions: M1, M2, S1, and S2. In condition M1, the subjects had to pronounce as soon as possible the first word of the predicate, that is, the verb. The other word of the predicate was to be produced in condition S1. In conditions M2 and S2 the required response was both words of the predicate in the order of a main and a subordinate clause, respectively. Thus, the conditions are named after the sentence type the participants had to complete.

Most important is that the subjects produced many successive responses within the same condition. Once they had got accustomed to a new condition—during a few preliminary trials—they were sure to receive 24 stimuli of the same sort: each sentence twice. Only after that a switch to another condition would be announced. This blockwise presentation enabled the subjects to activate the appropriate Search-and-Formulate program and to execute it on each successive trial.

The tasks were made clear to the subjects by first calling their attention to the word order ordained by the conjunction in an example sentence. In conditions M2 and S2 they were asked to pronounce the two predicate words in that order, whether or not it was the memorized word order. In the M1 and S1 conditions they were told that the word which, in the demanded order, occupied the first predicate position, would count as the correct response; pronouncing both words would be considered erroneous.

A few further details. Each subject participated in all four conditions, which were counterbalanced so as to exclude effects of practice or fatigue. The stimuli appeared on a CRT-screen connected to a PDP-11/45 computer that also controlled reaction time measurement. The experimenter's task was limited to explaining the instructions and checking correctness of responses. Reaction time (latency) was defined as the interval between start of stimulus presentation and onset of the spoken response word or word pair. A pilot study had shown that in the M2 and S2 conditions subjects do not hesitate or pause between words. They output the predicate as a single unit, even if the word order differs from the memorized order. In many respects (treatment of erroneous responses; a filler task between successive stimuli; interstimulus interval) the present experimental procedure is similar to the one described in Kempen (in press).

A total of 32 subjects (Dutch speaking university students) participated in the experiment. Half of them memorized M2 sentences (with conjunction *want*), the other half S2 sentences (with *omdat*). The groups of 16 were again split up into two groups of 8. The first of these received sentences of type (1) or (2), that is, having an object noun in their predicate phrases. For the second group, the object noun had been replaced by an adjective which served as an adverbial modifier to the verb, for example, *bite badly* instead of *bite cyclists*. Efforts were made to avoid adjectives that could also be taken as modifiers of the subject nouns.

I introduced this complication because the object nouns are likely to be more concrete than the verbs. Recalling abstract words has often been found more difficult than recalling concrete words. This factor might affect response latencies, too, and counteract the hypothesis under study. For instance, I predict that M1 responses will have shorter latencies than S1 responses. But the M1 responses are more abstract (verbs) than the S1 responses (nouns). I judged that adjectives on the average are less concrete than nouns.

Results. The hypothesis was nicely confirmed. The average reaction times (arithmetic means) for conditions M1, M2, S2, and S1 were 1279, 1317, 1315, and 1352 msec, respectively, in remarkably good agreement with the predicted pattern. The interaction between clause type (M versus S) and response length (1 versus 2 words) was statistically significant; $F(1, 28) = 5.82, p = .02$. Furthermore, the most important parts of the hypothesis, namely, that M1 < M2 and S1 > S2, are both true. This pattern is indeed generated by three out of the four participating groups of subjects (cf. Table 2).

Even so, this cannot be the whole story. Table 2 shows that word order of the memorized sentences exerted a considerable influence: if the subjects had to reverse this order, the reaction times increased. This indicates that they did not

TABLE 2
Average Reaction Times (Milliseconds)
for Main Conditions of the Experiment of Section IV[a]

Clause types	M				S			
Condition	M1	M2	S1	S2	M1	M2	S1	S2
Object noun	1207	1151	1228	1238	1242	1342	1284	1210
Adjective	1196	1253	1488	1472	1471	1525	1409	1341
Total	1202		1357		1395		1311	

[a]Each mean (not including the totals) represents about 175 observations.

always reproduce the predicate phrase from a representation of its meaning; apparently, they sometimes had a quicker access to the literal form of the predicate. And, of course, the hypothesis under study does not apply if subjects use this strategy.

Second, the subjects had more difficulty in switching from main to subordinate clause word order than the other way around: see the line labeled "total" in Table 2. The corresponding interaction is very significant: $F(1, 28) = 39.19, p < .00002$. This finding might open speculations about the psychological status of these two word orders within the predicate (not only in Dutch but also in German; needless to say that although the subordinate clause order is very difficult to learn for native speakers of English or French, Dutch and German speakers do not find it less normal and easy than the main clause order). Third, although the pertinent interaction is not nearly significant, the sentences with adverbial modifiers seem to give better results than the object noun sentences. This might be related to the abstractness factor discussed above.

Before turning to other data I have to point out that the predicted and obtained pattern of latencies, M1 < (M2, S2) < S1, does not follow from other leading theories on memory for sentences. Although Johnson (1970) does not consider within-sentence reaction time data, his model seems to predict that single word responses (M1 and S1) can be produced quicker than double word responses (M2 and S2). The opposite prediction, (M2, S2) < (M1, S1) is defendable too. During the memorization stage of the experiment, the predicates evolve into integrated memory units. Conditions M1 and S1 not only ask for their being retrieved but also broken apart. The latter process might increase the latencies of overt response production. Finally, one might try to interpret the results in terms of search through memory. Most theories on how to represent sentence meanings in conceptual or semantic networks would predict that, given an actor, it is easier to find the action than the object; or even that the object can only be found after first having retrieved the action. Theories like these lead to the predictions M1 < (M2, S2) and M1 < S1. But S1 > S2 does not naturally follow (see, also, Kempen, in press, footnote 2).

V. SYNTACTIC CONSTRUCTIONS AND LEXICAL STRUCTURES: FURTHER EXPERIMENTAL EVIDENCE

The notion of a syntactic construction as defined in Section II is related to what is known as the lexical structure of words. For instance, to say of a given word that it is a transitive verb is not only a statement about one aspect of its lexical structure but also about a certain class of syntactic constructions the word may appear in (predicate phrases, say, having a noun phrase which expresses the conceptual object). Because of this relationship, experimental data on the psychological effects of lexical structures are relevant here.

In the pertinent experiments the subject had to carry out memory tasks with transitive, intransitive, or middle verbs. (Middle verbs can be used both transitively and intransitively.) Polzella and Rohrman (1970) found that transitive verbs elicited a larger proportion of free associates belonging to the noun category than intransitive verbs did. They attributed this effect to the lexical structure of verbs in these categories. The lexicon specifies an object slot for transitive but not for intransitive verbs; nouns or noun phrases fit into that slot. Bacharach, Kellas, and McFarland (1972) pursued this idea in a free recall learning experiment. Subjects memorized pairs consisting of a consonant–vowel–consonant (CVC) trigram and a verb. The verbs were either transitive or intransitive; the CVCs either preceded or followed the verb. Each subject participated in only one of these four conditions (blockwise presentation; cf. Section IV). CVC–intransitive verb pairs, it was found, were easier to learn than CVC–transitive verb pairs if the trigram preceded the verb. No such difference between transitive and intransitive verbs obtained in the order verb–CVC.

The explanation went like this. In the conditions where trigrams came first, they took the role of subject phrase for the subsequent verb. If that verb was intransitive the CVC–verb pair made up a complete sentence. But not so if the pair contained a transitive verb; then, the object slot remained empty which presumably made such a pair more difficult to remember. In the order verb–CVC the transitive verbs were no longer at a disadvantage since their object slots were filled by the trigrams (Bacharach, Kellas, & McFarland, 1972).

But one aspect of the data is difficult to explain on the lexical structure hypothesis. Because transitive as well as intransitive verbs demand a subject phrase, one could argue that in the verb–CVC order both verb categories had slots left open. Whereas in the CVC–verb order one category (the intransitive verbs) had their environment completely filled in. Consequently, one would expect the order verb–CVC to produce, on the whole, slower learning than the CVC–verb order. But this difference does not show up.

The syntactic construction notion does not run into this problem. It considers verb–object sequences (without subject phrases) complete syntactic constructions, just as it does subject–intransitive verb sequences. The participants who tried to recall the verb–trigram pairs could make use of the Search-and-Formulate programs associated with these constructions. In the condition CVC–

transitive verb (in that order), the appropriate syntactic frame was made up of a verb and two nouns, one for the subject and one for the object. The latter noun, of course, did not figure in the syntactic frame for the CVC–intransitive verb condition. This length difference between the two frames provides a sufficient explanation for the recall difference observed in these conditions. Possibly, the open object slot interpretation is true at the same time. The Search-and-Formulate program running in the CVC–transitive verb condition had to work in a context of insufficient information.

A major weakness of the lexical structure notion has been uncovered by Kail and collaborators (Kail & Bleirad, in press; Kail & Segui, 1974; Segui & Kail, 1972). She pointed out that the lexical structure hypothesis makes wrong predictions for middle verbs. As indicated by their name, middle verbs take a position intermediate between transitive and intransitive verbs on the lexical complexity scale.

In a series of experiments, Kail had subjects memorize lists of transitive, middle, or intransitive verbs. Sometimes the verbs were presented in isolation, in other conditions they were embedded in sentences with one (subject) or two (subject and object) noun phrases. The results may be summed up as follows. The recall scores for middle verbs were never in between the scores for intransitive and transitive verbs. Instead, the middle verbs behaved either as transitive or as intransitive verbs, depending on whether or not they were followed by a noun phrase that could take the role of object.

One experimental condition deserves special attention. Subject–verb pairs–the verbs could be transitive, middle, or intransitive–were followed by a noun phrase printed on the next page of the booklet that contained the learning material. The noun phrases could be meaningfully interpreted as objects for the transitive and the middle verbs. By "integrating" these noun phrases into the preceding sentence fragment, the subjects could substantially reduce the memory load required by the learning material. In the case of an intransitive verb, they had to resort to the less efficient "segregation" strategy of memorizing the noun phrases as independent items. From a variety of recall measures Kail and Bleirad concluded that middle verbs gave rise to the integration strategy as readily as transitive verbs. But if middle verbs are inserted in a context of intransitive verbs, they behave as intransitive verbs and induce the segregation strategy. Unlike middle verbs, transitives and intransitives are not subject to context influences.

Kail and her co-workers explain these results by postulating a double-faced lexical structure for middle verbs. They are basically transitive verbs and in the absence of context influence they expect an object noun phrase. But in a context with mainly intransitive verbs, their intransitive side is activated.

Although I have no arguments which disprove this type of account, syntactic constructions probably provide a simpler explanation of Kail's data. I do need a context mechanism—compare the repetitive situations discussed in Section III;

the blockwise presentation needed in Section IV—but the special assumption that middle verbs are "basically" transitive verbs is superfluous. If middle verbs are regularly followed by noun phrases, then the participants mobilize the corresponding Search-and-Formulate program. If not, then they activate the "intransitive" Search-and-Formulate program which does not look for an object.

Thus, the appropriate level of explanation seems to be that of syntactic constructions, not of individual words. The lexical structure of a word influences recall performance only indirectly, namely, if it dictates what kind of Search-and-Formulate program the subjects execute.

VI. THEORETICAL OVERVIEW

After this long survey of experimental work, which appears to support the main theoretical notions of syntactic constructions and Search-and-Formulate programs, it is useful to summarize the human sentence production system outlined in this paper.

The sentence production system does not work according to the schedule: conceptualization first, then formulation. Instead, selection of conceptual content and determination of sentence form are heavily interdependent. Often, the speaker has available a syntactic construction that he knows will allow him to express what is on his mind, at the same time or even before he has definitely decided on the content of the sentence. This syntactic construction, then, shapes the content selection process. The interaction between conceptualization and formulation is made possible by Search-and-Formulate programs, of which I have sketched a few outlines.

How does the speaker know that a certain syntactic construction will fit in with what he wants to say? I mentioned two possibilities (but there must be more of them): repetitive situations where many messages of the same type of content have to be worded in succession, and scripts which specify both when the speaker will engage in speaking and which syntactic construction he can use. This idea of hooking up syntactic constructions with speech scenes in scripts is important because it contributes to the what-to-say and the how-to-say-it problems at the same time.

The syntactic formulation process does not always start with a full-fledged conceptual structure built by the Conceptualizer. What often seems to be the input to the Formulator is (a) a rudimentary conceptual structure only containing the core of the to-be-expressed content, and (b) some advice on which type of syntactic construction to use. The formulator must be able to search through memory for further content details. Finally, what has to happen if the syntactic advice turns out to be wrong? In order to do justice to the great flexibility the human language generation system obviously has, it seems obligatory to endow it with some sort of problem-solving mechanism that is able to reason about the applicability of the syntactic constructions it has in store. But writing about this topic requires many what-to-say and how-to-say-it problems solved first.

REFERENCES

Bacharach, V. R., Kellas, G., & McFarland, C. E. Structural properties of transitive and intransitive verbs. *Journal of Verbal Learning and Verbal Behavior,* 1972, **11,** 486–490.

Goldman, N. M. *Computer generation of natural language from a deep conceptual base.* Dissertation, Stanford University, 1974.

Johnson, N. F. The role of chunking and organization in the process of recall. In G. H. Bower (Ed.), *The psychology of learning and motivation,* Vol. 4. New York: Academic Press, 1970.

Kail, M., & Bleirad, G. Etude de quelque stratégies de codage mnémonique du matériel linguistique. *Bulletin de Psychologie,* in. press.

Kail, M., & Segui, J. Intégration mnémonique de séquences linguistiques. *Année Psychologique,* 1974, **74,** 157–170.

Kempen, G. *Syntactic constructions as retrieval plans.* Paper read at the Joint Meeting of The British Experimental Psychology Society and the Dutch Psychonomics Foundation, Amsterdam, April 1973.

Kempen, G. *De taalgebruiker in de mens.* Groningen: Tjeenk Willink, 1975.

Kempen, G. Syntactic constructions as retrieval plans. *British Journal of Psychology,* in press.

Levelt, W. J. M., & Kempen, G. Semantic and syntactic aspects of remembering sentences. In R. A. Kennedy & A. L. Wilkes (Eds.), *Studies in long term memory.* New York: Wiley, 1975.

Osgood, C. E. Where do sentences come from? In D. D. Steinberg & L. A. Jakobovitz (Eds.), *Semantics; an interdisciplinary reader in philosophy, linguistics and psychology.* Cambridge, England: Cambridge University Press, 1971.

Polzella, D. J., & Rohrman, N. L. Psychological aspects of transitive verbs. *Journal of Verbal Learning and Verbal Behavior,* 1970, **9,** 537–540.

Schank, R. C. Conceptual dependency: a theory of natural language understanding. *Cognitive Psychology,* 1972, **3,** 552–631.

Schank, R. C., & Abelson, R. F. Scripts, plans and knowledge. *Proceedings of the 4th International Joint Conference on Artificial Intelligence, Tbilisi, USSR,* 1975.

Segui, J., & Kail, M. Rôles des caractéristiques lexicales du verbe dans la rétention d'énoncés. *Année Psychologique,* 1972, **72,** 117–130.

Selz, O. *Über die Gesetze des Geordneten Denkverlaufs.* Zweiter Teil. Bonn: Cohen, 1922.

12
From Verbs to Sentences: Some Experimental Studies of Predication

Robert J. Jarvella

The Rockefeller University

The production of sentences is a human activity with significant cognitive, social, and linguistic aspects. Each of these areas has attracted the recent attention of behavioral scientists, and already some promising results bearing on specific questions in them are being achieved. Yet, absolutely speaking, our current knowledge of the process of producing sentences is quite minimal at all but the most peripheral levels. There is no attractive general theory available, and even a modest overview of the topic requires reference to concepts and methods from a variety of fields concerned with language and speech. Moreover, it is far from clear how the central process involved in making sentences—itself submerged from direct observation—might be best inferred from obtainable facts about its contexts and products.

In this paper, I have no such theory to propose, and will have relatively little to say about the results of others. Mainly, I will be looking at just the linguistic side to producing sentences. Even the perspective suggested for this may seem quite limited. For example, phonetic processes (including intonation) in the production of speech will be all but ignored. The studies which are reported here were begun almost five years ago, and the subjects were most typically asked to use English verbs of various kinds in sentences. On two occasions, some preliminary findings from the work were presented (Jarvella, 1972; Melamed & Jarvella, 1973). However, each of the general problems identified above helped to create delays in bringing it to a conclusion.

On the one hand, over a period of time my interests grew to include both the meaning of sentences and their external form. The more I thought about how production might be described to work at these levels, the more it seemed

275

advisable to take account of certain concepts from outside of psychology proper, especially from linguistics and philosophy. Various sources which have benefited my work are cited here without too great concern for their original context or whether they fit neatly together as a body of information.

On the other hand, the methodological approach which I adopted was used chiefly to collect a fair-sized sample of sentences, to try to interrelate some of their syntactic and semantic features and, if possible, account in part for the sentence latencies in production. It quickly became apparent, however, that data of this kind could be categorized and cross-classified in interesting ways that I just could not cover. By and large, the kinds of things I did happen to examine occurred early on in the sentences produced. Perhaps, because of this, I came away with the feeling that the beginnings of sentences may tend to serve a somewhat specialized function in both speaking and communication; that perhaps they can tell us something of value about how sentences come to be.

Following Miller (1970), I take it largely for granted here that sentences express judgments (as opposed to associations) by a process of predication; that this is a paramount fact to be explained about language behavior. But what exactly, or even approximately, is this process of predication like? Several plausible definitions come to mind. In English, for example, we sometimes mean that one thing is predicated of another. In this sense, predication may be viewed as a judgment itself—the mental act of asserting some property or relation, for instance, or of affirming some action, state, or quality. But when a sentence containing such judgments is spoken, it can also be regarded as an act of predication. Thus, predication can be thought of either as a cognitive process or a linguistic performance, the formation of verbal judgments or their expression. It is something which people do as they conceive of sentences and when they say them. In short, predication in English seems to refer to not one but two processes involved in talking.

The dual nature of predication may, I feel, be suggestive of how sentences are often produced. The two meanings that we have just considered seem to imply the possibility of similar, complementary stages in the sentence production process. Moreover, they also seem compatible with a more conventional distinction between sentence meaning and outward linguistic form. The working hypothesis chosen in this paper will therefore not be very surprising. Essentially, I will view the process of producing sentences as including two central components, one having to do with how linguistic judgments are formed and the other having to do with how they are expressed. These two major components are further viewed as being substantially serially ordered.

In the earlier stage, judgments are taken to be formed by mental operations which combine or join elements into particular formats. Here, we are concerned with partially formalizing the former definition of predication considered above. In order to label these types of elements and resulting structures, I will borrow some terms from symbolic logic. A quality which is predicated will be called a propositional function, or simply a predicate. A thing that it is predicated of, or applied to, will be called an argument. And the simplest type of resulting structure will be called a proposition.

This initial subprocess is conceived to operate largely by selection. Given the choice of some predicate, the problem would be to select appropriate arguments, and vice versa. As a view of predication, this is similar to that adopted by Miller (1970, personal communication), except that he assumes the process to normally involve choice of predicates first and arguments second. Generally, philosophers writing about language seem to attach a similar priority to predicates. Both Russell (1940) and Reichenbach (1947) propose (roughly) that propositions be constructed by substituting values for variables in propositional functions (or by binding them with quantifiers). In fact, this may be the more reasonable hypothesis, since predicates may be defined very widely for English, and while they are needed for predication to occur, particular arguments often are not. The present studies were partly intended to simulate early selection of predicates in the judgment-forming process.

The outcome of these hypothetical operations would be predicate—argument structures representing one or more linguistic judgments. By itself, however, this says little about what the predicate and argument elements being combined may be. Since the judgments that I am interested in characterizing are presumed to be linguistic, these elements will be taken to include abstract representations of lexical items and of their combinations. The judgments that we will be most interested in involve lexical items which are largely defined by language situations themselves or which indicate how (or how well) other propositional information is known.

Now consider the latter stage of the process. Here the judgmental structures being formed are considered to be translated or transformed into utterances. This subprocess would presumably incorporate English syntax in some form and place extreme constraints on the form of its output, namely, surface structure sentences spoken or written from left to right. However, as in the prior stage, certain choices would also be involved. For example, several grammatical constructions could potentially represent a given set of linguistic judgments, but usually only one would be used; the assignment of grammatical features to one judgment would tend to restrict the selection of features for other judgments; and so on.

Finally, what about the temporal relation between stages? At the outset, it was suggested that this be largely serial. This was partly for expository purposes, as simultaneous processing of the same or different (chunks of) information in the two stages is certainly conceivable. However, I presume that the second stage could not normally begin to function until it received some input from the first stage on which to operate. And in the case of many (perhaps most) sentences, I suspect there would be a nontrivial correspondence between the order in which judgments are formed and the order in which they are expressed. Like Kempen (this volume), I take for granted the presence of some mechanism such as a feedback loop to permit interaction and integration between stages.

The two linguistic components of sentence production that I have suggested culminate in different forms of predication, one quite implicit and the other usually overt. Yet, aspects of both components must in general be abstracted from performances of sentences actually used. In order to effectively study these two parts of the process, it may be necessary to provide research subjects with constraints on what they may talk about or say. As implied above, the current studies were largely aimed at getting people to incorporate particular predicates into their sentences.

If verbs express actions, states, or processes, as my dictionary suggests, then it seems likely that they have something important to do with predication. A central idea in this work, and I think still a fairly safe assumption, has been that verbs in English correspond roughly to (some of the) predicates underlying English sentences. Fillmore (1968) and Miller (1970), among others, have treated verbs as propositional functions which, in forming propositions, take noun phrases as their arguments. Various verbs (and words in other categories) have also been analyzed into complexes of more primitive but still verb-like predicates (see Miller & Johnson-Laird, 1976, for the most ambitious attempt of this kind). But although the relation between abstract predicates and superficial verb forms may often not be one to one, for a number of reasons it seems like a correspondence worth pursuing in production studies.

As Reichenbach (1947, Chapter 7) pointed out, English nouns and adjectives as well as verbs may at times function as linguistic predicates, but verbs tend to dominate among the words from these classes that can take multiple arguments (or which express relations versus properties). Loosely speaking, for example, intransitive verbs may be regarded as one-place predicates since they can take only subjects; transitive verbs also taking direct objects may be thought of as two-place predicates; and verbs which can take subjects and both direct and indirect objects can be considered three-place predicates. The use of verbs as predicates in sentences may also be more grammatically salient than for adjectives or nouns (for further relevant discussions, see Jesperson's, 1933, treatment of "predicatives"; Curme, 1947, on predicate nouns and adjectives).

If verb inputs to sentences can successfully convey their more judgment-like qualities to people, it should be feasible to manipulate the predicate structure underlying sentences and observe the superficial linguistic consequences. I will tentatively assume here that, through lexical memory, verbs can serve to initiate sentence production at a level corresponding to the selection of arguments. If this memory system is "organized to facilitate acceptable predications in grammatical speech [p. 187]," as Miller (1970) has proposed, people should at least experience no great difficulty in using verbs to form sentences. And if we are fortunate, perhaps they will intuitively recognize predicates or abstract verbs in what they are shown.

In applying linguistic predicates, a person would normally make contact with some real or hypothetical state of affairs. As Frege (1892) suggested, judgments might be thought of as transitions between propositions and their truth values.

At the judgment-forming level proposed here, linguistic inputs to sentence production are taken to arise in response to internal states and processes. Some activities of this kind would include processing of other sentences (that is, linguistic context), attention to other aspects of the visual or auditory environment, verbal or nonverbal thought, and so forth. Similarly, Russell (1940) has noted that sentences are normally expressions of speakers' beliefs. These, he suggests, have to do with mind–body conditions—with what is known or expected via memory, perception, inference, and the like. Information processing of these kinds could perhaps be characterized by perceptual and cognitive tests of the kind envisaged by Miller and Johnson-Laird (1976).

Perhaps the most serious limitation of simply giving subjects predicates to use in sentences is that there will usually be no way of telling if the sentences they produce are formulated to mean anything in particular. The aspect of forming and expressing propositions having to do with belief and knowledge might be largely forfeited to other concerns, with unknown consequences. Another major objection that might be raised to this kind of procedure is that it ignores the social nature of language use. The normal context for saying sentences is dialogue, and sentences used in conversations may usually have communicative functions other than just to inform. Sentences artificially elicited by lexical items in a psychological laboratory may bear a strange relation to things people otherwise say and their reasons for saying them.

On the other hand, sentence production in this kind of situation can be looked on more favorably. To a large extent, the usual cognitive and social concomitants of sentences may be such an established part of language behavior that in sterile contexts they are projected anyway and can be taken for granted. A somewhat opposite viewpoint, but one which is equally optimistic, would be that the more purely linguistic aspects of sentence production can best be studied by first stripping away its less linguistic features. Whether these limitations are thus real or only apparent, the usefulness of the present technique in revealing how predication may take place cannot easily be evaluated on an a priori basis. It seems worthwhile to at least try to initiate the production process using lexical items as input.

In the following section, I deal with a somewhat special case of linguistic judgments, and with how they might be converted into sentences. The case is largely that of judgments about other judgments. Learning how predicate–argument structures of this kind might be formed and realized through speech or writing was a principal goal of this research.

COMPLEMENT-TAKING VERBS

Some verbs can take full propositions as one or more of their arguments. In linguistics, these verbs are usually said to take sentence complements. In 1971, when this work was started, a number of insightful studies of complement-taking (or simply complement) verbs had recently become available (e.g., Ross, 1970; Vendler, 1970), and several of these provided classifications of the verbs which proved helpful in choosing dimensions among them that might be investigated experimentally (Rosenbaum, 1967; Kiparsky & Kiparsky, 1970). As best I can recall, my attention was drawn to the complement verbs for several different reasons.

One was what I felt was a strong tendency for these verbs to refer to subjective states and processes. Almost all verbs of perception, communication, learning, emotion, motivation, and thinking can take propositional arguments. Moreover, words like *listen* and *see, say* and *understand, remember* and *forget, delight* and *disappoint, want* and *need,* and *believe* and *know* seem to make up a substantial part of our everyday vocabulary for talking about cognition. In my original discussion of this research, I suggested the label "psychological verbs" for such words. Russell (1940) had also noted their psychological nature; that they are used to describe occurrences of believing, desiring, etc., which he called propositional attitudes. In any event, I think that the verbs of mind may be especially important words for us to understand in terms of their meaning and common usage. Carefully reasoned semantic analyses such as those proposed by Miller and Johnson-Laird (1976) may be most valuable for describing their meaning. But studies like the present ones should be useful in determining what people ordinarily describe these verbs as relating to in their sentences. That is, what are the persons, propositions, and other nominalizations commonly used as their arguments.

Take just persons and propositions. A second thing that interested me about complement verbs had to do with which of their arguments could be propositions and which could not. In the following phrases, the person A and the proposition P intuitively seem to have different underlying functions: A believes P, A expects that P, A needs to P, A is worried that P, and so on. As suggested above, such constructions could probably be further notated as, for example, BELIEVES (A,P). However, I was originally interested in these arguments in the context of Chomskyan deep structure (1965) rather than a predicate–argument formula. The arguments of interest are represented at the deep structure level by noun phrases used to define the relations "subject-of" and "direct-object-of": that is, noun phrases directly dominated by sentence and verb phrase nodes, respectively (Chomsky, 1965, p. 71). Following this grammatical model, Rosenbaum (1967) analyzed many English verbs as being capable of taking noun phrase complements (sentences) as their deep structure subjects or objects. In Fig. 1, some stylized phrase markers are shown for the two kinds of complementation, together with some examples of sentences which appear to have one kind of implicit structure or the other.

In general, one can verify that the complement verbs in the upper group of sentences are of the subject variety by asking the question "What plus the verb?" Thus, his going was what amazed me, your having come is what delights me, and

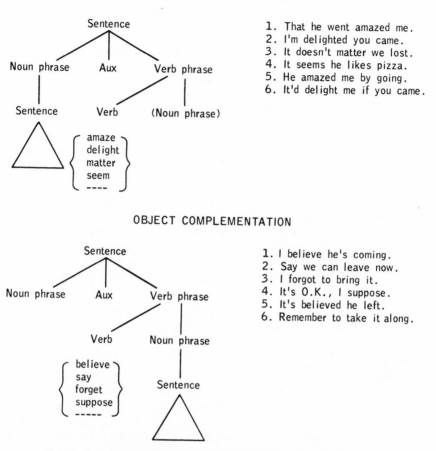

FIG. 1 Some hypothetical deep structures for sentences with complements.

that we lost is what doesn't matter. The answer will always be some form of a proposition. Similarly, one can tell that the complement verbs in the lower group of sentences are of the object variety by asking the question "What plus the passive form of the verb?" Thus, that he's coming is what is believed, bringing it is what was forgotten, and so forth. Again, the answer will always be some form of a proposition. This principle works, of course, because subjects of active voice verbs are taken to be deep subjects and subjects of passive voice verbs are taken to be deep objects.

McCawley (1970) and other linguists have argued that there are serious deficiencies to this form of deep structure. We need not review their arguments here, but I will note some respects in which deep and predicate—argument structure resemble each other and how they are different. Take, for example, the sentences from Fig. 1: "That he went amazed me" and "I believe he's coming." Using standard parenthetical notation, and ignoring tense and aspect, deep structures for these sentences might be shown by

$$((((HE)_{NP}((GO)_V)_{VP})_S)_{NP}((AMAZE)_V(ME)_{NP})_{VP})_S$$

and

$$((I)_{NP}((BELIEVE)_V(((HE)_{NP}((COME)_V)_{VP})_S)_{NP})_{VP})_S.$$

Their predicate–argument structure could be shown by AMAZE(GO(HE),ME) and BELIEVE(I,COME(HE)). Both types of representation are of psychological interest chiefly because they occupy a place in abstract sentence construction where lexical information is brought together and the meaning of the resulting expressions is defined from the configuration formed.[1]

However, both hierarchical and sequential features of the two types of structure are different. As suggested above, the major relations in deep structure are not defined between nominal elements and verbs, but between each separately and higher nodes in a phrase marker. For example, verbs and objects are grouped together to form a verb phrase node. The left-to-right order of nominal and verbal elements is also different in propositions and underlying sentences, or sentoids. As illustrated, a proposition is conventionally written with its predicate preceding an ordered series of its arguments enclosed in parentheses. But in a sentoid, the order of verb and noun phrase(s) corresponds to the relations subject–verb (–object).

Despite these differences, I will sometimes refer here not only to verbs as predicates, but to deep structure subjects and objects as if they are arguments; and to sentoids as if they are propositions. In fact, for my present purposes, it is not especially crucial which type of structure is taken to represent the configuration of judgments underlying a surface structure sentence. The principal question of interest can be phrased using either. Ultimately, this question concerns the partial order in which two propositions (sentoids) in this part–whole relation are formed and (then) expressed in sentences; if both propositions are fully formed before either is expressed, it boils down to just which is spoken or written first and which second.

Since we have considered two major kinds of complement verb, there are six possibilities for expression. The complement verb can precede its complement proposition in both cases, it can follow in both cases, or it can precede in either case and follow in the other one. For these particular kinds of sentences, the first alternative is roughly like saying that a deep structure representation is

---

[1] George Miller has pointed out to me that these two ways of describing sentences can be jointly represented by use of complex predicates formed by abstraction, or λ-conversion (see Church, 1956; Cresswell, 1973). In the expression $[\lambda x(\exists Y)(F(x,y))]$ (x), for example, (x), F, y, and $[\lambda x(\exists y)(F(x,y))]$ could correspond to a subject noun phrase, a verb, an object noun phrase, and a verb phrase, respectively. Semantic topic comment and surface structure subject–predicate distinctions could be captured similarly.

filled in and/or expressed sentoid by sentoid from top to bottom, or that the highest predicate is applied to its human argument before it is applied to its propositional argument. The second alternative is like saying the reverse of these. And the third alternative is like saying that a deep structure is filled in laterally from side to side, or that arguments of one kind (subject or object) are specified and/or expressed before arguments of the other kind.

In order to examine these various possibilities, I tried to determine if people would consistently use superficial sentences implying a single production strategy; whether they could easily adopt a different strategy under conditions that would make the more dominant one difficult to follow. The best way of asking this question seemed to be to obtain and contrast actual sentences formed with subject and object complements. To acquire a large enough sample of relevant sentences, I chiefly used an experimental design in which subject and object complement verbs were presented as lexical input to sentences, usually with another (noncomplement) verb presented before or after them to foster use of sentence complement constructions. (At least superficially, many complement verbs can take just nonpropositional arguments, as, for example, in "I believe the defendant.") When shown verb pairs, subjects were permitted to use either possible verb order in their sentences, or they were asked to maintain the order which they were shown. In this way, some were free to adopt a particular production strategy; others, I hoped, would be forced to produce sentences with the complement verb first ("It amazed me that he went"; "I believe he's coming") or with it second ("That he went amazed me"; "He's coming, I believe"). To what extent the order of clauses in such sentences can be taken to reflect the order of linguistic judgments made is a question considered in the general discussion.

A third and final interesting point concerning complement-taking verbs has to do with presuppositions sometimes invoked in their complements. Presupposition, as a concept bearing on sentence meaning generally and as a feature of complement constructions of certain verbs, was perhaps first recognized clearly by Frege. Frege (1892) pointed out that in declarative sentences, proper nouns are presupposed to designate something, whether the sentences make assertions or denials. For example, both "Kepler died in misery" and its negation, when used, presume reference to a particular person. In the same paper, Frege noted that there are particular convictions or truth values associated with the information expressed in complement clauses of some verbs but not others. More recently, each of these observations has been considerably refined.

Karttunen (1973) points out that the modern notion of presupposition has usually been stated in one of two related ways. There is a pragmatic viewpoint, in which presuppositions are ascribed to speakers. And there is a semantic one, according to which sentences themselves have presuppositions. Strawson (1952) appeared to recognize both of these senses. He notes that it would be "incorrect (or deceitful) . . . [p. 175] " for a speaker to utter a sentence such as "All John's children are asleep" unless he thought (among other things) that John had children; by using the sentence he would commit himself to their existence. In this pragmatic perspective, presuppositions may be thought of as sincerity conditions, or necessary features of contexts, for the utterance of sentences (Karttunen, 1973). On the other hand, presupposition can be defined semantically in terms of truth and falseness. According to Strawson, a statement S presupposes a statement S' if the truth of S' is a necessary condition for the truth *or* falseness of S. Or whenever S or not-S is true, S' is true (see van Frassen, 1971). In this sense, both "All John's children are asleep" and its negation presume that John has children. Logically, it would be contradictory to deny John's parenthood and either assert or deny the larger sentence.

Analyses of presupposition in English have been carried out largely in the context of subordinate clauses. Much of the work done has been on complement structures. A pioneering study was that of Kiparsky and Kiparsky (1970), who proposed a distinction between what they called "factive" versus "nonfactive" predicates. Semantically (or pragmatically), the difference they suggested between predicates of the two types was that only (speakers of) sentences formed with factives tend to presuppose that their complement propositions are true. For example, "surprise" is factive and "say" nonfactive. Either asserting or denying "John was surprised Mary left" presumes Mary left. But neither "John said Mary left" nor its negation necessarily makes such a presumption. More recently, it has been argued (see, for example, Karttunen, 1971, 1973) that just a simple categorization of complement-taking verbs along these lines may often be insufficient.

Grammatically, the Kiparskys noted that the noun "fact" could often be inserted at the beginning of factive complements; that gerunds could be used more freely with factive predicates; that only nonfactives tend to permit subject raising or require extraposition; and so on. In the initial study reported on here, the factiveness of complement verbs selected as stimulus items was not examined beforehand. But since it has grammatical consequences and might also be relatable to the selection of verifiable complement propositions in sentences, factivity was controlled for and considered as a variable in the remaining studies conducted. The question of where in the formation of sentences presuppositional judgments may enter is considered briefly near the end of this chapter.

THE EXPERIMENTS

Study 1

In this experiment and the next one, written sentences were collected from large numbers of college students. In this case, 120 students were tested. Each was presented either 20 individual verbs or 20 verb pairs and asked to use the verbs in sentences. Forty verbs were chosen as stimuli. Half of these were verbs taken from the appendix provided in Rosenbaum (1967). These included 10 transitive subject complement verbs and 10 object complement verbs. The subject complement verbs were *embarrass, delight, bore, amaze, dismay, disappoint, gratify, please, annoy,* and *interest.* The object complement verbs were *ask, believe, deny, remember, realize, tell, predict, think, announce,* and *know.* The other 20 verbs chosen were ones which do not ordinarily take sentence complements. Half of these were transitive (primarily "double-object" verbs) and the other half intransitive. The transitive noncomplement verbs were *send, buy, take, lend, retain, borrow, bring, sell, receive,* and *release.* The intransitive noncomplement verbs were *sit, die, depart, awake, emerge, arrive, live, rise, disappear,* and *sleep.*

The verbs were typed onto addressing labels individually and in pairs, with verbs within pairs separated by a blank space, comma, and another blank space. The labels were then glued one to a page into test booklets approximately 11 X 13 cm in dimension. Booklets were made up to contain five instances of a single verb type or five verb pairs drawn from two types. Forty subjects each completed one booklet of subject complement verbs, one of object complement verbs, one of transitive noncomplement verbs, and one of intransitive noncomplement verbs. The remaining 80 subjects wrote sentences with verb pairs. These were formed by permuting the two types of complement verb with the two types of noncomplement verb, also giving four types of booklet. For all subjects, all possible combinations of verbs from these types were used equally often. Half of the subjects were given the pairs in complement–noncomplement order and the other half in noncomplement–complement order. Item order within and between booklets was counterbalanced over subjects for both individual verbs and verb pairs using a Greco-Latin square.

All subjects were told that they should write down the first sentence that they thought of containing each verb or verb pair that they were given. Half of the subjects receiving verb pairs were told they could use the verbs in either order in their sentences, and the other half were told to maintain the left–right order they were given. In addition to writing five sentences in each of four test booklets, all subjects were instructed to record the time when they began and finished each booklet from one of several synchronized Lafayette GraLab timers present in the test room. In this way, 480 response intervals for completing particular five-sentence booklets were obtained along with the 2,400 sentences. Each verb was used in a sentence by 100 subjects, four times in combination with 20 other verbs and 20 times by itself.

The first group of results I will mention are ones that were obtained for mood, person, and tense. The sentences were classified for these features on the basis of punctuation and grammatical form; Table 1 summarizes what was found.

Sentence mood was decided mainly on the following basis. Sentences were considered to be declarative, interrogative, or imperative if they ended in a period, question mark, or exclamation point, and their main clause began with a

TABLE 1
Percentages of Moods, Persons, and Tenses in Some Sentences

	1st person	2nd person	3rd person
Sentences to single verbs (N = 800)			
Declaratives			
Past	6		13
Nonpast	24	2	20
Interrogatives			
Past		1	
Nonpast	1	5	
Imperatives			
Nonpast		27	
Sentences to pairs of verbs (N = 1,600)			
Declaratives			
Past	15		32
Nonpast	22	3	14
Interrogatives			
Past		1	
Nonpast		2	
Imperatives			
Nonpast		11	

subject noun phrase, a verb auxiliary or *wh-* word, or a main verb, respectively.[2] Overall, about 80% of all sentences written were declaratives, 4% were interrogatives, and 16% were imperatives.[3] But proportionally speaking, many more *non*declarative sentences were written with individual verbs than with verb pairs. For these items, about two and one half times (50 versus 21%) as many interrogatives and imperatives were produced with the object complement and transitive noncomplement verbs as with subject complement and intransitive noncomplement verbs. The same pattern distinguished verb types in sentences formed with pairs of verbs.

Grammatical person was scored as first, second, or third chiefly on the basis of surface structure subjects used. The great majority of sentences had personal pronouns as subjects, even when the implicit subjects of the imperatives were excluded from consideration. Overall, about 35% of surface subjects were first person (almost always singular "I"), 23% (including imperatives) were second person, and 41% were third person. Frequency of first person arguments in the main clauses of sentences was also determined. Together, "I" and "me" turned

[2] Note that the concept of mood being used here is somewhat different than the traditional one opposing indicative, subjunctive, and imperative.

[3] Unless otherwise noted, the only numerical differences considered in the text are significant differences. Tests used and levels of significance reached are therefore not given for particular instances. The data were in most cases evaluated using nonparametric analyses of variance by subjects or by items with a set at .05.

out to be used about equally often with each type of verb presented. To illustrate, the results for sentences formed with individual verbs were as follows. For subject complement verbs, only 3% of deep structure subjects were first person, but 43% of objects were first person. (And three fourths of these were superficial subjects.) For object complement verbs, 33% of deep structure subjects were first person, and 12% of sentences had first person indirect or direct objects. For intransitive noncomplement verbs, 37% of deep subjects were first person. And for transitive noncomplement verbs, 19% of deep subjects were first person and 23% of sentences had first person indirect or other dative objects.

Next, briefly consider verb tense. Again, this feature was considered only in the main clauses of sentences. Tense was scored as being past or nonpast using verb inflections and auxiliaries. Leaving imperatives aside, about the same percentage (40 versus 44%) of all sentences were written with past and nonpast tenses. The percentage of past tense verbs was about twice as great for sentences formed with verb pairs as individual verbs. Future verb forms were used in about 8% of sentences; in Table 1 they appear combined with other nonpast forms. About the same proportion of first and third person subjects had future verbs.

It is evident from Table 1 that mood, person, and tense were by no means independent features. Almost all interrogative as well as imperative sentences had second person subjects, usually with nonpast verbs. Within declarative sentences, second person subjects were fairly rare and nonpast verbs were dominant; nonpast verbs were also used with two thirds of first person subjects, but past tense verbs were used with three fifths of third person subjects. A more functional interpretation of these findings is considered later in this chapter.

A second group of results from this study concerns the use of complement constructions. A presented complement verb was scored as taking a sentence complement just in case there was a surface structure clause (including an overt verb) which was grammatically its underlying subject or object. Three types of finding will be mentioned: for frequency of complements used; for clause order used in these sentences; for complementizers used.

1. Three general results were obtained for complement frequency. First, sentence complements were much rarer when complement verbs were presented individually than when they were paired with other verbs. Most of the sentences produced for single verbs of all four types were simple, one-clause sentences; sentence complements were used in these cases with the complement verbs given only one fifth of the time. On the other hand, slightly over half of the sentences produced for verb pairs did have complements, with the complement verb usually incorporating the noncomplement verb. On the individual verbs, subjects averaged 1 min 38 sec per five-sentence booklet and wrote 1.6 clauses and 6.4 words per sentence. On verb pairs, subjects averaged 2 min 52 sec per booklet and wrote 2.4 clauses and 10.7 words per sentence.

Second, fewer complements were used with subject than with object complement verbs. The respective percentages were 15 versus 25% for individual verbs and 36 versus 66% for verb pairs. Booklets with subject complement verbs also took longer to complete than those with object complement verbs. The average difference was 15 sec per booklet for single verbs and 12 sec per booklet for verb pairs.

Third, complement frequency varied with verb order in pairs and instructions. When complement verbs were presented on the left in verb pairs, they took sentence complements 60% of the time, independently of the instructions given. When given on the right without order-preserving instructions, they were usually reversed and took complements 45% of the time. When given on the right and required to follow the noncomplement verb, they took complements only about 35% of the time. (This trend was fully consistent for subject and object complement verbs.) The average response time per five-sentence booklet in this last condition was 3 min 27 sec, versus about 2 min 40 sec in each of the others.[4]

2. Now consider clause order. A heavy bias toward main-complement order was essentially found in all conditions. Subject and object complement verbs presented individually almost always occurred before their sentence complements. When paired with noncomplement verbs, 80% of subject complement verbs and 90% of object complement verbs preceded their complements. Typically, these sentences contained just a main and a following complement clause. For example, this sentence form occurred in about half of all sentences produced when complement verbs were given on the left in pairs, and in about one third of the sentences when they were given second and free verb order was allowed.

As just indicated, the use of complement–main sentences was quite rare even in subject complementation. Generally, subject complements were postponed by extraposition, for example, leaving "it" as a surface subject in "It surprised me that he left," and sometimes by passivization as in "I was surprised that he left." When instructed to use subject complement verbs after the noncomplement verbs given, subjects did begin about half of their sentences with subordinate clauses. But only about one fourth of these were complements. The rest were largely time adverbials. To a lesser extent, sentences with noncomplement subordinations in this study also tended to begin with main clauses. For example, about twice as many main-clause-first as subordinate-clause-first sentences of this kind were written with the single verbs presented.

[4] Sentences formed when complement verbs were required to occur second were also slightly longer than sentences in the other two-verb conditions. Unlike the difference obtained here for one- versus two-verb stimuli, however, sentence length in this case and most later instances did not by itself offset the relatively large difference in latencies observed. In this example, only 8% more clauses and 15% more words were used, versus 30% more time.

3. The way in which main clauses were superficially linked to their complements was the third aspect of complementation examined. Function words which can serve this purpose are called complementizers. They include "that" (or ϕ where "that" is optional) used with finite verbs as in "He believed that...."; "to" used with infinitives as in "I was delighted to..."; various "wh-" words like "who" in "She wondered who..."; and prepositions used with gerunds. In the present sentences, complement verbs were often introduced by subjects. The most frequent complementizer used in these cases was "to," as in "I need/want/would like to...."

All complement verbs presented to subjects could be used with several types of complementizer. However, the distributions of complementizers used with subject and object complements were quite different. "To" was most frequently used (in 44% of cases) with subject complements, followed by "that" (22%). With object complements, this order was reversed; "that" (and ϕ) occurred three times as often (57 versus 19%) as "to." A wide variety of "wh-" words was also used with object complements, but with subject complement verbs, the only "wh-" word used resembling a complementizer was "when/if," as in "When he departed, I was amazed," or "If he would bring it, that would please me."[5] The remaining complementizers used with subject complements were prepositions (and ϕ) introducing gerunds; these forms were extremely rare in object complements.

The principle governing selection of most complementizers was also apparently different for the subject and object complements used. The former complements fell almost exclusively in declarative sentences; the main basis for selection seemed to be whether there was coreference between the object of the main clause and the surface subject of the complement clause. When there was, "to" was used, as in "It surprised him to awake" or "He was surprised to awake." Otherwise, "that" was usually used. On the other hand, for object complements, complementizer use seemed to be related to sentence mood. Miller and Johnson-Laird (1976) have observed that different complementizers tend to occur in indirect discourse with English verbs of stating, inquiring, and commanding. For example, "that" may be typically used to report what someone said, various "wh-" words to report what someone asked, and "to" in order to report what someone ordered. Two aspects of complementizer use from Study 1 were consistent with this observation. First, declarative, interrogative, and imperative sentences written with object complement verbs (half of which were speaking verbs) made most use of "that," "wh-" words, and "to" as complementizers, respectively. And second, most declaratives using "to" reported commands, and most imperatives using "wh-" words were requests to ask questions.

[5] Sentences of these kinds do not unambiguously contain predicate complements and were not counted as having them. However, they did occur fairly often when instructions called for subject complement verbs to be used to the right of noncomplement verbs, and would add about one fourth to the subject complement totals reported above.

Study 2

Both reference and factivity of the complement verbs used in Study 1 turned out to be largely confounded with the type of complement structures into which they could enter. In terms of content, the subject complement verbs seemed mainly to refer to arousal and emotion; the object complement verbs were mostly verbs of thought or language. In terms of factivity, the subject complement verbs were all more or less factive; of the object complement verbs, the thought verbs were mixed between factive (*know, realize*) and nonfactive (*think, believe*) and the speech verbs were basically all nonfactive.

To partly remedy these difficulties, the subject–object and factive–nonfactive dimensions of complement verbs were varied orthogonally in the second study conducted. Verb reference was also changed, by choosing a fully new set of complement-taking verbs for replicated complement–noncomplement verb pair conditions. However, although two complement verbs, one subject and one object, can sometimes be found which seem reasonably like converses (for example, in "I liked it" versus "It pleased me" or "It occurred to me" versus "I realized it"), no attempt was made to specifically match the verbs across conditions in this manner.

The 40 verbs used in Study 1 were again employed, along with 20 new complement-taking verbs drawn from Kiparsky and Kiparsky (1970). Half of the new verbs were intransitive. These subject complement verbs were, for factive, *suffices, matters, goes without saying, is well-known,* and *makes sense;* for nonfactive, *seems, happens, is in the works, is likely,* and *turns out.* As suggested, each was given in the third person present. The new object complement verbs were, for factive, *forget, bear in mind, be aware, take into account,* and *make clear;* for nonfactive, *suppose, anticipate, conclude, deem,* and *maintain.* Each of these verbs was also given in the form shown, as were those used over again from Study 1.

Ninety-six students were each presented 30 pairs of verbs and asked to use them in written sentences. These were typed in test booklets five pairs to a standard 21 X 28 cm page, with verbs within pairs set off as in Study 1. Verbs were combined into pairs on the following basis. First, the previously used subject and object complement verbs were paired randomly with each other. For these items, subject–object order was varied over pairs within subjects; order within pairs was varied over subjects. Second, the four groups of new complement verbs were each paired with all previously used noncomplement verbs. Each subject received six blocs of five verb pairs each. The first and sixth blocs contained the old complement verbs, and the four middle blocs contained the four groups of new complement verbs paired with old noncomplement verbs. Order between and within these middle blocs was counterbalanced over subjects using a Greco-Latin square.

As in Study 1, the complement–noncomplement verb pairs were presented to half of the subjects in one order and to the other half of the subjects in the opposite order. Again, subjects were instructed to write down the first sentence that they thought of that contained each pair presented. Half of the subjects were told they could change the order of the verbs given in sentences if they wanted, and the other half were instructed to maintain the order given. All subjects were told to record the time when they began and ended work on each bloc of verbs. In Study 1, a number of subjects had indicated difficulty in reading the clock face of the timers used; some made obvious errors recording their start and stop times. As a result, a digital procedure was used here instead; the experimenter simply recorded the elapsed time in 5 sec intervals on a blackboard. The data obtained in this way were 2,880 sentences and 576 response intervals for completing particular blocs of five sentences.[6]

Two groups of results for complement–noncomplement verb pairs based on the same scoring procedures replicated results from Study 1. First, frequency of complement constructions again varied with verb order and instructions. Sentence complements were used least often when complement verbs were required to occur after noncomplement verbs, in this case 47% of the time versus 65% in the remaining three conditions. Sentences in this condition were also produced most slowly. On the average, 2 min 54 sec were needed to complete a bloc of five sentences with mandatory noncomplement–complement verb order, versus 2 min 34 sec in the other three conditions. Sentences required to have this verb order on the average also contained about 10% more clauses and 3% more words.

Second, main–complement clause order was again dominant in complement constructions. Less than 5% of either subject or object complements preceded the new verbs. Two-clause main–complement sentences were used half of the time when complement verbs were required to fall first, and one third of the time when free verb order was permitted. Finally, unlike Study 1, there was no tendency for either fewer subject than object complements to be formed with the (respective) verbs given or for latencies to be greater for sentences formed with the subject complement verbs.

Sentences formed with the complement–complement verb pairs given took the shortest time of all to make up, an average of only 2 min 19 sec per five-sentence bloc. Over 80% of these sentences contained a complement construction based on one of the verbs given. Main–complement clause order was also dominant in these sentences, and about the same percentage of complements was used with the two kinds of verbs.

What effects did factivity have? Factive and nonfactive verbs used for the first time in this study took sentence complements about equally often. However,

---

[6] As in the previous experiment, this latency measure included everything subjects did between their start and stop times for each bloc of verbs.

sentences written with verbs of these two types were semantically or grammatically discriminable in a number of respects. For one thing, about five times as many factive as nonfactive complement constructions contained what might be called blanket assertions in their subordinate clauses. Such propositions included statements of general truths, moral precepts, social rules, and various proverbial sayings. Second, for the object complement verbs, about five times as many imperatives and related sentences with modal *should* or *must* were formed with factives as with nonfactives.

Third, as suggested by Kiparsky and Kiparsky (1970), the syntax of complement constructions was slightly different for factive and nonfactive verbs. Although subject complements were generally extraposed, this trend was more dominant for nonfactives. Over twice as many complement-clause-first sentences were used with the factive verbs. Similarly, only in the case of nonfactives were nominal constituents of lower sentences raised. (The almost sole use of gerundive complements with the verbs of emotion in Study 1 may have been another grammatical consequence of this factive–nonfactive distinction.) Finally, for object complement verbs, sentences with factives took longer to produce than sentences with nonfactives, a difference of about 20 sec per bloc of verbs. However, these sentences with factives, like the verbs themselves, were also considerably longer than those with nonfactives. The rate of production measured in words produced per second was about the same in the two cases.

The Melamed and Jarvella Studies

In Studies 1 and 2, large numbers of written sentences were collected along with a gross measure of time used in producing blocs of the sentences. In the present studies, smaller numbers of orally produced sentences were obtained along with multiple latency measures for each sentence. Measures of heart rate and skin resistance during production were also recorded.[7] Four oral sentence production tasks were used in an attempt to provide a better estimate of the locus of the previously obtained effects for complementation and determine their generalizability to other paradigms. The first task was an oral version of the verb-using task employed in Studies 1 and 2. The remaining tasks were question answering, sentence completion, and reading of sentences aloud.

In the verb-using task, following four practice items subjects were shown 20 pairs of verbs in which one verb was a complement verb and the other was not. The noncomplement verbs were the same as used previously, while the complement verbs were a subset of those used previously. The type of complement verb presented (subject versus object) and verb order in pairs (complement verb first versus second) were both varied within subjects. Instructions to use verb order

[7]The physiological data obtained in these experiments will be treated elsewhere in collaboration with Barbara G. Melamed.

freely or to maintain the order given were varied between subjects. For all subjects, 10 subject and 10 object complement verbs, balanced for factivity, were each presented 12 times with one transitive and one intransitive noncomplement verb.

In the questions task, subjects were shown 20 questions about everyday things. The questions all contained sentence complements and had main–complement clause order (for example, "Do you think it will rain today?"). One question was asked using each complement verb from the verbs task. Half of the questions formed with each type of complement verb were "wh-" questions and the other half were "yes/no" questions. Subjects were told to read each question silently and then answer it aloud using a complete sentence.

In the sentence completion task, subjects were shown 16 clauses, each of which began a sentence. Half of the clauses were main clauses and the other half were subordinate clauses. All main clauses contained complement verbs and could take sentence complements; half of these ended in a complementizer requiring a following complement. The subordinate clauses were sentence complements beginning with "that" or "for," and time adverbials beginning with "before" or "after." Subjects were told to say the beginning of each sentence out loud and make up their own ending for it.

In the sentence reading task, subjects were shown 20 sentences which had been written in the previous studies. One sentence was chosen using each of the complement verbs from the present verb-using task. The sentences varied in type of subordination (complement or noncomplement) and order of clauses (main or subordinate clause first) and were two or three clauses in length. In a number of sentences, slash marks were introduced to suggest hesitation pauses. Subjects were simply instructed to read each sentence aloud.

The stimuli for each task were printed on white addressing labels, glued onto sheets of cardboard, and presented in random orders using a wooden slant box such as devised by Levin (1966) for studying eye–voice span. The box contained a slot for inserting and withdrawing the cards, a low-power electric light, and a one-way mirror made transparent from the outside when the box's interior was illuminated. The subject was seated comfortably in a dimly lit test room and operated the box's light by means of a push button held in his preferred hand. (All subjects were right-handed.) After the experimenter had inserted the stimulus card into the apparatus for a given trial the subject turned on the light, processed the card according to the task, articulated a sentence response, and turned off the light. The experimenter then replaced the card, beginning another trial.

Throughout the experimental session, each subject's speech was tape recorded for later transcription, and the speech wave and button presses simultaneously recorded from an adjacent room using one channel of a Grapp Model 7 polygraph and paper speed of 2.5 cm/sec. Palmar skin resistance and raw EKG were recorded concurrently on other channels. The latency data described here were obtained by hand-measuring the polygraph record and converting from distance to time units. For each response sentence, three intervals were calculated—from the light-on point to the beginning of the utterance, for the duration of the utterance, and from the end of the utterance to the light-off point. These three intervals will be referred to as inspection times, utterance times, and shut-off times, respectively. The subjects were 24 college students. Half of the subjects performed only the verb-using task, and the other half did first that task and then the other three, with task order for the latter counterbalanced over subjects using a Latin square.

Table 2 presents a summary picture of the latency results for the four tasks. Sentence length was almost identical across conditions in average number of clauses used (2.4); sentences averaged 10 words for both using verbs and completing sentences ($SD = 3$) and 12 words for answering questions ($SD = 5$). The sentences read aloud averaged 9 words ($SD = 2$). It can be seen from Table 2 that inspection times were greatest for producing sentences from verbs and answering questions; they were of intermediate length for completing sentences; and they were smallest for reading sentences aloud. Utterance and shut-off times also were somewhat greater for using verbs and answering questions than for reading or completing sentences.

For individual tasks, large and reliable within-subject differences were found for both grammatical measures and latencies. The main grammatical factors analyzed were frequency of, and clause order in, complement constructions used. In the verb-using task, results for this variable were comparable to those observed previously. About twice as many complement verbs took sentence complements when required to precede the noncomplement verb presented as when required to follow it. When free verb order was permitted, a strong bias was observed for complement verbs to be used first and include the noncomple-

TABLE 2
Latencies (in seconds) for Some Sentences Produced Orally

Time interval	N	Using verbs		Task		
		Only 240	First 240	Answering questions 240	Completing sentences 192	Reading sentences 240
Inspection	Mean	5.1	5.9	5.9	4.2	1.8
times	SD	4.3	5.2	3.3	3.3	.9
Utterance	Mean	2.8	3.2	3.2	2.8	2.8
times	SD	1.1	2.5	1.9	1.4	1.0
Shut-off	Mean	.8	.7	.7	.5	.5
times	SD	.5	.4	.4	.3	.3

ment verbs in their complements. Each of these effects was obtained for both subject and object complement verbs, which were used with complements about equally often.

For response latencies, the following effects were obtained in the verb-using task. When verb order was fixed by instructions, total response time per sentence was about 2 sec greater for complement verb-second than complement-first items. Paralleling a result from Study 1, response times were more than 1 sec greater on the average for verb pairs with subject than with object complement verbs. Critically, however, this effect held principally (and hence with much greater magnitude) for sentences in which the complement verbs given had *failed* to take complements. There was no difference in time needed in producing the two types of main–complement sentences used. In line with this result, when verb order was not constrained, the largest response times occurred when complement verbs of both kinds were given in the first position but used after the other verb presented. Finally, unlike Study 2, there was no tendency for sentences with factive verbs (now balanced for length with nonfactives) to take longer to produce than those with nonfactive verbs. The direction of the difference, in fact, was in favor of faster factive complement constructions.

Now, consider performance in the other three tasks. About 70% of all questions asked elicited sentences with full complement constructions. Usually the complement verb from questions was repeated, and in the great majority of cases, main–complement clause order was retained. Sentence answers formed with subject and object complement verbs presented used this form about equally often. Total response times in answering questions, however, were more than 1 sec greater on the average for items with subject than object complement verbs. And all subjects in this task showed the same pattern in their latencies. Although this effect could be attributed to a few rather than all questions asked, and was found mainly for lengthy sentence responses, it nevertheless casts a further shadow over the feature(s) distinguishing the two types of verb in these experiments. Finally, "yes/no" questions in this task were answered more than 1 sec faster on the average than "wh–" questions.

In the sentence completion task, about 80% of the subject responses added a single clause to the one presented. When a complement clause was permitted but not mandatory (for example following "You would think" or "She was delighted"), it was usually provided. For latencies, it was found that subjects needed more than 1 sec extra on the average in both inspection and utterance intervals to finish sentences beginning with complements than to finish sentences beginning with main clauses taking or permitting complements. But sentences beginning with time adverbs (e.g., "Before you leave")—also subordinate clauses—took no longer to finish than the sentences with main clauses first.

Finally, although subjects occasionally made miscues in the sentence reading task, the grammar of the sentences spoken was of course predetermined. For all types of sentences, inspection times were almost exactly 1.8 sec. The only latency difference obtained was that utterance times were about .75 sec greater on the average for three-clause items than the two-clause sentences presented.

GENERAL DISCUSSION

Two groups of results obtained in these experiments seem to warrant further comment. One includes findings from Study 1 for mood, person, and tense, and the other includes the general results found for use of sentence complements.

Mood, Person, and Tense

The mood of sentences in English is correlated with the uses to which sentences are put. Although each of the three moods examined—declarative, interrogative, and imperative—can serve a variety of functions, the first is used most obviously to make statements or assertions, the second to ask questions or request information, and the third to give commands or request action. Similarly, grammatical person normally has deictic reference in actual speech situations. First person pronouns, including the surface structure subject "I," normally refer to the speaker of a sentence. Personal, as opposed to indefinite, "you" refers to just the person(s) addressed. And a third person subject usually refers to someone or something else spoken about. Verb tense also behaves deictically, tending to express when events mentioned in a sentence take place with respect to the time of its utterance. Generally, the past tense is used to mention prior events and nonpast tenses to mention current or future events.

In Study 1, it was shown that mood, person, and tense may interact in several ways. Specifically, it was found that second person subjects were rather dominantly used in interrogative sentences (as well as, presumably, in imperatives) but rarely used in declaratives. And while first person subjects were found to be used mostly with verbs in nonpast tenses, third person subjects occurred mainly with past tense verbs. Although these findings were obtained for only a fairly modest sampling of sentences, they make quite reasonable predictions about how mood, person, and tense may be correlated in spontaneous speech as well.

Consider the imperatives and interrogatives first. Along with previous writers, I have largely assumed that it is the addressee in an imperative of whom something is requested. An overt "you" may or may not be expressed (see Jesperson, 1933). If it is not, the second person subject may be assumed to be understood or, if imperatives include such a predication by definition, simply unnecessary (see Searle, 1975, for a relevant discussion). Similarly, the tense of imperatives is normally left unmarked, perhaps because as requests, these sentences automatically have reference to time following their utterance. (Consider sentences such as "Go away, *will* you!")

This kind of description of imperatives is quite standard. What is interesting about the present data is that over two thirds of the interrogative sentences produced also were in the second person present or future tense; but only a few percent of declaratives were second person. Why might this be? As Labov (1972a), Miller and Johnson-Laird (1976), and others have noted, people do say imperative and interrogative sentences to accomplish similar things. For example, both are used to request that someone do something. In this sense, perhaps a second person subject is predicated at some level in both; it is just usually more explicit in interrogatives. Moreover, the two kinds of sentences may be used fairly often to make functionally equivalent kinds of requests. Just like imperatives, interrogatives may comfortably be used to make requests for action (for example, "Will you close the door?" versus "Please close the door!"). And, conversely, imperatives as well as interrogatives may be used to solicit information (for example, "Tell me your name!" versus "What is your name?").

In declarative sentences, which was by far the most frequent mood used here, second person subjects were relatively rare. But this too does not seem at all unusual. If declaratives are most typically used to make statements or assertions, personal "you" would probably be expected to occur as a grammatical subject, or topic, in them only occasionally. Although the speaker might, for example, comment on the appearance of his listener, the latter is already knowledgeable about his own current or past behavior, experiences, and the like. Perhaps we should look especially carefully for second person declaratives to have other functions than simply asserting, for instance as requests, evaluations, instructions, suggestions, and so forth. In such sentences, a more particular purpose may usually be served. Even general statements formed with (indefinite) "you" as a subject might be categorized in this way. For example, the sentence "You can get killed crossing the street" might serve principally as a warning. Labov (1972b) has provided a similar type of example: if one party to a conversation says something about which he thinks the other party should know but he himself is not sure, the utterance is not heard as a statement of fact but as a request for confirmation.

Most of the sentences used in Study 1 were first or third person declaratives. But, generally speaking, opposing tenses were found for these two cases. While first person subjects were used primarily with nonpast verbs, third person subjects were used mainly with past tense verbs. It seems plausible that this final difference too had something to do with for what sentences like these may normally be used. Austin (1962), for example, suggests that sentences with which speakers perform what he called illocutionary acts will as a rule have "humdrum verbs in the first person singular present indicative active [p. 5]." More recently, Ross (1970), Gordon and Lakoff (1971), and others have forwarded abstract performative analyses for a wider variety of, if not all, sentences. It seems likely, moreover, that there is a general statistical tendency for personal judgments as well as illocutionary acts to be expressed in the first person present. (For a relevant discussion of ego perspective in sentence subjects, see Ertel, 1974, also this volume.) On the other hand, in opposition to this subjective orientation of "here—now—I" (Bühler, 1934) may be a complementary one. Narration and statements of fact may very well tend to be expressed in the third person past. It is interesting in this regard that the primarily nonfactive verbs of saying and thinking in Study 1 were used much more often with the first person present than were the factive verbs of emotion, with which "I" was usually used with a past tense.

To sum up, we can refer to Russell (1940). Russell describes three general purposes of language: to alter states of the listener; to express states of the speaker; and to indicate facts. The sentences from Study 1 suggest that there may often be rather superficial grammatical correlates for these concepts; mood, person, and tense may be jointly determined largely on the basis of communicative intent. Since these are also features indicated near the beginning of main clauses, they will be expressed very early in perhaps most sentences.

Sentence Complements

Early in this chapter it was hypothesized that, in the production of sentences, abstract lexical inputs are combined by an initial judgmental process to form linguistic propositions; that surface sentences result through the further intervention of a grammatical system on these underlying structures. In this final section, I will try to examine what the complement structures used here may imply about sentence production, first using grammatical derivations as a model and then in terms of the kind of hypothesis just summarized.

Several of the present findings did seem to confirm that people have a preferred way of writing and saying sentences with complements. First, sentences made up using complement—noncomplement verb pairs generally had main—complement clause order. In these sentences, a personal pronoun or "it" was usually the surface structure subject, followed by the complement verb given and the complementizer, and finally by a complement containing the noncomplement verb. Second, subjects did not freely alter this strategy and produce sentences with complement—main clause order when they were prevented by instructions from using the complement verb first. Rather, they tended to begin their sentences with other main clauses or noncomplement subordinations. Third, latencies for using verbs to produce sentences of these other types were considerably greater than for the favored main—complement sentences. And response latencies were also much greater for complement—main than main—complement sentences in which subjects were given the first clause and asked to supply an ending.

What do these results suggest? Early on in this research (Jarvella, 1972), I mostly took deep structures to represent linguistic concepts, however they might be formed, and tried to describe their possible mapping onto surface structures.

Fodor, Bever, and Garrett (1974) later interpreted that paper as concluding that speakers were constructing deep structure trees sentoid by sentoid from top to bottom. They (I think correctly) rejected this view, but it is instructive to consider what its implications would be as a kind of hypothesis about the mental derivation of sentences. In the *Aspects* version of generative grammar, as sentences are derived their underlying phrase markers are to a significant degree constructed from the top down. Only once a node has been formed by the application of some phrase structure rule can it be expanded by another such rule. By convention, of course, the branches in such trees are drawn as growing in a downward direction; any phrases that a given node dominates will fall somewhere beneath it.

Now the results mentioned above (and some others to be considered) might be thought to be compatible with a sentence-producing procedure (or class of derivations) in which deep phrase markers are derived one S-node at a time, beginning at the top of the tree. Unfortunately, however, underlying phrase markers are quite remote from superficial sentences, and this priority in development is not supportable at other linguistic levels. Even if we assume, contrary to the theory, that lexical items are introduced for each sentoid just following its phrase development rather than in a block following that for all sentoids, the grammar does not subsequently preserve this order in its operations. In fact, once all semantic content is expressed, it actually works in the opposite fashion as main–complement clause order might seem to suggest. Both in the conversion of deep into surface structures and of phonological into phonetic representations, various cyclic transformations have been proposed that apply earliest at the lowest levels of constituent structure present and work upwards (Chomsky, 1965; Chomsky & Halle, 1968).

Perhaps the strongest suggestion of top-to-bottom formation of deep structures in the present sentences was the fact that main–complement clause order was about as dominant for subject as for object complement constructions. Consistent use of any of the three remaining "mappings" (bottom to top, left to right, right to left) would predict a different pattern of results. However, again if we take the grammar seriously, something would have to be done to move subject complements to the right of their verbs so that they do not appear on the left in surface structure. But neither extraposition nor passivization appeared to make subject complement structures more complicated in production than object complement structures, which need not undergo such permutations. In Study 1, it did take subjects longer to make up sentences with subject than object complement verbs, but fewer complement constructions were used. No difference in either latency or complement use was obtained in Study 2, in which subject complement verbs were given in the present rather than the infinitive. And in the oral replication comparable to Study 1, a difference in latency was found, but was attributable to sentences produced without sentence complements.

Thus, there was no real indication that subject complements were deliberately postponed. In fact, subject complements appear to have been considerably simpler to use following their verbs than preceding them. Two possibilities seem to be suggested. Either the left-to-right property of deep structure in which subjects precede verbs and objects follow them is inconsequential in producing sentences like these. Or in this case, the underlying structures of sentences may have been rendered more accessible by permutations of their sentoids. Langendoen (1970) has suggested that linguistic transformations may actually facilitate verbal communication (that is, sentence interpretation) in this way. Perhaps they also facilitate speaking. And if cyclic transformations are in fact psychologically real in this performance sense, then perhaps one consequence of their bottom-to-top order of application is main–complement (or generally main–subordinate) clause order. In other words, main clauses may tend to occur first in spoken sentences partly because they are often (or belong to) the final or most recent constituents affected in derivations.

There is a third difficulty with the "top down" grammatical model of sentence formation. This is that complement clauses are just one kind of subordinated sentence. And the present studies showed that people postponed noncomplement subordinations less often than complement ones; often they would begin their sentences with noncomplement subordinations if denied the opportunity to first use the complement verbs they were given; they were able to finish sentences beginning with such noncomplement subordinate clauses in no longer than it took them to finish sentences beginning with main clauses. Rochester and Gill (1973) have also reported that relative clauses seem to cause people less difficulty in production than do noun phrase complements.[8] Thus, the downward sentoid by sentoid hypothesis would not appear to be as strongly supported for all kinds of sentences. In addition to grammatical rules operating on different sequences of sentoids at different levels, and perhaps making deep structures more accessible by transforming them, not all subordinate clauses are apparently equal.

Now consider the model of predication. Since generative grammars were not developed as performance models, it is natural that predication appears to offer certain advantages over the early stage of sentence derivation as a hypothesis about how sentences are produced. For instance, it begins by combining predicates and arguments into meaningful propositions rather than by introducing phrase structure which only at a later level can accept the expression of lexical

[8] Rochester and Gill also found that relative clauses occurred in many fewer complex sentences (13% of those they collected versus 65% for noun phrase complements). They did not, however, distinguish by argument or by position relative to the main verb between either type of subordination. Just like complements, relative clauses can often be postponed, for example, by passivization, or, with intransitive verbs, when there is no intervening noun phrase (as in "The man arrived who won the contest"). But to my knowledge, no study has been done showing that this is usually the case.

content. These predicates and arguments were identified in the introduction as abstract lexical items. However, it is not really clear what is the *appropriate* level of abstraction for them. The present experiments were carried out with the hope that a variety of English verbs might serve as good functional predicates. In this particular context, however, some of these verbs might have turned out to be either too superficial or too abstract.

Take, for example, a verb such as "surprise." On the one hand, it might be analyzed as incorporating other, more abstract linguistic predicates. For instance, "A was surprised that P," where A is a person and P a proposition, might be taken to presuppose HAPPEN(P) and LEARN(A, HAPPEN(P)) and to assert EXPECT(A, notHAPPEN(P)) and (vaguely) REACT(A). Miller and Johnson-Laird (1976) have used predicates of causation, perception, action, and the like to analyze a number of English verbs. If such primitives more accurately describe the meanings manipulated in the construction of propositions, the present studies of sentence production would appear to be too superficially oriented and perhaps irrelevant to that covert process. On the other hand, the past participles of verbs like "surprise" in these studies were often used with a form of "be," both with and without following sentence complements. In such sentences, these participial forms might be interpreted as adjectives rather than passivized verbs. But if adjectival rather than verb predicates were, in fact, what subjects were using in these cases, the deep structure subject versus object distinction would not apply psychologically to at least that proportion of the data obtained; it would probably be too abstract. (For a discussion of verb–adjective similarities, see Lakoff, 1970.)

Secondly, we might ask about the likelihood of predicates being applied "from the top down," or whether higher predicates could normally be chosen as abstract lexical items before their propositional arguments were formed. In other words, can complement verbs be predicated before their complements' verbs? When verb reference is considered, a definite problem seems to arise for this view. This is that complement verbs do tend to describe judgments about or processing of conceptualized events. Such predicates may be attached as we search for, reason about, or evaluate event-related information, and might often be found as part of what is remembered. However, it is not easy to see how people would describe their feelings toward, or support linguistic judgments of, something before having some idea of it in mind.[9]

This line of reasoning seems sound enough, but may fall slightly off–target if linguistic and other cognitive bases in sentence formation are held to be discrete. If they are, the argument suggested for prior specification of complement information might be taken to apply mainly at a conceptual level, and a speaker could be viewed as selecting higher lexical predicates before giving linguistic

---

[9] Nonetheless, it is possible that the main sentence production task used here allowed just this type of artificiality to occur.

form to their complements. For example, factive complements might be thought to express some of the background information a speaker uses in arriving at whatever assertions or requests he/she may make in such sentences (see also Bever, 1970). Such structures might sometimes develop with a person at first just thinking in the general domain of what become their presuppositions. That is, to presuppose something in a sentence may not imply that it be conceived of or predicated in advance linguistically. One possible advantage of such a separation of processes might be to permit the grammar–forming component to operate more freely from left to right. However, the problem might just be raised to a different level. To repeat, the mental operations which can be hypothesized to cast and manipulate the type of event-related information expressed in lower sentences seem to be of just the sort which complement verbs label.

In any case, an abstract process of predication such as suggested here would be compatible with the dominant main–complement type of sentence that was observed. As I have noted, superficial clause order in sentences by no means mandates a corresponding order of development at the level of propositions. In fact, since the logical forms I have suggested for meaning are superficially unlike *any* English sentences, they give no illusion of being closely related to canonical sentence form. Just as for deep structures, however, some sophisticated grammatical system would be needed to breach the gap between them and predications as observable linguistic performances. Main–complement clause order could perhaps be predicted if English sentences were superficially formed as well as spoken from left to right (see Yngve, 1960), but it seems unlikely at the present time that the variety and subtle interrelations among English sentence constructions could be captured by this type of production system.

I have nothing more to say about the form of the grammatical rules employed in producing sentences. It seems apparent, however, that a complete description of this component would need to take account in some way of the observed preferences of people to use particular kinds of clauses and sentences. For English, such strategies would probably include the preposing of human arguments and the postponing of abstract and sentential arguments, and perhaps generally of subordinations. The preponderance of main–complement type sentences found here is not the only known evidence supporting such biases. They are, for example, also suggested by work done using the cloze procedure and other sentence completion paradigms (for example, Clark, 1965; Clark & Begun, 1971; Jarvella & Sinnott, 1972).

Sentence production strategies could perhaps be categorized (and certainly cross-classified) according to the functions that they seem likely to serve. Some strategies would probably take advantage of general information-processing abilities of people as speaker–listeners and work around my limitations. But others could plausibly be concerned with aiding the communication process itself, with the speaker actually simplifying the listener's task. It was already implied that one function of placing the main clause of a sentence first might be to quickly convey information about mood, person, and tense. What if such a clause should also happen to be subsequently taking a complement? As Russell (1940) pointed out, propositional attitudes partly have the effect of expressing the degree of certainty or doubt that we may feel toward certain propositions. Since most utterances can be qualified or complementized after they begin, by a variety of grammatical means, Russell was wrong in suggesting that these attitudes are always or must be conveyed in main—complement form. However, a further benefit of using this clause order may be that it provides information about the reasoning being done about such later propositions as early as possible.

SUMMARY

A series of studies has been reported in which people were asked to make up sentences. The sentences were produced in response to English verbs presented one or two at a time, and to some questions and other sentences containing the verbs. Some 6,000 sentences collected in these ways were examined both in linguistic terms and for response latencies accompanying their production. The former analyses principally compared frequencies of occurrence of certain syntactic and semantic features. Results were reported for mood, person, and tense, and for sentence complement constructions. Questions, like imperatives, tended to occur in the second person nonpast, and statements in the first person present or third person past. In complement constructions, subjects appeared to strongly prefer using main—subordinate clause order, whether the complement present was abstractly a subject or an object noun phrase. The research was discussed in terms of a model for sentence production based on the formation and subsequent expression of linguistic judgments.

ACKNOWLEDGMENTS

This research was supported in part by Grant DAHC 15 from the Advanced Research Projects Agency, by Grant MH-22134 from the National Institute of Mental Health, and by Grant GM-21796 from the National Institute of General Medical Sciences. I am particularly grateful to George A. Miller and Sheldon Rosenberg for help, encouragement, and patience in seeing this work completed.

REFERENCES

Austin, J. L. *How to do things with words.* Cambridge, Massachusetts: Harvard University Press, 1962.
Bever, T. G. The comprehension and memory of sentences with temporal relations. In G. B. Flores d'Arcais & W. J. M. Levelt (Eds.), *Advances in psycholinguistics.* Amsterdam: North Holland, 1970. Pp. 285–293.

Bühler, K. *Sprachtheorie.* Jena: Fisher, 1934.

Chomsky, N. *Aspects of the theory of syntax.* Cambridge, Massachusetts: MIT Press, 1965.

Chomsky, N., & Halle, M. *The sound pattern of English.* New York: Harper & Row, 1968.

Church, A. *Introduction to mathematical logic.* Princeton, New Jersey: Princeton University Press, 1956.

Clark, H. H. Some structural properties of simple active and passive sentences. *Journal of Verbal Learning and Verbal Behavior,* 1965, 4, 365–370.

Clark, H. H., & Begun, J. S. The semantics of sentence subjects. *Language and Speech,* 1971, 14, 34–46.

Cresswell, M. J. *Logics and languages.* London: Methuen, 1973.

Curme, G. O. *English grammar.* New York: Barnes & Noble, 1947.

Ertel, S. Satzsubjekt und Ich-Perspektive. In L. H. Eckensberger & U. S. Eckensberger (Eds.), *Bericht über den 28 Kongress der Deutschen Gesellschaft für Psychologie, Band 1: Wissenschafts-theorie und Psycholinguistik.* Göttingen: Hogrefe, 1974. Pp. 129–139.

Fillmore, C. J. The case for case. In E. Bach & R. T. Harms (Eds.), *Universals in linguistic theory.* New York: Holt, Rinehart & Winston, 1968. Pp. 1–88.

Fodor, J. A., Bever, T. G., & Garrett, M. F. *The psychology of language.* New York: McGraw-Hill, 1974.

Frege, G. Über Sinn und Bedeutung. *Zeitschrift für Philosophie und philosophische Kritik,* 1892, 100, 25–50. Translated as "On sense and nomination" in H. Feigl & W. Sellars (Eds.), *Readings in philosophical analysis.* New York: Appleton-Century-Crofts, 1949. Pp. 85–102.

Gordon, D., & Lakoff, G. Conversational postulates. *Papers from the seventh regional meeting of the Chicago Linguistic Society, 1971,* pp. 63–84.

Jarvella, R. J. Starting with psychological verbs. Paper presented at the Symposium on Sentence Production, Midwestern Psychological Association, Cleveland, 1972.

Jarvella, R. J., & Sinnott, J. Contextual constraints on noun distributions to some English verbs by children and adults. *Journal of Verbal Learning and Verbal Behavior,* 1972, 11, 47–53.

Jesperson, O. *Essentials of English grammar.* New York: Holt, Rinehart & Winston, 1933.

Karttunen, L. *The logic of English predicate complement constructions.* Bloomington, Indiana: Indiana University Linguistics Club, 1971.

Karttunen, L. Presuppositions of compound sentences. *Linguistic Inquiry,* 1973, 4, 169–194.

Kiparsky, P., & Kiparsky, C. Fact. In M. Bierwisch & K. E. Heidolph (Eds.), *Progress in linguistics.* The Hague: Mouton, 1970. Pp. 143–173.

Labov, W. Rules for ritual insults. In D. Sudnow (Ed.), *Studies in social interaction.* New York: Free Press, 1972. Pp. 120–169. (a)

Labov, W. *Sociolinguistic patterns.* Philadelphia: University of Pennsylvania Press, 1972. (b)

Lakoff, G. *Irregularity in syntax.* New York: Holt, 1970.

Langendoen, D. T. The accessibility of deep structures. In R. A. Jacobs & P. S. Rosenbaum (Eds.), *Readings in English transformational grammar.* Waltham, Massachusetts: Ginn, 1970. Pp. 99–104.

Levin, H., & Turner, E. A. Sentence structure and the eye-voice span. In *Project literacy reports, VII.* Ithaca, New York: Cornell University, 1966.

McCawley, J. D. English as a VSO language. *Language,* 1970, 46, 286–299.

Melamed, B. G., & Jarvella, R. J. Some temporal and autonomic correlates of sentence production. *Journal of the Acoustical Society of America, 1973,* 53, 379(A).

Miller, G. A. Four philosophical problems of psycholinguists. *Philosophy of Science,* 1970, 37, 183–199.

Miller, G. A., & Johnson-Laird, P. N. *Language and perception.* Cambridge, Massachusetts: Harvard University Press, 1976.

Reichenbach, H. *Elements of symbolic logic.* New York: MacMillan, 1947.

Rochester, S. R., & Gill, J. Production of complex sentences in monologues and dialogues. *Journal of Verbal Learning and Verbal Behavior,* 1973, **12,** 203–210.

Rosenbaum, P. S. *The grammar of English predicate complement constructions.* Cambridge, Massachusetts: MIT Press, 1967.

Ross, J. R. On declarative sentences. In R. A. Jacobs & P. S. Rosenbaum (Eds.), *Readings in English transformational grammar.* Waltham, Massachusetts: Ginn, 1970. Pp. 222–272.

Russell, B. *An inquiry into meaning and truth.* New York: Norton, 1940.

Searle, J. R. Speech acts and recent linguistics. In D. Aaronson & R. W. Rieber (Eds.), *Developmental psycholinguistics and communication disorders.* New York: New York Academy of Sciences, 1975. Pp. 27–38.

Strawson, P. F. *Introduction to logical theory.* London: Methuen, 1952.

Van Frassen, B. C. *Formal semantics and logic.* New York: MacMillan, 1971.

Vendler, Z. Say what you think. In J. L. Cowan (Ed.), *Studies in thought and language.* Tucson: University of Arizona Press, 1970.

Yngve, V. H. A model and an hypothesis for language structure. *Proceedings of the American Philosophical Society,* 1960, **104,** 444–466.

13
One of Many Units: The Sentence

Daniel C. O'Connell

Saint Louis University

The simple phrase *the sentence as unit* would appear to be thoroughly innocuous and, on that score at least, an excellent starting point of agreement. It is the thesis of this chapter that the unexamined, often implicit use of the various concepts underlying *the sentence* has shed little light on theory or research in current psycholinguistics. In fact, far from serving any heuristic or integrative function, the concepts have led to a great deal of confusion. As always, the examination of per se nota concepts such as *unit* and *sentence* leads to many more questions than neatly packaged answers.

DEFINITIONS OF THE SENTENCE

The problem, of course, is that we all *do* know what a sentence is. The stereotypic school marm can wax eloquent about it, but so too can the stereotypic clod raise an eyebrow or utter a profanity in the face of a nonsentential utterance. So what's all the fuss?

Traditional Approaches

The standard, traditional, presumably neutral description of a sentence as "a combination of words which expresses a complete thought" can be traced back at least to the pre-Christian era (Ivic, 1965, p. 20). It should be noted, however, that the definition derives initially from an oral culture and refers to the "combination of sound elements which has a definite, independent meaning [p. 18]," as understood in the Aristotelian tradition. Applied *buchstäblich* within the written tradition which has arisen since the invention of printing, the above descriptions of a sentence could easily be understood of units such as the

307

paragraph, chapter, or volume. It is interesting to imagine a Greek philosopher having a multipaged Victorian sentence read aloud to him and being asked thereupon to vouch for its singular or unitary sententiality. Not a very good fit, one might suspect, and not entirely to be ascribed to the invention of the semicolon.

This is not to say that the sentence was unproblematic until the advent of printing. Ultimately the question must be reduced to one regarding the nature of human thought and its expression in discourse. What is a complete thought or a "perfect meaning" (Diaz, 1967, p. 264)? To oversimplify (though without intending to be facetious at all), no thought or meaning is worth its salt unless it *is* somehow incomplete, unfinished, imperfect. In other words, it is of the very essence of all human thought that it be a dynamic motion toward further integration, deeper insight, fuller contextualization. We are dealing with an intelligence which transcends any individual expression it may formulate. To be hyperbolic about it, actual human discourse always intends *simul* more than, less than, other than, and the same as what is formulated in any finite group of words identifiable as a sentence. The only definition I have been able to find that reflects such ideas about the sentence is one intended for schoolboys: "A sentence is a word or set of words revealing an intelligible purpose" (Gardiner, 1951, p. 98).

Now when that living sentence is decontextualized and isolated from its natural habitat of oral discourse by being written, by being set off by periods (or other punctuation), and by being analyzed solely in its internal structure, it has become metamorphized into a static linguistic entity, far more manageable, indeed, but at several removes from the realities of human thought and discourse.

This is not intended to serve as a criticism of the processes of abstraction essential to linguistics, but it should localize some of the misunderstandings that arise. There is a danger in using demonstrational materials rather than *corpora* (not without difficulties themselves) or actual discourse. The most famous of such demonstrational sentences, for example, *colorless green ideas sleep furiously,* demonstrates remarkably well only that some generative grammarians have themselves been too prosaic to recognize a perfectly legitimate sentence when they saw one.

If, then, we cannot decide what a complete thought is, if there are other units that fulfill the traditional definition of a sentence, if that definition is originally from an oral tradition and is now being applied largely to isolated, written sentences, and if the grammarian's intuitions about sententiality are themselves not inerrant, where do we go from here?

Linguistic Approaches

The problems should not be minimized; all sorts of systematic and ad hoc solutions have been invoked to settle the sentence in a quiet niche once and for all. A relatively recent working definition obviously ignores the reality of paragraphs and all other suprasentential units: "A sentence is a linguistic structure which is not a constituent of some larger one" (Barber, 1964, p. 279). The effort to imbed the sentence in some comprehensive linguistic system is clearly important. Such efforts range from Crystal's (1971, p. 202) conservative description as "one of the products of a grammar, and not something which we have when we begin," to Denes and Pinson's (1963, p. 12) neutral prescription that "sentences must make sense as well as satisfy the rules of grammar," to Martinet's (1960) definition:

> an utterance, all the elements of which are attached to a single predicate or to several coordinated predicates, and in this way we can dispense with the criteria of intonation in the definition, which is a real gain in view of the marginally linguistic nature of this phenomenon [p. 122].

to the generative or transformational definitions exemplified by that of Lyons (1970):

> The grammar is said to generate (and thereby define as "grammatical") all the sentences of the languages and to fail to generate (thereby defining as "ungrammatical") all the non-sentences, or "ill-formed" combinations of basic elements [p. 24].

The definition of sentence within a generative system introduces the notion of well-formed and ill-formed sentences. The latter are illegitimate in that they are not generatable. These concepts thrust us back once again to the differences between written and oral discourse. Depending on how orderly (sententially) oral discourse proves to be, we may find that the well-formed sentence applies to little more than the demonstrational materials of the linguists themselves. This is not to say that oral discourse is not structured, but only to question whether sentential analyses derived from written *corpora* and demonstrational materials will prove applicable to oral discourse. The matter of structure in oral discourse has been discussed by Labov (1970) and Brown (1973b) in this context. Suffice it to say at this point that the syntactic structure of oral discourse has not as yet been adequately described.

Empirical Approaches

We have little or no choice in empirically isolating sentences in written materials. If a writer isolates a word or group of words by proper punctuation, a sentence generally emerges. Oral discourse is quite another matter. Who is to say where one sentence ends and another begins? Do speakers use the sentence formally or otherwise, consciously or not, or somehow as the structural unit of production? Would they know necessarily, for example, whether they intended a semicolon or period in a specific location? The problems are legion.

The problem is difficult enough when the speaker himself transcribes into sentences what he has said; but for many reasons (including unavailability and illiteracy of the speaker), such a tactic may not be possible, or even desirable methodologically. One method of isolating the sentence has been based on the contention that "Sentences as distinct from clauses are marked by their temporal cohesion in spontaneous speech" (Goldman-Eisler, 1972, p. 103). This is a very far-reaching hypothesis, though Goldman-Eisler herself admits that it has exceptions, while arguing (rather circularly): "The rarity of such fluent transitions in spontaneous speech would indicate that in most cases a sentence presents the externalisation of a thought unit [p. 111]." What actually happened in this instance was that the *researcher* identified sentences on the basis of the combined criteria of temporal patterning and meaning. The concurrence of longer pauses and sentence boundaries is a necessary consequence of the methodology used—and of course of the implicit empirical definition of a sentence.

Goldman-Eisler also refers her psychological concepts of the sentence back to those of Wundt and finds her data consistent with an analytic theory of sentence production. Somehow the sentence is primary and the words secondary, just the opposite of a Markovian theory of word sequencing [p. 112].

Even more explicit in empirically defining the sentence in terms of intersentential pauses is Gardiner (1951, p. 207): "A pause after utterance is the mark of the finished sentence, and indeed there exists no more conclusive testimony that a sentence has come to an end." He adds that "human beings have such great experience in speaking and listening that they can readily judge what pauses are to be interpreted as evidence of the speaker's desire to conclude a sentence." That is exactly what Goldman-Eisler was doing, apparently without being aware of the circularity involved.

SOME RESEARCH EXAMPLES

Another example of the difficulties involved methodologically in using pauses initially to identify sentences and then arguing from the pauses as to how sentences are characterized pausologically in spontaneous speech can be found in Broen (1971):

> The coding that was done would only affect one set of results. These involve a determination of the frequency with which a sentence is followed by a pause. Many segments identified by this study as sentences would not be considered separate sentences by other criteria. Judges in this study did not consider them to be sentences, but judges in this study had a hard time agreeing on what were sentences.
>
> By coding this way most of the mothers' speech was grammatical. If we were to use the listener judgements, there would be few grammatical sentences [p. 30].

Broen's frankness is refreshing, but the methodological impasse is a formidable one.

More recently, Butterworth (1975) has made use of a method whereby independent judges were instructed to segment typed transcripts of spontaneous speech into semantic units or ideas. The author mentions quite explicitly of the typed transcripts: "They were in normal orthography, with the usual punctuation [p. 79]," but seems unaware that in so doing, he has already imposed on the transcript the researcher's own segmentation of ideas. Once again, implicit criteria for sententiality have been used unwittingly. Butterworth's conclusions must accordingly be considered largely artifactual: "Points in the transcripts where agreement was high among the judges were found to correspond with the beginnings of temporal cycles, and agreed semantic segments coincided with sentence or clause boundaries . . . [p. 75] ." Finally, the wide variation in semantic segmentation by the independent judges and their introspective reports regarding permissible alternative segmentation should give us further pause regarding the psychological reality conceptualized as *sentence*. Butterworth's evidence indicates that the sentence is psychologically *not* synonymous simply with the expression of a "single idea [p. 85] ."

SOME THEORETICAL CONSIDERATIONS

A very serious problem is pointed out succinctly by Jaffe and Feldstein (1970, pp. 2–3): "The serious study of dialogue patterns makes one poignantly aware that the largest unit dealt with in contemporary linguistics is at most the monologue and, more typically, the isolated sentence."

The limitation has not been indeliberate on the part of some. McNeill (1966) explicitly defines his domain of investigation as the individual sentence:

Let us think about a single sentence. By so restricting our attention, we eliminate discourse, dialogue, and the exchange of ideas, all of which are important questions for understanding the development of language. In return we shall gain relative simplicity without losing an accurate vision of linguistic knowledge [p. 34] .

He develops this theoretical stance at greater length as the theme of his later book:

Not only do children acquire knowledge of sentence structure—itself an important fact—but virtually everything that occurs in language acquisition depends on *prior* knowledge of the basic aspects of sentence structure. The concept of a sentence may be part of man's innate mental capacity. The argument of the book is designed to justify this assertion.

In brief, the argument is as follows. The facts of language acquisition could not be as they are unless the concept of a sentence is available to children at the start of their learning. The concept of a sentence is the main guiding principle in a child's attempt to organize and interpret the linguistic evidence that fluent speakers make available to him. What outside observers see as distorted or "telegraphic" speech is actually a consistent effort by a child to discover how a more or less fixed concept of a sentence is expressed in the language to which he has, by accident, been exposed.

This effort can be viewed as a succession of hypotheses that a child adopts concerning the form sentences take in the language around him. Children everywhere begin with exactly the same initial hypothesis: sentences consist of single words [McNeill, 1970, p. 2] .

The explanatory power of McNeill's insistence on the sentence as the key to the secret of man's innate mental capacity has always evaded this writer. As a philosophical concept, it can be—and has been—debated ad nauseam; but as psychological theory it fails the criteria of being either integrative or heuristic. And the reason should by now be clear: The concept of *sentence* is itself problematic, less well understood in a scientific sense, less agreed upon than the concepts it is used to explain. It does not contribute greater intelligibility to the discussion, despite all that has been said about it in recent decades of generative linguistics.

Brown (1973a, p. 203), on the other hand, approaches types of sentences without any commitment to a formalistic description of the sentence. And yet, Crystal (1974, p. 301) finds numerous unwitting assumptions on Brown's part regarding the defining properties of a sentence. He finds Brown's "basic" facts regarding sentences to be in fact highly controversial. Crystal localizes the difficulty in the way in which Brown understands child utterances to be "moving toward the adult form of language" and to be "identifiable as imperfect versions of one or another type of adult English sentence or constituent" (Brown, p. 203; cf. Crystal, p. 301). But for Crystal, if "perhaps all utterances are derived from implicit complete sentences" (Brown, p. 209), then Brown is well nigh boxed into a generative theory (Crystal, p. 302).

Contrary to McNeill, Brown (1973a) insists that a holophrase cannot be considered a one-word sentence because a sentence must be "a structural specification of relationships among elements [p. 154]." Again, as Crystal (1974, p. 305) points out, this is hardly a neutral, nonformalistic, atheoretical description of the sentence, even though the implications of his stance are not pursued by Brown.

Dore (1975) has reviewed the arguments for and against viewing the child's initial one-word utterances as holophrases:

> We suggest that an unresolvable theoretical stalemate exists because proponents on both sides of the controversy mistakenly assume the centrality of the notion SENTENCE in discussing holophrases. An alternative view of early language development, which takes the SPEECH ACT as the basic unit of linguistic communication, is offered as a solution to the problems with the holophrase controversy as it now stands [p. 21].

Once again, an antecedent notion of sentence is pinpointed as standing in the way of appropriate theory construction.

CONCLUSIONS

Much of the above discussion has been by way of examples from the literature. The evidence indicates that the concept of *sentence* and consequently the use of the sentence as an empirical unit are extremely complex and problematic. A universal prescientific concept has been erected into a scientific universal by various implicit metamorphoses. We would all do well to pursue some of the logical implications and empirical ramifications of our use of the concept *sentence* and be very suspicious of circularity in our identification or isolation of sentences—particularly those of other people.

Perhaps, we might heed the warning, *mutatis mutandis,* voiced by Lindsley (1975) regarding the production of simple utterances:

> First, it is not clear whether the degree of advance planning reflected in the constrained conditions of this laboratory task holds for naturalistic speech. Second, the exact details of the processing involved in speech must be explicated [p. 19].

The actual units involved in the production and reception of spontaneous oral discourse—of monologue, dialogue, and multilogue—whatever they may be, have as yet hardly been touched in any systematic empirical way.

REFERENCES

Barber, C. L. *The story of speech and language.* New York: Crowell, 1964.

Broen, P. A. *A discussion of the linguistic environment of the young, language learning child.* Paper presented at the American Speech and Hearing Convention, Chicago, Illinois, November 1971.

Brown, R. *A first language: The early stages.* Cambridge, Massachusetts: Harvard University Press, 1973. (a)

Brown, R. Schizophrenia, language, and reality. *American Psychologist,* 1973, 5, 395–403. (b)

Butterworth, B. Hesitation and semantic planning in speech. *Journal of Psycholinguistic Research,* 1975, 4, 75–87.

Crystal, D. *Linguistics.* Middlesex: Penguin Books, 1971.

Crystal, D. Review of *A first language: The early stages* by R. Brown. *Journal of Child Language,* 1974, 1, 289–334.

Denes, P. B., & Pinson, E. N. *The speech chain.* Murray Hill, New Jersey: The Bell Telephone Laboratories, 1963.

Diaz, Isidoro. *Diccionario de la lingua Espanola.* Madrid: Editorial Mayfe, S.A., 1967.

Dore, J. Holophrases, speech acts and language universals. *Journal of Child Language,* 1975, 2, 21–40.

Gardiner, A. H. *The theory of speech and language* (2nd ed.). London: Oxford University Press, 1951.

Goldman-Eisler, F. Pauses, clauses, sentences. *Language and Speech,* 1972, 15, 103–113.

Ivic, M. *Trends in linguistics.* The Hague: Mouton, 1965.

Jaffe, J., & Feldstein, S. *Rhythms of dialogue.* New York: Academic Press, 1970.

Labov, W. The study of language in its social context. *Studium Generale,* 1970, 23, 30–87.

Lindsley, J. R. Producing simple utterances: How far ahead do we plan? *Cognitive Psychology,* 1975, 7, 1–19.

Lyons, J. Introduction. In J. Lyons (Ed.), *New horizons in linguistics.* Middlesex: Penguin Books, 1970.

Martinet, A. *Elements of general linguistics.* Chicago: University of Chicago Press, 1960. (Copyright 1960 by the University of Chicago Press.)

McNeill, D. The creation of language. *Psycholinguistics Papers,* 1966, 27, 34–38. (Edinburgh University Press, publishers.)

McNeill, D. *The acquisition of language: The study of developmental psycholinguistics.* New York: Harper & Row, 1970.

Author Index

Prentice, J. L., 101, 102, *140*, 253, *257*
Pribram, K. H., 146, *167*

Q

Quadfasel, F., 24, *32*
Quirk, R., 116, *140*

R

Radulović, L., 92, 96, 132, 133, *140*
Ransom, E. N., 129, *140*
Reichenbach, H., 277, 278, *305*
Reid, L. S., 253, *258*
Retzius, G., 17, *34*
Reynolds, A., 65, *87*, 204, 206, *228*
Richards, M. M., 165, *167*
Riechert, T., 21, *33*
Riegele, L., 17, *34*
Roberts, L., 18, 21, 22, *33*
Rochester, S. R., 1, *12*, 65, 66, 70, 72, 83, 84, *87*, 196, 200, *228*, 300, *305*
Rohrman, N. L., 271, *274*
Rommetveit, R., 99, 101, 102, *140*, 163, 164, *167*
Rondot, R., 21, *33*
Rosch, E., 125, *140*
Rosenbaum, P. S., 212, *227*, 280, 285, *305*
Rosenberg, S., 217, *228*, 236, 237, *258*
Rosenthal, D., 85, *87*
Rosett, J., 23, *34*
Ross, J. R., 98, *138*, 280, 297, *305*
Rumelhart, D. E., 253, *257*
Russell, B., 277, 279, 280, 298, 303, *305*

S

Sabin, E. J., 11, *12*
Salzinger, K., *87*
Sanides, F., 17, 19, *34*
Saussure, F., 231, *258*
Schaltenbrand, G., 21, *34*, 57, *63*
Schank, R. C., 259, 261, 262, 264, *274*
Schlesinger, I. M., 96, *140*, 170, 180, 181, 183, 184, 185, 188, *193*, 233, *258*
Schwartz, J., 55, *63*
Schwenk, M. A., 253, *256*
Searle, J. R., 296, *305*
Sedlak, P. A. S., 132, *140*
Segal, E. M., 99, *140*

Segarra, J., 24, *32*
Segui, J., 272, *274*
Selnes, O. A., 16, 17, 23, 30, *34, 35*
Selz, O., 261, *274*
Shakow, D., 84, 85, *87*
Shapiro, H., 82, *85*
Shapiro, S. I., 215, 219, *228*
Sherman, S. M., 28, *34*
Siebenmann, F., 29, *34*
Silverman, G., 66, *87*
Sinnott, J., 302, *304*
Skarbek, A., 66, *86*
Slobin, D. I., 132, 133, *140*, 180, *193*, 249, *258*
Smith, H. L., 3, *13*, 198, *228*
Smith, J., 95, *139*
Stengel, E., 29, *34*
Stern, D. N., 51, 56, 59, *63*
Stern, G., *140*
Strange, W., 200, *228*
Strasburger, E. H., 17, *34*
Strawson, P. F., 283, *305*
Suci, G. J., 158, *167*
Sussman, H. M., 3, *13*, 28, *34*
Sutherland, N. S., 232, *258*
Svartvik, J., 116, 129, *140*
Szentagothai, J., 25, *32*

T

Tannenbaum, P. H., 65, *87*, 101, *140*, 158, 163, *167*, 197, 203, *228*, 253, *258*
Tannenhaus, M. K., 125, *138*
Tanz, C., 119, *140*
Taylor, I., 205, 209, *228*, 247, *258*
Teszner, D., 18, 30, *34*
Thompson, J. G., 102, *139*
Thorndike, E. L., 210, 217, 220, *228*
Thurston, S., 65, 84, *87*
Tirandola, G., 96, *138*
Trabasso, T., 249, *256*
Trager, G. L., 198, *228*
Turner, E. A., 101, 102, *140*, 163, 164, *167*, 293, *304*
Tversky, B., 252, *258*
Tzavaras, A., 18, 30, *34*

U

Umbach, W., 21, *33*

Subject Index